KNOWLEDGE EMERGENCE

KNOWLEDGE
EMERGENCE

Social, Technical, and Evolutionary
Dimensions of Knowledge Creation

EDITED BY

Ikujiro Nonaka

Toshihiro Nishiguchi

OXFORD
UNIVERSITY PRESS

2001

OXFORD
UNIVERSITY PRESS

Oxford   New York
Athens   Auckland   Bangkok   Bogotá   Bombay   Buenos Aires
Calcutta   Cape Town   Dar es Salaam   Delhi   Florence   Hong Kong
Istanbul   Karachi   Kuala Lumpur   Madras   Madrid   Melbourne
Mexico City   Nairobi   Paris   Shanghai   Singapore   Taipei   Tokyo   Toronto

and associated companies in
Berlin   Ibadan

Library of Congress Cataloging-in-Publication Data
Knowledge emergence : social, technical, and evolutionary dimensions of knowledge
creation / Ikujiro Nonaka, Toshihiro Nishiguchi, editors.
p.   cm.
ISBN 0-19-513063-4
1. Knowledge management.   2. Information society.
I. Nonaka, Ikujiro, 1935–   II. Nishiguchi, Toshihiro.
HD30.2 .K6363   2000
658.4'038—dc21   00-042795

9 8 7 6 5 4 3 2 1

Printed in the United States of America
on acid-free paper

Foreword

The Sasakawa Peace Foundation (SPF), a private nonprofit organization, was established in September 1986 for the stated purpose of "working for world peace through continual and concerted efforts to promote international understanding, exchange, and cooperation." SPF pursues this mandate by making grants in support of projects both in and outside Japan and by carrying out its own self-operated projects.

In April 1995, SPF initiated a three-year, self-operated project entitled "International Comparative Study of Knowledge Creation," in which three joint research groups, comprising eminent researchers and practitioners, were organized with an aim at exploring and finding solutions to issues related to knowledge creation. Their respective focus was placed on the following three themes: 1) organization and knowledge creation, 2) impact of technology advancement on knowledge creation, and 3) knowledge creation in relationship to suppliers.

Giving impetus to the project was a growing awareness of the strategic importance of knowledge as a key resource in the quickly approaching twenty-first century. Knowledge has unique properties, and many facets of its creation have yet to be fully explored. Knowledge is, for example, very different from tangible assets in that it can be possessed but not easily hoarded. Knowledge is also, in an inherent sense, a common good, and, as such, how to optimize its generation, transfer, and use is a challenge of far-reaching consequence to all human beings. In this context as well, the study of the mechanisms and dynamics of knowledge creation will provide essential keys for enhancing society in the twenty-first century.

With these challenges in mind, the project's joint research groups conducted their investigations and then met together in an international academic conference in Hawaii in December 1996 to report, discuss, and consolidate their results. The conference was jointly supported by SPF and the Japan-America Institute of Management Science (JAIMS). The substance of its presentations, discussions, and outcomes is compiled in the pages of this book.

For the instrumental guidance and assistance they provided the research groups over the course of this project, SPF wishes to express its deepest gratitude to Dr. Ikujiro Nonaka, Professor of Knowledge Science at Japan Advanced Institute of Science & Technology (JAIST), and to Dr. Toshihiro Nishiguchi, Professor of Management at Hitotsubashi University. We also wish to extend our sincere appreciation to Dr. Glenn K. Miyataki, President of JAIMS, who so generously gave of his time to assist us in organizing and convening the Hawaii conference. Furthermore, our thanks go to each of the paper contributors, whose names appear herein, for their helpful inputs in the compilation of this volume.

Finally, we would be very pleased if this book should contain useful hints or pointers for other individuals and groups grappling with the challenges of knowledge creation in various fields and domains.

Akira Iriyama
President,
The Sasakawa Peace Foundation

Contents

Contributors

Christina Ahmadjian Haas School of Business, University of California, Berkeley

Yasunori Baba Professor, Research into Artifacts Center for Engineering, University of Tokyo

Sigrun Caspary Associate Professor, Institute for Comparative Research into Culture and Economic Systems, Witten/Herdecke University

Michael A. Cusumano Professor, Sloan School of Management, Massachusetts Institute of Technology

Giorgio De Michelis Professor, Laboratory for Cooperation Technologies, Department of Informatics, Systems and Communication, University of Milan-Bicocca

Kazuo Ichijo Associate Professor, Faculty of Social Sciences, Hitotsubashi University

Martin Kenney Professor, Department of Human and Community Development, University of California, Davis and Senior Research Associate, Berkeley Roundtable on the International Economy, University of California, Berkeley

Linsu Kim Professor, Korea University and Chairman, Government Reform Council

Noboru Konno President, Column, Inc.

James R. Lincoln Professor, Haas School of Business, University of California, Berkeley

Toshihiro Nishiguchi Professor, Institute of Innovation Research, Hitotsubashi University

Kentaro Nobeoka Professor, Research Institute for Economics and Business Administration, Kobe University

Ikujiro Nonaka Professor, Japan Advanced Institute of Science and Technology

Stefan H. Thomke Associate Professor, Harvard Business School

Ryoko Toyama Assistant Professor, Japan Advanced Institute for Science and Technology

Georg Fredrik von Krogh Professor and Director, Institute of Management, University of St. Gallen

D. Eleanor Westney Professor, Sloan School of Management, Massachusetts Institute of Technology

Kenichi Yasumuro Professor, Kobe Commerce University

KNOWLEDGE EMERGENCE

1

Introduction

Knowledge Emergence

IKUJIRO NONAKA
TOSHIHIRO NISHIGUCHI

The importance of knowledge as a key source of competitive advantage is now well established in management studies, as suggested by the growing literature focusing on knowledge creation and transfer (Kogut and Zander, 1992; Nonaka and Takeuchi, 1995; Strategic Management Journal Winter Special Issue, 1996). However, although concepts such as tacit knowledge and organizational knowledge unify much of this emerging research, there remains much variety in terms of angles and approaches chosen to examine the knowledge-creation process. This book is no exception. A wide variety of concepts, hypotheses, and case studies are proposed, often in a tentative manner. This diversity reflects the advancement of the field of knowledge creation is still at an infant stage. It also reflects the complex and multidimensional nature of knowledge, making research on knowledge creation a difficult yet fascinating endeavor.

This book is the result of a conference held in Honolulu in December 1996.[1] During the three days of the conference, researchers from a wide range of academic backgrounds and nationalities exchanged insights and proposed new avenues of research. The conference was a fertile ground, or *ba*, as Ikujiro Nonaka and others would put it, for advancing the field of knowledge creation. At the same time, the event revealed the rich but compelling diversity of models and concepts used to characterize knowledge and knowledge creation. Such diversity can be stimulating but may also end up hindering the advancement of the field as a whole. On the other hand, too much convergence in concepts and approaches can be misleading, if not counterproductive, particularly when there is redundant and sterile use of buzzwords.

The aim of this book is precisely to reveal the richness and diversity of knowledge-creation research to the larger public, while at the same time attempting to identify common grounds that would lead to the emergence of a more unified field. This book offers a chance to assess and evaluate the state of our understanding on knowledge and knowledge creation and, hopefully, to help sustain the evolution of this fascinating field.

It is worth examining common characteristics that these essays share beyond their evident diversity. First, they are all grounded in extensive qualitative and/or quantitative research. Many of these essays include case studies of leading knowledge-creating companies in various countries (e.g., the United States, Japan, and South Korea) and industries (e.g., electronics, software, aerospace), which will be of particular interest to practitioners. Second, all the essays go beyond the mere description of knowledge-creation processes, suggesting both theoretical and strategic implications. Third, they all share, explicitly or implicitly, a view of knowledge creation and knowledge transfer as delicate processes, necessitating particular forms of support and "care" from management. Indeed, a fundamental thread uniting these essays is the idea that knowledge must be "nurtured" rather than "managed." In this sense, this book attempts to go beyond the often too narrowly focused literature on knowledge management. Hence the title, which refers as much to the emerging nature of the field as to the delicate nature of knowledge itself.

The book is divided into four parts. The two essays in Part I are highly conceptual and highlight key concepts of knowledge creation such as tacit knowledge, ba, and care. Parts II–IV contain a mix of conceptual discussions and empirical studies, often intermeshed. Part II focuses on the role of technology in knowledge creation; Part III on international knowledge-creation and knowledge-transfer processes; and Part IV on interorganizational dynamics. More detailed descriptions of the essays follow.

Knowledge, Ba, and Care

In the first essay, Ikujiro Nonaka, Noboru Konno, and Ryoko Toyama discuss the concept of ba and its application to the field of knowledge creation. *Ba*, a Japanese term difficult to translate in English, refers to a physical, virtual, and/or mental space shared by two or more individuals or organizations. The nature of a ba will condition social relationships among these social units and hence have a determining influence on the scale and scope of knowledge creation.

In previous work, Nonaka and his colleagues developed a model of knowledge creation based on a spiraling process of conversions between tacit and explicit knowledge, involving the four stages of socialization, externalization, combination, and internalization. This essay explores the possibility that each of these stages may be nurtured and supported by the design of an appropriate ba, a speculation based on case studies of Seven-Eleven Japan and Maekawa Seisakusho. Nonaka and his colleagues argue that the role of management in the knowledge-creation process should thus be to design and/or facilitate the emergence of an appropriate ba for each of the key stages rather than attempting to intervene directly in the knowledge-creation process.

The first essay demonstrates the importance of social relationships in organizations; in the second essay Georg von Krogh, Kazuo Ichijo, and Ikujiro Nonaka proceed to explore the role of *care* among individuals in the knowledge-creation process. The authors offer both a conceptual discussion and a case study based on the Japanese firm MYCOM. They argue that care can facilitate organizational knowledge development by nurturing trust among employees. High care organizations are characterized by employees who help each other, are accessible, have "attentive inquiry," high degrees of lenience, and share collectively the same value for care.

The authors identify four modes of knowledge creation, depending on whether there is low or high care and whether there is creation of individual or organizational knowledge. In low care organizations, individuals are largely left to their own to seize knowledge and consequently do not share their findings with others. Social knowledge under these conditions will be largely explicit, as employees do not engage in social interaction to share tacit knowledge. Instead, they transact explicit knowledge among each other, often on a give-and-take basis and under highly bureaucratic rules, which are respected but not necessarily understood. In high care organizations, by contrast, individuals are supported by a social network, making possible a process of bestowing of tacit knowledge by the individual, as well as the sharing of this tacit knowledge with other employees, through "indwelling." Rules are not only followed but also understood and agreed on by consensus.

Technology and Cooperation

The next five essays, while recognizing the importance of social interactions in the knowledge-creation process, focus on the tremendous impact of the emergence of new *information technologies* (IT) on business practices in general and on new product development in particular.

First, Yasunori Baba and Kentaro Nobeoka discuss the impact of computer-assisted design (CAD), computer-assisted engineering (CAE), and computer-assisted manufacturing (CAM) technologies, arguing that they will play an increasingly critical role in the future. Previous limitations on their use and efficiency are gradually being alleviated or eliminated; for example, the new three-dimensional CAD systems improve the efficiency of product developers' inductive, deductive, and abductive reasoning processes. As a result, IT is moving from a supportive to a central role in the knowledge-creation process.

The authors suggest that U.S. firms may be taking a lead in combining the power of IT with Japanese human-oriented approaches (e.g., lean production, cross-functional teams), which remain crucial in both the knowledge-creation and manufacturing processes. It has often been said that in the past, many Western firms wasted large investments in overly complex automation and logistics systems while their Japanese competitors successfully focused on exploiting the tacit knowledge of their workers and engineers. In other words, the Western firms were competing with technology against organization-oriented Japanese firms. However, with the elimination of many of the main bottlenecks in CAD/CAE/CAM systems and the concurrent absorption of Japanese human-oriented approaches by Western firms, firms such as Boeing that combine both modalities, may be gaining a substantial competitive advantage. With Western firms generally in advance of Japanese firms in the use of IT, a new era of mutual learning between East and West may be beginning.

An interesting point in this regard is that Boeing emphasizes colocation of project members despite having one of the most advanced computer networks in the world. Indeed, the need for face-to-face interaction among employees remains unchanged, along with the necessity to adapt organizations and skills to the needs of the new technologies. Japanese firms, many of which have emphasized the human element in knowledge creation and manufacturing, may still have an advantage in this area.

Next, Stefan Thomke discusses the implications of new computer simulation and prototyping technologies for knowledge creation. Competitive pressures to shorten product life cycles and accelerate time-to-market lead time while lowering development costs have increased remarkably in past years. As a result, there is increasing pressure to raise the efficiency of the *experimentation* process that is central to any development project, using the radically improved computer simulation and prototyping technologies. Experimentation involves several different modes with diminishing marginal returns, suggesting the need to determine the "optimal mode switching point" (OSP), for example, the point where the experimentation efficiency of computer simulation becomes lower than that of prototyping. Determining the OSP and adjusting the experimentation strategy accordingly will increase the rate at which design-related knowledge is created, which leads Thomke to argue that firms who do not change their strategies in this domain will be foregoing important gains from the new simulation and prototype technologies arriving on the market. Again, Thomke reminds the reader that the IT revolution requires new skills and capabilities along with organizational change to properly exploit the opportunities brought by technological change.

In the next essay, Martin Kenney takes a broader look at the implications of the emergence of time-to-market as a key variable of competition. He observes that the erosion of boundaries between users and producers and the acceleration of the pace of innovation and product changes call for a rethinking of the dominant design and architectural innovation models. Examining trends in both traditional producer goods industries and information technology industries, he finds time-to-market rapidity to be an increasingly key aspect of competition, surpassing price and quality in some cases. Kenney argues that knowledge creation is emerging as a pivotal process within economic activity and should therefore be put at the center of innovation models of researchers and strategies of firms.

One firm stands out as having succeeded in exploiting the opportunities brought on by the information age and the acceleration of innovation and product life cycles: Microsoft. Michael A. Cusumano discusses what he calls the synch-and-stabilize approach to product development used by Microsoft and suggests that this approach is central to the software giant's success. Using this approach, Microsoft promotes both *creativity*, a key factor for innovative knowledge creation, and *structure*, which assures that new product development is quick and cost competitive. In other words, Microsoft combines the flexibility and entrepreneurial spirit of the hacker culture from which it emerged with the structure and stability of a large modern firm. The basic elements of this approach are to continuously synchronize what employees are doing individually and as members of parallel teams and to periodically stabilize the evolving product features as the project proceeds. This puts order in the often chaotic nature of iterative software development yet allows specifications to evolve through experimentation and hacking away. The creativity of Microsoft employees is thus channeled toward popular, competitive, and profitable products, contributing to the company's continued success.

Giorgio de Michelis expands on Nonaka and Takeuchi's knowledge creation theory by focusing on processes instead of organizations. A key concept used here is that of the *cooperative process*, that is, the communicative relations that bind participants to each other and with the actions they are performing. The success of a cooperative process depends on the effectiveness of its actors and also on their capability to switch from one position to another when necessary. Indeed, in de Michelis's framework a given actor may be successively both a performer, that is, satisfying a request for action, and a customer, that is, making the request for an action. He shows that knowledge creation is a principal factor in allowing an increase in the value/cost ratio of a cooperative process as it enhances the capability of participants to manage complexity. He then argues that information and communication technologies should be designed to support this process, creating a space, or ba, where users can share and stock knowledge about the changing environment in which they are embedded. He presents a detailed case study of an Italian design academy to support his arguments.

International Knowledge Creation and Knowledge Transfer

In past years scholars have directed increasing attention to patterns of knowledge creation within multinational enterprises (MNEs), recognizing the potential advantages of global knowledge-creating networks. Based on analysis of a large-scale survey, D. Eleanor Westney finds that *cross-border knowledge creation* within MNEs is indeed extensive, calling for an examination of the relative efficiency of cross-border knowledge-creation processes. For example, estimating the relative effectiveness of fax, phone, video conferencing, e-mail networks, and face-to-face communications in the knowledge-creation process, Westney finds that the movement of people for short-, medium-, or long-term periods plays a key role in knowledge creation. Westney goes on to discuss several distinct cross-border knowledge-creation processes in terms of the *location* and *nature* of knowledge (i.e., generic or location-specific; tacit or explicit knowledge). She argues that a better understanding of these processes could permit firms to optimize resources by fitting cross-border communication and people-moving modes with knowledge-creation processes.

Next, Kenichi Yasumuro and Eleanor Westney look at the implementation by Japanese MNEs of Japanese organizational and knowledge-creation practices in foreign countries. They argue that many of the best Japanese firms are characterized by *front-line management*, where factories, R&D labs, and sales and marketing organizations are valued as key centers of knowledge creation. Key aspects of this approach include the diffusion of significant levels of discretion, response capability, and problem-solving responsibilities to front-line employees (e.g., factory workers, salespeople) and an egalitarian work culture that minimizes differences across organizational statuses and ranks. Not all Japanese firms adopt these practices, however. Based on an empirical survey, Yasumuro and Westney argue that this lack of consistency explains the uneven implementation of Japanese-style work practices by foreign subsidiaries of Japanese firms. In other words, firms that have highly developed front-line management practices in their home country organization are likely to have developed them overseas as well, while those who do not should not be expected to do better abroad.

Interorganizational Dynamics

In the next part the focus of interest shifts from *intra*organizational to *inter*organizational knowledge creation. Toshihiro Nishiguchi proposes a new model of knowledge creation based on the *coevolution* of interorganizational relations. Drawing on recent developments in complexity theory, he proposes a model where exploitation and symbiosis between organizations are perceived not as separate systems but as intertwined and nested within a twister. In this view, knowledge creation emerges through the destabilizing and dynamic interaction between the two systems. By contrast, traditional views have focused on the adaptation of organizations to environmental changes, neglecting the potential for interorganizational interaction to affect the very environment that surrounds them. In this new view, organizations are seen as entities with their own perception, consciousness, and memory whose interaction with other organizations can be a driving force that creates and maintains order within the social and economic system.

Sigrun Caspary and Toshihiro Nishiguchi continue this exploration of interorganizational dynamics, focusing on the case of the Japanese aircraft industry, where unique forms of interaction among government institutions and private companies play a central role. Although relatively small and focused on components rather than complete airplanes, Japanese aircraft manufacturers have come to occupy a critical position in the global aircraft industry. Based on in-depth analysis of several Japanese and international aircraft and engine development projects, Caspary and Nishiguchi argue that Japanese manufacturers such as Mitsubishi Heavy Industries (MHI) and Ishikawajima-Harima Heavy Industries (IHI) became attractive partners in international codevelopment projects (such as the development of the Boeing 777) because of unique manufacturing and product development capabilities. Low-cost and high-quality production capabilities were developed mainly through *intra*organizational transfers of manufacturing practices, as the main Japanese aircraft firms were all large and diversified conglomerates whose aircraft activity constituted only a small portion of their operations. The capability for product development, particularly intercorporate product development, was developed through interorganizational cooperation in various semigovernmental organizations sponsored by the Ministry of International Trade and Industry (MITI), whose overall role in the evolution of the Japanese aircraft industry actually appears to have been secondary. Intercorporate cooperation was necessary because each individual firm was too weak to carry out large-scale development projects on its own. This proved to be an advantage later as multifirm development projects became the norm in the aircraft industry, even for giants such as Boeing and General Electric. The Japanese mode of *inter*organizational knowledge creation, which emerged out of necessity more than strategy, thus helped Japanese firms enter the global aircraft industry as reliable and often indispensable partners.

James R. Lincoln and Christina Ahmadjian discuss interorganizational knowledge sharing in the Japanese electronics industry. Relative to the auto industry, buyer-supplier relations in the Japanese electronic industry tend to be less close and cooperative (e.g., during new product development). However, Lincoln and Ahmadjian suggest that a lot of informal knowledge sharing goes on among electronics firms nevertheless, mainly by way of extensive *shukko* (employee transfers) among firms. This generally overlooked practice is used to align the goals and operations of suppliers with those of the buyer, as well as to permit interorganizational transfers of tacit knowledge.

Finally, Linsu Kim discusses the emergence of Samsung as a global leader in memory chip manufacturing. He argues that previous research on knowledge creation has tended to focus too narrowly on advanced countries and/or pioneering firms. Kim uses the concepts of absorptive capacity and "co-opetition" along with Nonaka's knowledge creation model to show how Samsung orchestrated the equally important technological catching-up process. To raise its absorptive capacity, the firm used migratory knowledge (i.e., American-trained engineers and their tacit knowledge) to expand its prior knowledge base and proactively created internal crises and co-opetition among units to intensify employee effort. For example, by setting challenging goals for teams, Samsung intensified work pace and interaction among members, thus accelerating the process of knowledge conversion at the individual and organizational levels. With some differences, the evolution of Hyundai as a global player in the automotive industry appears to have followed the same pattern, suggesting the potential universality of the Samsung model for firms in developed countries. You may now proceed at will. Welcome to the *Knowledge Emergence* party!

Note

1. Japan-American Institute of Management Science/Sasakawa Peace Foundation Conference on International Comparative Study of Knowledge Creation, Honolulu, Hawaii, December 12–14, 1996.

References

Kogut, Bruce, and Ugo Zander. 1992. "Knowledge of the Firm, Combinative Capabilities, and the Replication of Technology." *Organization Science* 3: 383–97.

Nonaka, Ikujiro, and Hirotaka Takeuchi. 1995. *The Knowledge-Creating Company: How Japanese Companies Create the Dynamics of Innovation.* New York: Oxford University Press.

PART I
KNOWLEDGE, *BA*, AND CARE

2

Emergence of "Ba"

A Conceptual Framework for the Continuous and Self-transcending Process of Knowledge Creation

IKUJIRO NONAKA

NOBORU KONNO

RYOKO TOYAMA

In recent years, the importance of knowledge as a source of sustainable competitive advantage has been discussed by a myriad of authors (Drucker, 1993; Leonard-Barton, 1992; Nelson, 1991; Prahalad and Hamel, 1990; Quinn, 1992; Sveiby, 1997; Teece, Pisano, and Shuen, 1990; Toffler, 1990). Knowledge is undoubtedly an indispensable resource to create value for the next generation of society, industries, and companies.

Yet, despite all the discussions and attentions in both the academic and business worlds, very few have articulated how organizations actually create and manage knowledge. Many companies still seem to remain locked in the phase of building efficient and effective information technology (IT) systems when they try to "manage knowledge."

Although the terms "information" and "knowledge" are often used interchangeably, there is a clear distinction between information and knowledge. Information is a flow of messages, while knowledge is created by that very flow of information and is anchored in the beliefs and commitment of its holder.

Traditional management models focus on how to control the information flow and information processing within the organization. In such models, organizations are viewed as machines for information processing, which is a problem-solving activity centered on what is given to the organization, not what is created by it. This view, however, fails to capture the essence of organization as a knowledge-creating entity. Instead of merely solving problems, organizations create and define problems and then develop new knowledge to solve the problems by actively interacting with their environments and reshaping the environments and even the organizations themselves.

Hence, what "knowledge management" should achieve is not a static management of information or existing knowledge, but a dynamic management of the process of creating knowledge out of knowledge. In this essay, we argue that organizational knowledge creation is a continuous self-transcending process, which requires a new kind of management that goes beyond the traditional models of "management." In the following sections we discuss the basic concepts of the knowledge-creating process of an organization, how such a process is managed, and the organizational issues that arise in so doing.

SECI: The Continuous Self-transcending Process of Knowledge Creation

In traditional Western epistemology (the theory of knowledge), knowledge is defined as "justified true belief." However, this is an absolute, static, and nonhuman view of knowledge and fails to address the relative, dynamic, and humanistic dimensions of knowledge. Knowledge is context-specific and relational. Knowledge is dynamic, as it is dynamically created in social interactions. Knowledge is also humanistic, and it has both an active and a subjective nature. For the purposes of this study, we define knowledge as *"a dynamic human process of justifying personal belief toward the 'truth.'"*

There are two kinds of knowledge: explicit knowledge and tacit knowledge. Explicit knowledge can be expressed in words and numbers and shared in the form of data, scientific formulae, specifications, manuals, and the like. This kind of knowledge can be readily transmitted across individuals formally and systematically. Tacit knowledge, on the other hand, is highly personal and hard to formalize, making it difficult to communicate or share with others. Subjective insights, intuitions, and hunches fall into this category of knowledge. Difficult to verbalize, such tacit knowledge is deeply rooted in an individual's action and experience, as well as in the ideals, values, or emotions he or she embraces.

These two types of knowledge are complementary to each other, and both are crucial to knowledge creation. They interact with and change into each other in the creative activities of human beings. Understanding this reciprocal relationship between explicit knowledge and tacit knowledge is the key to understanding the knowledge-creating process. We call the interaction between the two types of knowledge knowledge conversion. Note that this conversion is a social process *between* individuals and is not confined to *within* an individual. Knowledge is created through such interactions among individuals with different types and contents of knowledge (Nonaka, 1990; Nonaka and Takeuchi, 1995).

There are four modes of knowledge conversion (whence the acronym SECI): (1) *socialization* (from tacit knowledge to tacit knowledge); (2) *externalization* (from tacit knowledge to explicit knowledge); (3) *combination* (from explicit knowledge to explicit knowledge); and (4) *internalization* (from explicit knowledge to tacit knowledge). Table 2.1 lists the factors that characterize the four knowledge conversion modes.

Socialization

We use the term "socialization" to emphasize the importance of joint activities in the process of converting new tacit knowledge through shared experiences. Since tacit knowledge is context specific and difficult to formalize, transferring tacit knowledge requires sharing the same experience through joint activities such as being

Table 2.1. The Factors That Constitute the Knowledge-Conversion Process

Socialization: From Tacit to Tacit

Tacit knowledge accumulation	Managers gather information from sales and production sites, share experiences with suppliers and customers, and engage in dialogue with competitors
Extra-firm social information collection (wandering outside)	Managers engage in bodily experience through management by wandering about and get ideas for corporate strategy from daily social life, interaction with external experts, and informal meetings with competitors
Intra-firm social information collection (wandering inside)	Managers find new strategies and market opportunities by wandering inside the firm
Transfer of tacit knowledge	Managers create a work environment that allows peers to understand craftsmanship and expertise through practice and demonstrations by the master
Externalization: From Tacit to Explicit (creating concepts)	Managers perform facilitation of creative and essential dialogue, the use of "abductive thinking," the use of metaphors in dialogue for concept creation

Combination: From Explicit to Explicit

Acquisition and integration	Managers engage in planning strategies and operations, assembling internal and external existing data by using published literature, computer simulation, and forecasting
Synthesis and processing	Managers build and create manuals, documents, and databases on products and services and build up material by gathering management figures and/or technical information from all over the company
Dissemination	Managers engage in planning and in implementation of presentations to transmit newly created concepts

Internalization: From Explicit to Tacit

Personal experience; real-world knowledge acquisition	Managers engage in "enactive liaisoning" activities with functional department by using crossfunctional development teams. Search and share new values and thoughts; share and try to understand management visions and values through communications with fellow members in the organization
Simulation and experimentation; virtual-world knowledge acquisition	Managers engage in facilitating prototyping and benchmarking and facilitate the challenging spirit within the organization; managers form teams as a model and conduct experiments and share results with the entire department

Source: Adapted from Nonaka, Byosiere, Borucki, and Konno (1994).

together, spending time, or living in the same environment. A quintessential example of socialization is traditional apprenticeship. Apprentices learn their craft not by spoken words or written textbooks but by observing, imitating, and practicing the works of their masters. Another example of socialization is the use of informal meetings outside the workplace by Japanese companies. Participants talk over meals and drinks, creating common tacit knowledge, such as a worldview, as well as mutual trust. Here, Nishida's (1921, 1970) concept of pure experience, which is related to Zen learning, is important.

In practice, socialization involves capturing knowledge through physical proximity. Knowledge is acquired from outside the organization through direct interactions with suppliers and customers. Capturing tacit knowledge embedded within the organization by walking around inside the organization is another process of acquiring knowledge.

Externalization

Through externalization, the process of articulating tacit knowledge into explicit knowledge, knowledge becomes crystallized, thus able to be shared by others, and becomes the basis of new knowledge. Through externalization, tacit knowledge is expressed and translated into such forms as metaphors, concepts, hypothesis, diagrams, models, or prototypes so that it can be understood by others. Yet expressions are often inadequate, inconsistent, and insufficient. Such discrepancies and gaps between images and expressions can help promote "reflection" and interaction between individuals.

In practice, externalization is supported by two key factors. First, the articulation of tacit knowledge involves techniques that enable one to express his or her own ideas or images both through deductive/inductive analysis and through abduction with figurative language, for example, metaphors, analogies, narratives, and visuals. Dialogues, that is, "listening and contributing to the benefit of all participants" (Bohm 1980), strongly support externalization. The second factor involves translating the tacit knowledge of customers or experts into readily understandable forms. This may require deductive/inductive reasoning or creative inference (abduction).

Combination

In combination, the process of converging explicit knowledge into more complex and systematic explicit knowledge, knowledge is exchanged and combined through such media as documents, meetings, telephone conversations, or computerized communication networks. Reconfiguration of existing knowledge through sorting, adding, combining, and categorizing can create new knowledge. In this mode, communication, diffusion, and systemization of knowledge are the keys. Combination can also include the "breakdown" of concepts. Breaking down a concept, such as a corporate vision, into operationalized business or product concepts also creates systemic, explicit knowledge. In the combination process, justification of knowledge takes place so as to form the basis for agreement and allows an organization to take practical concrete steps.

In practice, combination relies on three processes. First, explicit knowledge is collected from inside or outside the organization and then combined. Second, the new explicit knowledge is disseminated among the organizational members through presentations or meetings. Third, the explicit knowledge is edited or processed in the organization to make it more usable. Creative use of computerized communication networks and large-scale databases can facilitate this mode of knowledge conversion.

Internalization

Internalization, the process of embodying explicit knowledge into tacit knowledge, is closely related to "learning by doing." Through internalization, knowledge that has been created is shared throughout an organization. Internalized knowledge is used to broaden, extend, and reframe organizational members' tacit knowledge. When knowledge is internalized into individuals' tacit knowledge bases in the form of shared mental models or technical knowhow, it becomes valuable assets. This tacit knowledge accumulated at the individual level is in turn shared with others through socialization, setting off a new spiral of knowledge creation.

In practice, internalization relies on two dimensions. First, explicit knowledge has to be embodied in action and practice. Thus the process of internalizing explicit knowledge actualizes concepts or methods about strategy, tactics, innovation, or improvement. For example, training programs help the trainees to understand the organization and themselves. Second, explicit knowledge can be embodied through simulations or experiments to trigger learning by doing. New concepts or methods can thus be learned in virtual situations.

Knowledge creation is a continuous process. As we said earlier, knowledge is created through a continuous and dynamic interaction between tacit and explicit knowledge (see figure 2.1). Knowledges created through each mode of knowledge conversion interact with each other in the spiral of knowledge creation. For example, tacit knowledge about customers' needs captured through socialization may become explicit knowledge about a new product concept through externalization. Such a concept then steers the combination phase, where newly developed and existing component technologies are combined to build a prototype. The explicit knowledge expressed as the form of prototype is then turned into new tacit knowledge through internalization. The new tacit knowledge then triggers a new cycle of knowledge creation.

The interaction between tacit knowledge and explicit knowledge is not confined to one ontological level of knowledge-creating entity; for example, there are individual, group, organizational, and interorganizational levels. The organization has to tap into the tacit knowledge created and accumulated at the individual level, since tacit knowledge of individuals is the basis of organizational knowledge creation. The tacit knowledge created is *organizationally* amplified through four modes of knowledge conversion and crystallized at higher ontological levels. We call this the knowledge spiral, in which the interaction between tacit knowledge and explicit knowledge will become larger in scale as it moves up the ontological levels. Thus, organizational knowledge

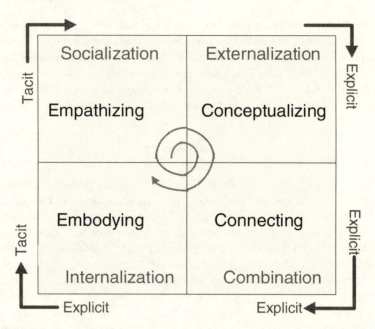

Figure 2.1. The SECI Process

creation is a spiral process, starting at the individual level and moving up through expanding communities of interaction, that crosses sectional, departmental, divisional, and organizational boundaries. A spiral emerges when the interaction between tacit and explicit knowledge is elevated dynamically from a lower ontological level to higher levels.

Knowledge creation is also a self-transcending process, in which one reaches out beyond the boundaries of one's own existence (Jantsch, 1980). In socialization, self-transcendence is fundamental since tacit knowledge can only be shared through direct experiences, which go beyond individuals (Nishida, 1921). For example, we empathize with our colleagues and customers in socialization, which diminishes borders among individuals. In externalization, an individual transcends the inner and outer boundaries of the self in the process of committing to the group and thus becomes one with the group. Here, the sum of the individuals' intentions and ideas fuse and become integrated with the group's mental world. In combination, new knowledge generated through externalization transcends the group in analogue or digital signals. In internalization, individuals access the knowledge realm of the group and the entire organization. This again requires self-transcendence, as one has to find oneself in a larger entity.

Ba: Platform for Knowledge Creation

Since knowledge is intangible, boundaryless, and dynamic and cannot be stocked, it has to be exploited where and when it is needed to create values. To exploit and create knowledge effectively and efficiently, it is necessary to concentrate knowledge at a certain time and space. We call such space ba (roughly translated "place"). By creating and managing ba, an organization can manage the knowledge-creating process effectively (Nonaka and Konno, 1998).

Based on a concept originally proposed by the Japanese philosopher Kitaro Nishida (1921, 1970) and further developed by Shimizu (1995), we define ba in knowledge creation as a platform where knowledge is created, shared, and exploited. It functions as a medium for the resource concentration of the organization's knowledge and of the individuals who own and create such knowledge. Ba collects the applied knowledge of the area and integrates it. It is from such a platform that a transcendental perspective emerges to integrate and create knowledge.

The most important aspect of ba is "interaction." Knowledge is created not just by an individual but through interactions among individuals and with the environment. For knowledge to be created organizationally, knowledge within a particular individual needs to be shared, recreated, and amplified through interactions with others. Ba is a space where such interactions take place. Therefore, the knowledge-creating process is also the process of creating ba, which means to create a boundary of new interaction.

Ba does not necessarily mean a physical space. In terms of the theory of existentialism, ba is a context that *harbors meaning*. The Japanese word *ba* denotes not only a physical space but a specific time and space, including the space of interpersonal relations. Hence, ba is a time-space nexus or, as Heidegger expressed it, a locationality that simultaneously includes space and time. Thus, we consider ba to be a shared time and space for emerging relationship among individuals and groups to create knowledge. It can be physical (e.g., office, dispersed business space), virtual (e.g., e-mail, teleconference), mental (e.g., shared experiences, ideas, ideals), or any combination of these. It can be a shared space and time (from face-to-face to virtual) for a project team, a space for informal dialogues, a space to share experiences with customers, a space for interdivisional cooperation, or a space shared by virtual companies.

To participate in a ba means to get involved and transcend one's own limited perspective or boundary. Within an organization, then, one can both experience transcendence in ba yet remain analytically rational, achieving the best of both worlds. Ba is the world where the individual understands him- or herself as a part of the environment on which his or her life depends.

Knowledge is embedded in ba, where it is then acquired through one's own experience or reflections on the experiences of others. If knowledge is separated from ba, it turns into information, which can then be communicated independently from the ba. Information resides in media and networks, while knowledge resides in ba.

There are four types of ba: originating, dialoguing, systematizing, and exercising. Each type supports a particular mode of knowledge conversion between tacit and explicit knowledge and offers a platform for a specific step in the knowledge spiral process. However, the respective relationships between single ba and conversions are by no means exclusive. Understanding the different characteristics of ba and how they interact with each other can facilitate successful knowledge creation. The characteristics of each type of ba are as follows.

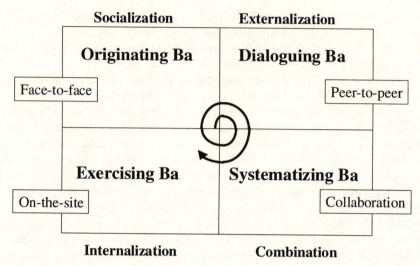

Figure 2.2. Four Types of Ba

Originating ba is the world where individuals share feelings, emotions, experiences, and mental models. An individual sympathizes or further empathizes with others, removing the barrier between self and others. Here emerges what Condon (1976) terms entrainment, which is similar to empathy and is defined as synchronizing behavior. To use epistemological metaphors, the guiding principle is "I love, therefore I am" (Nishida), as opposed to "I think, therefore I am" (Descartes). Care, love, trust, commitment, freedom, and safety emerge out of originating ba.

Originating ba often is the primary ba from which the knowledge-creation process begins, and this ba is associated with the socialization process. Physical, face-to-face experiences are the key in converting tacit knowledge into tacit knowledge. *Pure experiences, ecstasy,* or *being thrown into the world* are philosophical terms that describe such a subjective ontological field. A stress on open organizational designs and customer interfaces also provides strong ecological stimuli through direct encounter between individuals.

Dialoguing ba is more consciously constructed than originating ba. Selecting people with the right mix of specific knowledge and capabilities for a project team, task force, or crossfunctional team is critical. Through dialogue, individuals' mental models and skills are converted to common terms and concepts. Two processes are operating in concert. Individuals share the mental model of others but also reflect and analyze their own. This is the ba where Nishida's world and the Cartesian world interact in thought.

Dialoguing ba is the place where tacit knowledge is made explicit, thus it is associated with the externalization process. Dialogue is key for such conversions; the extensive use of metaphors is one of the conversion skills required. The importance of sensitivity for meaning and the will to make tacit knowledge explicit is recognized at companies such as Honda or 3M. Here dialoguing ba for collective reflection are institutionalized in the company culture. Initiators (conceptual leaders) are challenged to pursue their ideas.

Systematizing ba is a place of interaction in a virtual world instead of a sharing of space and time in reality. Here, combining new explicit knowledge with existing information and knowledge generates and systematizes explicit knowledge through justifying the concept throughout the organization. Cartesian logic dominates. Thus, the systematizing ba is associated with the combination phase.

The combination of explicit knowledge is most efficiently supported in collaborative environments utilizing information technology. The possibilities to construct and support systematizing ba through the use of on-line networks (intranet or internet), groupware, document tools, and databases have been growing rapidly over the last decade. This technological shift enhances the importance of this conversion mode.

Exercising ba supports internalization by facilitating the conversion of explicit knowledge to tacit knowledge. Focused training with senior mentors and colleagues consists primarily of continued exercises that stress certain patterns and the working out of such patterns. Through such self-refinement, knowledge is continuously enhanced by the use of explicit knowledge in real-life or simulated applications. The interaction that takes place in exercising ba is on-the-site, which means that it shares time and space. Rather than teaching based on analysis, learning by continuous self-refinement through on-the-job training or peripheral and active participation (Lave and Wenger 1991) is stressed in such a ba. Exercising ba synthesizes the transcendence and reflection through action, while dialoguing ba achieves this through thought.

The knowledge generated in each ba is eventually shared and forms the knowledge base of organizations. Moreover, ba exists at many ontological levels, and these levels may be connected to form a greater ba. Individuals form the ba of teams, which in turn form the ba of organizations. Then the market environment becomes the ba for the organization. The organic interactions among these different levels of ba can amplify the knowledge-creating process. The following case studies of Seven-Eleven Japan and Maekawa Seisakusho illustrate how organizations create knowledge by building and utilizing ba.

Case Studies: Knowledge Creation through Ba

Seven-Eleven Japan: Continuous Knowledge Creation through Four Types of Ba

Owned by Ito-Yokado, a Japanese supermarket chain, Seven-Eleven Japan is the most profitable convenience store franchiser in Japan. Its success is signified by its 1991 acquisition of Southland Corporation, the original franchiser of Seven-Eleven stores in the United States.

The success of Seven-Eleven Japan stems from its successful management of knowledge creation throughout the company. Although the success of Seven-

Eleven Japan has been often attributed to its extensive use of information technologies such as a state-of-the-art point-of-sales (POS) system, such systems are only a part of the system that Seven-Eleven Japan has built to create and exploit knowledge. By managing various ba and by continuous hypothesis-building and testing in such ba, Seven-Eleven Japan successfully creates knowledge.

The knowledge-creating process at Seven-Eleven Japan starts on the shop floors of the seven thousand Seven-Eleven stores. Store employees (in many cases part-time employees) accumulate tacit knowledge about customers' ever-changing needs through socialization with customers, for example, by engaging in dialogues with them. Long-term experiences in dealing with customers give store employees unique knowledge and insight in the local market and customers. They often say that they can just "see" how well certain items will sell in their stores; they cannot explain why, but say it's just their "feel" of the market based on their experiences.

To create and exploit such tacit knowledge about the market, Seven-Eleven Japan actively utilizes its stores as originating ba. Employees receive extensive on-the-job training (OJT) on the shop floor. Every new recruit is required to work at Seven-Eleven stores in various functions for about two years so as to accumulate experiences in directly dealing with customers and actually managing Seven-Eleven stores. Seven-Eleven Japan says that such OJT is the only way to keep its employees focused on serving its customers and does not use documented job manuals. Another instrument to create originating ba is the *burabura shain* (walking-around employee). These employees have the task of wandering around and socializing with customers in stores to discover new knowledge in the fields.

Such tacit knowledge about the customers is then converted into explicit knowledge through externalization. At Seven-Eleven Japan, the importance of making "hypotheses" about market needs at the shop floor is emphasized in every possible occasion. Since local employees are the ones who holds vast tacit knowledge about their customers and the local areas around their shops, Seven-Eleven Japan lets them build their own hypotheses about the sales of particular items by giving them the responsibility to order items. The responsibility is even given to part-time workers. For example, a local part-time worker can order more beer, on the basis of the knowledge that the local community is having a festival and that it is going to be a hot day.

To facilitate such hypothesis-building, Seven-Eleven Japan actively builds and utilizes dialoging ba, where tacit knowledge of local employees is externalized into explicit knowledge in the form of hypotheses through dialogues with others. For example, several part-time employees are responsible for ordering merchandise instead of just one manager. Each employee is responsible for certain merchandise categories, and through dialogues with others who are responsible for other categories, they can build hypotheses that fit changing market needs better.

Another instrument that facilitates hypotheses-building is the use of field counselors, who provide information and advice to store owners and employees to help them build their own hypotheses. Seven-Eleven Japan employs about fifteen hundred field counselors. Each is responsible for eight stores on average, each of which they have to visit at least twice a week. During these visits, field counselors engage in dialogues with owners and employees of local stores and give them advice in plac-

internalized again. This is a continuous process, as Toshifumi Suzuki, the CEO of Seven-Eleven Japan, affirms. "Day after day, week after week, I've been doing the same thing for twenty-five years—asking the employees what is wrong about our shops and how we can fix it." Such continuous knowledge creation through a well-laid system base on four types of ba is what created the success of Seven-Eleven Japan.

Maekawa Seisakusho: Organic Cohesion of Self-transcending Ba

Maekawa Seisakusho is a leading company that holds a 50 percent world market share in industrial freezers. Since its foundation in 1924, it has focused on specialized knowhow in basic, applied, and production technologies in industries that involve food and thermal technology.

Maekawa has a unique structure that can be described as a collective of many small "independent companies." Each of these independent companies is quite small, with twenty-five employees on average, while Maekawa in total employs two thousand five hundred people. Each of these small companies is established and classified by its product and/or market. Maekawa now consists of eighty such corporations in Japan and twenty-three outside of Japan. Each company either serves its local area or focuses on a specific market, for example, food, industrial freezers, or energy-related services. The purpose of this structure is to empower local organizations to cater to the specific needs of customers in niche markets as autonomous organizations. Each company is completely responsible for its own business and is self-sufficient, with a complete set of the functions it needs, from design to marketing.

However, Maekawa is not simply a holding company of many subsidiaries. Rather, its independent companies are ba where the self-transcending process is fostered in order to create knowledge, and the various ba are organically interrelated to each other to form Maekawa as a whole. Employees of Maekawa transcend the boundaries of self and organization when they participate in such ba to create knowledge.

At Maekawa, the importance of working with customers to satisfy their needs is always emphasized. Employees of Maekawa transcend the boundary between the organization and the market by "indwelling" in the customer's world. Instead of sitting at Maekawa's office, they often go out to customers to spend long hours with them. Masao Maekawa, the president of Maekawa Seisakusho, explains that this "getting out in the real world" is a way of "seamless co-experiencing" with customers (from a speech delivered at the Maekawa Sougou Kenkyuujo and Ba to Soshiki no Forum, 1996). He points out that it is vital "to indwell in the world of the customers to achieve oneness of subject and object" since it "helps to understand the needs of customers." Customers' needs and the knowledge necessary to solve their problems are often tacit, and customers cannot communicate them well to Maekawa's employees. Only by actually experiencing what customers are experiencing can one accumulate the knowledge needed to solve the customers' problems effectively.

ing orders and managing stores, as well as collecting information on each store. I a field counselor notices a unique hypothesis, such as new way to display merchandises at one store, he or she takes a note and shares that hypothesis with other stores.

The hypotheses built at the shop floor are disseminated throughout the company through various dialoguing ba. Field counselors report on the knowledge built at the stores they are responsible for to their zone managers, who then disseminate knowledge acquired from a field counselor to other field counselors. Zone managers from across Japan meet at the headquarters in Tokyo every week, where success stories and problems at local stores are shared with Seven-Eleven's top management and other zone managers. Field counselors also have meetings every week, where one thousand five hundred field counselors and five hundred staff members from the headquarters, including the top management, meet to share knowledge and information.

The cost to maintain such ba is not small. To hold such meetings in Tokyo every week, it has been estimated that Seven-Eleven Japan spends about 18 million dollars per year for traveling, lodging, and so on. However, Seven-Eleven Japan emphasizes the importance of face-to-face communication. Certain types of knowledge can be created and communicated only through *sharing* time and space together.

The hypotheses built at dialoging ba on market needs are then tested by the actual sales figures of the items. Successful and unsuccessful hypotheses are compiled at systematizing ba. Seven-Eleven Japan has built a state-of-the-art information system to collect, analyze, and utilize sales data, the company compiles systemic explicit knowledge about the market through the vast amount of data collected through its POS system.

Such explicit knowledge is immediately fed back to stores so that they can built new hypotheses that suit the reality of the market better. Graphic order terminals (GOTs), terminals that display the sales data analysis graphically and that place orders, are used at stores to help store employees to build hypotheses and to simplify and speed up the order process and delivery.

Compiled explicit knowledge is then internalized in store employees, field counselors, zone managers, and staff and managers at the headquarters. Utilizing POS data and its analysis, store employees test their hypotheses about the market every day at their local stores, which work as exercising ba. The organizational culture of Seven-Eleven Japan, which emphasizes the importance of serving the ever-changing needs of customers, is embedded in the mindsets and actions of the store employees through such continuous hypothesis-building and testing. The sales data and the stories of success and failures at shop floors are also shared among managers and field counselors through the meetings every week. Top management repeatedly emphasizes the importance of everyday efforts to make improvements and to adapt to market changes at such meetings. In such exercising ba, knowledge created in systematizing ba is justified by being compared to the reality of the world, and the gap between the knowledge and the reality then triggers new cycles of knowledge creation.

The internalization thus starts a new spiral of the SECI process. New hypotheses are built based on new tacit knowledge embodied in employees and managers. Hypotheses are then tested, and the results are fed back to the organization to be

The transcendence between organizational boundaries also occurs *within* Maekawa Seisakusho. Although Maekawa's independent companies are basically autonomous and self-sufficient, they are not isolated from each other. Some of the independent companies share the same office space. Members from different independent companies often spend time together to form informal relationships. Sometimes a new project or even a new independent company is created out of such relationships. When they encounter problems too large to deal with alone, a group of several independent companies are formed to find a solution together. The key in such interactions among independent companies is that they are created voluntarily, not by a plan or order from the headquarters. Maekawa Seisakusho as a whole is a coherent organization with various parts organically interacting each other.

This organic structure of Maekawa Seisakusho is modeled after a living organism, and it can be depicted as an "autopoietic system" (Maturana and Varela, 1980). Living organic systems are composed of various organs, which are again made up of numerous cells. Relationships between system and organs, and between organ and cells, are neither dominate-subordinate nor whole-part. Each unit, like an autonomous cell, controls all changes occurring continuously within itself, and each unit determines its boundary through self-reproduction. At Maekawa, autonomous individuals and independent companies set their task boundaries by themselves to pursue the ultimate goal expressed in the higher intention of the organization, that is, to serve customers.

Managing the Knowledge-Creating Process: Beyond "Management"

To manage the dynamic knowledge-creating process just described, managers are required to play different roles from those in traditional "management," which centers around controlling the information flow (von Krogh, Ichijo, and Nonaka, 1997; Nonaka and Takeuchi, 1995). To manage knowledge creation, leaders must manage ba by providing *knowledge vision* and by *building and energizing* ba, as follows.

Especially crucial to this management is the role of knowledge producers, the middle managers who actively participate in the process. The role of knowledge producers is similar to the role of key players in soccer a game in which "managing the space" is the key. In the game field, space is a strategic concept. Players have to "find" a space in the field and exploit such a space effectively to make a play. Players not only find such a space but also actively create one. A coach (top management) creates and exploits such a space based on a holistic view of the game as an "outsider." On the other hand, a key player has to play as an insider while sharing this holistic view with the coach. Such a space is unstable and quickly changes its shape throughout the game. The existence of such ba is not apparent to everyone. Only capable coaches and players can understand such ba and exploit it. Knowledge producers have to grasp such ba intuitively and exploit it so that the organizational members can interact dynamically with each other and/or with the environment to create knowledge.

Providing Knowledge Vision

For various ba in an organization to be effective platforms for organizational knowledge creation, they have to be strategically coherent under the "knowledge vision" of the organization. Knowledge vision defines what kind of knowledge the company should create and in what domain and synchronizes the entire organization. It also facilitates spontaneous commitments of the individuals and groups that are involved in knowledge creation. Knowledge vision also defines the value system that evaluates, justifies, and determines the quality of knowledge the company creates. In short, knowledge vision gives a direction to the knowledge-creating process and the knowledge created by it.

It is top management's role to articulate such knowledge vision and communicate it throughout and outside the company. Since knowledge is boundaryless, any form of new knowledge can be created regardless of the existing business structure of the company. Therefore, it is important for top management to articulate a knowledge vision that transcends the boundaries of existing products, divisions, organizations, and markets. It is then middle managers' role to break down the values and visions into concepts and images to guide the knowledge-creating process with vitality and direction. Middle managers remake reality, or "produce new knowledge," according to the company's vision.

Building and Energizing Ba

Ba can be spontaneously created, and it can be built intentionally. Leaders can facilitate knowledge creation by providing physical space, such as meeting rooms, or cyberspace, such as a computer network, or by promoting interactions among organizational members by using such means as task forces. It is also important for managers to "find" and utilize spontaneously formed ba, which changes or disappears very quickly.

However, building or finding ba is not enough for a firm to manage the dynamic knowledge-creating process. Ba should be "energized" so that the individuals or the organization can create and amplify knowledge through the SECI process. For that, the management has to supply necessary conditions to energize ba, such as autonomy; creative chaos; redundancy; requisite variety; and love, care, trust, and commitment.

Autonomy increases the chances of finding valuable information and motivating organizational members to create new knowledge. Not only does the self-organizing quality increase the commitment of the individuals, but also it can be a source of unexpected knowledge. By allowing members of the organization to act autonomously, the organization may increase the chance of introducing unexpected opportunities.

Creative chaos stimulates the interaction between the organization and the external environment. When chaos is introduced into an organization, its members face a "breakdown" of routines, habits, or cognitive frameworks. Winograd and Flores (1986) emphasize the importance of such periodic breakdowns as an opportunity to reconsider one's fundamental thinking and perspective. The continuous process of questioning and reevaluating existing premises by individual organizational members fosters organizational knowledge creation. While chaos is generated naturally when the organization faces a real crisis, such as declining market, it can also be generated intentionally when the organization's leaders try to evoke a sense of crisis among organizational members by proposing challenging goals. This intentional chaos, referred as creative chaos, increases tension within the organization and focuses the attention of organizational members on defining the problem and resolving the crisis situation.

Redundancy is absolutely essential for the knowledge spiral to take place organizationally despite its connotations of unnecessary duplication, waste, or information overload. In business organizations, redundancy refers to *intentional* overlapping of information about business activities, management responsibilities, and the company as a whole. Redundancy of information speeds up the knowledge-creating process in two ways. First, sharing redundant information promotes the sharing of tacit knowledge, because individuals can sense what others are trying to articulate. Second, redundancy of information helps organizational members understand where they stand in the organization, which in turn functions to control their direction of thinking and action.

Requisite variety allows an organization to cope with many contingencies. According to Ashby (1956), an organization's internal diversity has to match the variety and complexity of the environment in order to deal with challenges posed by the environment. Requisite variety can be enhanced by combining information differently, flexibly, and quickly and by providing equal access to information throughout the organization. When information differentials exist within the organization, organizational members cannot interact on equal terms, which hinders the search for different interpretations of new information.

Fostering love, care, trust and commitment among organizational members forms the foundation of knowledge creation. For knowledge (especially tacit knowledge) to be shared and for the self-transcending process of knowledge creation to occur, there should be strong love and caring among organizational members.

Conclusion

To summarize, the continuous and self-transcending process of knowledge creation, knowledge is created through the SECI process, involving the four modes of knowledge conversion: socialization, externalization, combination, and internalization of knowledge. With the conversion of tacit knowledge held by individuals into organizational knowledge, knowledge goes up, both in scale and at ontological levels.

The SECI process takes place at ba, where knowledge within a particular individual can be shared, recreated, and amplified through interactions with others. For an organization to create knowledge, leaders of the organization have to build and maintain and energize ba by providing enabling conditions of autonomy; creative chaos; redundancy; variety; and love, care, trust, and commitment.

Finally, we would like to bring up an issue of language as a future research topic. Language has long been thought as an "instrument of knowledge." By *language* here we mean tropes (such as metaphor, metonymy, synecdoche), "grammar," and "context" for knowledge, as well as nonverbal visual language, for example, design. Use of these kinds of language could offer a possible intellectual methodology for knowledge creation.

As semiotician Julia Kristeva has indicated, *articulating* language usually governs us when we recognize our ambience, like a dictionary of the world; *generating* language is uttered from direct experiences or by indwelling in reality. In other words, the former is the world of subjects or nouns, the latter is the world of predicates. Kristeva argues that the process of movement between the two brings forth a creative dynamism (1986).

These two aspects of language correspond to the tacit and explicit aspects of knowledge. They also represent individual (based on personal experiences) and group (based on common language) models of knowledge creation. The role of ba is to reconcile the contradiction of these two models and to create dynamics of knowledge creation. Ba is space where different views and models of people meet, contradict, and sometimes clash. Here "magic synthesis" of rationality and intuition in creativity occurs (Arieti 1976).

Each of the four modes of knowledge conversion requires different kinds of language for knowledge to be created and shared effectively. For example, nonverbal language, such as body language, is essential in the socialization process, as tacit knowledge cannot be expressed in articulated language. On the other hand, clear, articulated language is essential in combination process, as knowledge has to be disseminated and understood by many people in this process. In externalization, tropes such as metaphor, metonymy, and synecdoche are effective in creating concepts out of vast amounts of tacit knowledge. Therefore, knowledge leaders and producers should carefully choose and design language according to each mode of knowledge conversion.

References

Ashby, W. Ross. 1956. *An Introduction to Cybernetics*. London: Chapman and Hall.
Arieti, Silvano. 1976. *Creativity—The Magic Synthesis*. New York: Basic Books.
Bohm, David. 1980. *Wholeness and the Implicate Order*. London: Routledge.
Brown, John Seely, and Paul Duguid. 1997. "Organizing Knowledge," *California Management Review* 40(3): 90–111.
Drucker, Peter. 1993. *Post-Capitalist Society*. London: Butterworth Heinemann.
Condon, W. S. 1976. "An Analysis of Behavioral Organization." *Sign Language Studies* 63: 285–318.
Jantsch, Erich. 1980. *The Self-Organizing Universe*. Oxford: Pergamon Press.
Kristeve, Julia. 1986. *The Kristeva Reader*. New York: Columbia University Press.
Lave, Jean, and Etienne Wenger. 1991. *Situated Learning—Legitimate Peripheral Participation*. Cambridge, England: Cambridge University Press.
Leonard-Barton, Dorothy. 1992. "Core Capabilities and Core Rigidities: A Paradox in Managing New Product Development." *Strategic Management Journal* 13(5): 363–80.
Maturana, Humberto R., and Francisco J. Varela. 1980. *Autopoiesis and Cognition*. Dordrecht, Holland: D. Reidel.

Nelson, Richard. 1991. "Why Do Firms Differ, and How Does It Matter?" *Strategic Management Journal*, Special Issue, 12 (winter): 61–74.

Nishida, Kitaro. 1921. *An Inquiry into the Good*. Translated by Masao Abe, and Christopher Ives. (1990.) New Haven: Yale University Press.

———. 1970. *Fundamental Problems of Philosophy: the World of Action and the Dialectical World*. Tokyo: Sophia University Press.

Nonaka, Ikujiro. (1990). *Chishiki-Souzou no Keiei* (A theory of organizational knowledge creation). Tokyo: Nihon Keizai Shimbun-sha.

———. 1994. "A Dynamic Theory of Organizational Knowledge Creation." *Organization Science*, 5(1): 14–37.

Nonaka, Ikujiro, Phillipe Byosiere, Chester C. Borucki, and Noboru Konno. 1994. "Organizational Knowledge Creation Theory: A First Comprehensive Test." *International Business Review* 3(4): 337–51.

Nonaka, Ikujiro, and Noboru Konno. 1998. "The Concept of 'Ba': Building a Foundation for Knowledge Creation." *California Management Review* 40(3): 1–15.

Nonaka, Ikujiro, and Hirotaka Takeuchi. 1995. *The Knowledge-Creating Company*. New York: Oxford University Press.

Prahalad, C. K. and Gary Hamel. 1990. "The Core Competence of the Corporation." *Harvard Business Review* 68(3): 79–91.

Quinn, James Brian. 1992. *Intelligent Enterprise: A Knowledge and Service Based Paradigm for Industry*. New York: Free Press.

Shimizu, Hiroshi. 1995. "Ba-Principle: New Logic for the Real-Time Emergence of Information." *Holonics* 5(1): 67–79.

Sveiby, Karl Erik. 1997. *The New Organizational Wealth*. San Fransisco: Berret-Koehler.

Teece, David J., Gary Pisano, and Amy Anne Shuen. 1990. *Firm Capabilities, Resources, and the Concept of Strategy: Four Paradigms of Strategic Management*. Berkeley: CCC working paper no. 90–8 [sic].

Toffler, Alvin. 1990. *Powershift: Knowledge, Wealth and Violence at the Edge of the 21st Century*. New York: Bantam Books.

Von Krogh, Georg, Kaz Ichijo, and Ikujiro Nonaka. "Knowledge Enablers Facilitate Organizational Relationships: On Care and Indwelling." Japan-America Institute of Management Science Conference on International Comparative Study of Knowledge Creation, Honolulu, Hawaii, December 12–14, 1996.

Winograd, Terry, and Fernando Flores. 1986. *Understanding Computers and Cognition: A New Foundation for Design*. Reading, Mass.: Adisson-Wesley.

3

Bringing Care into Knowledge Development of Business Organizations

GEORG VON KROGH

KAZUO ICHIJO

IKUJIRO NONAKA

Care and the Knowledge-based Competence of a Firm

Social relationships in organizations have been drawing growing interest from the corporate world and management scholars and consultants. For example, radical corporate transformations have been affecting the implicit social contract between the individual and a firm. Top management of a large firm agonizes over how to accomplish an organizational renewal, facing the tradeoff between job security and organizational efficiency. Drastic transformation of a corporation can negatively affect its social relationships, thus damaging its organizational knowledge creation, one of its crucial competences. Despite this growing interest in the function and the role of social relationships in developing the competence of a firm, however, we still do not know what characterizes social relationships that enable the effective development of knowledge.

We believe that knowledge development, especially social knowledge development of organizations, cannot be taken for granted since knowledge is very fragile in them. Since individual knowledge can be easily killed, organizational knowledge development as social activity can be quite difficult or, in the worst case, impossible. Given this fragility, we argue that relationships in organizations must be given more attention. In this essay we explore "care" as one particular quality of organizational relationships that facilitates organizational knowledge development (von Krogh, 1998). We elaborate on how the presence or the absence of care will affect the development of organizational knowledge as well as individual knowledge. By focusing on care we can obtain more insights into social relationships in organizations.

At the beginning of this essay, we elaborate the roles and dimensions of knowledge in organization. In this analysis, we emphasize the necessity for the rediscovery of what knowledge means and how and why individuals and organizations know. From this theoretical perspective, we highlight the following characteristics of knowledge in organizations: individual and social knowledge; tacit and explicit knowledge; and a fundamental difference between understanding and agreement in organizations. It is our view that given these characteristics, more attention should be paid to the issue of social relationships as the crucial foundation for organizational knowledge development.

From this perspective on social relationship and its connection to organizational knowledge development, we develop our concept of care, describing in depth its fundamental argument with its theoretical background. We then describe how care contributes to knowledge development in organizations. We elaborate the four types of knowledge development in organizations using the condition of care (i.e., low or high) as its measurement. These four types are: seizing knowledge, transacting knowledge, bestowing knowledge, and indwelling knowledge. Each type is described in depth. Actual cases of the four types are included to help better understanding of them.

Finally, we refer to the limits of care for knowledge development. We describe potential impediments to and misuse of care in organizations. We then reflect again on why management should be concerned with care, that is, social relationships. Finally, we discuss further research on the concept of care and knowledge development.

On Knowledge in Organizations: Roles and Dimensions

Perspectives on Knowledge in Organizations

Most of the studies in our field have considered the concept of knowledge according a cognitivist notion. This is not strange, since the studies and theoretical arguments of our discipline to a large extent was founded on the work of March and Simon (1958) and Cyert and March (1963). Both of these works build on the idea of the organization being a machine for information processing and problem solving (Kilduff, 1992). Such a machine would need to acquire, store, and retrieve knowledge (Morgan, 1986).

For example, for many strategic management theorists these insights were revelations, allowing for clear and unambiguous descriptions of knowledge structures, managerial cognition, problem-solving behavior, and decision-making. Most strategic management research that is based on cognitivism views knowledge development as robust information-processing in the firm about an externally pregiven reality, like an industry. We argue, however, that the development of knowledge cannot be adapted to an externally pregiven reality, since this reality has yet to be created. Thus, the issue of creating future competitive advantages necessitates a new set of assumptions about knowledge.

Recently, strategic management research has focused more on organizational and individual knowledge. According to the resource-based theory of the firm (e.g., Wernerfelt 1984, Peteraf 1993), resources characterized by high value, rarity, imperfect substitutability, and imperfect imitability could give rise to sustainable competitive advantages and hence to superior industry performance. In this vein, knowledge can be seen as a potential source of sustainable competitive advantages.

Potential differences in resource characteristics beg another question, however. Recent works not only establish the importance of physical capital, human capital, and organizational capital but also isolate knowledge and focus its role in competitive strategy (Collis, 1994). The need to isolate knowledge from other resources essentially comes from its origin and nature; knowledge is created in the thinking and acting of individual organizational members, and it is further shaped by the social processes of an organization. Still, the previous literature on resources has not readily considered alternative explanations for knowledge and cognition at the level of fundamental assumptions. Taking a new turn could mean shifting attention to a new epistemology, a rediscovery of what knowledge might mean, and how, and why individuals and organizations know.

The Roles and Dimensions of Individual Knowledge

Knowledge can be observed and distinguished on two levels, the individual and the social (e.g., Nonaka and Takeuchi, 1995; Lyles and Schwenk, 1992; Berger and Luckman, 1966). Individual knowledge emerges from individual observations, movements, actions, and communications in the world, and it is closely linked to the senses, ranging from smelling and hearing to watching and touching. As individuals we use these inputs to our personal knowledge development by forming distinctions, categories, and concepts (Lakoff and Johnson, 1980). In this sense, individual knowledge is embodied (Varela, Thomson, and Rosch, 1991). Embodied knowledge also implies that knowledge development is closely linked with emotions. In confronting situations, we tend to use all of what we are rather than just what we know (Dreyfus, 1996). Experiences can be positive or negative, delightful or painful, revealing or concealing.

Knowledge enables individual organizational members to make sense of an organizational world, to make judgments about it, to move about in it, to imagine possible actions, and to enact effectively. Since knowledge is embodied, the organizational world as it is (and not as it appears), for the individual depends on previous individual experiences. Any experience, ranging from watching a presentation to meeting a friendly personnel consultant, will shape the way the individual knows the organizational world. In this sense, knowledge is not representing an objective, externally pregiven world, as assumed by the classical cognitivists (von Krogh and Roos, 1995). Rather, knowledge brings forth a world for the individual (Maturana and Varela, 1987).

Furthermore, as noted by a number of authors in fields ranging from management, economics, and computer science to the philosophy of science (Nonaka, 1991, 1994; Nonaka and Takeuchi, 1995; Dreyfus, 1979; Polanyi, 1958; Arrow, 1962; Callon, 1994), there is a distinction between tacit and explicit knowledge. Since individual knowledge is embodied, not all knowledge can be a reference point for statements to be made by the individual. Explicit knowledge develops through a process of thematization (see, for example, Schutz and Luckman, 1985/1989); a language is learnt, words are being carefully selected for an experience, this linguistic choice is tested, misconceptions are corrected in interaction with others, new words are being invented to better convey experiences in the eyes of the individual, and so on. Explicit knowledge can shape the knowledge development of others through writing and reading, as well as talking and listening, for example, in a teaching situation. On the other hand, tacit knowledge escapes this process of thematization, either because it would be too exhaustive to linguistically convey all personal experiences or because some experiences do not lend themselves to thematization.

In an organization, embodied tacit and explicit knowledge should allow for effective individual action, for example, solving a particular task. Various kinds of task solution might have been developed over the years of confronting the task or might be invented on the spot. Task solution assumes quite a particular role in our individual lives. Successful task solutions form rules for the individual. The novice has few rules for solving a particular task, whereas the expert can transcend established rules and imagine new rules for the task with great vigilance and enthusiasm (Dreyfus and Dreyfus, 1986). Although they could be, the concept of such rules should not be constrained to explicit and formalistic rules, like an organizational job description. "Rules" are meant in a wider sense to encompass varied, subtle, unarticulated, and emergent rules, tied to personal experiences.

The Roles and Dimensions of Social Knowledge

Unlike individual knowledge, social knowledge is not guaranteed through the physiological mechanisms associated with human cognition. Whereas individual knowledge is embodied and imparted through the process of life, social knowledge does not lodge in a physical space. Social knowledge takes on a life of its own (von Krogh and Roos, 1995). Social knowledge is shared among organizational members. Based on individual experiences of shared organizational events, social knowledge allows organizational members to share rules in the form of practices, like how to successfully manage projects (Brown and Duguid, 1991); traditions, like how to address people in the company; and languages, like how to use the word "*strategy*" at management meetings. In this sense, social knowledge brings forth an organizational world that is accessible to the individual organizational member and lends itself to individual knowledge development. Individual knowledge is needed for the creation of an organizational world, and this world, in the form of social knowledge, is in turn needed for the creation of individual knowledge about this world.

Social knowledge can be both explicit and tacit (Nonaka and Takeuchi, 1995). First, social knowledge allows for explicit claims about knowledge to be made in an organization. Whereas such claims presuppose social knowledge of language and concepts, their grounds or warrants may be well hidden in individual or social knowledge. Social knowledge is explicit but hidden for a particular group. For example, a vice-president in a pharmaceutical company might claim to a group of R&D staff that investments in biotechnological hormone production will be vital to corporate survival, while the ground for this claim, that a competitor is two years away from launching a biotechnologically produced growth hormone, is shared only among top management.

Second, social knowledge might also be tacit, bringing forth rules of tradition and practice that are observable but not possible to thematize. The key mechanism for utilizing this social knowledge for individual knowledge development is through socializing, involving extensive training and tutoring of organizational members in which the novices learn the skills of the incumbents (Nonaka and Takeuchi, 1995).

Rules of traditions and practices are also grounded in the value system of the organization. Before experiences of shared events can be transformed into sustainable rules, there are collective judgments on the value of these events and corresponding rules. Occasionally, however, in devising new practices or traditions, experiences might escape value judgments (Argyris, 1993), forming into counterproductive ways of performing tasks or viewing the world. In trying to make new events the basis for more effective traditions, organizational members might also experience how existing traditions prevail and become entrapping for acceptable social knowledge (Levinthal and March, 1993). These entrapping traditions can function as barriers to the development of new social knowledge. Because of tacit social knowledge, grounds and warrants might be well hidden; for this reason social knowledge is not always what it seems to be.

Assuming that social knowledge is shared knowledge, an overlooked distinction in the studies is that between agreement and shared understanding. As argued by von Krogh, Roos, and Slocum (1994), most studies, in fact, do equate the two or view social knowledge as agreement. As we will show, such a conception can be highly misleading, especially if tacit knowledge is the object of inquiry. Shared understanding is social knowledge of how to follow certain rules, be it a tradition or language. An organizational member in a consultancy understands the company ethical values, leading him to destroy confidential news and other material about his client to protect him against disclosure.

Shared understanding is quite different from agreement, however. Agreement is knowledge of shared rules among organizational members, not necessarily presupposing the ability to follow such rules. For example, the consultant rookie might know about the ethical values but not understanding them might disclose some sensitive rumors to a former university pal from one of the client's competitors. As will be shown, agreement and understanding are fundamental elements in knowledge development processes.

Since knowledge is of a social and individual character, explicit as well as tacit, and since there is a fundamental difference between understanding and agreement in organizations, we cannot escape the issue of social relationships, which form the organizational world and hence knowledge. Given this importance of social relationships, the following research question is generated: What characterizes organizational relationships that enable effective knowledge development in business organizations? We argue that care is the answer. Knowledge development, especially social knowledge development of the organization, cannot be taken for granted, and relationships in organizations must be given more attention. Knowledge development is fraught with emotions, misunderstandings, misconceptions, and so on. Care, which involves patience, emotional forbearance, and so forth, is the remedy for such difficulties.

Hereafter we explore care as one particular quality of organizational relationships and how the presence or the absence of care affects the development of individual and social knowledge.

The Concept of Care

The concept of care in organizational relationships has strong philosophical underpinnings, although instances of it seem to be quite rare in contemporary mainstream philosophy. Foucault (1972) argued that care for the self became a theme among Greek and Roman philosophers. Care for the self meant that the individual should train the body and the mind through both physical exercises and reflection. The challenge of personal reflection on experiences, first conducted in solitude then communicated through conversations or writing, was key to self-cultivation. The classical philosophers believed in self-cultivation as a means to form better social individuals who understood the importance of truth (Foucault, 1972).

Both Mayeroff (1971) and Gaylin (1976) discussed the concept of care and how it relates to philosophical streams as well as social practice. Noddings (1984) viewed caring as a form of feminine rationality that would have strong implications for ethical practice, moral stance, and education. Care is typically seen as a function of motherhood, the mother's provision of good living conditions for her family.

Organization studies provide contributions to a practical understanding of the concept of care. Researchers have studied relationship between givers and recipients of care in organizations that have care as a part of or a basis for a particular service (Lyth, 1988; Pines and Aronson, 1988; Shapiro and Carr, 1991). Such studies have focused on care in the relationships between patient and doctors, teacher and student, religious leaders and followers, as well as social workers and the less privileged (Kahn, 1993). The studies share a common assumption: that care recipients should experience that they are being cared for and cared about and that this is a key to their healing (Kahn, 1993; Sarason, 1985). Care has been mostly associated with providers and receivers who have relatively clear roles: one strongly needs care, for example, a homeless person, and the other commands the resources necessary to provide care, for example, a Salvation Army worker.

In devising a more general concept of care applicable to the study of organizational knowledge development, insights can be drawn from a host of literature from personality psychology, sociology, and social psychology—with one reservation, however. The literature on care providers and care-based institutions assumes a clear and stable functional relationship between care provider and care receiver. The relationship between doctor and patient is clearly defined in terms of both authority and expertise, as well as process, including the steps of illness, diagnosis, remedy, prescription, and supervised healing. It may not be very effective to describe care in organizational relationship according to these categories, since there are no specific functions for care providing and no explicit roles relating to care receiving and since one person might both be a receiver and provider of care. Care characterizes a process of interaction between receiver and provider and should not be understood in terms of roles and functions. In general we can talk of more or less care in organizational relationships.

Dimensions of Care in Organizational Relationships

First, as a relationship quality, care can but does not necessarily entail concrete action in ways of helping another. Dependent on the needs of the care recipient, care can just refer to presence and intimacy without action. On the one hand, care can be sufficient for helping behavior to occur (Egan, 1986). In helping another, a care provider may reassure him of his worth, provide information and support valuable for task execution, integrate him socially, give him guidance in task resolution, give him the opportunity to nurture another, and enhance attachment and social bonds between the helper and the helped, as well as helping him to choose what outputs of a task performance will be presented to a larger audience (see Cutrona et al., 1994; Sarason, Pierce, and Sarason, 1990). On the other hand, helping behavior is not necessary for care to be a relationship quality. For example, if a teacher believes that a student will enhance her understanding of a text if left alone without further intervention, her care for the student will lead her to do so.

Further, the social psychology literature assumes that help occurs in an exchange relationship. Helpers expect to receive some amount of help in return for their service. The principle of reciprocity (Gouldner, 1960) suggests that greater help received increases the level of help returned (Eisenberger, Cotterell, and Marvel, 1987). Greenberg and Westcott (1983) even suggest that it is customary for some people to believe that they put other people in debt by returning more help than people gave them.

Second, the propensity to help as a quality of a relationship, even if no exchange is expected, leads to a central question: Does care require an altruistic (as opposed to self-interested) personality? Such a personality would be inherently other-oriented in making choices—taking the perspectives of the other—sympathetic toward others needs, and, to a large extent, able to assume social responsibility (Staub, 1974; Eisenberg, Cotterell, and Marvel, 1987). In an organization, there clearly will be organizational members with highly developed altruistic personalities and others who act more in self-interest. Hence, it is imperative to find out how even individuals who are more self-interested could develop the ability to care.

A possible answer would be that the values of an organization tend to structure behavior by forming the basis of expectations of organizational members. Newcomers into an organization tend to appropriate such values and comply with expectations or, alternatively, to exit the organization (March, 1988; Luhmann, 1991). Batson, Bolen, Cross, and Neuringer-Benefiel (1986) suggested that altruistic behavior in a situation where someone needs help is more likely when it is difficult for helpers to escape from the situation. One reason could be the loss of self-image in the eyes of potential observers. Hence, when the values of the organization lead to expectations to care in relationships among organizational members, even the self-interested personality might care for those who are in need of help, if only to avoid loss of face with potential observers. Alternatively, the self-interested personality might decide to exit the organization, finding another organization with a value system that supports a different set of expectations, for organizational values tend to prevail over time, forming sustainable structures of expectations (March, 1988).

Third, in a longitudinal, inductive case study of job burnout among human service workers, Kahn (1993) identified behavioral dimensions of caregiving. His first assertion is that the distinguishing characteristic of care can be seen in its accessibility. Care in organizational relationships involves not only the propensity to help but also access to the potential helper. Accessibility means people in organizations allow time and space for connection (Kahn, 1993). Time spent on listening to the concerns of others is time well spent. Hence, we can talk of more or less accessibility among organizational members.

Fourth, in some instances, people who seek help may voice their needs to one another in an organization, but this cannot be automatically expected. A care concept is needed that extends beyond mere propensity to help and focuses on proactive behavior. To this end, Kahn (1993) also suggested inquiry and attention as dimensions of care. Since inquiry naturally involves cognitive attention, and since attention in care should have the quality of empathy and dialogue, we suggest that the two be collapsed into *attentive inquiry*. This is a vigilant search for events where help is needed, an active inquiry into the needs for help, both emotional and factual, and the design of a diligent helping intervention. Attentive inquiry extends beyond the mere recognition of issue symptoms, for its goal is to provide a shared understanding between help provider and help receiver of the underlying causes an issue. Attentive inquiry characterizes a genuine interest in the lives of other organizational members.

A quality of successful inquiry is that agents have the ability to compassionately take the perspective of another and convey their own understanding of this perspective (Braaten, 1983; Kahn, 1993). Since experiences are not (fully) accessible to another organizational member, this is a matter of attitude rather than transcendental cognition. Attentive inquiry involves not only the active engaging in a dialogue on needs and help but also respect of the other's standpoint, as well as the active appreciation of his or her ideas and insights. We can talk of more or less such attentive inquiry occurring in organizational relationships.

Fifth, the dimensions of care developed thus far have been in the realm of activities and values. However, because emotions are an integrated part of all task-performing activities in an organization (Sandelands, 1988), these dimensions have to be complemented with the emotional side to care. Care cannot only refer to helping behavior in a concrete task, but must also refer to a more general concern with the well-being of other human beings.

As Haslam (1994) argued, people frequently judge social relationships on the basis of emotional categories, and their emotions might affect the formation of cooperation in general. One person might judge another to be passive and timid, or cooperative and warm; hostile and hardheaded or cunning and competitive; trusting and respectful or dominant and assertive; introverted and detached or outgoing and cheerful (see also Brunswik, 1956). For care to flourish in organizational relationships, that is, if help will be offered, and if accessibility can be expected, the helper must be competent, warm, trusting, respectful, and available in an ongoing way.

Emotion can be defined as a subjective feeling state (Ashforth and Humphrey, 1995: 99) toward another person. In addition to a propensity to help reinforced by organizational values, there can be a genuine subjective feeling state of desiring to offer support to other organizational members beyond what is expected. Care has to extend beyond the understanding and empathy of another person (Kahn, 1993) to the tolerance of apparently intolerable behavior. The caring organizational member recognizes that intolerable behavior can have many causes. For example, lacking knowledge of organizational dress codes, a newcomer may turn up in a sweatshirt and shorts for a department meeting, causing distress among other department members. In an effort to aid the newcomer, rather than dismissing his personality and behavior as unacceptable, the others explain to him the dress code and its history.

Emotion can also partly be prescribed in terms of feeling rules in an organization, which set expectations to emotional behavior (Humphrey and Ashforth, 1994). This insight led Van Maanen (1991) to describe the Disney theme parks with the term "*smile factory*," since service personnel are expected to appear content, happy, ongoing, service-minded, and smiling. Feeling rules create emotional recipes in which a variety of sometimes unexpected organizational behaviors can be accommodated and allow organizational members to suppress their instant negative emotions by adopting trained patterns of emotional expression.

Lenience, as a dimension of care, includes compassionate, accommodating, and favoring behavior toward others. As suggested by Ashforth and Humphrey (1993) feeling states in an organization can be described in terms of breadth, that is, the spectrum of situations that would be associated with a particular emotion, and depth, for example, the number of nuances that are associated with a particular emotion. More lenience in organizational relationships implies that organizational members have fine nuances to emotionally categorize an event and respond to these events in a compassionate and tender way. More lenience also implies that an increasing number of different events are approached with lenience.

The Impact of Care in Knowledge Development

As a quality of organizational relationships, care has five dimensions. Depending on an overall score on these dimensions, we can distinguish between high and low care in an organization. High care would characterize relationships where there is a great propensity to help, high accessibility of individuals, an extensive attentive inquiry, and high lenience and where care is a shared value among organizational members. Low care, on the other hand, characterizes relationships where there is a low propensity to help, organizational members do not make themselves accessible to one another, attentive inquiry is restricted, organizational members exhibit impatience and lack of lenience towards others, and care is not a shared value among organizational members.

Individual and social knowledge development under conditions of high and low care takes four forms: seizing, transacting, bestowing, and indwelling (see table 3.1), as follows.

Seizing Knowledge under Conditions of Low Care

Seizing of knowledge is the type of individual knowledge development that takes place under conditions of low care. In a low care situation, there is a low propensity to help, there is reduced accessibility, and attentive inquiry is lacking. First, the individual cannot expect that his or her knowledge development and task performance will be attentively observed by other organizational members. Nor can he or she expect to be asked helpful questions indicating mutual personal interests and willingness to help. There are no shared organizational values that would direct a

Table 3.1. Knowledge Development Processes

Care	Knowledge	
	Individual	Social
Low	Seizing	Transacting
High	Bestowing	Indwelling

proactive helping behavior. In the event where a task cannot be performed satis-factorily and the individual seeks help, he or she has low accessibility to other col-leagues at various levels of the organization.

In this situation the individual is "left to his or her own devices" with very little or no assistance or interest from colleagues. Since knowledge is embodied, he or she will autonomously seek to orient his or her knowledge development toward achiev-ing effective task performance. According to Merleau-Ponty (1963), in developing knowledge about the world, the individual seeks to get a maximum grip of a situa-tion, be it in fastening two metal plates, getting a view of computer screen, lifting a basketball from the floor, getting the right angle for viewing a painting in a gallery, or placing a deck chair to get the best view of the ocean. In the process of seizing, the individual "left to his or her own devices," will seek to get the maximum grip of a task in order to achieve a personal understanding of the task at hand and possible task solutions. The individual will use established rules to solve existing and new tasks and will experiment with new rules to more effectively master existing situa-tions as well as to cope with new situations. The individual will dwell with these rules; faulty as they might be, they are the only ones he or she knows about or at least knows how to practice.

In the absence of attentive inquiry, there are few requirements and opportunities for thematization during knowledge development. Whereas the individual might share the end result of a knowledge development process, this final thematization can never accurately convey all the intricacies and obstacles of a work process, so the lis-tener can gain only a partial understanding of successful task performance at best (Brown and Duguid, 1991). Since thematization is limited in a seizing process, it can be expected that knowledge that is developed will be predominately tacit, residing in the individual as embodied, private knowledge.

Since low care in organizational relationships also is characterized by egoistic as opposed to altruistic behavior, it can also be expected that knowledge development, rather than being intended to serve the collective, will be a means to gain power and influence in organizational relationships. For one to gain power, however, one's individual understanding or knowledge of how to practice has to become part of social knowledge. As argued later, since individual knowledge developed through seizing is predominantly tacit, this poses some major problems for individual power acquisition, since others have to rely on cues rather than oral argumentation about what is known.

Darrah (1995) gives an excellent example of seizing in a case study on training offered to production workers of a computer manufacturer. In response to productivity problems and demands from the workers to be up-skilled, the company introduced a major training program. Before the program was launched, there was shared agreement among company managers, foremen, supervisors, and workers, that novices' individual knowledge development on the shop floor should be restricted because of fear of lost productivity if too much time was given to such development. Most novices would given a short tour of the manufacturing facility and instructed by a more experienced worker or supervisor for as little as fifteen minutes. Beyond that, no further attentive inquiry was conducted by experienced workers or supervisors. Under such conditions, novices were "left to their own devices," trying to figure out the rules for task performance and how to follow them. Moreover, playfulness and overt experimentation was prohibited. Any knowledge development was not to interfere with production quotas.

No written descriptions of disk drive components or other parts or of the product as a whole were accepted on the shop floor. Such descriptions were considered a sign of an incompetent worker. It was an agreement among the manufacturing staff that anybody should understand the manufacturing process without having to periodically consult technical drawings, since this typically would lead to unnecessary delays.

The case reveals limited accessibility and strong reservations toward helping behavior. It was considered pestering for novices to ask more experienced workers for help, so novices were often left frustrated with unresolved problems. Furthermore, more experienced workers did not want to share their accumulated understanding of tasks and the overall manufacturing process. Typically each worker went through a cumbersome process of developing embodied, tacit knowledge of rules that allowed him or her to cope with separate tasks at the production line. Moreover, through success in such knowledge development, workers also gained prestige, power, and influence in the eyes of other workers. More highly skilled workers expressed concern that those with lower skills would learn how they performed their work, a situation they thought would be unfair since the latter had not earned that knowledge. (Darrah, 1995:33).

In reading this case as a process of seizing, one is further reminded of the hidden damages of production quotas and productivity goals. Indeed, the norms of rationality often seduce men and women into committing profoundly antisocial acts; the division of labor and the repetitiveness of task performance distance one from the effects of one's behavior; the division of authority fragments responsibility; organizational ideologies justify otherwise repugnant acts; and so forth, so that role occupants may remain emotionally disaffected from their acts (Ashforth and Humphrey, 1988:105).

Transacting Knowledge under Conditions of Low Care

Transacting knowledge is the type of social knowledge development that takes place under conditions of low care. In a low care situation, in sharing their knowledge with others, individuals are forced to follow certain protocols whereby they convey their messages in a clear and unambiguous way (see Grice, 1975). Individuals cannot expect help from others to find the most suitable means of expression of their individual experiences. In general, there is little interest in the particulars of individual knowledge, beyond what is of value to social knowledge and the task performance of a group. If such help is received to express personal experiences, the helper will expect favors and assistance to be returned at some later point in time (Gouldner, 1960).

In the process of transacting knowledge, little or no time is allowed to explore new individual ideas. Individual particulars succumb to the maxim "Think straight, talk straight." Low accessibility among organizational members means, further, that time pressure is critical in knowledge development. Knowledge that can be developed fast is of high value.

Under conditions of low care, bureaucratic rules and procedures substitute for the qualities of personal relationships (Foner, 1995). Processes of transacting knowledge are regulated by formal rules and procedures rather than informal personal relationships. Bureaucracy establishes expertise and regulates the flow of knowledge in an organization. A number of specialists without spirit, designated by organizational hierarchy and function (Weber, 1958), define and legitimate social knowledge and transact this knowledge to lesser or different experts. Experts have normative ties to other organizational members; they transact knowledge because they feel they ought to, given the tasks they have at hand. Moreover, expertise is normally associated with fast task execution and clear unambiguous claims about knowledge (Dreyfus and Dreyfus, 1986), requiring only so much access to organizational members as prescribed by organizational procedures.

Development of new social knowledge is also subject to value judgments. Certain claims pass for knowledge while others do not. Occasionally, social knowledge will be formed through a process of negotiations (Lyles and Schwenk, 1992), in which individuals (recognized as experts) will seek power by achieving social acceptance for the value of their personal knowledge. Social knowledge will be formed through a process in which individuals make conflicting claims about knowledge on the basis of differences in their own personal experiences. Occasionally, individuals will also strategically construct polarizing debates in order to increase their power (Barth, 1995). These debates are rooted more in the personal benefits of disagreeing with others than in the felt differences of personal experience. To reiterate: social knowledge is not always what it seems to be.

The kind of social knowledge that results from this process of transacting will be predominantly explicit, for two reasons. First, since access is limited, social knowledge develops under time constraints, hence there is no time to engage in an iterative process of dialogue that would be needed to make tacit knowledge explicit (see Nonaka and Takeuchi, 1995). Second, since the power resulting from expertise requires recognition from other organizational members, the expert (or expert-to-be) has to make his or her claims explicit.

The explicitness of social knowledge, however, does not automatically mean that all social knowledge is shared throughout the organization. Occasionally, groups of experts will keep secrets; they will protect explicit knowledge from other groups in order to keep their power. However, when social knowledge becomes contested, as it does when the organization confronts a new situation (Lyles and Schwenk, 1992), these groups will be forced to reveal what they know in order to reconfirm their status of expertise.

Social knowledge resulting from a process of transacting will tend to be agreement among organizational members on rules for task execution rather than a profound understanding of how to follow these rules. The rules are contested and negotiated, but once shared agreement has been reached, the rules form explicit expectations to behavior. This does not automatically imply that individual organizational members know how to follow these rules. The rules will again be subject to processes of seizing where individual organizational members will interpret the rules and make sense of them in the local context of their work. Social knowledge will not always be of much use to individuals in their individual task execution. Nevertheless, it remains the only knowledge that is truly shared (see Argyris and Schon, 1978; Brown and Duguid, 1991). Even if the individual develops some tacit understanding that these rules have flaws, she encounters a problem when trying to share this insight with other organizational members because of the lack of attentive inquiry. Again, in interpretation and execution the individual is "left to his or her own devices."

In the case of the computer manufacturer (Darrah, 1995), there are numerous examples of transacting processes. Once the problem of low manufacturing productivity was identified, production management proposed a training program in which manufacturing and product development engineers would act as teachers. The training program can be seen as a process of transacting in which the engineers represent the established expertise. Hence in the training sessions the flow of knowledge was directed from the engineers to the workers. Essentially reluctant to share their expertise but still motivated by the normative ties that were valid for the organization and the productivity issues, the engineers gave a short and dispassionate overview of their own work and the production process. They would describe production as a disembodied process in which the workers were substituted for functions and ideal rules of production.

The workers, sometimes reluctant to voice their concern in public because they feared repercussions, did not recognize the process as it was theoretically described by the engineers. After the training sessions, the workers often claimed that their practical knowledge, for example, of how to assemble a disk drive, was much better and more effective than that of the engineers. Nonetheless, the aim of transacting knowledge about production was not to achieve a better understanding of how to manufacture computers but rather to come to a shared agreement on what a smooth, flawless, and efficient production process should look like. There were few opportunities in the training program for workers to share their personal experiences of flaws in the production process and thereby to contest the established social knowledge. A key reason was that since personal notes of a worker were forbidden on the shop floor, a worker would have to rely on his memory of the problems. In the short time allowed for questions and answers in the training sessions, the workers found it generally hard to structure and convey their personal experiences with the production process. There was no lenience on the part of the engineers for listening patiently to work-related problems. Bounded by the tacitness of their experiences, the workers could not claim any expertise to the engineers, even in the most detailed parts of manufacturing.

On the part of the engineers there was in general little attentive inquiry that could have re-mediated this problem. The experts kept their power as a result of their command of a supposedly comprehensive knowledge and full description of the production process. Since the workers remained the group with supposedly less knowledge, no shift in power was taking place between the trainers and the workers during the sessions.

The training program was generally considered a failure. Productivity did not increase much after the sessions were ended, and the workers still felt that they had to cope individually with manufacturing problems that were not commonly understood by the engineers and supervisors. The director of manufacturing left the company because of, among other reasons, the failure of the training program to produce the expected results.

Bestowing Knowledge under Conditions of High Care

Bestowing knowledge is the type of individual knowledge development that takes place under conditions of high care. Unlike seizing, bestowing characterizes individual knowledge development where organizational members make themselves mutually accessible and relate to each other in lenient, helpful, and attentive ways, the individual is not left alone to develope knowledge on how to solve tasks but is generally supported by a social network of organizational members (see Pagel, Erdly, and Becker, 1987). Shared values of care in an organization direct helping behavior to any place where help is needed. Where the task cannot be performed satisfactorily, both the individual task performer and other organizational members are expected to develop knowledge on new solutions in common. In asking for help, the individual task performer will be met with interest and lenience. Organizational members also proactively ask if help is needed in order to improve task performance.

Individual knowledge development is a personal journey. In the case of bestowing, however, this journey is accompanied by helpful colleagues recognizing that enriched personal experience depends not only on individual capability but also on a ring of support. As already mentioned, personal knowledge development is associated with positive and negative emotions like satisfaction with a completed task or uncertainty with a future task. In bestowing knowledge, these emotions can be expressed freely and will be appreciated by other organizational members as part of a process of knowledge development.

While organizations often lack a vocabulary for expressing emotive activities and subjective experiences (Sandelands, 1988), care in organizational relationships allows such a vocabulary to evolve. Anger, joy, compassion, and so on are thematized and acquire a status on their own. There are few strict feeling rules regulating emotion with respect to a task's execution.

In a process of bestowing, the individual develops personal understanding of the task at hand and possible task solutions. As in the case of seizing, he or she will use established rules to solve existing and new tasks and will experiment with new rules to more effectively master existing situations as well as to cope with new situations.

Unlike with seizing, however, the individual is not necessarily captured by these rules. Other organizational members caring for individual and organizational task performance will inquire attentively into current practices and help to improve on these. In bestowing, because of the inquiry and dialogue, the individual is caught up in a process of thematizing his or her own experiences. In helping others, thematization is even reinforced (the master has to thematize certain personal experiences for the apprentice). In this respect, bestowing is also quite different from seizing, where thematization is left to the end of a learning process and where power acquisition is a strong imperative to convey knowledge. Because of the continuous attentive inquiry and thematization, we would expect individual knowledge to be both of a tacit and explicit nature.

MYCOM's development of a deboning machine is a good illustration of bestowing knowledge (and also of indwelling knowledge, described hereafter). MYCOM, a comprehensive thermal and food engineering company headquartered in Tokyo, with a 50 percent share of the world market for industrial freezers, released TORIDAS, a very innovative automatic chicken deboning machine, to the market in 1994. The machine's performance is quite high; it can debone a chicken leg in four seconds, or nine hundred legs an hour. It is four times faster than manual deboning. In addition, the machine makes possible a considerable increase in the yield of the deboning process of 1.8 to 2.0 percent. Because of this deboning performance and yield increase, the machine has been acclaimed by the food processing industry, whose main concerns are the reduction of production and personnel costs. The machine was introduced to the market in May 1994, and one hundred were sold during the first year. Considering the relatively high market price of 18 million yen per unit, the machine has been remarkably well received by the market.

The development of TORIDAS, however, was not very easy and took fourteen years, with an investment of more than 1 billion yen, including labor costs. In the first phase of development, the project members tried to develop the machine using the technology of mechanical electronics. Although they had been advised by manual deboners not to cut the meat, they still stuck to inventing a meat-cutting machine. They believed it was the only way to develop a deboning machine, using their knowledge and expertise about mechanical electronics. The project members in the first phase of development ended up with an inefficient deboning machine.

In the second phase of development, a young development engineer who regularly visited some chicken-processing factories for his tasks in developing freezers and other machines made a breakthrough. He looked at the prototype, which clumsily cut chicken meat off the bone by force. The machine's movements were completely different from manual deboning work he had watched at chicken-processing factories. He concluded that the development concept had been fundamentally wrong and decided to experience deboning work for himself.

At MYCOM, no specific training program for young engineers is conducted. Instead, young engineers are encouraged to visit the plants of MYCOM's customers, observe how they work, and finally increase engineering skills through this observation. MYCOM's corporate mission is "innovation in fields," and the respect for tacit knowledge to realize innovation is defined as its corporate value. How much they work following this corporate mission and value is the evaluation criteria of MYCOM's engineers.

Therefore, that MYCOM's young engineer asked a chicken-processing company to let him work at its factory. The idea was to master deboning skills, under the guidance of the factory's deboners, using his own hands and eyes. Through this "training and practice" at the factory, he learned the knack of stripping chicken meat off the bone after cutting the tendons. The point was that deboners cut only tendons. What they do next should be described not as "cutting the meat off the bone" but as "stripping the meat from the bone."

This young engineer then demonstrated manual deboning for the project leader in the first phase, saying: "the chicken meat can be taken from the bone without cutting it off." The project leader, who was aware of the faulty concept in the first phase of the development and the limits of knowledge about mechanical electronics, saw the demonstration of the young engineers and thought that "he really had something!" He believed that it could be a highly viable alternative that he had not been able to find. Then the project leader decided to officially restart the project. This conceptual change from "cutting off" to "stripping off" was a real breakthrough for the project, which eventually led the project members to success.

To sum up, at MYCOM, the development of individual knowledge is facilitated by its corporate value. The activity of young engineers in "fields" is supported by the value. The results of this activity also are supported by organizational sharing, the same corporate value. This value on sharing at MYCOM facilitates the mutually supportive behavior among MYCOM members. This relationship, the one that takes place under conditions of high care, was crucial for the young engineer to find the core concept for innovation.

Indwelling Knowledge under Conditions of High Care

Indwelling knowledge is the type of social knowledge development that takes place under conditions of high care. High care indicates a situation where organizational members share the same values of learning. They share attentive inquiry and a high propensity to help. Knowledge is being shared not for the egoistic purpose of gaining power but for the purpose of solving tasks effectively. Organizational members make themselves accessible to each other for small questions and for major inquiry about rules and tasks. They share knowledge freely, not constrained by personal interests of maintaining power. Continued cooperation increases positive mutual feelings among participants in knowledge development (Lawler and Yoon, 1996).

Care provides for a safe environment that welcomes attempts at expressing new personal understanding. Generally, some personal understandings take considerable experimentation to become explicit; unlike transacting, indwelling allows for that: inventing new words, displaying insecurity, conveying hunches, drawing on humor, laughing, playing, and so on. Where some efforts go astray, organizational members show lenience by accepting errors and failures and allowing for repeated attempts. Cooperation under conditions of such experimentation is secured by personal commitment to continue the development of social knowledge (Orbell, Dawes, Van de Kragt, 1988).

Under conditions of high care, the effective functioning of organizational relationships substitutes for bureaucracy (Foner, 1995). Bureaucratic rules are not needed to secure the exchange of insight and development of knowledge; this exchange is naturally motivated through a strong mutual interest of organizational members in common task execution. Likewise, because it is legitimized by the value system of the organization, care-based behavior will be more important than complying with rules and procedures, making personal helping behavior a virtue of organizational life. Expertise will still prevail, but it will be a kind of passionate expertise, eager to find opportunities to help others.

Unlike transacting, a process of indwelling creates not only agreement on rules but also shared understanding of how to follow and make use of rules. Because organizational members do not push their self-interest, discussions about rules takes the form of dialogue rather than advocacy (von Krogh and Roos, 1995). Experts come to share not just an abbreviated part of their experiences with attempting certain task solutions but errors, failures, and aborted attempts. In the dialogue with others, they also come to revise their understanding of which rules worked and which rules did not work. The resulting knowledge of rules is more profound.

High care also has a positive impact on shared understanding of rules. Knowledge of how to apply and practice certain rules can only be achieved through learning by doing. Indwelling characterizes a process in which organizational members assume tutorship functions and help others learn how to practice rules of effective task execution. High lenience coupled with attentive inquiry allows repeated trials and errors coupled with joint reflections on why certain practices works and other do not. Access is also key in establishing shared understanding. Without it, organizational members would be left to their own devices to find a good practice of rules and would be forced to find a maximum grip of the situation that does not foster shared understanding.

The social knowledge that results from indwelling is both explicit and tacit. It becomes explicit as organizational members thematize and share their personal experiences, argue about tasks and rules, try out certain rules, and reflect on them (see Nonaka and Takeuchi, 1995). Explicit social knowledge comes in the form of agreement on rules, for example, of concepts, designs, drawings, specifications, statements, claims, and products, and understanding of how to follow these rules, for example, of product development procedures, job descriptions, quality procedures, strategic planning procedures, and so on.

Because knowledge of how to practice and invent rules is also knowledge of how to relate to fellow human beings, tacit social knowledge becomes an intrinsic element of organizational relationships. The way organizational members come to behave toward each other, the practice of attentive inquiry, the way help is requested, their patter of helping behavior, lenient responses, mutual accessibility, and so on, become in themselves social tacit knowledge about how to practice rules of interpersonal behavior. Where transacting knowledge must rely on bureaucracy for social knowledge to develop, indwelling knowledge relies on the quality of interpersonal relationships.

The second phase of the development of TORIDAS offers a good illustration of indwelling knowledge. In the beginning of the second phase, which was initiated by the deboning experience of the young engineer, the project members, on the basis of this experience, came to an agreement that deboning work could be mechanized by analyzing the work by human hands and translating it into mechanical movements. From this agreement they developed the following hypotheses. First, deboning work by human hands would have to be fully grasped as prerequisite knowledge. Second, the work would be broken down into several very simple actions. Then they would try to translate these actions into mechanical actions that could be combined in a single machine. Unlike the first stage of the project, which was totally based on mechanical electronics, the second stage focused on integrating human work skills into mechanical electronics.

Therefore, all the project members of the team started learning about chicken legs and learning deboning work from scratch beside professional deboners at chicken processing factories.

After mastering deboning skills under the guidance of professional deboners, the team members started breaking down manual deboning work into phases. Through this procedure, deboning skills acquired by and embodied in the team members were articulated and transformed into explicit knowledge. In the end, deboning work was broken down into eight mechanical phases. The prototype was completed in 1992. Since it was a totally new invention from scratch, it took the project team a rather long period of time to complete the product. The product was completed and released to the market in May 1994.

The project members not only created agreement on the rules but also developed shared understanding of how to follow and make use of the rules. By sharing the experience of deboning work, the project members came to reverse their understanding of which rule that worked and which rule did not work. The fact that MYCOM completed the development and that the machine was really innovative illustrates the fact that the type of knowledge that results from the indwelling process is more profound than the alternative types.

Each of the four processes discussed here is associated with a particular resulting knowledge: tacit and explicit, understanding or agreement (see table 3.2).

Limits to Care

There are limits to care for organizational knowledge development. First, it is not easy to consistently pursue knowledge development using the concept of care. This is because care is based on a person's implicit understanding of a need to help. In order to implicitly understand that their colleagues are in need of help, organizational members have to pay attention well to their colleagues, an activity that demands a significant amount of power and commitment from organizational members. Given the hectic world of business, organization members can easily devote themselves to their own work, becoming less concerned with their colleagues. Therefore, the fundamental way to overcome the limit of care for organizational knowledge development is to firmly establish the concept of care as a value in the mindset of organization members. For that purpose, the idea of always being concerned with one's colleagues and the intention for knowledge development

Table 3.2. Knowledge Development Outcome

Knowledge	Process			
	Seizing	Transacting	Bestowing	Indwelling
Individual	Yes	Yes	Yes	Yes
Social	No	Yes	No	Yes
Understanding	Personal	Not shared	Personal	Shared
Agreement	No	Shared	No	Shared
Tacit	Yes	No	Yes	Yes
Explicit	Limited	Yes	Yes	Yes

based on the care relationship should be strongly shared among organizational members.

Second, care can be misused as the strategy of overhelping. We may overhelp others by ignoring what they really need. Care can be used as the strategy of taking others to their own party. Too much care can push for agreements. With such overhelping relationships, organizational knowledge either is not developed or is not well managed.

The organizational relationship based on the care concept should be reciprocal. We care for others, and others care for us. If this reciprocal characteristic of care is not well understood, care can be misused as a strategy of manipulative politics in the organization. Or care can motivate learned helplessness in people if they are always cared for without actively caring for others.

On the other hand, in the reciprocal relationships of care, we have respect for the need of others whom we care for. If we are being overhelped, we recognize the importance of respecting the real needs of others by our own experiences. Through the reciprocal relationship of care, we recognize what unique capabilities others may have and what they may need to complement those capabilities. Organizational relationships based on care thus facilitate the complementary relationship among organizational members, facilitating in turn the integration of a variety of unique individual capabilities. As the product of reciprocal relationship of care, trust is developed among organizational members. Thus care is crucial enabler for developing trust in organizations.

Why Organizational Relationships Matter

Why should management concern itself with questions of organizational relationships? As we said initially, knowledge in organizations is very fragile. Organizational knowledge development starts from individual experiences. Individual organization members may develop a new product/service concept or idea through observation or creative thinking. This idea or concept should be shared by other organization members so that organizational knowledge can be developed from individual observation and thinking. For that purpose, other organization members must actively listen to what individual organization members say, that is, they must show interest in their personal experience. However, this process of sharing does not happen naturally, there are many obstacles to it. Organizational members may not show any interest in the experience of others. Bosses may kill their subordinates' ideas. The source of innovation may be easily destroyed in the social process.

Care has an epistemological status since it is intimately connected to why and how organizations know. Care plays a pivotal role in organizational knowledge development at two levels, the individual level and the organizational level. First, individuals have to discover sources of innovation that they might develop. In this sense, knowledge development is caring about our own observation, reflecting on it, nurturing it despite possible criticism, and bringing it to the people whom you believe might have an interest in it (Von Krogh and Roos, 1996). Second, organizational members should respect the individual experiences of their colleagues. Caring means that organizational members withhold negative value judgments on the new insights that come so spontaneously to all of us. Individual organizational members should care for their own insights and those of others.

Further Research

What should be the focus of further research on the concept of care and knowledge development? This essay discusses how care facilitates organizational knowledge development internally (i.e., within organizations). Care should also be studied in the relationship between organizational members and external members (e.g., customers). How care for customers facilitates organizational knowledge development is one of the most promising research focuses. It will also be interesting to study the relationship between care within organizations and care outside organizations and how this relationship contributes to the development of knowledge of a firm. An internally high care organization may or may not be an externally high care organization. Are there any externally high care organizations that are internally low care? We hope to pursue these research questions in the future.

References

Argyris, Chris. 1993. *On Organizational Learning*. Cambridge, Mass.: Blackwell.

Argyris, Chris, and Donald A. Schön. 1978. *Organizational Learning*, Reading, Mass.: Addision-Wesley.

Arrow, Kenneth J. 1962. "The Economic Implications of Learning by Doing." *Review of Economic Studies* 29: 155–73.

Ashforth, Blake E., and R. H. Humphrey. 1993. "Emotional Labor in Service Roles: The Influence of Identity." *Academy of Management Review* 14: 20–39.

———. 1995. "Emotion in the Workplace: Appraisal." *Human Relations* 48: 97–125.

Barth, Fredrik. 1995. "Other Knowledge and Other Ways of Knowing." *Journal of Anthropological Research* 51: 65–8.

Berger, Peter L., and Thomas Luckman. 1966, *The Social Construction of Reality: A Treatise in the Sociology of Knowledge*. New York: Doubleday.

Braaten, Sheldon. 1983. "Assymetric Discourse and Cognitive Autonomy: Resolving

Model Monopoly through Boundary Shifts." In *Problems of Levels and Boundaries* edited by A. Pedretti and A. de Zeeuw. Princeton, N.J.: Princelet Editions.

Brown, John Seely, and Paul Duguid. 1991. "Organizational Learning and Communities-of-Practice: Toward a Unified View of Working, Learning and Innovation." *Organization Science* 2: 40–57.

Brunswik, Egon. 1956. *Perceptions and the Representative Design of Psychological Experiments*, Berkeley: University of California Press.

Callon, Michel. 1994. "Is Science a Public Good?" *Science, Technology, and Human Values* 19: 395–424.

Collis, David J. 1994. "Research Note: How Valuable are Organizational Capabilities?" *Strategic Management Journal*, Special Issue 15 (Winter): 143–52.

Cutrona, Carolyn E., V. Cole, Nicholas Colangelo, Susan G. Assouline, and D. W. Russel. 1994. "Perceived Parental Social Support and Academic Achievement: An Attachment Theory Perspective." *Journal of Personality and Social Psychology* 66: 369–78.

Cyert, Richard Michael, and James G. March. 1963. *A Behavioral Theory of the Firm.* Englewood Cliffs, N.J.: Prentice-Hall.

Darrah, Charles N. 1995. "Workplace Training, Workplace Learning: A Case Study." *Human Organization* 54: 31–41.

Dreyfus, Hubert L. 1979. *What Computers Can't Do: The Limits of Artificial Intelligence.* New York: Harper and Row.

———. 1996. "Response to My Critics." *Artificial Intelligence* 80: 171–91.

Dreyfus, Hubert L., and Stuart E. Dreyfus. 1986. *Mind over Machine.* New York: Free Press.

Egan, Gerard. 1986. *The Skilled Helper.* Monterey, Calif.: Brooks/Cole.

Eisenberg, Nancy, G. Carlo, D. Troyer, G. Switzer, and A. Speer. 1991. "The Altruistic Personality: In What Context is it Apparent?" *Journal of Personality and Social Psychology* 61: 450–8.

Eisenberger, R., N. Cotterell, and J. Marvel. 1987. "Reciprocation Ideology." *Journal of Personality and Social Psychology* 53: 743–50.

Foucault, Michel. 1972. *The Care of the Self.* New York: Vintage Books.

Foner, Nancy. 1995. "The Hidden Injuries of Bureaucracy: Work in an American Nursing Home." *Human Organization* 54: 229–37.

Gaylin, Willard. 1976. *Caring.* New York: Knopf.

Geertz, Clifford. 1973. *The Interpretation of Cultures.* New York: Basic Books.

Gouldner, Alvin Ward. 1960. "The Norm of Reciprocity: A Preliminary Statement." *American Sociological Review* 25: 161–78.

Greenberg, M. S., and D. R. Westcott. 1983. "Indebtness as a Mediator of Reactions to Aid." In *New Directions in Helping*, edited by Jeffrey D. Fisher, Arie Nadler, and Bella M. De Paulo. New York: Academic Press. Pp. 85–112,

Grice, H. Paul. 1975. "Logic and Conversations." In *Syntax and Semantics: Speech Acts* edited by Peter Cole, and J. L. Morgan. New York: Academic Press. Pp. 41–58.

Gunther McGrath, R., I. C. MacMillan, and S. Venkatarama. 1995. "Defining and Developing Competence: A Strategic Process Paradigm." *Strategic Management Journal* 16: 251–75.

Haslam, N. 1994. "Categories of Social Relationship." *Cognition* 53(1): 59–90.

Humphrey, R. H., and Blake E. Ashforth. 1994. "Cognitive Scripts and Prototypes in Service Encounters." In *Advances in Services Marketing and Management: Research and Practice*, 3, edited by T. A. Schwartz, D. E. Bowen, and S. W. Brown. Greenwich, Conn.: JAI Press. Pp. 175–99.

Kahn, W. A. 1993. "Facilitating and Undermining Organizational Change: A Case Study." *Journal of Applied Behavioral Science* 29: 32–55.

Kilduff, Mark. 1992. "Performance and Interaction Routines in Multinational Corporation." *Journal of International Business Studies* 23: 133–45.

Lakoff, George, and Mark Johnson. 1980. *Metaphors We Live By*. Chicago: University of Chicago Press.

Lawler, Edward. J., and J. Yoon. 1996. "Commitment in Exchange Relations: Test of a Theory of Relational Cohesion." *American Sociological Review* 61: 89–108.

Levinthal, D. A., and James G. March. 1993. "The Myopia of Learning." *Strategic Management Journal* 14: 92–112.

Luhmann, Niklas. 1991. *Soziologische Aufklaerung*. Frankfurt: Suhrkamp.

Lyles, Marjorie, and Charles R. Schwenk. 1992. "Top Management, Strategy and Organizational Knowledge Structures." *Journal of Management Studies* 29: 155–74.

Lyth, Isabel Menzies. 1988. *Containing Anxiety in Institutions: Selected Essays*. London: Free Association Books.

McGrath, G., I. MacMillan, and S. Venkataraman. 1995. "Defining and Developing Competence: A Strategic Process Paradigm." *Strategic Management Journal* 16: 251–75.

March, James G. 1988. *Decision and Organizations*. Oxford: Blackwell.

March, James G., and Herbert A. Simon. 1958. *Organizations*. New York: Wiley.

Maturana, Humberto R., and Francisco J. Varela. 1987. *The Tree of Knowledge*. Boston: Shambhala.

Mayeroff, Milton. 1971. *On Caring*. New York: Harper and Row.

Merleau-Ponty, Maurice. 1963. *The Structure of Behavior*. Boston: Beacon Press.

Morgan, Gareth. 1986. *Images of Organization*. Beverly Hills, Calif.: Sage.

Noddings, Nell. 1984. *Caring: A Feminine Approach to Ethics and Moral Education*. Berkeley: University of California Press.

Nonaka, Ikujiro. 1991. "The Knowledge Creating Company." *Harvard Business Review* (November-December): 96–104.

———. 1994. "A Dynamic Theory of Organizational Knowledge Creation." *Organization Science* 5: 14–37.

Nonaka, Ikujiro, and Hirotaka Takeuchi. 1995. *The Knowledge Creating Company*. New York: Oxford University Press.

Orbell, J.M., Robyn M. Dawes, and A. J. C. Van de Kragt. 1988. "Explaining Discussion-Induced Cooperation." *Journal of Personality and Social Psychology* 54: 811–19.

Pagel, M. D., W. W. Erdly, and J. Becker. 1987. "Social Networks: We Get by with (and in Spite of) a Little Help from Our Friends." *Journal of Personality and Social Psychology* 53: 793–804.

Peteraf, M. 1993. "The Cornerstones of Competitive Advantage: A Resource-Based View." *Strategic Management Journal* 14: 179–91.

Pines, Ayala M., and Elliot Aronson. 1988. *Career Burnout*. New York: Free Press.

Polanyi, Michael. 1958. *Personal Knowledge*. London: Routledge and Keegan Paul.

Sandelands, Lloyd E. 1988. "The Concept of Work Feeling." *Journal for the Theory of Social Behavior* 18: 437–57.

Sarason, Seymour B. 1985. *Caring and Compassion in Clinical Practice*. San Francisco: Jossey-Bass.

Sarason, Barbara R., Gregory R. Pierce, and Irwin G. Sarason. 1990. "Social Support: The Essence of Acceptance and the Role of Relationships." In *Social Support: An Interactional View*, edited by Barbara R. Sarason and Gregory R. Pierce. New York: John Wiley. Pp. 97–128.

Schutz, A., and Thomas Luckman. 1985/1989. *The Structures of the Life-worlds*. Vols.1 and 2. Evanston, Ill.: Northwestern University Press.

Shapiro, Edward R., and A. Wesley Carr. 1991. *Lost in Familiar Places*. New Haven: Yale University Press.

Staub, Ervin. 1974. "Helping a Distressed Person: Social, Personality, and Stimulus Determinants." In *Advances in Experimental and Social Psychology*, vol. 7, edited by L. Berkowitz. New York: Academic Press. Pp. 293–341.

———. 1978. *Positive Social Behavior and Morality: Social and Personal Influences*. New York: Academic Press.

Van Maanen, John. 1991. "The Smile-Factory: Work at Disneyland." In *Reframing Organizational Culture*, edited by Peter J. Frost, Larry F. Moore, M. R. Louis, C. C. Lundberg, and J. Martin. Newbury Park, Calif.: Sage. Pp. 58–76.

Varela, Francisco J., Evan Thompson, and Eleanor Rosch. 1991. *Embodied Mind: Cognitive Science and Human Experience*. Cambridge, Mass.: MIT Press.

von Krogh, Georg. 1998. "Care in Knowledge Creation." *California Management Review* 40(3): 133–53.

von Krogh, Georg, and Johan Roos. 1995. *Organizational Epistemology*. New York: MacMillan.

———. 1996. *Managing Knowledge: Perspectives on Cooperation and Competition*. London: Sage.

von Krogh, Georg, Johan Roos, and K. Slocum. 1994. "An Essay on Corporate Epistemology." *Strategic Management Journal*, Special Issue (summer) 15: 53–71.

Weber, Max. 1958. *The Protestant Ethic and the Spirit of Capitalism*. New York: Scribner.

Wernerfelt, Birger. 1984. "A Resource-Based View of the Firm." *Strategic Management Journal* 5: 171–80.

PART II
TECHNOLOGY AND COOPERATION

4

The Influence of New 3-D CAD Systems on Knowledge Creation in Product Development

KENTARO NOBEOKA
YASUNORI BABA

The management of knowledge creation is considered one of the key factors in the management of new product development. In the past, differences in knowledge creation capabilities at the organizational level were primarily attributed to the quantity and quality of human interactions that were facilitated by the appropriate organizational management (Nonaka, 1994; Kogut and Zander, 1992). Although organizational interactions continue to be important, the use of information technologies (ITs), including design, engineering, and manufacturing (CAD/CAE/CAM), is becoming a much more critical factor for organizational knowledge creation in product development.

Traditionally, ITs have been considered tools that support product development processes with organizational management positioned in the center. However, it appears that in the future IT will play a much more critical role and in some cases it will actually lead the changes in new product development processes. The purpose of this essay is to outline how the newest generation of information technologies will play this key role in terms of their effect on the knowledge-creation process.

New CAD technologies coupled with new organizational structures and processes that are designed to complement the new ITs have only just begun the fundamental change that they will make in the core concept of traditional product development activities. Most of the firms we have studied are currently implementing these initial changes. We will lay out the key issues these firms both have been struggling with and will have to consider in the immediate future.

The effective utilization of ITs in the product development process is part of a larger trend in which Japanese *human-oriented* approaches are being integrated with Western *systematic-rationality-oriented* practices. Japanese manufacturing and product development processes in the assembly industries have been recently recognized worldwide as best practices. The core of their competitiveness has been attributed to continuous improvements made by multiskilled workers who have utilized their extensive experiences in the factory and to extensive interactions among different groups of engineers and workers. In the Japanese best practices model, an importance has been attached to both the *workplace* and to the *actual product* in which knowledge at the manufacturing site is highly regarded. Knowledge and skills improve as the result of an accumulation of experiences gained through direct contacts with artifacts (we define artifacts as humanmade objects) and through active interpersonal exchanges. It is thought that both tacit and articulated knowledge are created mainly through these experiences and exchanges (Nonaka, 1994).

This human-oriented approach, in which manufacturing and product knowledge is created by sharing a common "field," has enabled Japanese firms to interpret and apply technology flexibly to varying environments. A common field has been nurtured by the cooperation between engineers and workers, and the implementation of concurrent engineering has been based on the smooth exchange of information between design engineers and manufacturing engineers. With this human-oriented approach, computers were introduced only as a supportive role.

However, changes are taking place in both the IT and the economic environment that are affecting the competitiveness of the Japanese workplace and human-oriented manufacturing model. The first notable change is the rise in the absolute standard of computer capabilities. From the economic standpoint, there is the entry into the world market of newly industrializing countries such as the eastern European countries, China, and other Asian countries where labor costs are much lower than in Japan. In addition, because of the increasingly intensifying competition, standards of competition with respect to the speed and efficiency of product development have been raised to unprecedented levels.

In the Western systematic-rationality-oriented model, development and production processes are integrated primarily through the use of IT. These processes reflect the Western model of knowledge creation and problem-solving, which is based on pragmatism and an intellectual tradition of analytic rationality. In this model, possible options are analyzed using clearly defined objectives, and the decision-making is a rational process that follows the comparison and review of these options. The ideal state of this systematic-rationality-based model is the systematic management of processes in a decentralized computer environment that utilizes digital information. For example, this approach could enable the establishment of a global production system in which real-time integration of a firm's worldwide development and production activities can be achieved.

Although for a number of technical and organizational reasons the potential capabilities of IT have not yet been fully realized in the creation of such a worldwide decentralized development and production system, it appears that technical and managerial changes are taking place that will enable the creation of such a system. The limitations in IT that prevented their effective support of the Western systematic-rationality-oriented model are being solved through new generations of IT such as three-dimensional (3-D) CAD. The introduction of new organizational systems, involving, for example, the simplification of organizations and the downward transfer of managerial authority, is also being driven by the need for faster and more rational decision-making processes.

This essay suggests implications for both U.S. and Japanese manufacturers. United States firms appear to be the leaders in integrating the U.S. and Japanese approaches. Leading U.S. manufacturing firms have already begun to learn and adopt aspects of the Japanese model, according to recent studies (Ellison, et al., 1995; MacDuffie and Pil, 1996). Japanese manufacturers, on the other hand, appear to be lagging significantly behind U.S. firms in the effective implementation of IT. However, although both sets of firms are approaching the problem from different directions, it appears that they have the same goal in mind. This essay argues that in both the U.S. and Japanese approaches, the new generation of 3-D CAD systems is the key to successfully introducing the new paradigm of product development.

The next section reviews the evolution of CAD technologies and it defines the key aspects of the new generation of 3-D CAD systems. We then describe two types of conceptual models for knowledge creation in product development, one supported by traditional 2-D CAD systems and the other led by the new 3-D CAD systems. Next, we discuss potential contributions and benefits that the new 3-D CAD system may provide in the product development process. We provide a brief description of the Boeing 777 project as a leading example of how the new generation of 3-D CAD systems can be effectively utilized. Next, we briefly explain usage of CAD systems in the Japanese automobile and shipbuilding industries. Finally, we discuss the necessary managerial changes for successfully introducing and fully realizing the benefits of the new CAD systems in the product development process.

This study is primarily based on a 1995 and 1996 field study done in Japan. We interviewed about fourteen managers and engineers in three shipbuilding firms, twenty-two in four automobile firms, eleven in two aircraft firms, and seven in a chip manufacturer. It is very appropriate to study the implementation of CAD in these industries, since they have been the leading users of advanced CAD applications for mechanical products (Kaplinsky, 1982). It is also important to recognize that the influences of CAD tools on design and organizational processes varies greatly depending on the products that are developed (Liker et al., 1992). Our detailed case studies regarding the automobile, shipbuilding, and chip manufacturers, available elsewhere, also include detailed descriptions of the firms (Baba and Nobeoka, 1996).

The Evolution of CAD Tools for Product Development

In order to consider the influence of CAD on the product development process, it is necessary both to describe the evolution of CAD tools and to define the specific characteristics of the newest generation of them that will enable the realization of a more effective knowledge-creation process within the product development process. Using an example from the Japanese automobile industry, table 4.1 summarizes the three stages in the evolution and the application of CAD systems to product development.

In the beginning of the first stage, called the introduction stage, design engineers began to use CAD tools; almost simultaneously, manufacturing engineers began to use (NC) machines and CAM tools. In this stage, design engineers used CAD tools primarily as an electronic drafting board. The use of CAD significantly improved the efficiency and preciseness of drawing, particularly when engineers were able to develop drawings based on existing ones.

Manufacturing engineers were also able to reduce the number of engineering hours in the design of dies by using digital design data that was received from de-

Table 4.1. An Evolution of CAD Usage in New Product Development

Stage	1. Introduction	2. Diffusion	3. Integration
CAD System	2-D/3-D mixture	2-D/3-D mixture	3-D
Primary purpose	Efficiency in drawing data transfer to NC machines	Diffusion and learning more efficiency and smoother data transfer	Real concurrent engineering
Relationship with traditional product development process	Support for efficiency in drawing and data usage for NC machines	Support for efficiency in drawing and data usage for NC machines	Fundamental change in process
Period (in the case of automobile)	1970–1985	1985–1995	1995–

sign engineers. However, even when components were designed using early versions of 3-D CAD, manufacturing engineers needed to transform the data rather extensively before an effective die design was realized.

In the second stage, called the learning and diffusion stage, design engineers learned to use CAD tools more efficiently, and the tools continued to be adopted in greater numbers. Figure 4.1 shows the diffusion pattern of CAD terminals at a major Japanese automobile firm in which the diffusion pattern follows the classic S-curve. It took several years for this firm to increase the number of CAD terminals to a sufficient level whereby the diffusion speed slowed down. There are about three thousand design engineers in total at this firm. On the basis of our interviews with three other Japanese automobile firms, although there are minor differences in terms of time, we have concluded that this pattern is not unique to one firm.

Understandably, CAD usage has gradually increased as the benefits of CAD tools to designers and engineers have continued to increase—from four perspectives.

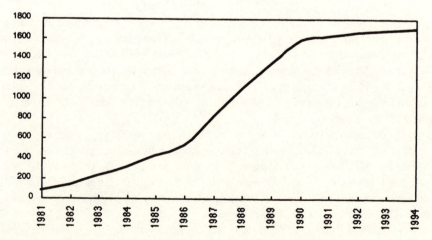

Figure 4.1. Number of CAD Terminals at a Japanese Automobile Firm

First, engineers gradually learned to use CAD tools more effectively and efficiently. Salzman (1989) has reported that it usually takes a relatively long period of time for engineers to learn how to make the most of CAD tools. Second, the CAD technologies continued to improve, in terms of user interface, speed, and stability of the system. Both the learning by designers and the technological improvements gradually improved the benefits of CAD tools over manual drawing boards and helped diffuse CAD systems.

Third, there was also a continuous improvement in data transferability from one application to others. For example, it became much easier to transfer design data into NC data. It also became less time-consuming to create a CAE simulation model using design data. Fourth, because the benefits from CAD tools are greatest when designers can reuse existing drawings, the potential for realizing benefits from CAD increased as more designs were accumulated. Therefore, the benefit of the CAD tools for designers improved as a function of time and experience, and CAD tools continued to diffuse during the second stage.

However, in spite of these improvements, CAD tools were not considered a truly integrated product development tool during this stage in most firms. One of the major reasons for the lack of integration was attributed to the mixture of 2-D and 3-D CAD applications. Different applications are used depending on the different component characteristics even within the development of a single product. For example, among automobile components, exterior body panels began to be designed using 3-D CAD very early, primarily because they had complex curves and needed 3-D representation. However, most other functional components, such as the suspension, engine, and transmission, continued to be designed in 2-D CAD, although 3-D models were sometimes used for simulation in CAE.

When only the efficiency of drawing designs is considered, there are many types of components that do not benefit much from 3-D drawings. It takes many more hours to design components using 3-D CAD, at least until the engineers become fully accustomed to 3-D tools. Although the use of 3-D CAD can provide potential benefits to other functional groups, such as manufacturing and suppliers, each functional group has pursued the improvement of its own efficiency as opposed to improvements in the system-level performance for the entire product development process.

In the third stage of the evolution of CAD technology, called the integration stage (see table 4.1), all components are designed using 3-D CAD tools, which usually feature 3-D solid modeling features. The same 3-D CAD data are shared by all the engineering functions, including styling and component designers, analytical engineers, and manufacturing engineers. For example, the 3-D data that are created by design engineers can be shared and used by manufacturing engineers. In addition, all the components are digitally assembled as a finished product in an early stage of the development project before a real prototype can be available. Digitally assembled data have information regarding topological relationships among the different components as well as manufacturing requirements. Finally, the integrated CAD systems also include the capability for sharing the latest digital data between different computer terminals. Therefore, all the engineers involved in a development project can see the latest design that is being worked on by other engineers.

This essay focuses on the influence of this third stage on knowledge creation in product development. Whenever we use terms like *the new 3-D CAD system*, or *3-D CAD model*, we are referring to this third stage. Although 3-D CAD is not technologically new to this stage, digital preassembly and the sharing of digital data among all engineers is new at this point.

Knowledge-Creation Models: 2-D and 3-D CAD Models

In the process of knowledge creation, specific processes of identifying and solving problems play an important role. In order to properly consider the influence of CAD systems on knowledge creation in the product development process, we will first summarize different types of problem-solving processes.

In solving problems, people use several types of logic and reasoning. We classify the logical ones into the following three forms: deduction, induction, and abduction. The first two are widely used in categorizations of human logic; the third, abduction, was originally advocated by Charles S. Peirce, a nineteenth-century pragmatic philosopher, and has been discussed in some studies (Hartshorne and Weiss, 1978).

We argue that because the 3-D CAD system supports the abductive reasoning process of engineers, as well as the deductive and inductive reasoning processes, it will have a fundamentally different impact on knowledge creation in product development from that of the earlier CAD systems. The earlier versions basically only supported deductive and inductive reasoning processes through their analytical and data-processing capabilities.

In the abductive reasoning process, a person forms a hypothesis that he or she believes provides a unified explanation for the various observed data. Nakajima (1995) argues that the synthesis of knowledge or knowledge creation in designing new products, the diagnosis of design problems, and the product maintenance processes can all be categorized as abductive reasoning processes.

Yoshikawa (1993) uses an example of house design to explain the abductive reasoning process. Selecting a design from an unstructured set of alternatives can be considered a major part of the abductive reasoning process. A client expresses his or her desires for the structure, budget, and so on. There may also be conditions related to the circumstances of the land and regulations that should be satisfied in the design of the new house. An architect designs the house on the basis of the client's needs and conditions, as well as his or her knowledge of architectural technology. The architect first develops a domain where all the needs and conditions are satisfied. He or she then considers design alternatives within the domain. A client's desires and conditions must be clearly converted to the architecture-related forms so that the architect can judge whether particular design alternatives fall within the domain. Another way to state this is that a major part of the process of designing a house are the attempts to create hypotheses and to verify whether a particular hypothesis consistently fulfills all the requirements. These actions can be classified as an abductive form of reasoning.

Once the domain has been defined (i.e., the design objective and demands have been fully defined), the designer forms a mental picture of a completed design. In this stage of the design process, engineering or architectural theories, although they provide intellectual support, do not bring about a solution. For example, in the case of developing a photocopying machine, although theories in electrostatic engineering, photoconducting material science, and control engineering all provide a design engineer with knowledge for carrying out deductive reasoning, this knowledge by itself does not bring about a concrete design solution. It is also necessary for the designer to search for a design solution by considering hypothetical design alternatives. Although these search activities partially utilize deductive reasoning, they are actually abductive reasoning processes (Nakajima, 1995).

A series of recent studies in economics and business administration have revealed that abductive reasoning is acquired through learning by doing or by accumulating aesthetic perceptions nurtured by professional experiences (von Hippel, 1994; Dosi, Marengo and Fagiolo, 1996; Tyre and von Hippel, 1997). These studies have emphasized that although abduction may accompany a jump in logic and may occasionally lead to wrong hypotheses, human beings can learn from abduction processes and mistakes. When they make mistakes, they find differences between their perceptions and realities. Based on the differences, they modify their mental and intellectual models. They continue this process until the hypothesis is deductively corroborated and objectively recognized as correct.

These abductive reasoning processes can be considered a major part of the learning process. Social scientists may be interested in the roles of abduction in learning and knowledge-creation processes; from engineering and computer scientists may be more interested in the mechanism of the abductive reasoning process.

Although this discussion has focused on unstructured problems whose solution may require abductive reasoning, there are also many structured problems to be solved in product development, problems that can be successively solved mainly through deductive reasoning and sometimes through induction. Computer support is obviously effective and useful for this type of problem-solving. When a designer verifies the viability of a deduced design plan, he or she can analyze a series of design parameters with the support of a database in which designing and drafting rules are encoded.

As seen in such an *expert system*, it is possible to support deductive reasoning through the systematization of information found in the operation manuals of experts. The knowledge base of an expert system comprises a congregation of if-then rules. If problems fit within these rules, a solution can be found through reasoning that traces a tree structure of rules. When manufacturing knowledge is built into the database, even in metal mold processing where a craftsman's technique was traditionally required for the delicate finishing process, it is possible for NC data fed into CAM equipment to replace skills embodied in a craftsman. In addition to expert systems, automatic fuzzy control is also effective for deductive reasoning, and as for support for inductive reasoning, a neuron system that promotes modeling by a built-in self-organizing function is known to be effective.

In the 2-D CAD model of knowledge creation, there must be a preexisting problem structure that has been developed using an abductive reasoning process. Solutions are then obtained through a series of deductive and inductive reasoning processes that can be supported by a 2-D CAD model. Information created in this process is stored in a computer-supported database as digital design and manufacturing information. Product data are then transformed into concrete artifacts by transferring NC data into CAM equipment.

Thus, even in the 2-D CAD model, computer support has significant benefits for knowledge creation. However, its limitations are also apparent. In the case of an expert system, unless conditions regarding problem-solving meet the if-then rules, no solution can be obtained. Computer support is useful only when prespecified routines are sufficient for problem-solving. Otherwise, the 2-D CAD tools are unable to support abductive reasoning processes and can only support the engineer's design analysis processes.

The new 3-D CAD systems, however, can potentially support an engineer's abductive reasoning process. The key features of the new 3-D CAD systems that enable the support of abductive reasoning are full visualization of products, digital assembly, simulation, and shared databases.

Full visualization of products, in which hypothesis formation can be carried out in 3-D CAD, enables engineers to engage in more advanced abductive reasoning than with the 2-D CAD tools (Young, 1987; Adler, 1989; Robertson et al., 1991; Robertson and Allen, 1992, 1993). Three-dimensional design enables engineers to more effectively create and compare designs to their design objectives (Salzman, 1989).

The new 3-D CAD system also has advantages in its ability to quickly carry out a number of iterations in the formation and verification of a hypothesis. Analysis and simulation functions built in the new 3-D CAD systems enable faster verifications of various hypotheses than experiments with real prototypes. This capability contributes to abductive reasoning through the expansion of deductive reasoning premised on hypotheses.

There is also a contribution to abduction capabilities at the organizational level. Human interaction and human collaboration have a positive influence on recognition activities, especially in problem-solving and abduction (Nonaka and Takeuchi, 1996). The 3-D CAD model supports these types of organizational knowledge creation activities. Under the computer-supported environment in the 3-D CAD model, all the information is expressed in a common form, so that everyone concerned can more quickly respond to each other. Sharing design ideas with other engineers enables an engineer to confirm a design from a variety of different viewpoints and to resolve design conflicts with others. Furthermore, the presentation and briefing capabilities made possible by the simulation functions of 3-D CAD increase the ability to communicate key tradeoffs to other functions within (e.g., multiple functions) and outside the firm (e.g., suppliers and customers).

In the new 3-D CAD system, the various types of simulation that can be conducted can reduce the number of design problems that might occur later in the development process. Knowledge obtained through such computer support can be molded into a unified expression and stored in a database, making use of the characteristics of the 3-D CAD. This requires the establishment of a common language between different specialties in order to eliminate the duplication of efforts.

In the 3-D model, the abduction ability of engineers, as well as the organization, may be improved through their experiences with product development in the computer-supported environment. Acquisition of design knowledge from in-depth understanding of what is being designed enhances an individual's and subsequently an organization's abduction ability. Knowledge of alternatives in the design specifications also raises an engineer's abduction capabilities.

In addition, in the 3-D CAD model, pieces of knowledge are constantly recombined and reintegrated through digital assembly and simulation. Relationships between different subsystems are clearly defined in the assembly feature of the 3-D system. The systematized knowledge is transferred into artifacts. The process of frequent integration of different pieces of knowledge is also an abduction process. This capability is also useful in the development of multiple products that utilize different combinations of the same subsystems. For example, firms can enter various product market segments efficiently, as shown in the case study of Boeing (discussed hereafter). This process results in increased returns in product development and decreased marginal development costs (Arthur, 1989). Many industries face competitive markets where more product variations must be developed and products are constantly becoming obsolete. In this situation, capabilities that enable the development and accumulation of integrated systematized knowledge are important competitive tools (Nobeoka and Cusumano, 1997).

The incentive to introduce this kind of computer support cannot be obtained from a short-term or locally optimized perspective. It can be realized only through a long-term perspective. Further, an improvement in a firm's innovative ability requires the strengthening of knowledge infrastructures in which knowledge is constantly being broken down into narrow skills and recombined into new forms of knowledge in an abductive reasoning process.

The importance of the human's role in abduction will remain unchanged. Sharing of the same information (unified expression of knowledge) by all those concerned is made more effective by the use of 3-D CAD. However, in order to systematically unify individual abductions so that they bring about concrete results, the individuals must make a conscious effort to understand the intentions of other members in the team and develop a common perspective and mental model. There must be face-to-face communication through co-location in order to establish their objective. From this standpoint, it is understandable that Boeing (see hereafter) and Microsoft (Cusumano and Selby, 1995), which have some of the most advanced computer-supported environments in the world, emphasize co-location of project members.

Influence of the New 3-D CAD System on Product Development

Four groups of factors determine how the new generation of 3-D CAD tools have a strong influence on knowledge creation in product development: 3-D visualization, digital preassembly, simulation, and communication, and coordination.

3-D Full Visualization

When all components are designed in 3-D CAD, engineers can access much more relevant information during the drawing process by seeing and working on the entire form of the component. Engineers can see the entire design from any perspective, whereas in 2-D CAD they can see only a component from a few fixed perspectives. In addition, surfaces can be shaded and lines removed to improve visualization. Two-dimensional designs are often too complicated, with too many lines, which can easily confuse even skilled designers (Lynch, 1988).

Engineers can also draw more details and exact shapes with 3-D CAD, enabling them to consider the design from a multifunctional perspective. For example, the manufacturability of components can be more effectively considered in 3-D design since it enables more details of component shapes to be defined and represented. There are also designs that can only be created with 3-D design processes. For example, designers can much more effectively evaluate the aerodynamic characteristics of automobiles through the use of 3-D drawing tools (Lynch, 1988).

The use of 3-D design requires completely different drawing skills from 2-D design. Designers do not have to transform their ideas for new components into two dimensions—this historically being one of the major parts of "designing." The 3-D drawing process is more like clay work. Although it requires a different set of skills, some perhaps more sophisticated, requiring appropriate training and experiences, it can enhance knowledge-creation capabilities in engineering.

Simulation

It is much easier to perform simulation analysis of such considerations as thermal stress, mechanical stress, and vibration, on a 3-D than on a 2-D design. Since most types of engineering simulation require 3-D modeling, designers must first translate a 2-D design into three dimensions, which is time-consuming and costly. Therefore, simulation is rarely carried out when only 2-D CAD tools are available and when prototypes, which are also time-consuming and costly, are made and tested.

A combination of 3-D solid modeling and user-friendly CAE applications also enables design engineers to conduct analysis by themselves, as opposed to having specialists carry out the simulation analysis. When engineers can carry out both the design and simulation activities they are able to consider the design from more perspectives and thus knowledge creation is enhanced.

Digital Preassembly

The digital integration of components, usually called digital preassembly, is also a form of simulation. It enables engineers to view an assembled set of components before physical prototypes are made. Real prototypes are costly and time-consuming to build; in addition, it is usually not possible to manufacture a prototype before all of the drawings are completed to a certain level. According to a component designer at Kawasaki who worked on the development of the Boeing 777, with digital preassembly he was able to begin making a digital assembly that included components being designed by other engineers when he had only a very rough idea of the component for which he was responsible.

Digital preassembly helps engineers create a more systemwide view of the final product, particularly when the components are designed by engineers from different functional or component groups. Engineers can look for interferences and the goodness of fit between relevant components during the early stages of product development, whereas it is often almost impossible to see interferences when engineers use only 2-D designs.

One can also use 3-D designs to analyze a product's kinematic behavior, which is also almost impossible with 2-D design. This analysis includes the ease of assembly; for example, engineers can see how easily workers can reach and assemble certain components by using a digital prototyping feature in a 3-D solid modeling application. According to one automobile engineer we interviewed, in an average product development project that uses 2-D design, about 70 percent of design changes during the project are necessitated by component interference problems. Coordination between engineers is usually not sufficient to catch interference problems because such problems, particularly those that occur during the product's kinematic operation, often occur where the engineers do not expect them to happen.

Of all the benefits of 3-D design, digital preassembly may have the most influence on product development processes. In developing a new product that consists of numerous interdependent components, many researchers have argued that knowledge about system integration plays a key role with respect to product integrity (Clark and Fujimoto, 1991). These authors have argued that it is important for all engineers, particularly engineers who are responsible for different components, to coordinate their design activities from an early stage of product development, even before physical prototypes are available.

Furthermore, new product knowledge is often created through the interactions among engineers who work on different parts of the product. The way in which components relate to each other is a critical element to so-called architectural innovations (Henderson and Clark, 1990), where the structure of the product is completely changed by the innovation. Digital preassembly may facilitate the implementation and perhaps the identification of such architectural innovations.

Communication and Coordination

The three factors just discussed all contribute to an improvement in coordination and communication among component designers, as well as among engineers from multiple functions such as design, manufacturing preparation, analysis, and experiment. Communication and coordination are the key factors that determine the effectiveness of concurrent engineering. Concurrent engineering can be implemented successfully only when people from different functional groups share similar knowledge and language. The new 3-D CAD system provides these different functions with this common knowledge and language, which significantly improves coordination and communication effectiveness among engineers. Components drawn in 3-D and prototypes assembled digitally can be a common means to which all different functional engineers refer during the product development process.

Conversations in front of a 3-D CAD designs often differ significantly from those in front of a white board or engineering drawing (Robertson and Allen, 1993). The CAD representation of the design can be quickly changed during the conversation. Given this common reference, fewer misunderstandings occur, and conversations are more effective (Robertson and Allen, 1993). According to one automobile engineer, when 3-D representation is not available before physical prototypes are made, there are problems with the quality of discussion and information exchange. Members who specialize in testing or manufacturing are often not able to provide meaningful feedback with 2-D drawings since they are not very familiar with visualizing actual components when looking at a 2-D design.

The ability to include in 3-D a component's design details, for example, back views and rounded corners, also supports communication between design and manufacturing engineers. Manufacturing engineers are often interested in the detailed shape of a component that cannot be sufficiently represented with 2-D drawings. In addition, because 3-D data can be used directly by manufacturing engineers for the development and design of dies, this kind of data is transferred more quickly and frequently from design to manufacturing than 2-D data (Robertson and Allen, 1993).

Boeing

One of the best and most famous examples of a successful implementation of the 3-D CAD model is the development of the Boeing 777. The project was conducted as an international joint development led by Boeing and involving five Japanese aircraft manufacturers. A number of case studies have been written on this project; this discussion focuses on how the 3-D CAD model was implemented and how it changed the way the organization works.

Boeing uses the term *preferred process* to describe its new development process, which was first implemented with the development of the Boeing 777. The main features of this new process are: (1) concurrent product definition; (2) design build teams, (3) digital product definition; and (4) digital preassembly. The first two features are associated with organizational and process changes; the latter two are associated with the 3-D CAD system.

Concurrent Product Definition (CPD)

Concurrent product definition involves the determination of the key design features for each component. As a core element of achieving concurrent engineering, CPD was conducted through concurrent operations among different design groups and among various functions such as design, test, production, and materials. Interferences between components, manufacturability, and product functionality were considered by all relevant project members from the very beginning of the project. Although these activities were also supported by the new CAD system, most project members from both Boeing and the suppliers were co-located in Seattle during the CPD stage.

Design Build Team (DBT)

Beginning with the CPD stage, many teams were created to facilitate smooth coordination among various functions. In the 777 project, more than two hundred fifty teams were created in total. While most of these DBTs were focused on specific component areas, teams were also created for specific engineering issues, such as aerodynamics.

A hierarchy of DBTs was created in order to systematically manage the project. There were upper-level DBTs that contained leaders of lower-level DBTs. Although this hierarchy was created, it was much more flexible than the product development organizations that had been previously used at Boeing.

Digital Product Definition (DPD)

All components were defined using 3-D CAD data, and these digital data were designated the only medium for component definition in the 777 project. The latest data were made available to most project members in order to have real-time coordination between them. Access to data was determined by managerial level and group membership.

Digital Preassembly (DPA)

Digital pre-assembly was conducted from the very beginning of the development process. In order to simultaneously check for interference and manufacturability problems, DPA was conducted even when there was only a rough idea of the size and shape of the component.

The four characteristics just described represent a combination of both Japanese human-oriented and U.S. systematic-rationality-oriented practices, including IT. Before implementing the new development process, Boeing conducted an activity it called "Learn the Japanese way," in which it extensively studied the Japanese manufacturing and development model through visits to Toyota and shipbuilding companies. In this study, Boeing learned the importance of crossfunctional teams that are created at the very beginning of a project, which Toyota calls front-loading. The front-loading of activities enables the inclusion of other functional perspectives at the beginning of the development project. In previous Boeing development projects, design engineers, who held a great deal of power in Boeing, were allowed to conduct their work in a designer-centered fashion with little attention to downstream processes. One purpose of implementing the DBTs was to remedy this power relationship so that the designers and the production people could exchange information and ideas on an equal footing from the early stage of development. The introduction of DBTs and the CPD enabled the concurrent drawing of designs, production instruction charts, and tool charts.

However, Boeing went beyond the traditional Japanese knowledge-creation model, partly since it was armed with much more sophisticated CAD systems than most Japanese firms. Digital preassembly facilitated crossfunctional communication. According to some Japanese automobile engineers, even when they want to discuss design issues at the very beginning of a project, manufacturing and testing people sometimes cannot participate in the discussion unless they have a physical representation such as a prototype or a view of a digital preassembly.

An additional problem often found in Japanese firms, which was handled well by Boeing, concerns the distribution of power among project members. In the Japanese projects, the more experience an engineer has, the greater respect he or she receives and thus the more likely his or her recommendation is to be implemented. Although experience and correctness are often related, experienced people do make mistakes. In Boeing's DBTs, the digital preassembly and simulation activities made it possible to make decisions more on the basis of logic than just experience.

The performance of the Boeing 777 project was in many ways superior to past Boeing projects. First, there were 75 percent fewer design changes than in previous projects. Design changes for both design improvement and for design error corrections were reduced. A large portion of the changes for design improvement are typically caused by demands outside the design function; they range from manufacturing to customer service changes. The CPD and DBT activities enabled a reduction in this type of design change. Design error corrections, which are typically caused by parts interference problems, were reduced through digital preassembly.

Other benefits included reduced engineering hours and a reduced number of prototypes, including mockups. Although the work load for project designers increased, since they were responsible for both producing 3-D drawings and for producing the final design that incorporates manufacturing requirements and testing results, a reduction in engineering changes enabled a reduction in the number of total engineering hours. Further, a full-scale mockup was not needed.

Finally, the development method used for the 777 project has made it easier to develop subsequent aircraft that are similar to the 777 model. While reuse of a component design was also easy when engineers used 2-D CAD, the new 3-D CAD system featuring digital preassembly makes it possible to also reuse subassembly designs. The basic aircraft, with a passenger capacity of three hundred and a cruising range of five thousand miles, was first developed in May 1995. It was followed by a long cruising-range aircraft with a cruising range of seven thousand miles in December 1996. A stretched-body aircraft with a passenger capacity of more than three hundred fifty was also introduced in May 1998. Effective applications of the system knowledge to multiple products are becoming a more important factor for the competition in many other industries (Nobeoka and Cusumano, 1997).

Although the development of the Boeing 777 aircraft is an excellent example of the 3-D model we are advocating in this paper, we recognize that there are some characteristics of aircraft development that make the 3-D model easier to implement in this than in other industries. In the aircraft industry, the design architecture and the structure of components are relatively standardized. A standardized manufacturing and assembling structure exists—called work breakdown structure (WBS)—and is shared by most firms in the industry. In the WBS, all the work required for aircraft development is broken down into a tree structure. Through experience in joint development projects, both domestic and international, in which the main contractor subcontracts work to cooperating firms, a common WBS has emerged among many firms. This WBS includes standard individual operations, standard durations of time, and standard combinations of different operations. This WBS has probably made it easy for Boeing to introduce the 3-D model not just internally but also with all its suppliers.

The Japanese Automobile and Shipbuiliding Industries

Automobile

The automobile firms we interviewed in Japan are struggling to introduce the new 3-D CAD system like the one Boeing used in its 777 project, but they have not reached the level of Boeing in terms of both the system's introduction and its effective usage.

The most critical factor that has delayed the adoption of the new 3-D CAD system at the Japanese firms is the tendency to consider local rather than total optimization. Each functional group tends to consider only its local efficiency. For example, it takes much longer to develop a 3-D design than a 2-D design, particularly initially. Therefore, most engineers do not have an incentive to introduce 3-D design tools because doing so would lower their productivity.

The benefits of 3-D design can be realized at the project level, where digital preassembly and smooth data transfer between design and manufacturing engineers helps reduce engineering changes and improve the product's manufacturability. However, the Japanese automobile firms we interviewed have not yet introduced 3-D CAD in this manner. They are now using 3-D CAD as a prime design tool only for body design, where there are benefits at both local and project levels. It is almost impossible to draw body designs in 2-D form because they have complex 3-D curves.

A different situation exists for the chassis and power train, however. Two of the three firms still primarily use 2-D tools for the chassis and power train, as shown in table 4.2. Engineers for the chassis and power train at these firms mentioned that it is usually much easier for them to design these components in 2-D form. It would take many more engineering hours using 3-D design. At the firm that has introduced 3-D CAD design for the chassis (including the suspension and brakes), the CAD system includes a digital preassembly system for both body and chassis components. According to one system engineer, the digital preassembly feature has made the introduction of the 3-D CAD system effective. Engineers can refer to the latest versions of other relevant components, thus facilitating the implementation of concurrent engineering.

Table 4.2. CAD Systems at Three Major Japanese Automobile Manufacturers

	Firm A	Firm B	Firm C
Body	3-D wire-frame and surface	3-D wire-frame and surface	3-D wire-frame and surface
Chassis	2-D	2-D	3-D wire-frame
Power train	2-D	2-D	2-D

Shipbuilding

The Japanese shipbuilding firms began to introduce concurrent engineering in the 1970s by changing their managerial and organizational processes. They introduced the concept of beginning the downstream processes (e.g., purchasing components and materials and preparing production processes) before completing the upstream processes (e.g., receiving orders from customers, defining technical specifications, and proposing ship models). By using concurrent engineering, the complete processes usually required between one and a half and two years. In order to manage this process, firms relied on a few skilled engineers who drafted the production layout and processes, as well as coordinating the entire design and production processes.

These engineers were familiar with the entire operation, ranging from business planning to design, analysis, and production. Seventy percent of their work was spent on the coordination of different functional departments. In the late 1970s, one of the largest shipbuilders in Japan, Firm A, learned the concept of computer-supported concurrent engineering from General Electric. In 1979, the firm replaced most of its drafting boards with a 2-D CAD system from Computer Vision. The introduction of these CAD systems shortened the design portion of the process by thirty percent. However, the CAD systems were only used in the design process as an electronic drafting board and were not linked to the downstream processes, which included detailed parts drawing and blueprinting. Therefore, the 2-D CAD systems did not help integrate the entire development process.

In 1981, Firm A started to develop a custom 3-D CAD system in order to better integrate its processes and to enhance its concurrent engineering capabilities. Firm A decided to partially base this new system on the CATIA CAD software system. Forty engineers were assigned to develop the new system, and the total budget for its development was originally planned as five billion yen. However, the internal 3-D CAD development project has not been as successful as hoped. The actual costs are double the original budget, and in twelve years the project has only managed to meet the initial technological requirements.

In 1989, a joint R&D consortium, called Zosen (Shipbuilding)-CIMs, was established by seven major shipbuilding firms, including Firm A, to develop a new CAD/CAM system. All the member firms had difficulties in their in-house development of 3-D CAD systems, which led five of them to decide to purchase a packaged system, while Firm A and another firm continued their in-house development efforts. The seven-firm consortium did, however, manage to create a framework in which the role of CAD/CAM systems in shipbuilding operations was drafted. The consortium also developed some basic common systems that could be shared by all member firms in spite of the different types of systems that were being introduced by each firm.

Through its participation in the consortium, Firm A improved its design and production efficiency. In particular, an automated drafting tool enabled Firm A to reduce the ratio of direct labor to total labor cost from 30 to 20 percent. However, the development efforts of the new system are not considered to be fully successful. First, the efforts have not changed the entire process of developing and producing ships, particularly when compared to other examples of IT-based changes in the development process, such as the revolutionary changes at Boeing. The new system did not integrate the entire shipbuilding operations; while the system fully supports the design and blueprinting processes, it does not cover the preparation of specific assembly procedures and welding methods.

Second, the benefits from the reduction of direct workers did not match Firm A's total investment on system development. This suggests that the internal development of custom CAD systems does not seem to be an appropriate strategy. Technologies at the worldwide CAD vendors have been advancing more quickly than Firm A realized when it began its development of the custom CAD systems in 1981. A manager at Firm A reported that engineers may have had too much pride in their internal engineering capabilities, since the Japanese shipbuilding industry had been the world leader for a number of years. This overconfidence is partly responsible for the large investment in the custom CAD/CAM system. Engineers were also unwilling to purchase technologies, particularly from foreign vendors who are still the major suppliers of these systems. They felt that it would be difficult for them to effectively work with foreign companies. These factors probably had a negative influence on implementing more extensive changes in the shipbuilding processes.

Influences on Organizational Requirements

There needs to be a good fit between development tools such as CAD systems and organizational processes for firms to perform well (Adler, 1989; King and Majchrzak, 1996). Many studies have argued that unless certain organizational changes are made, the potential benefits of CAD cannot be achieved (Adler, 1989; Huber, 1990). In order to successfully introduce the new 3-D CAD system, two important factors should be considered with respect to organizational management: development of multiskilled engineers and restructuring of functional task structure.

Development of Multiskilled Engineers

Two skill changes are needed in order to benefit from the sophisticated features of the new 3-D CAD system. First, individuals need to unlearn old skills and replace them with new skills. For example, with 2-D design, a significant design skill is the ability to convert design ideas into 2-D drawings. With 3-D design, the conversion to 2-D drawings is unnecessary and 3-D solid modeling skills become essential.

Second, in order to fully utilize 3-D solid modeling, designers also need to have skills that previously only existed in other functional groups. With 3-D solid modeling, component designers can both draw details of components and can incorporate manufacturing requirements more extensively in the design than with 2-D design tools. However, in order to do this effectively, component engineers need more knowledge about manufacturing requirements.

Similarly, design engineers can also perform simulation analysis rather easily using CAE in combination with 3-D solid modeling. In particular, simulation analysis has become much easier to carry out with new CAD features such as automated

Finite Element Analysis (FEA) modeling. If design engineers are also to conduct the simulation analysis, the potential cost for coordination between the designers and CAE specialists can be saved. However, traditional design engineers do not usually have the proper knowledge to do CAE analysis.

Thus, multiskilled design engineers will enable organizations to more effectively utilize the new 3-D CAD tools through effectively integrating tasks that used to be done by multiple people and multiple functions. In addition, even if the multiskilled design engineers do not actually perform these tasks, organizations will benefit from the existence of such engineers. King and Majchrzak (1996) have argued that because engineers in different functions have different skills, knowledge, and culture, it is traditionally difficult for them to share a single representation. However, a 3-D solid modeling and digital assembly feature could be the single common representation for multiple functions.

Restructuring of Functional Task Structure

Traditional division of functions or tasks is based on traditional development tools. The new 3-D CAD system requires a new division of tasks, which will lead to a new process and a new organization. In particular, multiple tasks that used to be performed by different functional engineers can be conducted by a single function of engineers in the 3-D CAD model.

According to the automobile engineers we have interviewed, as CAD systems become more sophisticated, more tasks can be done by upstream functions. Many tasks traditionally done by manufacturing engineers are now expected to be done by design engineers. For example, using 3-D CAD, component engineers can design more of the component design details that in the case of 2-D CAD are designed by manufacturing preparation engineers. Design engineers are also expected to perform more CAE analyses, which used to be done separately by CAE engineers.

While there is still a mixture of 2-D and 3-D design in most automobile firms, in the new 3-D CAD systems, designers will have to draw all components in 3-D form. In this case, a number of different tasks will be integrated into one task through the common CAD tool. One possible change in task structure is depicted in figure 4.2. For example, task processes 1 and 2 could be considered design and testing or design and manufacturing preparation. Each task is now performed by a separate functional group. However, in order to fully realize the benefits from the new 3-D CAD tools, a single functional group may have to be responsible for multiple tasks.

In spite of these needs for organizational changes, some of the automobile engineers we interviewed argued that it will be difficult to change an organizational structure that has been maintained for decades. The engineers pointed out two potential problems. First, there may be resistance from functional groups mainly because of power issues. Second, engineers and managers need to learn more skills and knowledge to perform the converged task processes. Nonetheless, as seen in the Boeing example, a new organizational structure that integrates multiple task functions is necessary in order to benefit from the new system.

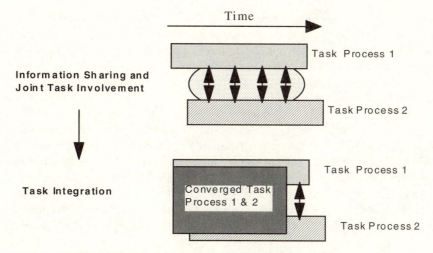

Figure 4.2. Potential Needs of Changes in Task and Organizational Structure

Conclusion

The new 3-D CAD systems are playing a central role in the creation of new product development processes. They have the capability to improve the knowledge-creation processes of engineers, which has been considered a critical element in a firm's product development capabilities. Earlier versions of CAD systems were thought of as tools that improve efficiency within a traditional product development process. This change in the role of CAD systems in product development has been made possible through technological improvements in the tool. It is only since 1990 that 3-D solid modeling CAD has been capable of effective use for the entire product development process, including the design, testing, and manufacturing of many components. Now, the most important issue is how firms can make the most of the new 3-D CAD tools. Firms will have to clearly understand the new tool's potential benefits and will have to change their product development processes.

In the 3-D CAD design model, IT contributes not only to the improvement of the efficiency of inductive and deductive reasoning processes, but also to the abductive reasoning process at both the engineering and organization levels. The abductive reasoning process is a key mechanism for knowledge creation in product development. The contribution of the 3-D CAD model to the abductive reasoning process is primarily enabled by the combination of three features of the new 3-D CAD tool: full visualization of components, as well as the entire product, during the design process; a digital preassembly capability that features topological information among components; and a simulation capability that enables quick and frequent iterations of trial and error. These three features improve the coordination and communication among engineers through an integrated data format in 3-D and a networked exchange of information.

In order to effectively implement the new 3-D CAD model, firms need to have a system-level perspective to integrate all the related operations. In addition, the new tool will definitely require engineers to have new skills. In particular, they need integrated skills that previously existed in multiple functions. There may also need to be fundamental changes in the task-partitioning structure for design, testing, simulating, and manufacturing preparation.

The leading firms in the introduction of the new 3-D CAD model are U.S. firms, such as Boeing. While many U.S. firms have been implementing the Japanese human-oriented approaches, many Japanese firms have begun to implement the Western systematic-rationality-oriented approaches represented by the technological characteristics of the 3-D model. We consider this situation the beginning of an era of mutual learning for the United States and Japan. In order to create a new product development paradigm for the twenty-first century, active mutual learning among different industries, countries, and cultures is essential.

Acknowledgments An earlier and shorter version of this chapter appeared in: Baba, Yasunori and Kentaro Nobeoka, 1998. "Towards knowledge-based product development: The 3-D CAD model of knowledge creation." *Research Policy* 26: 643–659.

We are indebted to Jeffery Funk, Hiroyuki Yoshikawa, Naomasa Nakajime, Tetsuo Tomiyama, Takashi Kiriyama, Yasushi Umeda, Ikujiro Nonaka, Michael Cusumano and Stephan Thomke and the participants on "International Comparative Study of Knowledge Creation" Conference for their comments. We thank the Sasagawa Peace Foundation for funding research that initiated the thinking behind this paper.

References

Adler, Paul. 1989. "CAD/CAM: Managerial Challenges and Research Issues." *IEEE Transactions on Engineering Management* 36(3): 202–16.

Arthur, Brian. 1989. "Competing Technologies, Increasing Returns, and Lock-in by Historical Small Events: the Dynamics of Allocation under Increasing Returns to Scale." *Economic Journal* 99: 116–31.

Baba, Yasunori, and Kentaro Nobeoka. 1996. "21-seiki gata Chishiki Soshutsu: Johogijyutu no Senryaku Riyo" (Knowledge creation in the twenty-first century: A strategic usage of information technology). Unpublished report to Sasagawa Foundation, Tokyo.

Clark, Kim, and Takahiro Fujimoto. 1991. *Product Development Performance: Strategy, Organization, and Management in the World Auto Industry*. Boston: Harvard Business School Press.

Cusumano, Michael, and Richard W. Selby. 1995. *Microsoft Secrets*. New York: Free Press.

Dosi, Giovanni, Luigi Marengo, and Giorgio Fagiolo. 1996. "Learning in Evolutionary Environment." Department of Economics, University of Rome. Mimeographed.

Ellison, David, Kim Clark, Takahiro Fujimoto, and Young-suk Hyun. 1995. "Product Development Performance in the Auto Industry: The 1990s Update." Unpublished working paper, International Motor Vehicle Program, Massachusetts Institute of Technology.

Hartshorne, Charles, and Paul Weiss. 1978. *Collected Papers of Charles Sanders Peirce*. Cambridge: Harvard University Press.

Henderson, Rebecca, and Kim Clark. 1990. "Architectural Innovation: The Reconfiguration of Existing Product Technologies and the Failure of Established Firms." *Administrative Science Quarterly* 35: 9–30.

Huber, George. 1990. "A Theory of the Effects of Advanced Information Technologies on Organizational Design, Intelligence, and Decision Making." *Academy of Management Review* 15(1): 47–71.

Kaplinsky, Raphael. 1982. *Computer-Aided Design*. London: Frances Printer.

King, Nelson, and Ann Majchrzak. 1996. "Concurrent Engineering Tools: Are the Human Issues Being Ignored?" *IEEE Transactions on Engineering Management* 43(2): 189–201.

Kogut, Bruce, and Udo Zander. 1992. "Knowledge of the Firm, Combinative Capability, and the Replication of Technology." *Organization Science* 3(1): 383–97.

Liker, Jeffery, Mitchell Fleischer, Mitsuo Nagamichi, and Michael Zonnevylle. 1992. "Designers and their Machines: CAD Use and Support in the US and Japan." *Communications of the ACM* 35(2): 77–95.

Lynch, Michael. 1988. "The Externalized Retina: Selection and Mathematization in the Visual Documentation of Objects in the Life Sciences." *Human Studies* 11: 201–34.

MacDuffie, John-Paul, and Frits Pil. 1996. "Performance Findings of the International Assembly Plant Study." Unpublished working paper, International Motor Vehicle Program, Massachusetts Institute of Technology.

Nakajima, Masaya, ed. 1995. *Chishiki Shi San no Saikochiku* (Reconstruction of knowledge assets). Tokyo: Nikkan Kogyo Shimbun.

Nobeoka, Kentaro, and Michael Cusumano. 1997. "Multi-Project Strategy and Sales Growth: The Benefits of Rapid Design Transfer in New Product Development." *Strategic Management Journal*, 18(3): 169–86.

Nonaka, Ikujiro. 1994. "A Dynamic Theory of Organizational Knowledge Creation." *Organization Science* 5(1): 14–37.

Nonaka, Ikujiro, and Hirotaka Takeuchi. 1996. *The Knowledge-Creating Company*. New York: Oxford University Press.

Robertson, David, and Thomas Allen. 1992. "Managing CAD Systems in Mechanical Design Engineering." *IEEE Transactions on Engineering Management* 39(1): 22–31.

Robertson, David, and Thomas J. Allen. 1993. "CAD System Use and Engineering Performance." *IEEE Transactions on Engineering Management* 40(3): 274–82.

Robertson, David, Karl Ulrich, and Marc Filerman. 1991. "CAD and Cognitive Complexity: Beyond the Drafting Board Metaphor." *Manufacturing Review* 4(3): 194–204.

Salzman, Harold. 1989. "Computer-Aided Design: Limitations in Automating Design and Drafting." *IEEE Transactions on Engineering Management* 36(4): 252–61.

Sebeok, Thomas, and Jean Umiker-Sebeok. 1980. *"You Know My Method": A Juxtaposition of Charles S. Peirce and Sherlock Holmes*. Bloomington, Ind.: Gaslight.

Tyre, Marcie, and Eric von Hippel. 1997. "The Situated Nature of Adaptive Learning in Organizations." *Organization Science* 8(1): 71–83.

von Hippel, Eric. 1994. "'Sticky Information' and the Locus of Problem Solving: Implications for Innovation." *Management Science* 40: 429–39.

Yoshikawa, Hiroyuki. 1993. "Proposal for Artifactual Engineering: Aims to Make Science and Technology Self-Conclusive." Paper presented at the First International Symposium on Research into Artifacts (RACE), University of Tokyo, October 26–28.

Young, Lawrence F. 1989. "The Metaphor Machine, a Database Method for Creativity Support." *Decision Support and Idea Processing Systems* 3: 309–17.

5

The Impact of Technology
on Knowledge Creation

A Study of Experimentation in Integrated Circuit Design

STEFAN H. THOMKE

Experimentation is fundamental to the creation process of new engineering knowledge as it advances the engineer's understanding in the form of new analytical concepts and new ways of thinking (Vincenti, 1990). The rate at which such knowledge is created and transferred can create new competitive advantage (Nonaka, 1994; Nonaka and Takeuchi, 1995); thus, improvements in the efficiency of experimentation should be of great interest to firms. This paper focuses on experimentation in an area where new knowledge plays a very important role—product design and development—and demonstrates how the efficiency of experimentation (and, as a result, the rate at which design-related knowledge is created) can be radically affected by the use of new and greatly improved technologies such as computer simulation and rapid prototyping.[1]

I will show that a given experiment (and the related trial and error learning) can be conducted in different "modes" (e.g., computer simulation and rapid prototyping) and that managers and designers will find it economical to determine the optimal switching point between these modes so as to increase overall development efficiency. This is confirmed by a large-scale empirical study of the experimentation process in the design of integrated circuits, using two different technologies: (1) field-programmable logic devices (FPLDs); or (2) application-specific integrated circuits (ASICs). In comparing different experimentation strategies for a large number of analogous design projects, it was found that the former technology (FPLD), an approach that utilizes many prototype iterations, outperformed the latter (ASIC) by factor of 2.2 (in person-months), and over 43 percent of that difference can be attributed to differences in experimentation and the related learning strategies. These findings are important to managers in many other development fields that involve knowledge creation with the aid of different experimentation modes: software development, chemical process development, and pharmaceutical drug development, to name a few.

I begin by discussing experimentation and the related knowledge creation process. Next, I describe how new modes of experimentation can be leveraged to increase development performance. I then describe research methods and present empirical findings from integrated circuit design. Finally, discuss the implications for managerial practice and theory.

Knowledge Creation by Experimentation

Experiments play an important role in the creation of new science and engineering knowledge. Indeed, studies of product development show experimental trial and error (or, more precisely, trial, failure, learning, correction, and retrial) as a significant feature of design and the creation of such engineering knowledge (Marples, 1961; Allen, 1966; Simon, 1969; Bohn, 1987; Vincenti, 1990; Adler and Clark, 1991; Smith and Eppinger, 1997; Wheelwright and Clark, 1992; Pisano, 1996; Iansiti, 1997). I adopt this view of design and, more specifically, define an experimental cycle as consisting of the following steps:[2]

(1) Design: One conceives of or designs an experiment.
(2) Build: One builds the (physical or virtual) apparatus needed to conduct that experiment.
(3) Run: One runs the experiment.
(4) Analyze: One analyzes the result.

If the results of a first iteration are satisfactory, one stops. However, experimentation is usually a matter of repeated trial and error. That is, if analysis shows that the quality of a design can be improved cost-effectively, one modifies one's design on the basis of what one has learned and "iterates" or tries again. It is precisely during this last step where much new knowledge about cause and effect can be created and then be applied to the next iteration. For example, one might (1) conceive of and design a new, more rapidly deploying airbag for a car; (2) build a prototype of key elements of that airbag, as well as any special apparatus needed to test its speed of deployment; (3) run the experiment to determine actual deployment speed; and (4) analyze and understand the observed result. If the results of a first deployment are satisfactory, one stops. However, if analysis shows that the results of the deployment test are not satisfactory, one modifies the airbag design on the basis of what one has learned from the test and the analysis and "iterates" again.

The Experimentation Process

As an aid to study experimentation and the related learning process, I define the efficiency of an experiment as *the economic value of information learned during an experimental cycle, divided by the economic cost of conducting the cycle.* (Economic cost in this definition includes monetary cost and the opportunity cost of time.) When an experiment is costly (inexpensive) and the incremental economic value of information learned is small (large), its experimental efficiency is low (high). Note that in the definition, experimentation efficiency involves not only attributes of the experimental technology itself but attributes and choices made by the experimenter. For example, if a particular designer is ineffective or less able to analyze an experiment (e.g., for lack of experience) and therefore benefits less from new available information, the experimental efficiency will be lower than for someone more experienced (*ceteris paribus*). Also note that experimentation efficiency is not a static measure, as it can change as a function of time and the development path chosen. The following subsections discuss in greater detail the cost and benefits one typically finds in the experimentation process.

Experimentation Cost The economic costs of conducting an experimental cycle typically involve the cost and time of using equipment, material, facilities, and engineering resources. These costs can be as high as millions of dollars, for example, for a prototype of a new car used in destructive crash testing, or as low as a few dollars, for example, for a chemical compound used in pharmaceutical drug development and made with the aid of combinatorial chemistry (Thomke, von Hippel, and Franke, 1998). I will discuss some of these costs by reference to the four-step experimental cycle defined earlier.

The cost of building (step 2) an experimentation model depends highly on the available technology and the degree of accuracy that the underlying model is intended to have. For example, modern computer-assisted design (CAD) tools can sometimes interface to computer software that converts a design directly into a simulation model. In such cases, the cost of building a model is relatively low, as it consists mainly of the investment in conversion tools (fixed cost) and the time required to operate them (variable cost). Furthermore, experimentation models can have varying degrees of fidelity with respect to reality (Bohn, 1987; Wall, Ulrich, and Flowers, 1991). The value of using "incomplete" models in experimentation is both to reduce investments in aspects of the real that are irrelevant for the experiment and to control out some aspects of the real that would affect the experiment in order to simplify the analysis of the test results (step 4). Thus, a model of an airplane used in wind tunnel experiments has no internal design details—these are both costly to model and [mostly] irrelevant to the outcome of wind tunnel tests. Sometimes a model to be built is incomplete because one cannot economically incorporate all relevant aspects of the "real" or does not know them. The incompleteness of a model can lead to unexpected design errors when a given model being used in testing is replaced by a different (and more accurate) model or by the real design in the real environment for the first time.

The cost of analyzing (step 4) the results from step 3 (run) depends to a significant degree on access to test-related information and the availability of tools that aid in the problem-solving process. For example, consider the discovery of an error during prototype testing and the series of following diagnostic steps to identify the error cause(s). Sometimes a designer has a thorough understanding of a tested prototype and finds the error's cause very quickly. Very often, though, subtle errors make the analysis very difficult, especially in cases of great complexity and poor engineering knowledge of causal relationships between system inputs and outputs. As a result, designers have to rely on diagnostic tools and problem-solving methods to aid in their analysis of error symptoms. The use of computer simulation is a very effective analysis tool, since it gives a designer quick access to virtually any information within the realm of the underlying simulation model. In contrast, an analysis of data from prototype testing is more difficult, since access to error-related information is typically limited. For example, consider that a real car crash happens very quickly—so quickly that the designer's ability to observe details is typically impaired, even given high-speed cameras and well-instrumented cars and crash dummies. In contrast, one can instruct a computer to enact a virtual car crash as slowly as one likes, and one can zoom in on any structural element of the car that is of interest and observe the forces acting on it and its response to those forces during a crash.

Experimentation Benefit The benefit of an experiment is the economic value of information that one derives from the experimental cycle. Such information can be of great value if it aids in the identification of severe design errors or uncovers a new and much improved design solution. As an example, consider the detection, analysis, and removal (elimination) of design errors. An error is a problem in the external operation of a design (operational failure) that is caused by an internal design error. Thus, error elimination consists of finding such operational failures (detection), determining the internal design error that causes the failure (analysis), and modifying the design as to remove the internal error (removal). The process of error elimination is fundamental to the design of new products, and research on product development has shown that it accounts for a significant part of total design cost. (Boehm [1981] studied the effort distribution of several software design projects and found that about 40 percent of total design effort is devoted to the detection and elimination of errors.) Not identifying design errors and its consequences can sometimes have catastrophic outcomes, as demonstrated by the *Challenger* disaster in 1986 (Hauptman and Iwaki, 1991), or can jeopardize the commercial success of an otherwise well-designed product, as demonstrated by the well-publicized problems with the Intel Pentium processor (Uzumeri and Snyder, 1996). Thus the economic value of detecting an error can be great but is usually difficult to determine prior to actually detecting the error. As very complex designs are usually not completely error free when they reach the time of release, designers sometimes resort to heuristics that try to estimate the economic value of finding and removing an error and compare it to the cost of continuing experimentation. For example, Cusumano and Selby (1995) reported that software designers at Microsoft track four error categories that approximate economic severity. Errors of severity 1 cause the product to halt, and therefore all such errors need to be found (very high economic value of information), whereas errors of severity 4 are minor (e.g. cosmetic), and their elimination is of lower economic significance.

Experimentation Modes

Experimentation can be conducted in different *modes*, and the absolute and relative efficiencies of these modes play an important role in development performance and the rate at which new design knowledge is created. As experimentation modes are often driven by technological innovations, it is particularly important to managers to track new developments in this area. Recently, new experimentation modes have been emerging that are radically affecting the absolute and relative efficiencies of experimentation and, as a result, overall design efficiency and the creation of design-related knowledge. I will illustrate this by reference to two such modes: computer simulation and rapid prototyping.

Computer simulation is used as a substitute for "real experimentation" in fields ranging from the design of drugs (e.g., rational drug design) to the design of mechanical products (e.g., finite element analysis) to the design of electronic products (e.g., computer simulation of digital circuitry). An experimenter typically uses simulation in steps 3 and 4 of an experimental cycle: running an experiment and analyzing the result. The ability to usefully substitute a simulation for a "real" experiment requires, of course, a simulation model that is accurate from the point of view of a given experimentation purpose.

Simulation can have both advantages and disadvantages relative to testing a physical prototype. As an illustration, consider a real explosion in a prototype cylinder of a gasoline-powered car engine, which may take milliseconds, while a detailed and less accurate simulation of the same explosion might take minutes or hours on a powerful computer. On the other hand, the analysis of an experiment carried out in simulation is typically much richer. For example, one can only collect data from the combustion in a car engine cylinder at a few points via instrument probes. But one can obtain information from a simulated explosion on variables such as gas temperature and shock wave propagation at any location and at any point in the evolution of the explosion. This allows experimenters to get much more and much better data per experimental run. Thus subsequent experiments can be designed to be more efficient.

Rapid prototyping is used by developers to *quickly* generate an inexpensive, easy-to-modify (and often physical) prototype that can be tested against the actual use environment and allows "real" experimentation. Rapid prototyping techniques can be found in areas ranging from mechanical designs (e.g., stereolithography, three-dimensional printing) to the design of integrated circuits (e.g., FPLDs) to the design of software (e.g., emulation of user-interfaces) (Carey and Mason, 1986; Sachs et al., 1992; Boehm, Gray, and Seewaldt, 1984; von Hippel, 1994). Rapid prototyping is *often* an inexpensive and fast way to achieve step 2 (build) in an experimental cycle while preserving the advantages of "real" experimentation—higher degrees of accuracy and experimentation speed (step 3) with respect to a given experiment. The utilization of such rapid prototyping techniques has resulted in significant improvements in development time and cost. With increased competition and shorter product life cycles, accelerated time-to-market and lower development cost have become increasingly important to product success (Clark and Fujimoto, 1991; Smith and Reinertsen, 1991; Wheelwright and Clark, 1992), and rapid prototyping aids in achieving such improved performance.

Experimentation Strategies

If new experimentation modes are affecting the absolute and relative efficiencies of experimentation (and the rate at which new design knowledge is created), then how can managers and designers change their experimentation strategies such that overall performance improves? The following subsections describe a model of *how* these modes drive experimentation efficiency and introduce the concept of an optimal mode switching point (OSP). The following discussion of technological innovations and their impact on experimentation strategies serves as a foundation for the empirical study presented in the next section.

Optimal Mode Switching as an Economic Experimentation Strategy

As a design progresses and experimental cycles are repeated within a given mode, I propose that the efficiency of experimentation decreases because of diminishing marginal returns from experimenting in that mode and that different modes decrease at different rates. This view is strongly supported by empirical evidence from studies on bug detection in software engineering, which found similar relationships (Boehm, 1981; Shooman, 1983; Cusumano and Selby, 1995).

In the following discussion I assume that:

- The compared modes can detect the same or at least a large group of common errors as a design evolves. This may not always be true for all cases, as modes are sometimes designed to exclude aspects that are irrelevant to the experiment (e.g., wind tunnel experiments will not reveal internal airplane design problems) or contain models that focus on a single class of errors (e.g., logic simulation in integrated circuit design). If there is *no* overlap between error categories, any decreases in one mode's efficiency would leave the other mode's efficiency unchanged.
- The rate of new error introduction is negligible compared to the rate of error detection and removal. If errors are introduced at a significantly higher rate (but smaller than the rate of error elimination), the efficiency would still be decreasing but at a slower rate.
- As designers learn between projects, the mode trajectories can change from project to project but are still declining. For example, a more experienced engineer may be able to "drive out" a mode much more quickly by eliminating all design errors with fewer iterations.

As an example, consider the use of computer simulation in the detection and elimination of design errors. During each simulation cycle, design errors will be detected and, if the error cause can be determined and removed, eliminated. With an increasing number of simulation cycles, the cumulative number of design errors eliminated is increasing and the pool of residual errors tends to decrease. Therefore the mean time between errors detected increases, implying that the number of tests to be run until another error is detected also increases. The overall effect is a monotonically decreasing error detection rate, resulting in an increase in run time cost for a given return. Thus, the marginal return (errors detected per iteration) from simulation diminishes as a function of experimental cycles. Similarly, if a designer conducted experimental cycles with the aid of prototype testing, she would also experience diminishing returns but, because prototype tests run significantly faster than simulated tests in this particular example, at a slower rate (see figure 5.1). In general, we find that prototype tests do not always execute experiments faster than computer simulation (e.g., simulating fatigue life performance in aircraft). However, one can still find many cases where run time differences are many orders of magnitude, even with rapid increases in computational speed. (Examples are thermal combustion in engines, crash tests of automobiles, timing-specific behavior in integrated circuits.)

As the efficiency trajectories of available experimentation modes differ, one would conceivably start experimentation with the mode that is most efficient under initial experimental conditions. Then, as a design progresses and the mode's marginal returns diminish, there may be a point (the OSP) where the trajectories intersect and where switching to another [more efficient] mode will be an economical strategy (see figure 5.1). I call such a strategy mode switching. Like the curves that il-

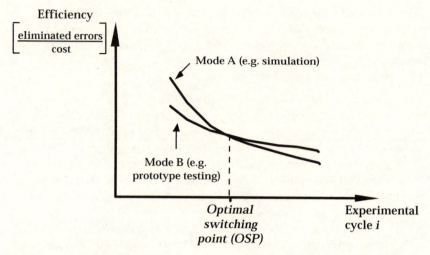

Figure 5.1. Switching between Two Experimentation Modes (Illustration; modes can detect same category of errors)

lustrate diminishing returns in economic theory, the smoothness depicted in figure 5.1 looks much "rougher" at the microlevel, resulting in occasional "spikes," or discontinuities, that would suggest reswitching to previously used modes. (Occasional reswitching was observed during my studies of integrated circuit design.)

As a general example, consider the use of computer simulation and prototype testing in design once more. Computer simulation is usually more efficient with respect to experimental step 2 (building a test model), step 4 (analysis of error symptoms), and step 1 (design modification). In contrast, full prototypes are more accurate and in many cases can execute test runs (step 3) much more rapidly than simulation can. But since the number of design errors is usually high prior to starting experimentation, the mean-time between errors detected tends to be small, thus most designers will find it economical to start with simulation. As a design progresses and the error detection rate of simulation declines, the efficiency of continuing to simulate will at some point fall below the efficiency of prototype testing. Thus, designers will find it economical to switch from simulation to prototype testing *exactly* where their efficiency trajectories intersect (the OSP) and continue iterative experimentation with prototype testing. I propose that finding the OSP can result in significant improvements in development efficiency and the rate at which design-related knowledge is created.

The Impact of New Technologies

Technological innovations can have a direct impact on the cost and the time of experimental trials or on the value of information learned from an experiment. For example, consider the changes that one would expect if the cost and time of building (or modifying) a test model can be reduced (e.g., through the use of rapid prototyping technologies). Recall that during experimental step 2, models are built to test design solutions that are generated during step 1 (design). Since efficiency is a function of cost and time, one would expect reductions in the cost and time of building a test model to have an effect on the efficiency of conducting an experimental cycle. (I assume that these changes result from innovation sources exogenous to a particular design process and that changes in model accuracy are negligible.) Thus one would expect the efficiency trajectory of prototype testing to shift outward and, as a result, the OSP to shift in favor of prototype testing. Figure 5.2 illustrates such a shift in the OSP between simulation and prototype testing, given that an exogenous innovation has resulted in a reduced *build* cost and time for design prototypes.

As a general example, consider the dramatic improvements in the cost and time of prototyping that have resulted from rapid prototyping technologies. By significantly reducing the cost and time to build a physical model prototype of a design, they have significantly improved steps 1 (design) and 2 (build) of an experimental cycle. At the same time, we have observed an increased use of rapid prototyping (relative to other experimentation modes) at earlier points in a design process. Using the model presented in figure 5.2, I propose that this shift in the OSP in favor of rapid prototyping has been partially caused by the (exogenous) change in the cost and time to build prototypes.

Research Methods and Findings

The empirical investigation concentrates on the integrated circuit (IC)–based systems design industry, a field chosen because of (1) its overall economic significance (the overall IC market is over $100 billion per year, and ICs can be found in most

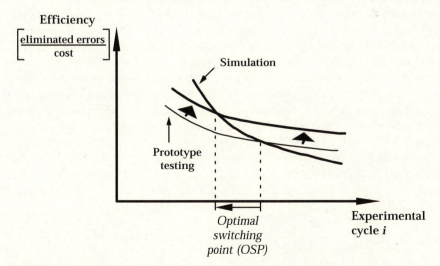

Figure 5.2. The Impact of a Decrease in the Cost of Building Prototypes on the Optimal Mode Switching Point (Illustration; modes can detect same category of errors)

products today, ranging from communications networks to children's toys) and (2) the fact that it has benefited greatly from the availability of dramatically improved experimentation modes, such as computer simulation and the rapid prototyping of integrated circuits. (Computer simulation enables designers to model and simulate complex system behavior prior to committing to an—often expensive—hardware prototype. In contrast, rapid prototyping provides designers with a low-cost, rapidly available prototype that can be used to run faster and more accurate experiments.)

I elected to focus the study on the design of integrated systems with the aid of two technologies: (1) systems containing ASICs, where the cost and time of building and modifying a prototype is *high*, and (2) systems containing FPLDs, where the cost and time of building and modifying a prototype is *low* ("rapid prototyping," as described earlier). The cost of building or modifying an ASIC prototype can easily exceed tens of thousands of dollars because of fixed manufacturing costs (known as nonrecurring engineering [NRE] costs), which are typically amortized over many units. FPLD prototypes are usually very inexpensive (a few hundred dollars) and can often be erased and reprogrammed when necessary but face higher variable cost when large volume production is required. One also finds that lead times for an ASIC prototype typically exceed one week, whereas FPLD prototypes can be produced (programmed) almost instantly. This is of particular concern to users of integrated circuits, who usually come from the fast moving high-technology industry where time-to-market drives project performance.

While ASIC technology has been available to designers for more than a decade, modern FPLDs are a relatively new technology; they were invented in the late 1980s and have rapidly improved since then (Walker, 1992). Today's FPLDs are not able to meet the complexity and speed requirements of very high performance integrated circuit designs, but they are quite capable of serving as a substitute for ASICs at the middle and low end of the integrated circuit design spectrum.

Data on mode switching strategies were collected in a two-stage process. First, I followed a grounded research approach, during which I conducted a field study at a local high-technology firm (Glaser and Strauss, 1970). Over a period of three months, I conducted over thirty extensive interviews with designers and constructed a database with twenty-four design error case histories. The interviews and the data allowed me to verify the significance of experimentation strategies in integrated circuit design and to develop an in-depth technical understanding of simulation and prototype testing in design practice. Second, I developed a detailed mail questionnaire that was used to collect data on experimentation strategies from several hundred designers throughout the United States (Judd, Smith, and Kidder, 1991). The data analysis employs statistical analysis to determine if in fact the differences in prototyping cost and time result in different experimentation strategies and, if so, whether this has an impact on overall development efficiency.

Data Collection

A mail questionnaire was used to learn about designers' decisions and experiences during switching between computer simulation and prototype testing in the design of integrated circuit–based systems. The questionnaire was sent to one thousand designers who were selected from the subscriber database of *Integrated Systems Design*, a leading technical industry journal that focuses on issues related to ASIC- and FPLD-based design. The sample was divided into two groups (five hundred FPLD designers and five hundred ASIC designers), which were randomly chosen from a pool of designers who qualified for the survey. Because of a significant difference in the cost and time to build and to modify a design prototype, I hypothesized that the two groups' switching behavior varies significantly.

The questions and their phrasing were strongly influenced by preliminary findings in the extensive three-month field study and a questionnaire pretest. The pretest of the questionnaire was conducted with the aid of two networking technology design groups (one FPLD and one ASIC group) at a company in Maryland, and a detailed discussion of the questions ensured that designers in both groups understood them as they were intended (Judd, Smith, and Kidder, 1991). The questionnaire pretest was mailed to one thousand designers (five hundred ASIC designers and five hundred FPLD designers) in August 1994. In sixteen cases the addressee could not be reached or had left the company. Of the 984 designers reached, 463 returned the questionnaire. Sixty-one questionnaires had to be discarded because the designers felt that their background and experiences did not allow them to answer the questions with high confidence. Eleven questionnaires arrived after the analysis had been completed and were therefore not included in the study. The remaining 391 yielded a response rate of 39.74 percent (38.53 percent for ASIC designers; 40.93 percent for FPLD designers). A comparison of the respondents' length of design experience resulted in no significant difference between the groups; both had been designing integrated circuits for an average of ten years. (Some designers had experience in both ASIC and FPLD technology.)

As some of the measured variables can be influenced by design complexity and ASIC designs are on average more complex than FPLD designs, I extracted two subsamples that were compared along several complexity measures, and no statistically significant complexity difference was found along these dimensions. Where appropriate, results of the study were compared using these subsamples only.[3]

Study Findings

It was proposed that the efficiency of experimentation modes (and the resulting learning rates) can decrease at different rates and that, as a result, designers will find it economical to determine the OSP between these modes. As changes in the cost to build (and/or modify) experimentation models cause a movement of the experimental mode's efficiency trajectory and thus a shift in the OSP, designers will find that adjusting their mode-switching strategies in the direction of the new OSP will result in significant improvements of experimentation efficiency (hence the rate at which design-related knowledge is created). As shown hereafter, the data strongly support these propositions.

To test for differences in overall performance of FPLD and ASIC design projects, I asked designers to provide an estimate of design effort required in the completion of their last design project (in person-months) and of how the design team's effort was distributed among five different design phases: (1) design specification, (2) design development, (3) design verification, (4) design prototyping, and (5) prototype evaluation.

An analysis of *project performance* data shows that FPLD designers needed an average effort of 8.15 person-months to complete their projects while ASIC designers needed 17.94 person-months (significance of mean difference: $p < 0.01$; see table 5.1). As we will see, at least 43% of this difference can be attributed to the different mode switching strategies discussed earlier. If one considers that design effort correlates highly with time-to-market (quite often, these projects are completed by teams consisting of one to two members) and that product life cycles in this industry are very short, then a difference of such magnitude can be regarded a significant competitive advantage for a firm.

A close examination of design effort (table 1) shows that the overall performance difference is driven by earlier phases of a project: (1) design specification, (2) development, and (3) verification. FPLD designers required significantly less resources than ASIC designers in all these three phases, while no significant difference was found for design prototyping and evaluation.

Design specification accounted for 23.4 percent of the total design performance difference. FPLD designers chose to spend significantly less effort on design specification than their ASIC counterparts (significance of mean difference: $p < 5\%$). While design specification does not involve computer- or prototype-assisted experimentation, this finding does suggest a connection between the degree of specification and the expected cost of making design changes. Thus, if the cost and time of modifying a design is low, designers are less inclined to invest effort in reducing the risk of facing design changes—after all, they can change them at a relatively low cost (*ceteris paribus*). This ability to make changes at low cost and time results in higher design flexibility and can have a significant impact on overall design performance (Thomke, 1997). This finding is also consistent with studies of "prototype-driven" design approaches in software engineering, where short specification phases combined with early prototypes for user feedback were instrumental in accelerating

Table 5.1. A Comparison of Design Effort by Design Phases and by FPLD and ASIC Design Technologies

Variable	FPLD			ASIC			P-value (T-test)
	Mean	St.Dev.	n	Mean	St.Dev.	n	
Design effort (person-months)	8.15	5.75	47	17.94	17.98	31	0.006**
Due to (1) design specification	1.08	0.93	47	3.37	4.91	31	0.015*
Due to (2) design development	2.74	2.70	47	5.48	6.38	31	0.030*
Due to (3) design verification	1.52	1.30	47	5.75	6.03	31	0.001**
Due to (4) design prototyping	1.20	1.23	47	1.26	1.59	31	0.856
Due to (5) design evaluation	1.60	1.69	47	2.07	2.40	31	0.353

Samples are for designs of comparable complexity. Only data from interviewees that responded to all six questions were analyzed. * = $p < 0.05$ P-value: ** = $p < 0.01$; (Test: independent samples of unequal variances).

software projects and increasing user satisfaction (Alavi, 1984; Boehm, Gray, and Seewaldt, 1984; Cusumano and Selby, 1995).

Another 28 percent of the total performance difference can be attributed to *design development*. ASIC designers spent significantly more effort on development than FPLD designers (significance of mean difference: p < 5%). From field observations, it appears that much of the additional effort that ASIC designers invest is related to the high cost of finding errors during prototype testing. First, ASICs are more carefully designed so as to reduce the likelihood of running into problems during prototype testing. Second, as a means of minimizing the risk of failure, ASIC vendors require thorough design documentation, which in turn requires additional preparation time by the designer. In contrast, FPLD designers can come up with a design solution and quickly move to experimentation (via simulation or prototype testing) as a means of getting rapid feedback and to generate new knowledge about their designs.

Design verification, where most experimentation activity and the related switching between simulation and prototype testing occurs, accounts for 43.2 percent of the total performance difference. FPLD designers (mean performance: 1.52 person-months) were by a factor of 3.8 more effective than their ASIC counterparts (mean performance: 5.75 person-months, significance of mean difference: p < 1%; see table 5.1). I submit that the difference is due to early switching to prototype testing by FPLD designers and thus being able to move to a higher efficiency trajectory more quickly. Interestingly, the higher number of FPLD prototype iterations that resulted from early switching did not lead to significantly higher effort during design evaluation—the phase where most prototype testing occurs (p > 10%).

To verify that ASIC designers did in fact go through fewer prototype iterations (i.e., switched to prototype-driven experimentation much later than FPLD designers), I asked designers to give a numerical count of the number of prototype iterations undertaken in their last project. The variable "number of prototype iterations" (table 5.2) shows that on average, FPLD designers used 13.90 prototype iterations before the design was complete while ASIC designers used 1.49 prototype iterations (significance of mean difference: p < 0.001; samples contain designs of comparable design complexity).

Finally, one may ask why designers would choose to select ASIC technology if FPLD technology was technically feasible and allowed faster and more efficient development. A number of alternative explanations were discovered during the field study. First, designers chose to stay with ASIC technologies because at large volume production, lower variable cost for ASICs would provide significant savings that

Table 5.2. A Comparison of Prototype Iterations in FPLD and ASIC Design projects

Variable	FPLD			ASIC			P-value (T-test)
	Mean	St.Dev.	n	Mean	St.dev.	n	
Number of prototype iterations	13.90	14.77	51	1.49	1.48	33	0.000

A prototype iteration occurs whenever the designer makes a change to any part of the physical design prototype and subsequently verifies it.

are "traded against" a more inefficient and slower development process. This is supported by data from the two subsamples analyzed: on average, FPLD designers eventually produced 1,581 units whereas ASIC designers had average production volumes of 113,232 units. However, a number of small firms have recognized this opportunity and started to specialize on supplying a conversion path from FPLD to ASIC designs. (Designers would use FPLD technology to develop their integrated circuits, have a specialized firm convert it to an ASIC design, and then run volume production in an ASIC foundry.) This has started to result in a gradual migration away from ASIC design technology where FPLDs are feasible alternatives and large production volumes are required. Second, ASIC designers are reluctant to switch to a technology they often consider "inferior," as it requires them to make an investment in acquiring different skills and, if they became FPLD designers, often a career track with lower pay, less peer recognition, and fewer opportunities to grow (e.g., moving into high-end design projects). Nonetheless, market forces are pushing toward a proliferation of FPLD technology in the low-to-moderate integrated circuit design segment, for many of the reasons described in this paper.

In summary, the data offer strong evidence for a positive link between the performance of a design project and its related experimentation and learning strategy. While the survey cannot determine cause and effect, it can be concluded that experimentation strategies represent an important connection between problem-solving efficiency and overall product development performance.

Discussion

Innovation practitioners and managers are now adopting and using new experimentation technologies such as computer simulation without an explicit understanding of the change in experimentation economics that can follow and the consequent change in economic development and learning strategies that may result. One objective of this essay is to help managers and researchers to understand the impact of new and improved experimentation techniques on design performance and the generation of design-related knowledge and to formulate managerial actions that would motivate designers to take full advantage of these changes in experimentation economics. One such strategy is the determination of an OSP that can result in significant improvements of design performance and the efficiency at which design-related knowledge is created. Thus, managers will find it economical to provide design resources that aid in the determination of mode switching points and to devise managerial actions so as to move designers' switching behavior as close as possible to the optimal point. The emergence of new technologies and methods such as simulation raises a number of important issues, as follows.

Managing Knowledge Integration

Effective product development requires both that all the organizational groups involved develop the appropriate specialized capabilities and that the efforts and technologies are effectively integrated (Katz and Allen, 1988; Hayes, Wheelwright, and

Clark, 1988). In the context of switching between experimentation modes, we sometimes find that the switching involves a hand-off between organizational groups that have specialized knowledge in the use of a particular experimentation mode. Such a hand-off is likely to occur with some bias unless the interaction and integration of these groups is *managed* effectively at both the individual and organizational level.

Consider the use of computer simulation and prototype testing in integrated circuit design once again. In large design projects, one sometimes finds that simulation and prototype testing is assigned to different design groups and that the knowledge and skills of these groups is highly specialized. Thus switching between experimentation modes will require a formal hand-off between these two groups but will often result in hand-off "biases." Quite often, design groups that specialize in simulation know little about prototype testing (and vice versa), and groups do not have access to real-time information about each other's experimentation activities. An objective evaluation of the optimal mode switching (or hand-off) point, however, requires both knowledge and information on both activities. Or, as functional groups are often organized around design technologies and thus have investments in these technologies (e.g., skills, career paths, etc.), it is not unusual for these groups to compete with each other. For example, I have found in many firms that groups that specialize in prototype testing often try to compete with groups that specialize in computer simulation—many times leading to hand-off "biases," since both groups have to work together (e.g., the simulation group tries to demonstrate the goodness of simulation by handing off an error-free—but excessively simulated—design to prototype testing). Because the group interface is so important to effective product development and learning, it is imperative for managers to understand the dynamics of intergroup competition and ensure that an effective integration of all relevant knowledge takes place.

Model Building and Knowledge Creation

As firms are adopting and using new technologies such as computer simulation, firms will have to make substantial investments into the generation of new models based on what they know about a given field of application or physical phenomena being modeled. For example, consider that the discipline and accuracy required in building and improving crash models for crash simulation has led to an increased knowledge stock of the underlying crash dynamics (Thomke, 1998b). Interestingly, there are some parallels to research on the history of process control (Jaikumar, 1988) and its interaction with the evolution of knowledge (Jaikumar and Bohn, 1992). Jaikumar found that with increased identification, measuring, and gaining localized control of processes, system developers were able to extract general principles that can be applied to many domains different from the process being controlled (Jaikumar, 1988).

The rapid emergence of computer simulation will require large investments in the development and building of mathematical models, which, in turn, can result in much deeper and more broadly applicable knowledge of the physical phenomena being modeled. Thus I propose that the discipline required in developing computer models will lead to advantages that go beyond making simulation models available to users. It may also take a firm's R&D knowledge from tacit (Polanyi, 1958) to explicit—a process that Nonaka and Takeuchi (1995) have defined as "externalization." Not surprisingly, this knowledge conversion process carries high significance, as "among the four modes of knowledge conversion, externalization holds the key to knowledge creation, because it creates new, explicit concept from tacit knowledge" (Nonaka and Takeuchi, 1995: 66). Explicit knowledge lowers the cost of information transfer, or stickiness, making information easily transferable within and between firm boundaries (von Hippel, 1994). As firms are currently adopting advanced simulation capabilities, research on the emergence of knowledge as a function of modeling activities may provide researchers with new and deeper insights into individual and organizational knowledge-creation processes.

Notes

1. This paper has been adapted, with significant modifications, from Stefan Thomke, "Managing Experimentation in the Design of New Products," *Management Science* 44: 6 (1998).

2. Similar building blocks to analyze the design and development process were used by other researchers. Simon (1969: chap. 5) examined design as series of "generator-test cycles." Clark and Fujimoto (1988) and Wheelwright and Clark (1992: chap. 9, 10) used "design-build-test" cycles as a framework for problem-solving in product development. I modified the blocks to include "run" and "analyze" as two explicit steps that conceptually separate the execution of an experiment and the learning that takes place during analysis.

3. As mentioned earlier, for projects of low to moderate complexity and average speed requirements, integrated circuit designs can often be developed using either technology (ASIC or FPLD), with differences remaining mainly in the volume production cost of ICs. Using input from design engineers, the subsamples were carefully selected to occupy a complexity and performance spectrum where both technologies were feasible choices to designers. Even though the subsamples represented designs that were considered of lower complexity and speed, they accounted for 30.5 percent of the research study's FPLD-based designs and 25.2 percent of all ASIC-based designs. Thus it is reasonable to assume that projects from both subsamples are of similar complexity and that an objective comparison of project performance can be conducted.

References

Adler, Paul, and Kim Clark. 1991. "Behind the Learning Curve: A Sketch of the Learning Process." *Management Science* 37 (March 1991): 267–81.

Alavi, Maryam. 1984. "An Assessment of the Prototyping Approach to Information Systems Development." *Communications of the ACM* (June 1984): 556–63.

Allen, Thomas J. 1966. "Studies of the Problem-Solving Process in Engineering Design." *IEEE Transactions on Engineering Management*, EM-13, no. 2: 72–83.

Boehm, Barry. 1981. *Software Engineering Economics.* Englewood Cliffs, N.J.: Prentice-Hall, 1981.

Boehm, Barry, Terence Gray, and Thomas Seewaldt. 1984. "Prototyping versus Specifying: A Multiproject Experiment." *IEEE Transactions on Software Engineering* (May 1984): 290–302.

Bohn, Roger. 1987. "Learning by Experimentation in Manufacturing." Working paper no. 88-001, Harvard Business School.

Carey, T., and R. Mason. 1986. "Information System Prototyping: Techniques, Tools, and Methodologies." *New Paradigms for Software Development*, Washington, D.C.: IEEE Computer Society Press.

Clark, Kim, and Takahiro Fujimoto. 1991. *Product Development Performance.* Boston: Harvard Business School Press.

Cusumano, Michael, and Richard Selby. 1995. *Microsoft Secrets.* New York: Free Press.

Einspruch, Norman, and Jeffrey Hilbert. 1991. *Application Specific Integrated Circuit (ASIC) Technology.* San Diego, Calif.: Academic Press.

Eisenhardt, Kathleen, and Behnam Tabrizi. 1995. "Accelerating Adaptive Processes: Product Innovation in the Global Computer Industry." *ASQ* (March 1995): 84–110.

Glaser, Barney, and Anselm Strauss.1970. *The Discovery of Grounded Theory: Strategies for Qualitative Research.* Chicago: Aldine.

Hauptman, Oscar, and George Iwaki. 1991. "The Final Voyage of the Challenger." case no. 9-691-037, Harvard Business School.

Hayes, Robert, Steven Wheelwright, and Kim Clark. 1988. *Dynamic Manufacturing.* New York: Free Press.

Iansiti, Marco. 1997. *Technology Integration: Making Critical Choices in a Turbulent World.* Boston: Harvard Business School Press.

Jaikumar, Ramchandran. 1988. "From Filing to Fitting to Flexible Manufacturing: A Study in the Evolution of Process Control." Working paper no. 88-045, Harvard Business School.

Jaikumar, Ramchandran, and Roger Bohn. 1992. "A Dynamic Approach to Operations Management: An Alternative to Static Optimization." *International Journal of Production Economics* 27: 265–82.

Judd, Charles, Eliot Smith, and Loise Kidder. 1991. *Research Methods in Social Relations.* Fort Worth, Tex: Harcourt Brace Jovanovich.

Katz, Ralph, and Thomas Allen. 1988. "Organizational Issues in the Introduction of New Technologies." In *Managing Professionals in Innovative Organizations*, edited by Ralph Katz. Cambridge, Mass.: Ballinger. Pp. 442–56.

Leonard-Barton, Dorothy. 1995. *Wellsprings of Knowledge.* Boston: Harvard Business School Press.

Lockhart, Daniel. 1984. *Making Effective Use of Mailed Questionnaires.* San Francisco: Jossey-Bass.

Marples, David L. 1961. "The Decision of Engineering Design." *IRE Transactions on Engineering Management* 2 (June 1961): 55–71.

Miles, Matthew, and Michael Huberman. 1984. *Qualitative Data Analysis.* Beverly Hills, Calif.: Sage.

Nonaka, Ikujiro. 1994. "A Dynamic Theory of Organizational Knowledge Creation." *Organization Science* 5 (February): 14–37.

Nonaka, Ikujiro, and Hirotaka Takeuchi. 1995. *The Knowledge-Creating Company.* New York: Oxford University Press.

Nonaka, Ikujiro, Katsuhiro Umemoto, and Dai Senoo. 1996. "From Information Processing to Knowledge Creation: A Paradigm Shift in Business Management." *Technology in Society* 18: 203–18.

Pisano, Gary. 1996. *The Development Factory*. Boston: Harvard Business School Press.

Polanyi, M. 1958. *Personal Knowledge: Towards a Post-Critical Philosophy*. Chicago: University of Chicago Press.

Sachs, Emanuel, et al. 1992. "CAD-Casting: Direct Fabrication of Ceramic Shells and Cores by Three Dimensional Printing." *Manufacturing Review* 5(2): 117–26.

Shooman, Martin. 1983. *Software Engineering: Design, Reliability, and Measurement*. New York: McGraw Hill.

Simon, Herbert A. 1969. *The Sciences of the Artificial*. 2nd ed. Cambridge, Mass.: MIT Press.

Smith, Preston, and Donald Reinertsen. 1991. *Developing Products in Half the Time*. New York: Van Nostrand Reinhold.

Smith, Robert, and Steven Eppinger. 1997. "A Predictive Model of Sequential Iteration in Engineering Design." *Management Science* 43(8): 1104–1120.

Suh, Nam. 1990. *The Principles of Design*. New York: Oxford University Press.

Takeuchi, Hirotaka, and Ikujiro Nonaka. 1986. "The New New Product Development Game." *Harvard Business Review* (January-February): 137–46.

Thomke, Stefan. 1997. "The Role of Flexibility in the Development of New Products: An Empirical Study." *Research Policy* 26: 105–19.

———. 1998a. "Managing Experimentation in the Design of New Products." *Management Science* 44 (6): 743–62.

———. 1998b. "Simulation, Learning and R&D Performance: Evidence from Automotive Development." *Research Policy* 27: 55–74.

Thomke, Stefan, Eric von Hippel, and Roland Franke. 1998. "Modes of Experimentation: An Innovation Process and Competitive Variable." *Research Policy* 27: 315–32.

Uzumeri, Mustafa and Charles Snyder. 1996. "Information Technology and Accelerated Science: The Case of the Pentium Flaw." *California Management Review* 38 (2): 44–63.

Vincenti, Walter. 1990. *What Engineers Know and How They Know It*. Baltimore: John Hopkins University Press.

von Hippel, Eric. 1994. "'Sticky Information' and the Locus of Problem Solving: Implications for Innovation." *Management Science* 40 (4): 429–39.

von Hippel, Eric, and Marcie Tyre. 1994. "How 'Learning By Doing' Is Done: Problem Identification in Novel Process Equipment." *Research Policy* 19, (1): 1–12.

Walker, Rob. 1992. *Silicon Destiny: The History of Application Specific Integrated Circuits and LSI Logic Corporation*. Milpitas, Calif.: C.M.C.

Wall, Matthew, Karl Ulrich, and Woodie Flowers. 1991. "Evaluating Prototyping Technologies for Product Design." Working paper no. 3334-91-MSA, Sloan School of Management, Massachusetts Institute of Technology.

Wheelwright, Steven, and Kim, Clark. 1992. *Revolutionizing Product Development*. New York: Free Press.

6

The Temporal Dynamics of Knowledge Creation in the Information Society

MARTIN KENNEY

> In 1993, Gates melodramatically told his software developers "there's not a single line of code here today that will have value, say, in four or five years time"
>
> Randall Stross, *The Microsoft Way* (1996)

Knowledge creation is playing an ever more central role in capitalist economies, and business organizations must constantly create new knowledge to guarantee survival. To be a competitive firm in the contemporary economy it is necessary to continually innovate. Industries and firms that formerly were in comfortably protected, slowly evolving markets are being swept into accelerated change. Nonaka and Takeuchi (1995) were, perhaps, the first authors to reflect on how knowledge is created, but, equally important, they zeroed in on the fundamental importance to today's firms of creating new knowledge or, put differently, of innovating. To compete, a firm must be transformed into an organization mobilized for knowledge creation. This paper reflects on the changing temporal dynamics of innovation on products, which are crystallizations of the state of knowledge in the firm at a particular moment. Products, released from the knowledge-creation process, become static, while the firm rushes into the future.

With knowledge in its various manifestations as the increasing arbiter of value, innovation (i.e., new knowledge creation) has become the key to success in the global marketplace. The dedication of organizations and the increase in the number of organizations dedicated to continuous innovation are having profound effects on the world economy. Product development cycles are being shortened, and there is an acceleration of new product introduction. In the process, the market value of products is increasingly transient, and the length of the commercial usefulness of products is declining. At the heart of the transience of a product's value is the growing centrality of knowledge creation and innovation in the value-creation process. In the contemporary world economy, the value of the purely physical components and inputs such as raw materials is dropping while the value component, consisting of design and "software," is correspondingly increasing. As a result of this tendency, products are becoming "dematerialized." This tendency is most apparent in the electronics-related industries, such as personal computers, software, and data communications, but is no longer confined to high-technology sectors.

The result is that a number of manufacturing sectors have temporal dynamics that resemble the rate of change in the high-fashion garment and shoe industry. This essay argues that these temporal dynamics are intimately connected with the increasing application of electronics and, more precisely, information processing to other industries. Electronics, or the provision of information-processing power, is the vehicle for something more significant, that is, the increasing importance of creating new products. The routinized portions of intellectual activity are being turned over to the computer. This unleashes a powerful tendency to delegate routine calculations to machinery. In the same way that power machinery earlier freed humans from the limits of their muscles, thereby speeding production, information-processing power is freeing the human mind to become more active in the knowledge-creation process.[1]

This essay examines the implications of the acceleration of knowledge creation and its impacts on business. The remaining sections briefly examine the contemporary dynamics of capitalism, arguing that the acceleration is embedded within the increasing importance of knowledge creation. The second section describes the impact of changing temporal dynamics on the producer goods industry, a critical sector because of its central role in manufacturing, where rapid change has become the norm. The third section describes the supercharged pace of change in the personal computer (PC) industry. The fourth section examines the quintessential knowledge-creation industry, computer software. In software, product physicality is rendered virtually nil, while the knowledge component is nearly total. The fifth chapter speculates on the applicability of the knowledge-transience linkage to the transmutation of computer networks into the Internet. The concluding section discusses the implications of the increasing centrality of knowledge creation and the temporal dynamics of firms.

Knowledge Creation and the Contemporary Economy

The importance of knowledge creation in what many have termed the Information Age is recognized by many scholars (Nonaka and Takeuchi, 1995; Leonard-Barton, 1995). Drucker (1993) argues that we are now in a postcapitalist society in which knowledge and creativity have replaced labor and capital as the source of value. Beyond these theoretical treatments, some empirical research on the implications of these developments is being done. For example, Zuboff (1988) points out that today's automated machinery creates information constantly, yet it is the work of human beings to transform this into knowledge. Put more properly, only human beings can transform information into knowledge. In the transformation of information, people are actually involved in analyzing symbols. Reich (1991) called the persons involved in these activities symbolic analysts. This formulation captures an important component of the changing nature of work. Frenkel and colleagues (1995) argue that more and more workers as part of the work process are dealing with "symbolic and systematic representation(s) of material reality." These representations are attributable to their use of software that models reality on the basis of algorithms.[2]

In the 1990s, there has been an explosion of interest in the innovatory process. And yet, only a few explicitly consider the temporal aspects of the innovation process. The one that pays the greatest attention to the innovation process has developed a stylized account of a cyclical innovation process that begins with a technological discontinuity, which results in great uncertainty and ferment (Anderson and Tushman, 1990). Eventually, the period of ferment ends, and a dominant design emerges (Suarez and Utterback, 1995). With the emergence of the dominant design, innovation does not end, rather the trajectory shifts into more predictable paths, including incremental product and process innovations, until another technological discontinuity emerges. This model provides a convenient and useful stylized history of technological development.

Explanations of technology cycles was pioneered by Abernathy and Clark (1985) and Clark (1985), who generalize from a case study of the automobile to argue that innovations can usefully be thought of as belonging to four innovation cells: architectural, niche, regular, and revolutionary. In these schema, hereafter model 1, the types of innovations are classified on two axes: whether they conserved or disrupted a firm's existing competencies and whether they conserved or disrupted the firm's relationships with its customers. Later, Henderson and Clark (1990) modified this schema (model 2) to classify innovations on the basis of whether the innovation reinforced or overturned core design concepts or changed the linkages between core concepts and components. In the earlier formulation the focus was on the firm, internally or externally. In the second formulation the focus changed to the product and tried to understand the implications of changes in the product for the firm. In model 2 an architectural innovation was redefined as an innovation that "changes the way in which the components of a product are linked together, while leaving the core design concepts untouched." With the emergence of this architectural innovation, evolution usually continues along an incremental process and product improvement cycle. In addition to their new concept of the architectural innovation, Henderson and Clark (1990) added two other types of innovation. The first, which they call radical innovation, is the complete substitution of one genre of products, such as horse-drawn buggies, with another—automobiles. In the second, modular innovation, the core design concept is changed, for example, the substitution of the digital for the analog telephone receiver set, but this does not disrupt the relationships between the different parts of the phone system (though here it is not clear that this was not a radical innovation, because it unleashed the ability to transform the phone into a much more powerful instrument). Model 2 has some elements of a technology cycle in it; however, it is not nearly as explicit as in the dominant design literature or in model 1. Model 2 explicitly considers the impact of the innovation on a firm's knowledge.

Whereas the dominant design literature described a cyclical motion, model 2 is not nearly as deterministic as Model 1 in temporal evolutionary terms. On the other hand, it does bring the firm as a repository of knowledge back into the discussions of innovations and the effects of innovations on the knowledge. However, in another sense, these models seem somewhat lacking when describing the contemporary competitive environment. The accelerated pace of change can mean that the concatenation of simple incremental product innovations can destroy a firm's competencies just as surely and perhaps more quickly than an architectural or radical change. This paper, while not contradicting these models, aims to return the dynamic of knowledge creation to the center of the discussion rather than treating knowledge as a passive component.

To build another basis of understanding the acceleration, it is necessary to recognize that products have an intellectual component and a physical component. The relative balance between the physical value added and the intellectual value added is shifting inexorably toward the intellectual. Many of the fastest growing firms, such as Microsoft, Intel, Oracle, and Cisco, are so successful because their businesses are based much more on the knowledge intensity than on the physical content of their products. In quite another way, retailers such as the Gap are delivering a fashion look that people want. In effect, they are creating knowledge about what the market wants. In yet another way, the value that the shoemaker Nike adds is in the knowledge of shoe design and marketing. The materiality of the shoe is almost less relevant. The "goods" these companies produce are largely dematerialized, in the sense that the value of the material component is relatively minor compared to the value attributable to the knowledge embedded in the product.

To illustrate the importance of the knowledge and the accelerated temporal dynamic, an example from the semiconductor industry is interesting. A semiconductor sold in 1999 will, by the middle of 2001, have lost more than 50 percent of its value. Some semiconductors will no longer be available, having been replaced by improved products with much greater functionality. According to an article in *Electronic News* (1996), "[t]he life span of an IC [integrated circuit] made by a big player is short. There's only about 18 months to four years while a firm like Motorola ramps up production, places a circuit in a system and manufactures the circuit at volumes high enough to keep it profitable." After four years, the market value of the knowledge congealed in the semiconductor will be only valuable as a replacement part.

The unusual aspect of these knowledge-intensive products is their extreme transience. A semiconductor is extremely resistant to physical degradation but not temporally based obsolescence. Because of the speed of new knowledge creation, the market demand for a particular semiconductor model is transient; as a commodity having market value, it is here today and gone tomorrow (for an excellent discussion of this, see Hutcheson and Hutcheson, 1996). The semiconductor soon becomes worthless even though it retains full functionality.

In the early twenty-first century, the fastest growing industrial sectors are the ones in which knowledge creation is most central. The Fordist period, in which consumer durables manufacturing, that is, of highly physical products, was the leading sector is giving way to an environment in which the focal economic sectors are those based on the creation and manipulation of information. When purchasing an automobile, its physical function of transporting you is of great interest, that is, you expect it to convey you somewhere, safely and reliably. In the case of computer software, you expect it to manipulate symbols in a virtual spreadsheet (it is not a physical spreadsheet) or a virtual document or a virtual game or to direct a device to perform functions such as printing letters or spreadsheets. Another task might be to order metal-cutting equipment to undertake a particular cut and send visual representations of the cutting to a monitor. Software is, in a sense, ethereal; it (in itself) does not do anything physical. In contrast to the automobile, software is immaterial and thus very easy to communicate, improve, and so on.

The distinction between a product's physicality and its embedded knowledge is, of course, artificial, for these are but two perspectives on a product's fundamental unity. Even the most disembodied product, computer software, to be transmitted and used requires the physical flow of electrons, magnetic impulses on a hard or floppy disk, or pits on a CD ROM sensed by a laser beam. Thus, though the software's physicality is minimal, its physicality still exists—for human knowledge and creativity must be transmitted and actualized in the physical world or, put differently, embodied in a medium.

Traditional Producer Goods Industries

It was for the traditional complex assembled product industries that dominant design and models 1 and 2 were created. However, more recently these industries have also been drawn into the knowledge-creation dynamic. The increasing significance of the intellectual component of products is having an important effect on the rate of change in traditional industries such as machine tools and producer goods. The market value of these goods is increasingly dependent on the software and integrated circuitry components, though the product is not yet treated as a modular assemblage, as in the case of the PC.

The normally staid world of producer goods is experiencing a change in the locus of value in its highly complicated and expensive machinery. Historically, these machines had life expectancies measured in decades and were considered durable assets. Thirty years ago, these machines were freestanding and used little or no electronics. Change was gradual and confined to steady incremental improvements. The knowledge of how to create value with these machines was located in the machine operators. The knowledge embedded in the machines was increasing, but at a rather slow rate.

The linkage of the machines with the information-processing ability of electronics transformed the economics of owning manufacturing machines. The electronics and software permit a more rapid improvement in machine performance than was possible when improvements were based on redesigning only the physical features of the machine. This means that newer models are being introduced more quickly and have significantly more functionality than their predecessors. John McDermott, vice-president of Rockwell Automation's standard drive business, described the changes in the industrial motor starter business, which until the recent application of semiconductors had changed only very slowly for nearly one hundred years:

> As the technology changes faster, the life cycle of our products drops. . . . Both features and costs are impacted so greatly by technology that if you don't have a new product within four years, you're not competitive. . . . If you have a three-year development window and four-year product life cycle, you're in tough shape. (Bassack, 1996:30)

Though not yet accelerated to the speed of change in the electronics and software industry, these mundane businesses are also experiencing a pervasive acceleration.

The ubiquity of distributed computing power has transformed an important part of the machining industry into an extension of the electronics and software industry. Machining centers are a large machines containing many components and materials, all of which, of course, are embodiments of human knowledge. For example, extremely sophisticated bearings capable of continuous speed when the 15,000 rpm cutting tool goes from air to cutting metal embody enormous amounts of knowledge (Lee, 1996). It was the application of integrated circuits in controller boxes that changed the development pace of the machine tool industry (Yamazaki, 1995).[3] This application of electronics to machine tools, or what the Japanese call mechatronics makes it possible to update a machine by rewriting the software (Schodt, 1988; Kodama, 1991), Integrated circuitry and software are becoming ever more significant value-added components of a machine tool. For example, at Mori Seiki, one of the largest machine tool builders in the world, the value of the software and electronics in the machines has increased from 20 percent of the total value to a current 30 percent (Mori, 1996). The important point here is that the software and the computer controller are the most knowledge-intensive components (but, emphatically, not the only components that have significant amounts of embodied knowledge) of the machine tool.

As more and more of the operations of the machine tool are automated, they also produce data in an electronic form. This provides opportunities of on-line computer monitoring. Now the machine tool has two outputs: the work piece and electronic data. Recently, Mori Seiki developed a system whereby information from the user's machine can be communicated to a computer, which can transfer information regarding malfunctioning to Mori Seiki's technical center for problem diagnosis or to another point for remote machining control. This means that the most knowledgeable people in the world, the tool's producers and designers, can participate in trouble-shooting. Moreover, it makes the user-designer relationship, which von Hippel (1988) argues is so important for improvement, even closer.[4] However, there are possibilities to go even further; for example, now software could be downloaded to the user's machine from anywhere, including third party vendors. With the increasing ability to quickly provide new software, change in the machine tool industry can be expected to become increasingly rapid.

Rapid change is not confined to the traditional machining industries. It is pervasive. For example, printed circuit board (PCB) component insertion machines are so fast that the insertion head is merely a blur as it inserts components fed from a tape reel (Mody, Suri, and Tatikonda, 1995). In this segment, the rapidity of improvement in insertion machines and the shrinking size of the components means that the machines also rapidly lose value (Kawai, 1992). The result is that designers must constantly develop new and improved models.

The importance of time is reflected by Douglas Elder, the Singapore-based managing director of Asia operations for the U.S. semiconductor test equipment maker Teradyne, when he said that price and quality were no longer the main sales features in the electronics industry; rather "the differentiating value is now cycle time.

. . . Many sales are now made on the basis of how soon the product can be delivered" (Bordenaro, 1996). Price, which used to be an all-important criteria, is no longer entirely central.

Production equipment loses its market value so quickly that it is becoming an ever greater business cost. Profits must be made quickly before the equipment has lost its value. This gives real meaning to the term "speed-based" competition. The introduction of electronics has made machines more productive, but simultaneously, due to accelerating technological change, productive life decreases. Factories are under extraordinary pressure to operate constantly, because physical depreciation no longer bears any relationship to obsolescence. Interestingly, this is matched by an environment in which markets often emerge and either disappear or explode in very short periods. In periods of slower change, depreciation and obsolescence had a relatively tight linkage, simplifying management decision-making about timing the replacement of capital goods. Now, the previous relatively stable linkage has been broken, and intensifying competition forces all companies to accelerate the introduction of new capital equipment.

The integration of electronics into production machinery increased functionality and speed; however, its pervasive effect on the rest of the economy simultaneously operated to decrease the machine's effective productive life. Even for the rather traditional industries such as machine tools, time has become an ever more central facet of the competitive environment. These developments are placing ever greater pressure on managers to actively manage the one-way arrow of time.

Personal Computers

Of all the products of the information age, the personal computer is probably definitional. The power of the PC is its neutrality—it can host many different functions. It can be an entertainment vehicle, a controller for machine tools, an information storage device, a switchboard router, a television receiver, a word processor, a spreadsheet, a telecommunications device, and/or a database manager. It is not imprinted in necessarily deterministic ways. It is universal receptacle, into which human creativity can pour the software concretizations of various ideas.[5]

Of all the products consumers and businesses purchase, the PC is the one that becomes obsolete most quickly. The pace of change in PCs is so rapid that it is nearly impossible to have a state-of-the-art machine. Time, in the PC world, is measured in months and even in weeks.

An important reason that the PC can change so quickly is that it is extremely modularized (Langlois, 1992). The various components that make up a PC can be mixed and matched in an enormous number of combinations from a wide variety of vendors. The result is that the PC's evolution is driven by change in each of its major components, and many of these are evolving at breakneck speed. As a result, the PC is also evolving at an exceptionally rapid rate. Moreover, as one component evolves it quickly makes the other components, in Thomas Hughes's terms, a reverse salient providing significant profitability for the product that ameliorates the salient (Hughes, 1983). As an illustration, the average life of a PC model is approximately three months, after which its price is dramatically reduced so as to remove it from the retailer's inventory.[6]

The PC is fascinating case study because it is ubiquitous. Moreover, because of the PC's modular construction, it is possible to see quite plainly the components that are rapidly changing and those less rapidly evolving. As table 6.1 indicates, certain components such as the case, the mouse, and the keyboard exhibit minimal improvement and negligible price decreases. The price/performance changes are concentrated in the components that have the highest value added and the least materiality and require the most R&D.

The innovations in the electronics industry are incessant and cumulatively dramatic. For example, the areal density of information storage in Winchester hard disk drives is increasing at 50 percent per annum. For example, in 1989, 40-megabyte hard drives were standard; in 2000 five-gigabyte hard drives are considered small. Semiconductor memory capacity doubles even more rapidly, every eighteen months. However, the price per chip or disk drive remains roughly constant. As a result, price per bit of information processed or stored decreases exponentially, and consumers can purchase ever more powerful information systems at a roughly constant price.

As I mentioned earlier, not all PC components experience such rapid price evolution. For example, monitors evolve somewhat more slowly, even though new programs such as Windows 95, 3–D graphics, desktop publishing, and CAD-CAM applications are driving a move to larger, better resolution monitors. The other force that is beginning to force the rather sedate pace of the monitor industry is the rapidly evolving flat panel display industry. In flat panel displays, technological innovation and product introduction more resembles the integrated circuitry industry than the tube-based monitor industry. The picture tube is the last major tube still being produced in the electronics industry.

The PC industry is the quintessential example of an industry in which time has become an absolutely critical component of the industrial dynamics. Accelerated knowledge creation is directly coupled with rapid price declines. Any specified model is a perishable item. Steve Haslett, Hewlett-Packard's Asia Pacific marketing director for servers, PCs, laptops, and related products, uses a graphic analogy to indicate the growing importance of logistics to PC sales.

> In this industry there is a horrendously short life cycle—if a product doesn't move from the chip to the customer in ninety days, like a banana, it goes rotten very fast. . . . It is estimated that computer products lose 1 percent of their value every day they sit on a warehouse shelf or a retail shelf. . . . If we can put the high-value parts in at the last minute, we will be able to help retain value and reduce costs. (Bordenaro, 1996)

Each company must try to decrease its cycle time to remain competitive. The rapidity of price declines in computers has created a situation in which personal computer producers often cannot assemble and sell the systems before some components decrease in value. To cope, computer assemblers are reorganizing their global production networks to maximize proximity to customers. Ten years ago, personal computer motherboards were often completely assembled in then low-wage Asian

Table 6.1. Value of the Components of a Personal Computer, 1990 and 1996

PCs Circa December 1990			
COMPAQ 389/33	**Price**	**Build Your Own PC**	**Price**
Motherboard	$ 1,100	Motherboard	$ 1,100
2MB RAM	$ 100	2MB RAM	$ 100
VGA Monitor - 14"	$ 350	VGA monitor - 14"	$ 350
2MB memory board	$ 375	2MB memory board	N/A
Video board	N/A	Video board	$ 135
84MB hard drive	$ 275	80MB hard drive	$ 550
1.4MB floppy drive	$ 58	1.4MB floppy drive	$ 70
Keyboard	$ 45	Keyboard	$ 68
Mouse	N/A	Mouse	$ 50
Case	$ 53	Case	N/A
Power supply	$ 135	Power supply	$ 61
Total parts cost	**$ 2,491**	**Total parts cost**	**$2,484**
List price	**$10,698**		

Source: Infoworld 1990

PCs Circa December 1996			
Dell 200 MHz Pentium Processor (bundled)		**Build Your Own PC**	**Price**
Pentium Pro motherboard		Pentium Pro motherboard	$ 809
64MB RAM		64MB RAM	$ 549
SVGA trinitron monitor 17"		SVGA trinitron monitor 17"	$ 995
2MB video card		2MB video card	$ 239
4.2 GB hard drive		4.2 GB hard drive	$ 899
8X CD-ROM drive		8X CD-ROM drive	$ 99
28.8 fax modem		28.8 fax modem	$ 149
Various software		N/A	
		Power supply	$ 49
		Case	$ 51
		Keyboard	$ 59
		Mouse	$ 35
		Floppy drive	$ 28
Total cost	**$3,449**	**Total cost**	**$3,961**

Compiled from various vendors
Source: Computer Shopper 1996

countries such as Taiwan. The completed boards or even completed PCs were shipped to the United States. Recently, because microprocessors (MPUs), disk drives, and dynamic random access memory (DRAM) decline in value so rapidly, firms are altering their production location decisions. They still insert more slowly evolving components onto the motherboard in Asia, but now they add the MPUs and DRAMs near the customer right before shipment. Even more recently, because of increasing automation, the obsolescence of even more traditional components, and the rapidly changing marketplace, some firms have begun assembling the entire motherboard close to the final customer. For example, Intel has recently become the largest motherboard producer in the world, doing much of its assembly in the Portland, Oregon, area. The reason for Intel's decision is that the evolution of other components such as Basic Input/Output System (BIOS) chips and graphics chips is also quickening, and it is no longer much more economical to use low-cost labor.

Intel can achieve savings by inserting its newly made MPU right onto the board, thereby eliminating a sales step. This is because in the three to four weeks it takes to ship a completed motherboard or completed PC to the United States from Asia, it may have lost 20 percent of its total value.[7] Michael Dell, the president of Dell Computers, described the situation his company faces.

> The equipment to build the machines is relatively indiscriminant [*sic*]. It doesn't care where it sits, and time-to-market is really important. Labor is not a really important factor in the production of motherboards, particularly in high-end machines. If you're talking about low-end machines, which we don't participate in, you might have to build them in Taiwan to get the cost ratio. But then you have the question of, if you put it on a boat for thirty days and have the devaluation of materials, it's going to be much worse than if you built it close to the market. (Dell 1996)

The rapidity of change and the corresponding devaluation of their product means that the transience of value has become a central concern for PC industry managers.

Software and Value Creation

Software is an interesting commodity, because the physical portion of its value is trivial, and this makes the material component of production trivial. But timing in the software industry is critically important; missing a generation can place a software company so far behind the market that it is very difficult to recover. As a result, from one perspective, software appears to be a service, while from another it clearly is a product. Software (like musical recordings) need only be produced once; further reproduction is trivial. More than any other product, the relative cost difference between production and reproduction is the greatest in software. Normal goods require significant quantities of capital and labor to produce more units. Most other products, though not all—exceptions are recorded music and books—are "consumed" upon usage.[8]

Software, as a set of instructions that direct a machine to undertake a sequence of actions or, put differently, a tool that can be loaded onto a computer to perform various activities such as processing words or numbers, has its value almost entirely embodied in its code. The disk (or media) on which the software is imprinted is only a very small portion of its total value.

Software operates forever—but it is very time sensitive, in contrast with machines, which have a discrete life expectancy in the sense of how many production cycles can be performed before they wear out. In other words, a machine has physical constraints. In contrast, software has virtually none. Software, therefore, should be timeless. However, in the marketplace it has only a limited life expectancy, before it is replaced by an upgrade with greater functionality.

The speed of change is astonishing. For example, Microsoft operates on a one-year cycle for minor upgrades and a two-year cycle for major feature and architectural changes. Operating systems are scheduled for major changes on a three- to four-year cycle (Cusumano and Selby 1985:191). Semiconductor design software is on six-month major upgrade cycles.

The cost of software applications has also decreased dramatically. For example, word processing was first available as part of a dedicated system for about $7,000 to $10,000 per machine in the 1970s. It was also available from an extremely expensive mainframe or minicomputer terminal. In the mid-1980s a superior word processing system was available for approximately $500 on a PC costing approximately $5,000. In the 1990s, word processing has been reduced to a function in a suite of productivity applications worth approximately $100 and operating on a $2,500 machine. One observer believes the next step is that "the word processor is likely to become a feature in the operating system with almost no explicit economic value (Mcnamee, 1996:76)." In word processing software, little new knowledge is being created. Word processing programs are now products containing largely old knowledge, with new releases providing limited further functionality.

It is in software that the most purified form of mental labor is expressed. The physical aspect has been reduced to a minimum and may even be reduced further, if the current discussion of delivering software over the Internet actually comes to fruition. It may no longer be necessary to go to a store to purchase a CD ROM; the software could be downloaded directly from the Internet to your computer. This is the goal of the current discussions of building an information appliance. Instead of an appliance dedicated to a single function, such as a toaster connected to a power delivery network, the information appliance would be connected to an information delivery network. The acceleration of change that is so prevalent in the electronics world would now be linked directly to the home consumer. Software upgrades would be delivered directly to the end-user's computer as they become available—further quickening the pace in the industry.

Software is characterized by extremely short product cycles. This is possible because its creation is largely free of material constraints in its production. However, software quickly falls prey to obsolescence. Entire product categories such as word processing software lose value as they become old knowledge available nearly for free.

Knowledge and the Internet

In 1993, Bill Gates, the Rockefeller of the late twentieth century, thought that the Internet was not of critical importance to Microsoft. Then in 1995 he wrote his famous "Internet tidal wave" memo, and Microsoft was completely reoriented to participate in and capture the dominant spot on this tidal wave (Stross, 1996). That Microsoft, a veritable monopolist, could become concerned indicates how inherently fluid positions are in economic sectors based on knowledge creation.

The Internet forms the core of a significant new economic space in the continuing movement of the global economy from a physical basis to a knowledge and in-

formation basis. It is simultaneously contributing to an important new acceleration. The Internet is a vast unregulated, uncontrolled mass of information, images,
and opinions accessible almost immediately to any computer owner with a connection (that can be had at quite low cost). Through the Internet, information that would
have taken much time to find is now quickly available. Much of these materials are
not for sale—they are provided for free. For example, many major companies put their
press releases directly onto their Internet servers so that anyone can access them. This
means that a computer can have access to press releases and corporate earning reports nearly simultaneously with reporters and professional analysts.

There are also many commercial sites on the Internet that cost money to access.
Given the relative immaturity of the Internet, it is hard to draw any firm conclusions about its future, but some tentative observations are possible. Even though
no one can be sure what the system will look like when it is mature, businesses such
as stock trading, bookstores, and computer stores have already gone on-line.[9] This
dramatically accelerates the process of acquiring many goods, and such products
can then be drop-shipped from anywhere in the world using the various courier
services. Market barriers are often also eased by the minimal startup costs, here
again contributing to an acceleration of the realization of an idea.

The dematerialization that the Internet represents is extremely powerful. It is
no longer necessary to disseminate information in the physical medium of paper,
floppy disks, or CDs. Information can now be communicated through electronic
impulses or beams of light (fiber optics). This availability of information accelerates the information flow and communication that can facilitate new knowledge
creation.

Software firms using the Internet have developed a new business model. The
companies with the most used Internet software, Netscape (Navigator) and Microsoft (Explorer) initially provided their software free to users in an effort to capture
market and "mind" share (Lewis,1996:70). Similarly, the "search engine" companies, such as Yahoo! Lycos, and DEC Altavista also provide their software and databases for free. From the perspective of traditional economics, this practice seems
foolhardy and even perverse, though recently some economists, such as Arthur
(1994, 1996), have begun a rethinking of traditional economic concepts to encompass the value added from knowledge creation and the increasing returns in infor-
mation- and communication-intensive industries.

Companies are giving the software away because of the need to quickly establish
a market presence and capture market share. If their product becomes a standard,
adopters become customers for the rapidly arriving upgrades or spinoff products.
This business model is possible because as Jim Clark, the chairman and founder of
Netscape, said,

> [t]he Internet is low cost. We proved that by using the Internet to distribute our
> first product, and we were able to build a customer base of ten million users in just
> about nine months. Our only expense was the engineering cost of making the pro-
> gram. . . . So we see this potential for low-cost distribution of any kind of intellec-
> tual property—whether software, or pictures, or movies, or compact disks, or any-
> thing that can be represented as bits. (1995:70)

As the product is dematerialized, the costs of distribution drop dramatically, while the speed increases markedly.

The Internet also gives companies such as Netscape a route to users that circumvents traditional channels. Knowledge creation has spread to a "virtual" community, because of the practice of posting experimental versions of new software on the Internet. Then the consumers actually create knowledge by using it and communicating the results back to the company. Here, the community of users actually creates knowledge for the firm. This speeds the testing process, while simultaneously creating a market for the finished product. This integrates a subset of customers directly into the product development process.

Distributing software gratis over the Internet was pioneered by John McAfee with his antivirus software. McAfee has said, "If you give software away and assist people as well, you're almost bound to make money" (Leon, 1997). His strategy is to capture users and lock them in. After McAfee's companies get five million users, they change their "marketing" and start to charge for upgrades and add-ons. Since computers and networks are constantly evolving, the customers actually evolve with the software in the form of upgrades. The tempo of the users merges with that of the software developers. This occurs because the software soon becomes obsolete. The value created by this model is enormous. In the case of the McAfee antivirus product, the venture capital firm Summit Partners invested $5 million in his first company and took out $100 million.

In the Internet market space, product evolution has been extremely rapid. For example, Netscape Communications, the main provider of Internet software, was established only in February 1993 but already by June 1996 had already issued its third full upgrade of its Navigator software. Netscape develops a new product generation annually. This is also true of its Internet server software. Moreover, it has already made four acquisitions of other software companies to broaden its product line (Netscape Communications Company, 1996).

It is not only the data communications software industry that is evolving extremely rapidly. The increased number of Internet users has accelerated the pace of change in data communications hardware as well. New switches, routers, and data servers are released constantly (Burg and Kenney, 1995). Though these companies appear to be hardware companies in that they deliver physical products, the bulk of the value is embedded in their integrated circuits and the product design. Switches installed two years ago are already overloaded and need to be replaced by those with higher capacity. With the increasing communication of data, system overloads constantly pressure users to upgrade to keep the performance of their networks from degrading.

The acceleration in the amount of data being communicated over networks is so powerful, and change occurs at so many levels, that even the most sophisticated hardware firms find it difficult to innovate rapidly enough. In response, as table 6.2 indicates for Cisco Systems, the largest computer networking company, the larger companies purchase firms to secure access to new knowledge. Upon purchase, it is the larger firms' interest to drive that technology into the mainstream as quickly as possible. Eric Benhamou, the president and CEO of 3Com Corporation, another major computer networking company, believes that

Table 6.2. Cisco's Acquisitions, 1993–1996

Company	Date	Purchase price ($millions)
Netsys	1996	79
Granite Systems	1996	220
Telebit	1996	200
Nashoba Networks	1996	100
Stratacom	1996	4,000
TGV Software	1996	115
Grand Junction	1995	348
Network Translations	1995	N/A
Combinet	1995	114
Internet Junction, Inc.	1995	6
Kalpana	1994	204
Newport Systems Solutions	1994	91
Lightstream Corp.	1994	120
Crescendo Inc.	1993	95

Source: Cisco Systems Inc. 1996.

[i]f all [change] was fairly static, if the pace of change was relatively slow, you wouldn't have to buy companies to create this integration. You could rely on third-party integrators whose job it is to take products from different companies and make them work together. The problem is that these networks grow and change so fast that even if you manage to freeze different vendors in one moment in time and get their products to interoperate well, two years downstream, each one of the products may have evolved on its own vector and the whole infrastructure [would] no longer be coherent. (Benhamou, 1995:46)

In an industry in which the product's value is so knowledge-intensive and changing so quickly, companies can be formed to create discrete pieces of knowledge-intensive (in this case, usually software-intensive) hardware. The value is so high and the pressure of change is so overwhelming that startups are purchased by the larger companies to secure control of the product and gain a few months. For example, the computer networking applications area not only is changing fast but also is expanding in so many directions that even firms in the center of its development cannot internally pursue all the possible expansion paths.

"It's weird," said Joe Kennedy, cofounder of the five-month-old startup Rapid City Communications, a developer of gigabit intranet switches in Mountain View, California. "What used to be two-and-one-half years for a startup's business cycle is now being condensed to between six and nine months." For instance, Rapid City accelerated its plans to hire a VP within the first six months of being in business. The company will announce its new VP at the end of the month. (Bournellis 1996:1)

Competition is so intense and the technology is changing so rapidly that a startup must be jumped up even more quickly or it might miss the market. There can be little doubt that the Internet/data communications field is experiencing the rapid growth characteristic of a Schumpeterian new economic space. It seems possible that it will settle into the more stable phase that Abernathy and Clark (1985) identify as occurring after an architectural innovation becomes established. However, thus far there seems to be one fundamental difference from earlier periods; namely, the technical change in underlying industries of integrated circuitry, communications bandwidth, and data storage continues at logarithmic rates. The current acceleration gives little signs of slowing. The Internet provides every indication of continuing this process as ever more activities move on-line.[10]

Discussion

This essay explored some of the interconnections between knowledge creation and temporal dynamics. The dominant design and architectural innovation models provide insights into the phases of the innovation process. Model 2 posed the question of how a particular innovation might affect the core competencies of a firm. Model 2 distilled the dynamism of knowledge creation into the more static concept of effect on a core competency. Neither Model 1 nor Model 2 fully captured the temporal dynamics of highly knowledge-intensive industries. In many of the industries that are critically concerned with knowledge creation, the boundaries between users and producers are eroding. Moreover, some of the innovation dynamics operating are so accelerated that it is difficult to separate the incremental from the modular and architectural.

As knowledge creation becomes the focal point of our thinking about economic activity, managers face an environment with two attributes: increased emphasis on knowledge creation and a transience of existing products and knowledge. The acceleration in new knowledge creation speeds up the devaluation of the concrete results of knowledge creation, the products. In electronics and computer networking, knowledge creation is rapid and the pace of change is dramatic. For managers, understanding and operating at the industry's speed is the difference between success or extremely rapid failure.

Often management is simply riding on the tiger's back. Even industry leaders such as Intel and Microsoft have every reason to be paranoid (Grove, 1996), as the pace of change is engulfing all firms. For the more slowly evolving sectors of the economy, innovations such as the Internet may accelerate and transform their businesses (witness the case of on-line bookstores). Firms face unique challenges, as management of labor and capital is as critical as the management of knowledge and time.

Acknowledgments The author thanks Charles Edquist, Kristian Kreiner, and the participants of seminars at the Copenhagen Business School and Linkoping University for helpful comments. I also thank James Curry, Raghu Garud, W. Richard Goe, Rob Grant, Jack Kloppenburg, Nicos Mouratides, Toshihiro Nishiguchi, J. C. Spender, Urs von Burg, and one anonymous reviewer for their comments. Special thanks must be given to Takuji Hara for his pointed and insightful criticisms. I also thank the participants of the IBM Japan-Mitsubishi Bank Conference and the Conference on the Comparative Study of Knowledge Creation.

Notes

1. It is important to be careful not to assume that humans need no longer be concerned with the material. As material beings, we must continue to work with the material, but it is our minds working through our hands that is the critical feature. When the mind is no longer working through the hands, that is, mindless labor, the work is now suitable for machines. For a further discussion of this, see Kenney (1996).

2. For an insightful discussion of the tradeoffs between computer modeling and physical prototyping, see Thomke herein.

3. For an examination of the creation of computer numerically controlled (CNC) machine tools in the United States, see Noble (1984).

4. At higher speeds these tools become more efficient and accurate.

5. Charles Babbage was perhaps the first economist to see this (Rosenberg, 1994).

6. The fashion industry has similar turnover cycles. In this industry product lifecycles are notoriously short. The value-added is clearly in the design (creativity), and that is devalued extremely quickly, as cheap copies are created and the new season's fashions are released.

7. It is interesting to note that four to six weeks it takes to deliver a computer ordered from a mail order firm such as Dell or Northstar provides them with a significant competitive advantage because of the decrease in component cost between order and payment and delivery.

8. Musical recording is fascinating because two tendencies have been at play in its technological evolution. The first tendency has been toward ever greater fidelity, for example, from records to CD ROMs. The second tendency has been toward increased ease of copying.

9. For the package delivery firms, such as Federal Express, the changes in purchasing facilitated by the Internet create a burgeoning market (Lappin, 1996).

10. An interesting example of the Internet's acceleration of information flow is the rapidity with which Intel was forced to recall the flawed Pentium in 1990 (Uzumeri and Snyder, 1996).

References

Abernathy, William, and Kim Clark. 1985. "Innovation: Mapping the Winds of Creative Destruction." *Research Policy* (14): 3–22.

Anderson, Philip, and Michael Tushman. 1990. "Technological Discontinuities and Dominant Designs: A Cyclical Model of Technological Change." *Administrative Science Quarterly* 35: 604–33.

Arthur, W. Brian. 1996. "Increasing Returns and the New World of Business." *Harvard Business Review* (July–August): 100–9.

———. 1994. *Increasing Returns and Path Dependence in the Economy*. Ann Arbor: University of Michigan Press.

Bassack, Gil. 1996. "Silicon Invigorates Industrial Control." *Electronics Business Asia* (July): 29–30.

Benhamou, Eric. 1995. Interview. *Upside* (August): 38–51.

Bordenaro, Michael. 1996. "Supply Chains: From Static to Dynamic." *Electronics Business Asia* (December): 63–65.

Bournellis, Cynthia. 1996. "Cisco's $220M Gigabit Ethernet Move." *Electronic News* (September 9): 1, 10.

Burg, Urs von, and Martin Kenney. 1995. "Silicon Valley and the Creation of the Computer Networking Industry" (in Japanese). *Hitotsubashi Business Review* 42(4): 15–44.

Clark, Jim. 1995. Interview. *Red Herring* (November): 70–74.

Clark, Kim. 1985. "The Interaction of Design Hierarchies and Market Concepts in Technological Evolution." *Research Policy* 14: 235–51.

Cusumano, Michael, and Richard Selby. 1995. *Microsoft Secrets.* New York: Free Press.

Dell, Michael. 1996. Interview. *Electronic Business Asia* (March): 49.

Drucker, Peter. 1993. *Post-capitalist Society* New York: HarperBusiness.

Electronics News. 1996. "Pitting the Davids against the Semiconductor Goliaths." (September 23): 1.

Frenkel, Steve, Marek Korczynski, Leigh Donoghue, and Karen Shire. 1995. "Reconstituting Work: Trends towards Knowledge Work and Info-normative Control." *Work, Employment and Society* 9(4): 773–96.

Grove, Andrew S. 1996. *Only the Paranoid Survive: How to Exploit the Crisis Points that Challenge Every Company and Career.* New York: Currency Doubleday.

Henderson, Rebecca, and Kim Clark. 1990. "Architectural Innovation: The Reconfiguration of Existing Product Technologies and the Failure of Established Firms." *Administrative Science Quarterly* 35: 9–35.

Hippel, Eric von. 1988. *The Sources of Innovation.* New York: Oxford University Press.

Hughes, Thomas. 1983. *Networks of Power.* Baltimore: Johns Hopkins University Press.

Hutcheson, G. Dan, and Jerry Hutcheson. 1996. "Technology and Economics in the Semiconductor Industry." *Scientific American* (January): 54–62.

Kawai, Makoto (General Manager, Circuits Manufacturing Technology Laboratory, Matsushita Electric Industrial Corporation). 1992. Interview by author. Kadoma, Osaka, Japan, December 3.

Kenney, Martin. 1996. "The role of Information, Knowledge and Value in the late Twentieth Century." *Futures* 28(8): 695–707.

Kodama, Fumio. 1991. *Analyzing Japanese High Technologies: The Techno-paradigm Shift.* London: Pinter.

Langlois, Richard. 1992. "External Economies and Economic Progress: The Case of the Microcomputer Industry." *Business History Review* 66 (Spring): 1–50.

Lappin, Todd. 1996. "The Airline of the Internet." *Wired* 4(12): 234–40, 282–90.

Lee, Jay. 1996. "Status on Research and Production Practices in Industrial Machinery and Machine Tools Industry in Japan." Report memorandum #96-1, National Science Foundation, Tokyo Office, (January 19).

Leon, Mark. 1997. "Bright Idea or Loose Bulb?" *Red Herring* (January): 52–53.

Leonard-Barton, Dorothy. 1995. *Well-Springs of Knowledge.* Boston: Harvard Business School Press.

Lewis, Ted. 1996. "Surviving the Software Economy." *Upside* (March): 66–79.

Mcnamee, Roger. 1996. "Fishing on the Internet Sea." *Upside* (February): 74–81.

Mody, Ashoka, Rajan Suri, and Mohan Tatikonda. 1995. "Keeping Pace with Change: International Competition in Printed Circuit Board Assembly." *Industrial and Corporate Change* 4(3): 583–613.

Mori, Masahiko (Managing Director, Corporate Planning and Administration Department, Mori Seki Co., Ltd.). 1996. Letter to the author, July 18.

Netscape Communications Company. 1996. Corporate Information Package.

Noble, David. 1984. *Forces of Production.* New York: Knopf.

Nonaka, Ikujiro, and Hirotaka Takeuchi. 1995. *The Knowledge-Creating Company.* New York: Oxford University Press.

Reich, Robert. 1991. *The Work of Nations.* New York: Knopf.

Rosenberg, Nathan. 1994. *Exploring the Black Box.* New York: Cambridge University Press.

Schodt, Frederik. 1988. *Inside the Robot Kingdom: Japan, Mechatronics, and the Coming Robotopia.* Tokyo: Kodansha International.

Stross, Randall. 1996. *The Microsoft Way.* Reading, Mass.: Addison-Wesley.

Suarez, Fernando, and James Utterback. 1995. "Dominant Designs and the Survival of Firms." *Strategic Management Journal* 16: 415–430.

Thomke, Stefan. 1996. "The Impact of Technology on Knowledge Creation: A Study of Experimentation and Learning in the Design of New Products." Paper presented at conference, "International Comparative Study on Knowledge Creation: Implications for Business Enterprises of the Twenty-first Century." Japan-America Institute for Management Science. Honolulu, Hawaii, December 13–15.

Uzumeri, Mustafa, and Charles Snyder. 1996. "Information Technology and Accelerated Science: The Case of the Pentium Flaw." *California Management Review* 38(2): 44–63.

Yamazaki, Kazuo (Professor, Department of Mechanical Engineering, University of California, Davis). 1995. Conversation with the author, May 18.

Zuboff, Shoshona. 1988. *In the Age of the New Machine.* New York: Basic Books.

7

Focusing Creativity

Microsoft's "Synch-and-Stabilize" Approach
to Software Product Development

MICHAEL A. CUSUMANO

This essay discusses how Microsoft, the world's largest producer of personal computer (PC) software, focuses the creativity of its engineers through a very specific product development process. Much of this paper is based on material adapted from Cusumano and Selby, 1995. The first section discusses the culture that dominates Microsoft's product development teams, which tries to balance structure with flexibility in the design process. The second section outlines the basic concept underlying Microsoft's approach to design, development, and testing: allow teams and individuals to be creative but frequently synchronize and periodically stabilize the design changes that they are continuously making. The third section discusses the specific strategies and principles that Microsoft uses to implement this "synch-and-stabilize" development philosophy. The next section returns to the theme of combining structure with flexibility in software development. The conclusion summarizes ways in which Microsoft's approach contrasts to more conventional "sequential" styles of product development.

The Microsoft Development Culture

Product developers need to understand actual or potential customer needs, as well as generate new knowledge or understand existing knowledge about product concepts, relevant technologies, components, and other elements that go into product design, construction, and delivery. In this sense, product development is a form of structured knowledge creation (see Nonaka and Takeuchi, 1995). Strategies or practices that promote structure in the work of product teams, as well as those that promote creativity in their thinking, are both necessary because companies generally want to create products that customers want to buy—and to do so in competitively short periods of time and with competitive levels of cost.

Although not every team operates in identical ways, one aspect of the product development culture at Microsoft is the attempt to balance creativity with structure in the design, development, and testing processes. An excellent description of this mix of structure and creativity is provided by Dave Maritz, a former tank commander in the Israeli army, who headed the MS-DOS/Windows testing group. Maritz described how he and other Microsoft managers try to focus creativity by imposing only enough direction and ironclad rules—resembling the discipline of the Israeli military—so that individuals and teams work together toward the common goal of getting a new product out the door:

> In the military, when I was in tank warfare and I was actually fighting in tanks, there was nothing more soothing than people constantly hearing their commander's voice come across the airwaves. Somebody's in charge, even though all shit is breaking loose. . . . When you don't hear [the commander's voice] for more than fifteen minutes to half an hour, what's happened? Has he been shot? Has he gone out of control? Does he know what's going on? You worry. And this is what Microsoft is. These little offices, hidden away with the doors closed. And unless you have this constant voice of authority going across the e-mail the whole time, it doesn't work. *Everything that I do here I learned in the military. . . . You can't do anything that's complex unless you have structure. . . . And what you have to do is make that structure as unseen as possible and build up this image for all these prima donnas to think that they can do what they like.* Who cares if a guy walks around without shoes all day? Who cares if the guy has got his teddy bear in his office? I don't care. I just want to know . . . [if] somebody hasn't checked in his code by five o'clock. Then that guy knows that I am going to get into his office. (Interview with Dave Maritz, former test manager, MS-DOS/Windows, April 15, 1993. Emphasis added.)

Focusing creativity is especially important for firms competing in fast-paced industries such as PC software. There are so many technical innovations or new feature ideas that managers in PC software companies often cannot predict the direction of specific technologies or customer requirements more than six months to a year in advance. The explosion of interest in the Internet and the World Wide Web, as one case, took even Microsoft managers with great surprise in late 1995. To respond to this new technology, within merely a few months CEO Bill Gates had to make major changes in strategic direction, product development plans, marketing tactics, and organizational structure (Rebello, 1996).

The Internet is only one recent example. In general, it appears that companies in markets characterized by rapid rates of change in technology and user requirements often need extreme levels of flexibility in strategy, technical capabilities, people, and organizational structure and processes simply to cope with the new knowledge that their personnel must rapidly create and understand. At the same time, firms in fast-paced markets still seem to need a stable vision to guide strategic, technical, and financial investment decisions.

In the case of Gates and Microsoft, the vision since the company founding in 1975 has been to dominate the desk-top computer software market, whatever form this might take. Not even Bill Gates knew how this vision would play out and take the company through successive waves of mass markets—from programming languages to character-based and then graphical operating systems, individual user applications, commercial applications, multimedia, on-line publishing, the Internet, and various other related businesses. (For a discussion of the evolution of Microsoft's strategy, see Cusumano and Selby, 1995: chap. 3.) Nonetheless, product development processes and outcomes at Microsoft have quickly adapted to these changes in technology and market needs.

Microsoft and other PC software firms have gradually been adding more structure to the way they organize teams and technical functions, such as specification, development, and testing, at least partly in response to the need to manage larger teams, handle more complex development tasks and technologies, and get products debugged and stabilized faster. PC software products now consist of hundreds of thousands and even millions of lines of source code and require hundreds of people to build and test over periods of one or more years. As the world's largest producer of PC software, with approximately twenty thousand employees, more than two hundred products, and annual revenues of around $8 billion, Microsoft has probably tackled more PC software projects than any other PC software company. Some of its products, such as Windows 95 (which contains more than 11 million lines of code and had a development team of hundreds of programmers and testers), rival the complexity of many systems produced by makers of software for mainframe computers and telecommunication systems.

Microsoft's general philosophy has been to maintain its roots as a highly flexible, entrepreneurial company and *not* adopt too many of the structured software-engineering practices commonly used by software producers for mainframe computers or U.S. Department of Defense applications. Rather, Microsoft has tried to "scale-up" a loosely structured small-team (some might say "hacker") style of product development. The objective is to get many small parallel teams (three to eight developers each) or individual programmers to work together as one relatively large team, in order to build large products relatively quickly but still allow individual programmers and teams freedom to evolve their designs and operate nearly autonomously. These small parallel teams evolve features and whole products incrementally, while occasionally introducing new concepts and technologies. Developers are free to innovate as they go along, however; therefore, they must synchronize their changes frequently so that product components all work together. For example, a team developing a drawing feature must continually synchronize its changes with the teams developing the file management and printer control features so that users can save and print the objects that they draw.

Frequent Synchronizations and Periodic Stabilizations

In our 1995 book *Microsoft Secrets*, Richard Selby and I observed Microsoft over a two-and-a-half-year period, conducted in-depth interviews with thirty-eight key people (including Bill Gates), and reviewed thousands of pages of confidential project documentation and "postmortem" reports. We identified a relatively consistent approach to product development and decided to label this the synch-and-stabilize approach. The essence is simple: continually *synchronize* what people are doing as individuals and as members of parallel teams, and periodically *stabilize* the evolving product features in increments as a project proceeds, rather than once at the end of a project.

Microsoft people refer to their techniques variously as the milestone, daily build, nightly build, or zero-defect process. (The term "build" refers to the act of putting together, or "integrating," partially completed or finished pieces of a software product during the development process to see what functions work or what problems exist, usually by completely recompiling and linking the source code components and executing a simple automated regression test.) These techniques address a problem common to many firms in highly competitive, rapidly changing industries: two or three people can no longer build many of the new, highly complex products; they require much larger teams, and the team members must also invent and innovate as they develop the product. Team members thus need to create components that are interdependent but difficult to define accurately in the early stages of the development cycle. In these situations, projects must find a way to proceed that structures and coordinates what the individual members do while allowing them enough flexibility to be creative and evolve the product's details in stages. To save time and produce better features, the development approach should also allow developers to test the product with customers and refine their designs during the development process.

In a variety of industries, many companies now use prototyping as well as multiple cycles of concurrent design, build, and test activities to control iterations as well as incremental changes in product development. (See examples in Wheelwright and Clark, 1992.) In the computer software community, since the mid-1970s, researchers and managers have talked about "iterative enhancement," a "spiral model" for iterating among the phases in project development, and "concurrent development" of multiple phases and activities. (See Basili and Turner, 1975; Boehm, 1988; Aoyama, 1993.) Many firms have been slow to adopt these ideas formally. Nonetheless, the basic idea shared among these approaches is that users' needs for many types of software are so difficult to understand, and that changes in hardware and software technologies are so rapid, that it is unwise to attempt to design a software system completely in advance. Instead, projects should iterate as well as concurrently manage several design, build, and testing cycles while they move forward to completing a product.

This iterative as well as incremental and concurrent-engineering style contrasts to a more sequential or "waterfall" approach to product development. In the waterfall approach, projects attempt to "freeze" a product specification, create a design, build components, and then merge these components together—primarily at the end of the project in one large integration and testing phase (figure 7.1). This approach to software development was common in the 1970s and 1980s (see Royce, 1970). It remains a basic model for project planning in many industries. (See Wheelwright and Clark, 1992, as well as, e.g., Urban and Hauser, 1993; Ulrich and Eppinger, 1995.) The waterfall model has gradually lost favor, however, because companies usually build improved products if they can change specifications and designs, get feedback from customers, and continually test components as the products are evolving.

As a result, a growing number of companies in software and other industries—including Microsoft plus many others—now follow a process that iterates among design, building components, and testing, as well as overlapping these phases and containing more interactions with customers during development. Many companies also ship preliminary versions of their products, incrementally adding features

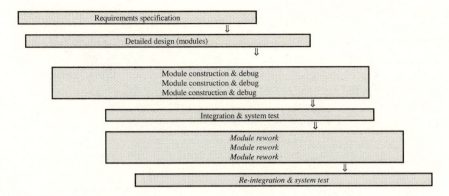

Figure 7.1. Simplified Waterfall Development Process

or functionality over time in different product "releases." In addition, many companies integrate pieces of their products together frequently (usually not daily, but often biweekly or monthly). This is useful to determine what works and what does not, without waiting until the end of the project—which may be several years in duration.

Key Strategies in Microsoft's Development Process

Two specific implementation principles best characterize the techniques that make the synch-and-stabilize style of product development work: (1) *focus creativity by evolving features and "fixing" resources* and (2) *do everything in parallel with frequent synchronizations.*

Microsoft uses the first strategy—*focus creativity by evolving features and "fixing" resources*—to define products and organize the development process. While having creative people in a high-technology company is important, it is often more important to *direct* their creativity. Managers can do this by getting development personnel to think about features that large amounts of people will pay money for and by putting pressure on projects by limiting their resources, such as staffing and schedule. Otherwise, software developers run the risk of never shipping anything to market. This risk especially becomes a problem in fast-moving industries, when individuals or teams have unfocused or highly volatile user requirements, frequently change interdependent components during a project, and do not synchronize their work as they go along.

Microsoft teams begin a project by creating a "vision statement" that defines the goals for a new product and prioritizes the user activities that need to be supported by the product features (figure 7.2). Product managers (marketing specialists) take charge of this task, which they do while consulting program managers, who specialize in writing up functional specifications of the product. Next, the program managers, in consultation with developers, write a functional specification that outlines the product features in sufficient depth to organize schedules and staffing

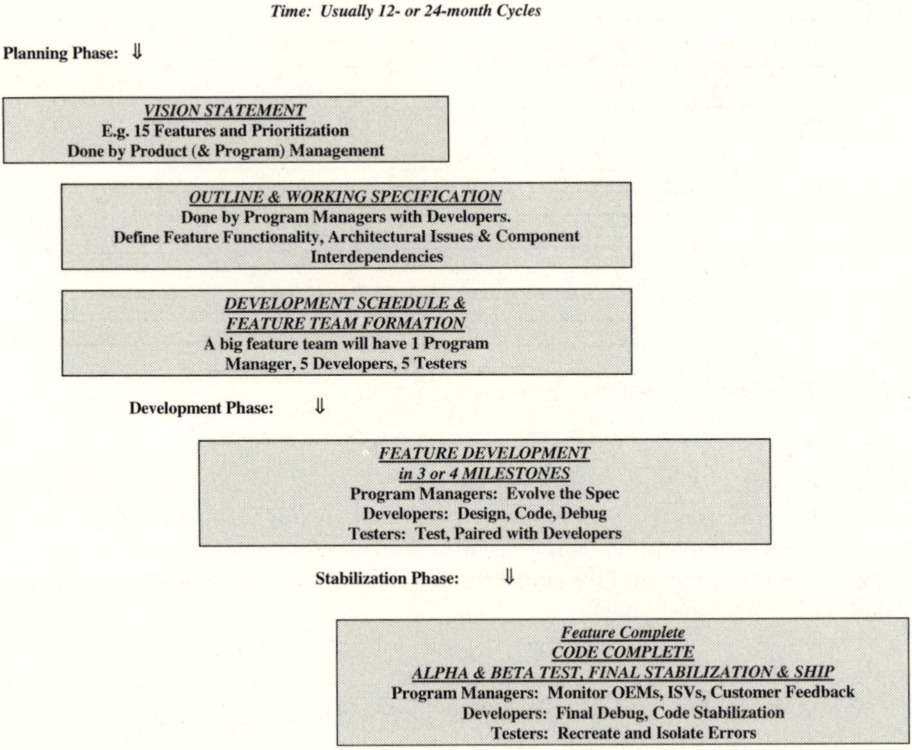

Time: Usually 12- or 24-month Cycles

Planning Phase: ⇓

> **VISION STATEMENT**
> E.g. 15 Features and Prioritization
> Done by Product (& Program) Management

> **OUTLINE & WORKING SPECIFICATION**
> Done by Program Managers with Developers.
> Define Feature Functionality, Architectural Issues & Component
> Interdependencies

> **DEVELOPMENT SCHEDULE &**
> **FEATURE TEAM FORMATION**
> A big feature team will have 1 Program
> Manager, 5 Developers, 5 Testers

Development Phase: ⇓

> **FEATURE DEVELOPMENT**
> **in 3 or 4 MILESTONES**
> Program Managers: Evolve the Spec
> Developers: Design, Code, Debug
> Testers: Test, Paired with Developers

Stabilization Phase: ⇓

> *Feature Complete*
> **CODE COMPLETE**
> **ALPHA & BETA TEST, FINAL STABILIZATION & SHIP**
> Program Managers: Monitor OEMs, ISVs, Customer Feedback
> Developers: Final Debug, Code Stabilization
> Testers: Recreate and Isolate Errors

Figure 7.2. Microsoft's "Synch-and-Stabilize" Development Process

allocations. But the specification document does not try to decide all the details of each feature or to lock the project into the original set of features. During product development, the team members will revise the feature set and feature details as they learn more about what should be in the product. Experience at Microsoft suggests that the feature set in a specification document may change by 30 percent or more.

The project managers then divide the product and the project into parts (features and small feature teams) and divide the project schedule into three or four milestone junctures (sequential subprojects) that represent completion points for major portions of the product (figure 7.3). All the feature teams go through a complete cycle of development, feature integration, testing, and fixing problems in each milestone subproject. Moreover, throughout the whole project, the feature teams synchronize their work by building the product, and by finding and fixing errors, on a daily and weekly basis. At the end of a milestone subproject, the developers fix almost all errors that have been detected in the evolving product. These error corrections stabilize the product and enable the team to have a clear understanding of which portions of the product have been completed. The development team may then proceed to the next milestone and, eventually, to the ship date.

Microsoft also structures projects into sequential subprojects containing prioritized features, with buffer time (20 to 50 percent of total alloted time) within each

Time: Usually 2 to 4 months per Milestone

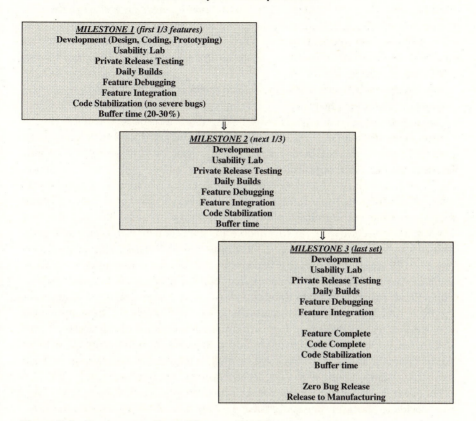

MILESTONE 1 *(first 1/3 features)*
Development (Design, Coding, Prototyping)
Usability Lab
Private Release Testing
Daily Builds
Feature Debugging
Feature Integration
Code Stabilization (no severe bugs)
Buffer time (20-30%)

MILESTONE 2 *(next 1/3)*
Development
Usability Lab
Private Release Testing
Daily Builds
Feature Debugging
Feature Integration
Code Stabilization
Buffer time

MILESTONE 3 *(last set)*
Development
Usability Lab
Private Release Testing
Daily Builds
Feature Debugging
Feature Integration

Feature Complete
Code Complete
Code Stabilization
Buffer time

Zero Bug Release
Release to Manufacturing

Figure 7.3. Development Phase Milestone Breakdowns

subproject to allow people time to respond to unexpected difficulties or delays or to add features during the project. Short vision statements and outline specifications are used, rather than complete product specifications and detailed designs, before coding because teams realize that they cannot determine in advance everything that the developers will need to do to build a good product. This approach leaves developers and program managers room to innovate or adapt to changed or unforeseen competitive opportunities and threats. Particularly for applications products, development teams also try to come up with features that map directly to activities that typical customers perform, and this requires continual observation and testing with users during development. In addition, most application product designs have modular architectures that allow teams to incrementally add or combine features in a straightforward, predictable manner.

Managers generally allow team members to set their own schedules but only after the developers have analyzed tasks in detail (half-day to three-day chunks, for example) and asked developers to commit personally to the schedules they set. Managers then "fix" project resources by limiting the number of people they allocate to any one project. They also try to limit the time projects spend, especially in applications like office or multimedia products, so that teams can delete features if they fall too far behind. (Cutting features to save schedule time is not always possible with operating systems projects, however, where reliability of the system is more important than features and where many features are closely coupled and cannot be so easily deleted individually.)

Microsoft uses the second strategy—*do everything in parallel with frequent synchronizations*—to manage the process of developing and shipping products. The objective here is to bring some discipline to the development process without trying to control every moment of every developer's day. Managers in many different companies talk about making their companies less bureaucratic, more innovative, and faster to react through organization and process "reengineering" and "restructuring" so as to speed up product development. But complex products often require large teams of hundreds of people, not small teams of a dozen or fewer engineers; and large teams can make communication and coordination extremely difficult and slow. Large-scale projects are simpler to schedule and manage if they proceed with clearly defined functional groups and sequential phases and precise rules and controls. This approach, however, may excessively restrain innovation and may underemphasize the importance of synchronizing work frequently. Communication and coordination difficulties across the functions and phases may also result in the project taking more time and people to complete than projects that overlap tasks and make people share responsibilities and work in small, nimble teams. What Microsoft tries to do, then, is allow many small teams and individuals enough freedom to work in parallel yet still function as one large team. The teams also adhere to a few rigid rules that enforce a high degree of coordination and communication.

For example, one of the few rules developers must follow is that, on whatever day they decide to check in their pieces of code, they must do so by a particular time, such as by 5:00 P.M. (as Dave Maritz mentioned in the earlier quotation). This allows the team to put available components together, completely recompile the product source code, and create a new "build" of the evolving product by the end of the day or by the next morning and then start testing and debugging immediately. (This rule is analogous to telling children that they can do whatever they want all day, but *they must go to bed at 9:00 o'clock*.) Another rule is that if developers check in code that "breaks" the build by preventing it from completing the recompilation, they must fix the defect immediately. (This actually resembles Toyota's famous production system, where factory workers stop the manufacturing lines whenever they notice a defect in a car they are assembling; see Cusumano, 1985.)

Product teams also test features as they build them from multiple perspectives, including bringing in customers from "off the street" to try prototypes in a usability lab. In addition, nearly all Microsoft teams work on a single physical site with common development languages (primarily C, with some C++), common coding styles, and standardized development tools. A common site and common language and tools help teams communicate, debate design ideas, and resolve problems face-to-face. Project teams also use a small set of quantitative metrics to guide decisions, such as when to move forward in a project or when to ship a product to market. For example, managers rigorously track progress of the daily builds by monitoring how many bugs are newly opened, resolved (such as by eliminating duplicates or deferring fixes), fixed, and active.

Beyond "Hacking": Combining Structure with Flexibility

Some people may argue that Microsoft's key practices in product development—daily synchronizations through product builds, periodic milestone stabilizations, and continual testing—are no more than process and technical "fixes" for a "hacker" software organization that is now building huge software systems. I do not really disagree, but we also think that Microsoft has some insightful ideas on how to combine structure with flexibility in product development—and thereby *focus creativity*.

Actually,the term "hacker" is not necessarily a bad word in the PC industry. It goes back to the early days of computer programming in the 1960s, when long-haired, unkempt technical wizards would sit down at a computer with no formal plans, designs, development processes, or testing procedures and just "bang on" a keyboard and "hack away" at coding (see Levy, 1984). This approach worked for small computer programs that one person or a small handful of people could write—such as the first versions of DOS, Lotus 1-2-3, WordPerfect, Word, or Excel. It became unworkable as PC software programs grew into hundreds of thousands and then millions of lines of code.

Formal plans and processes existed first in the mainframe computer industry, where software systems had grown to this million-line-plus size even by the end of the 1960s (see Cusumano, 1991). Yet PC software companies have been unwilling to give up their traditions and cultures completely. Nor would it be wise for them to do so, given the rapid pace of change in PC hardware and software technologies and the need for continual innovation.

No company has taken advantage of the exploding demand for PC software better than Microsoft. Similarly, I believe, no PC software company has done a better job of keeping some basic elements of the hacker culture while adding just enough structure to build today's and probably tomorrow's PC software products. It continues to be a challenge for Microsoft to make products reliable enough for companies to buy, powerful enough so that the products' features solve real-world problems, and simple enough for novice consumers to understand. To achieve these somewhat conflicting goals for a variety of markets, Microsoft still encourages some teams to experiment and make lots of changes without much up-front planning. Projects generally remain under control, however, because of how teams of programmers and testers frequently synchronize and periodically stabilize their changes.

Since the late 1980s, Microsoft has used variations of the synch-and-stabilize approach to build Publisher, Works, Excel, Word, Office, Windows NT, Windows 95, Internet Explorer, and other products. Of course, the synch-and-stabilize process does not guarantee on-time or bug-free products. Creating new, large-scale software products on a precisely predicted schedule and with no major defects are extremely difficult goals in the PC industry. Microsoft and other PC software companies also try to replace products quickly and usually announce overly ambitious deadlines, which contribute to their appearance of being chronically late. Nonetheless, without its synch-and-stabilize structured approach, Microsoft would probably never have been able to design, build, and ship the products it now offers and plans to offer in the future.

Microsoft resembles companies from many industries that do incremental or iterative product development as well as concurrent engineering. It has also adapted software engineering practices introduced earlier by other companies (such as various testing techniques) and has "reinvented the wheel" on many occasions (such as concluding the hard way that accumulating historical metric data is useful to analyze bug trends and establish realistic project schedules; see Selby, 1990). Microsoft is distinctive, however, in the degree to which it has introduced a structured hackerlike approach to software product development that works reasonably well for both small- and large-scale products. Furthermore, Microsoft is a fascinating example of how culture and competitive strategy can drive product development and the innovation process. The Microsoft culture centers around fervently antibureaucratic PC programmers who do not like a lot of rules, structure, or planning. Its competitive strategy revolves around identifying mass markets quickly, introducing products that are "good enough" (rather than waiting until something is "perfect"), improving these products by incrementally evolving their features, and then selling multiple product versions and upgrades to customers around the world.

Conclusion: The Contrast with Sequential Development

The principles behind the synch-and-stabilize philosophy thus add a semblance of order to the fast-moving, often chaotic world of PC software development. There are no "silver bullets" here that will solve major problems with a single simplistic solution. Rather, there are specific approaches, tools, and techniques, a few rigid rules, and highly skilled people whose culture aligns with this approach. As I've suggested, several elements distinguish synch-and-stabilize from older, more traditional sequential and more rigid styles of product development (table 7.1).

First, as is becoming more common in software and other industries, Microsoft does not follow a sequential "waterfall" process. It does not treat product development and testing as separate phases done one after the other, albeit with iterations back and forth if things do not proceed exactly according to plan. Rather, Microsoft teams *do development and testing in parallel*. The process is similar to how individuals might "hack away" at designing, coding, and testing as they go. It also resembles "concurrent engineering" practices in other industries that overlap many activities and phases.

Second, Microsoft does not try to write and "freeze" a complete functional specification and detailed design up front in a project, before starting to build the product's components. Rather, Microsoft *allows specifications to evolve*—adding or cutting features, experimenting with design details—as projects proceed and test the evolving product. The complete specification is more an *output* of a project than an *input* to the development process. Microsoft also has no real detailed design phase or documentation; *the code is the detailed design and the documentation.* This is, again, typical

Table 7.1. Synch-and-Stabilize versus Sequential Development

Synch-and-stabilize	Sequential process
Spec, development, testing in parallel	Separate phases in "waterfall" sequence
Vision statement and evolving spec (spec = output, not input)	Complete spec and detailed design before coding
Prioritized features built in 3–4 milestones	Build all pieces of a product simultaneously
Frequent synchs (daily builds) and intermediate stabilizations (milestones)	One "late and large" integration and test phase at project end
"Fixed" ship dates and multiple release cycle	Feature and product "perfection"
Customer feedback during development	Feedback as input for future projects
Large teams work like small teams	Many individuals work in functional groups

of a hacker approach rather than a "mature" software organization, even though many firms end up with specifications and designs that evolve considerably over the course of a project. We think Microsoft has particularly effective mechanisms to allow specifications to evolve but keep changes more or less under control.

Third, Microsoft does not try to build all the pieces of a product simultaneously, for example, by breaking down a detailed design and assigning all the modules or features to different people and teams. Rather, Microsoft *breaks up a design into features, prioritizes them, and then builds clusters of features* in three or four milestones. Teams usually work on the most important features in the first milestone, the second most important features in the second milestone, and so on. For products where features are not so closely coupled, projects will drop features from the last milestone if they fall too far behind in the schedule.

Fourth, Microsoft does not try to bring together all the pieces of a product for the first time in one late and large integration and system test phase at the end of a project. This occurs if a project builds all pieces in parallel and has no way to synchronize or test them together during the development process. Rather, Microsoft uses the concept of frequent builds to *synchronize the work of many individuals and teams on a daily or weekly basis*. It also uses the concept of *milestone subprojects to stabilize subsets of features* in three or four increments. These practices resemble the "incremental builds" used in other firms. Nonetheless, we think Microsoft stands out for how well it has refined and institutionalized this style of development.

Fifth, Microsoft does not necessarily try to complete and perfect every feature initially proposed at the beginning of a project. Rather, and particularly with applications products, Microsoft will set *time and personnel limits* and *establish goals for reducing the most severe bugs*. Teams will wait until the next "release" of the product to add features they could not complete in the previous project or to fix minor bugs that they did not detect or could not fix. In this way, Microsoft now *avoids the common dilemma of working and reworking a product in an endless cycle of changes, additions, and bug fixes*. Other software firms have multiple release cycles, as do companies in industries that put out annual or frequent "model changes." Microsoft, though, has pushed this style of development and marketing to a fine art. It has even brought the annual model change idea to software—hence the names Windows 95 and Office 95. (Of course, this strategy of annual models will backfire or at least become an embarrassment if Microsoft cannot predict schedules accurately enough to finish within a given year.)

Sixth, Microsoft does not wait to collect and utilize customer feedback until projects finish and market a product. Rather, Microsoft *continuously incorporates customer feedback throughout the development process.* This begins with analyses of users in the product planning phases and continues with the testing of prototypes in a usability lab and the delivery of prerelease versions to beta-test sites. Furthermore, Microsoft sends to the development groups detailed weekly reports on customer inquiries made to the product support organization. This information affects future product designs as well as features currently under development.

Finally, Microsoft does not allow developers to write software as if no one else existed in the company. Nor does Microsoft build software with huge teams divided into designers, developers, and testers working sequentially in separate departments, "handing off" work to the next phase in accordance with lots of fixed procedures and the requirement to document everything they do. Rather, Microsoft develops software in multifunctional teams and does a number of things to *make large teams work like small teams* in the sense that teams and individuals have a great deal of freedom to invent and change their designs as they proceed in a project because of the integration and project management techniques that Microsoft uses. As I've discussed, this results in an ability to *focus creativity,* which is especially important in fast-moving markets where firms need to invent while designing as well as deliver something quickly and then rapidly incorporate feedback from customers.

References

Aoyama, Mikio. 1993. "Concurrent-Development Process Model." *IEEE Software* (July): 46–55.

Basili, Victor R., and Albert J. Turner. 1975. "Iterative Enhancement: A Practical Technique for Software Development." *IEEE Transactions on Software Engineering,* SE-1 (4): 390–96.

Boehm, Barry W. 1988. "A Spiral Model of Software Development and Enhancement." *IEEE Computer* (May): 61–72.

Cusumano, Michael A. 1985. *The Japanese Automobile Industry: Technology and Management at Nissan and Toyota.* Cambridge: Harvard University Press.

———. 1991. *Japan's Software Factories: A Challenge to U.S. Management.* New York: Oxford University Press.

Cusumano, Michael A., and Richard W. Selby. 1995. *Microsoft Secrets: How the World's Most Powerful Software Company Creates Technology, Shapes Markets, and Manages People.* New York: Simon and Schuster.

Levy, Steven. 1984. *Hackers: Heroes of the Computer Revolution.* New York: Anchor.

Nonaka, Ikujiro, and Hirotaka Takeuchi. 1995. *The Knowledge-Creating Company.* New York: Oxford University Press.

Rebello, Kathy. 1996. "Inside Microsoft: The Untold Story of How the Internet Forced Bill Gates to Reverse Course." *Business Week* (July 15): 56–70.

Royce, Winston W. 1970. "Managing the Development of Large Software Systems," *Proceedings of IEEE WESCON* (August): 1–9.

Selby, Richard W. 1990. "Empirically Based Analysis of Failures in Software Systems." *IEEE Transactions on Reliability* 39(4): 444–54.

Ulrich, Karl, and Steven Eppinger. 1995. *Product Design and Development*. New York: McGraw-Hill.

Urban, Glen.L., and John R. Hauser. 1993. *Design and Marketing of New Products*. Englewood Cliffs, N.J.: Prentice-Hall.

Wheelright, Steven C., and Kim B. Clark. 1992. *Revolutionizing Product Development*. New York: Free Press.

8

Cooperation and Knowledge Creation

GIORGIO DE MICHELIS

Today there is general consensus on the idea that organizations cannot get and/or maintain effectiveness without continuous organizational changes allowing them to maintain their structural coupling with a highly turbulent, highly complex environment. However, the characterization of factors rendering an organization capable of getting and/or maintaining its effectiveness through organizational changes remains a controversial issue. This point is the most relevant one for those such as myself whose interest lies in designing effective computer-based support systems for cooperation among people working together.

In contrast to the inventors and/or promoters of business process reengineering (BPR; Hammer, 1990; Hammer and Champy, 1993; Davenport, 1993), other scholars have paid attention to the capability of organizations to learn and/or sustain their members' learning (Argyris and Schoen, 1978, 1996; Senge, 1991) or to create knowledge (Nonaka and Takeuchi, 1995), considering learning the necessary condition for any organizational policy that advocates continuous changes in order to face the growing complexity of the market.

Without radicalizing the opposition between the two approaches—quite recently even the BPR side has recognized the relevance of the human factor in organizational effectiveness (Hammer, 1996; Davenport et al., 1996)—I am with the learning side because, as I will show, cooperation is a matter of communication, learning, and knowledge sharing.

More precisely, this essay aims to understand the type of support computer-based systems may offer to knowledge creation processes (Nonaka and Takeuchi, 1995). In order to reach this objective, I develop the theoretical framework proposed by

This essay presents research that has been conducted with the financial support of the European Community within the Esprit LTR project, DESARTE. Draft versions of this paper were presented at the Toshiba Chair Symposium "Human Oriented Information Technologies and Complex Systems," organized in Tokyo by Keio University in November 1996, and at the Conference on Comparative Study on Knowledge Creation organized in Honolulu (Hawaii) by the Jaims and Sasakawa Peace Foundation in December 1996. The case study at Domus Academy was conducted together with Eliana Covarrubias and Edmundo Leiva-Lobos of the Cooperation Technology Laboratory of the University of Milan and Claudio Moderini and Marco Susani of Domus Academy and discussed in depth with Ina Wagner and Rüdiger Lainer of the Vienna group of the Desarte Project. My sincere appreciation goes to all them. Finally, Alessandra Agostini and Monica Divitini deserve special thanks for their careful reading of various drafts of this paper.

Ikujiro Nonaka and Hirotaka Takeuchi, grounding this framework on the practice of cooperation and focusing it on processes instead of organizations. I therefore propose the integration of their knowledge creation model with the cooperative process model developed at the University of Milan-Bicocca (De Michelis, 1995a, 1995b, 1997).

This work offers three main theoretical contributions: (1) the four knowledge transformation types defined by Nonaka and Takeuchi are characterized in terms of the positional relations between the actors of a cooperative process. This enforces their grounding at the level of the practices of the actors; (2) it is shown that knowledge creation is one principal factor allowing an increase in the value/cost ratio of a cooperative process since it enhances the capability of managing its complexity. In this context, complexity is considered not a generic property responsible for the nondeterminacy and unpredictability of the postmodern society but a property generated by the increase of communication characterizing it; (3) it is argued that knowledge creation does not require the support of large information bases and sophisticated information-processing and -retrieval systems; rather, it requires the information and communication technology to create a space that supports, with continuity, openness, and multiplicity, the awareness of its users with respect to the continuously changing context in which they are embedded.

Finally, the approach offered here is extended to the analysis of knowledge creation within organizations performing various cooperative processes concurrently, where knowledge creation among organization members must also be considered. Within this framework a case study has been conducted at a laboratory for industrial design: namely, Domus Academy, which can be considered an emblematic Italian school of design. This case study offers some insight into one of the most peculiar aspects of Italian industry (world leader in the creation of clothes, furniture, and accessories).

Industrial design is a rather creative and complex activity, where knowledge creation is a continuously ongoing process permeating both the cooperation between the designers and their relations with the customers. On the one hand, an industrial design laboratory must pay attention to the way in which its members are capable of learning from their own and others' experiences in order to improve the quality of their performances and develop the company style; on the other, it must continuously improve their capability to understand customer needs and communicate the design results to its clients. As will be seen later, from the knowledge creation viewpoint, industrial design can be considered a paradigmatic process where most critical issues appear in very clear terms.

Cooperative Processes

From the viewpoint of its work practice, a group of persons engaged in a common performance is not an organizational structure (even if innovative enterprises today recognize groups as their basic microorganizational units); rather, it is a social aggregate cooperating in a work process, participating in a cooperative process (De

Michelis, 1996). As a social phenomenon, a cooperative process is complex: the group involved in it is a network of social relationships that cannot be reduced to any functional and/or hierarchical model. Despite any attempt to plan its evolution with respect to its expected outcome, what its history will be is unpredictable. The participants in a cooperative process in fact change from time to time, since some actors may leave it and new ones join it, while some actors have a temporary engagement in it. Moreover, while performing, they change their understanding, their image of the requested actions, their ways of performing these actions, their mutual agreements in a history of successes and failures, all in a common experience of action, communication, and learning.

A cooperative process can be characterized by the communicative relations binding its participants to each other and with the actions they are performing (Winograd and Flores, 1986; Keen, 1991; Medina-Mora et al., 1992; De Michelis and Grasso, 1994; De Michelis, 1995a, 1995b, 1997). The relevance of communication and language practices within organization has also been advocated by proposers of an action perspective within organizational theories (Nohria, Gulati, 1994), who stress the role of managerial rhetoric in shaping the organizational structures and of the interplay between contingent actions (bricolage) and organizational structures to drive change.

The basic communicative relations within a cooperative process are therefore the conversations giving rise to the cooperative process itself, where the customers (i.e., those who have a condition to be satisfied) and the performers (i.e., those who can satisfy it) reach an agreement on the actions to be performed and share the evaluation of their execution. The actions performed within a cooperative process are, in fact, embedded in the conversations between its customers and its performers: they are performed through their *collaboration*.

But a cooperative process is not characterized only by the relations between its customers and performers, by their collaboration. Since a cooperative process, if not a trivial one, has more than one customer and more than one performer, the relations (conversations) among the customers and the relations among the performers are also relevant and play important roles, giving rise to other forms of cooperation (more details about the latter, which can be characterized as two different forms of *codecision*, can be found in: De Michelis, 1996); this issue will be taken up again hereafter.

The terms *customer* and *performer* can generate some confusion in the reader, since they are generally used to define the roles of market actors. Nonetheless, probably because of the fact that the classic economy market model permeates the rhetoric of organizations (Nohria and Gulati, 1994), it is difficult to find alternative names for the concepts introduced here. It is therefore necessary to clarify the different way in which they are used here.

In this context, customer and performer do not define *roles*; rather, they define *positions*. A customer is not a person who has the role of making requests to the performers within a cooperative process. Although this is what reveals the market in the classic economy, it does not capture the essential features of cooperative processes. On the contrary, it is the fact of making a request for action that puts a person in a customer position. In other words, it can be said that making a request for action means assuming a customer position and that agreeing to satisfy a request for action means assuming a performer position. Whenever within a conversation a person negotiates the satisfaction of a request or makes reference to it, she is occupying a customer position; conversely, whenever she negotiates the action she has to perform to satisfy a request or makes reference to it, she is occupying a performer position.

The three forms of cooperation just mentioned correspond therefore to three types of (positional) relations, distinguished from one another by the positions occupied by those participating in them. When two persons are conversing about a common request or about a common performance, they are codeciding (De Michelis, 1996); when they are negotiating a performance, they are collaborating.

Cooperative processes are to some degree recursive: within a cooperative process, in fact, the actors can consider each action to be performed as a cooperative process in itself. Moreover, in order to make a requested action possible, frequently either the performers themselves or the customers too may be requested to perform some new actions. These actions can be negotiated not only within conversations between customers and performers but also within conversations among the customers and among the performers: therefore, the relations between the actors of a cooperative process have a continuously changing nature, since they change together with their objects (with the request for action to which they make reference). Any breakdown occurring to a performer while she is performing an action, for example, induces her to make a request for help, shifting her temporarily from a performer to a customer position. In the same way, if a customer is requested to provide some information characterizing the context in which the performance she requires falls, then she temporarily becomes a performer, changing her position. The success of a cooperative process depends not only on the effectiveness of its actors in all their positional relations but also, and to a greater extent, on their capability to switch from one to another when necessary.

Whenever an event in the cooperative process induces one of its actors to make and/or to receive a new request for a performance, she may move from one position to another, changing her relations with the other actors accordingly. These movements are so rapid and frequent that a strong continuity is needed between the different positions an actor of a cooperative process may occupy.

The recursiveness of a cooperative process also generates a problem of granularity affecting both the understanding and the behavior of its actors: if within a cooperative process a group of actors opens a subcooperative process in order to get an action done that is necessary for the successful completion of the larger process, then, while cooperating, those actors can be in different positions with respect to the main process and its subprocess. In this unavoidable situation they may not interpret their mutual positions consistently, since some make reference to the main process and its condition of satisfaction and others to the subprocess. Understanding customer and performer as mobile positions and not as fixed roles is the only way to allow rapid solutions of such inconsistencies, through the explicit negotiation of the level of granularity that needs to be taken into account.

Both customers and performers, therefore, are in all senses participants in the cooperative process; they cooperate in it consuming (some of) their resources and creating together its value. Even if the value of a cooperative process depends on the condition of satisfying customers, it is not created by the performers for the customers. Again, the classic economics model says that it is, but from our point of view this is a rather mystifying abstraction and simplification. In what sense is the value a "value"? How can value and cost be compared? In very general and abstract terms, the value of a cooperative process can be characterized by the increase of the potential for action it generates; and its cost can be characterized by the potential for action it extinguishes.

The knowledge—the practical knowledge, the knowledge for action—generated within a cooperative process is the principal component of its value. For both customers and performers, a successful cooperative process generates new knowledge: thanks to it, the former become able to overcome the problem for which they asked help, while the latter increase their experience, improving their effectiveness in future performances as well as their public reputation. Nelson and Winter in their evolutionary economics (1982) and Nonaka and Takeuchi with their knowledge-creating organization model (1995) offer many arguments to support this point.

There is a direct link connecting knowledge creation and communication in a cooperative process. Through their conversations the participants in a cooperative process learn, both individually and together, and share an experience constituting them into a whole, into a community (the concept of community of practice has deeply inspired this observation; see Lave and Wenger, 1991; Brown and Duguid, 1991; Cook and Brown, 1998). Despite the fact they occupy different positions in it, they share a space (physical and/or virtual; this point cannot be explored further here; for some hints on it, see De Michelis, 1996), a set of artifacts (tools, resources, documents, and/or information), a language (De Michelis, 1995a, 1995b), the knowledge of the world they live in and of the possibilities it opens, the history of the cooperative process in which they participate, and the value they create within it. Sharing an experience reflects itself in sharing the knowledge created and used in it: participating in a cooperative process, being a member of a group, can only be obtained through a learning process (see Lave and Wenger, 1991).

Knowledge Creation within Cooperative Processes

Considering learning within cooperative processes as a knowledge-creation process (Nonaka and Takeuchi, 1995) offers new insights about both organizational memory (Walsh and Ungson, 1991) and organizational learning (Argyris and Schoen, 1978, 1996; Senge, 1991). On the one hand, it focuses on the dynamic nature of the knowledge organizations use while performing, avoiding its reduction to the information they store in electronic and/or physical archives; on the other, it avoids the reduction both of learning to adaptation and of social to individual learning.

Knowledge-creation processes within organizations have been characterized by Nonaka and Takeuchi (1995) in terms of tacit and explicit knowledge transformation processes. As mentioned, they are interested not in knowledge per se but in the process through which knowledge is continuously created, modified, updated: the emphasis is, therefore, on the practice through which the members of a work group (or of a whole organization) increase their ability to perform individually and collectively. Their attention is focused on pragmatic knowledge, on knowledge for action, both when it is embodied in the capabilites of the group members (tacit knowledge), and when it is described in documents and/or information bases (explicit knowledge). Instead of considering new knowledge as something that is added to the previous, they conceive it as something that transforms it, and therefore knowledge creation is performed through knowledge transformation. As shown in figure 8.1, the two types of knowledge taken into consideration by Nonaka and Takeuchi give rise to four types of knowledge transformation processes, characterizing four types of social interaction. The effectiveness of a work group depends on its capability to keep all four types of transformation active.

Consider knowledge creation within cooperative processes. Tacit knowledge is indirectly exhibited by the actors of a cooperative process when they are performing (i.e., when they are in the performer position), while explicit knowledge is exhibited when they declare a condition they need to be satisfied (i.e., when they are in the customer position). On the one hand, a person performing an activity that falls within her domain of competence knows how to do it, even if she generally does not know how to explain it; and, in the social dimension, a group of persons performing effectively together are able to interact and/or synchronize silently without spending time explaining to one another what each must do. On the other hand, no person can make a request for a performance to another person (i.e., can be in the customer position)

	Tacit knowledge *to*	Explicit knowledge
Tacit knowledge	Socialization	Externalization
from		
Explicit knowledge	Internalization	Combination

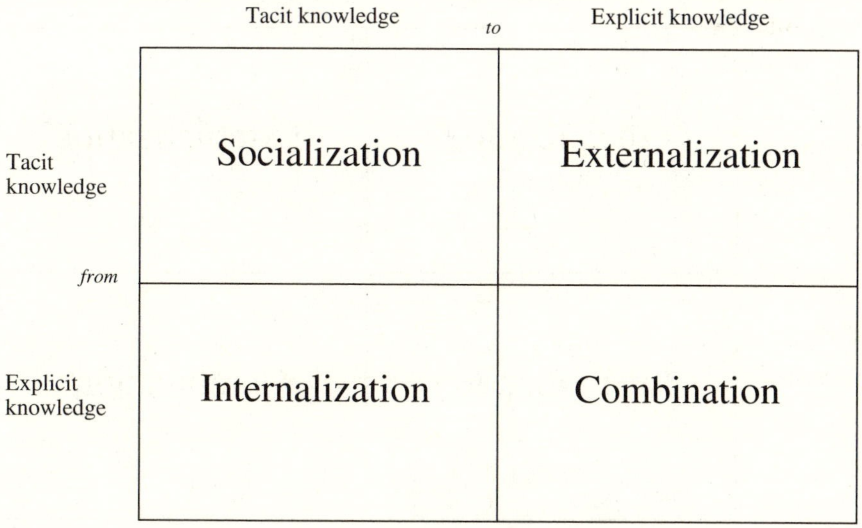

Figure 8.1. Knowledge transformation processes (from Nonaka & Takeuchi, 1995)

without making explicit her request in a document or at least in some precise words that could be formalized in a document; tacit customers do not exist!

The four types of knowledge transformation proposed by Nonaka and Takeuchi can therefore be coupled with the types of positional relations that bind the actors of a cooperative process (figure 8.2) already discussed.

Externalization and internalization both occur within a customer-performer relationship. Successful cooperation requires that within customer-performer interactions both internalization and externalization occur: if externalization is missing, then the customers do not get any value from the performance of the performers; if internalization is missing, then the performers cannot understand the conditions of satisfaction to be met. Internalization and externalization characterize the mutual learning between customers and performers within a cooperative process. In other words, they characterize the cooperation.

Socialization and combination are also relevant in complex cooperative processes, since they are, respectively, the processes through which performers and customers absorb complexity without spreading it into the process itself. On the one hand, through socialization the performers maintain their capability to cooperate smoothly and effectively, changing their synchronization in accordance with the changes of the spatial and temporal context and of the condition of satisfaction of the customers. On the other hand, through combination the customers get and maintain their agreement on the request they make to the performers.

Finally, recall that the actors of a cooperative process continuously change their mutual positions while performing. Accordingly, each knowledge trasformation type cannot be taken into account alone, disconnected from the others: successful socialization may require that externalization, internalization, and/or combination

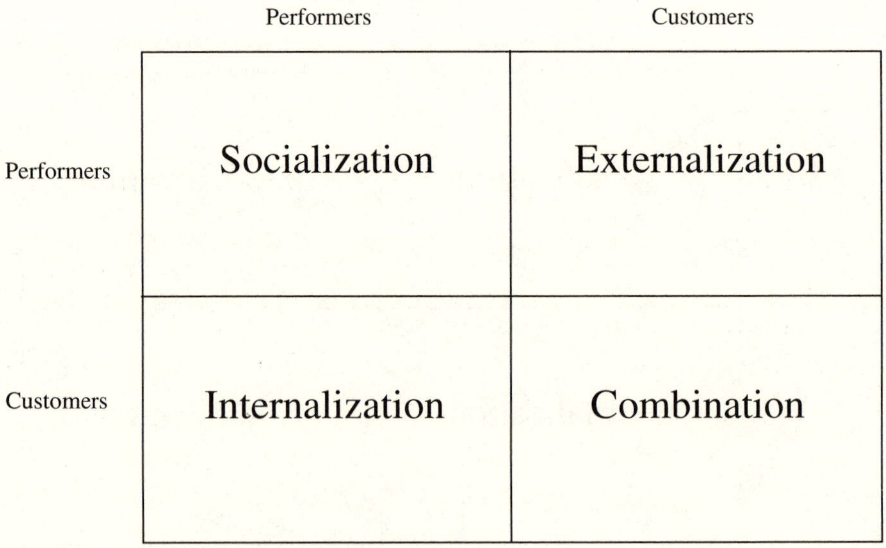

	Performers	Customers
Performers	Socialization	Externalization
Customers	Internalization	Combination

Figure 8.2. Customers and Performers and Knowledge Transformation

are performed effectively, and so on. This fact offers a new argument to sustain the need for organizations to become effective in all four knowledge transformation types, which has been already underlined by Nonaka and Takeuchi (1995). Moreover, it indicates that supporting any knowledge trasformation type requires supporting the other ones too and, last but not least, supporting a smooth switching between them.

Knowledge Creation within Organizations

What I have said up to this point focuses on the single cooperative process, analyzing and discussing how its members develop cooperation and knowledge creation. But the actors of a cooperative a process are also members of organizations, and this fact influences their behavior and therefore, if and how they they cooperate and create knowledge. Two problems related to this point arise from the organizational membership of the participants in a cooperative process: on the one hand, the organizations to which they belong do have other members performing other cooperative processes, and knowledge-creation processes should to a certain degree involve them too; on the other hand, the participants in a cooperative process do not belong to the same organization, and any organization is distinguished by its own knowhow and knowledge creation capabilities.

The case when the performers of a cooperative process constitute one whole organization, so that they are always participating in any of its knowledge creation processes, is a very simple, extreme case. Generally, an organization is concurrently involved in several cooperative processes, and each of its members is participating only in some, so that knowledge-creation processes are not involving all of them and therefore knowledge sharing within the organization becomes critical. What is needed is the capability to extend any knowledge-creation process occurring within a cooperative process so as to involve all members of the organization (more precisely, all members of the organization who have similar competencies). Training programs within an organization, as well as information and communication programs, are generally devoted to fulfilling this requirement, but they may fail to reach their objective and in fact frequently do so. As clarified earlier, participation in a knowledge-creation process is more than access to the documents (to the explicit knowledge) created within it or listening to a presentation describing a cooperative process and its achievements; rather, there must be a participation, as direct as possible, in the performances of the cooperative process in a way that activates all four types of knowledge transformation. Training and information programs, therefore, are effective with respect to this objective to the extent they are strictly integrated with the ongoing processes and to the extent they are occasions for crossfertilizations between the different ongoing cooperative processes, allowing any member of the organization peripheral participation (Lave and Wenger, 1991) in any one of them.

Knowledge sharing is always partial between different organizations, since their identities are characterized by their different (in terms of areas of competence, past experiences, work habits, objectives, and rules and procedures) knowledge-creation capabilities. It is useful, therefore, to distinguish, within a cooperative process, the knowledge through which customers and preformers share their common experience, and the knowledge through which the organization of the performers improves its capabilities in view of future performances. Merging and/or confusing these two knowledge-creation processes is dangerous, since imposing a generalized participation in a knowledge-creation process may affect its effectiveness, reducing its professional and organizational specificity. Moreover, any organization participating in a cooperative process may be interested in separating its internal knowledge-creation processes with respect to those involving other organizations in order to make an asset of part of the knowledge it creates. Any organization should separate, when needed, its internal knowledge-creation processes from those involving its clients. But separating them does not mean keeping separate the knowledge that is created within them: on the contrary, if and when internal knowledge-creation processes are distinguished by those involving both performers and customers, then great attention must be paid to the mechanisms granting a continuous interchange between them.

In general, therefore, knowledge-creation processes are more complex than those analyzed in the previous sections, since there is no one-to-one relation between any of them and the cooperative process within which it occurs. Instead, they introduce a high degree of multiplicity and autonomy to that process.

Cooperative Processes for Industrial Design: an Italian Case History

Domus Academy is a private educational institution dealing with innovation in industrial design. Its main and traditional activity is offering postgraduate and professional courses in various design-related areas (industrial design, fashion design, service design, interface design, design management) at its school and at customer sites. Domus Academy may be considered representative of the Italian school of design. Many of Italy's most highly reputed fashion and industrial designers teach its courses. The student body is very international (more than 60 percent of them come from abroad, increasingly from America and Asia).

In recent years, in order to support the educational activities and to develop a new business area, the Domus Academy's Research center was created. Here research projects in design-related areas are carried on, and innovative design projects are performed for several customers. The Research Center is currently well established, and several projects on different subjects are ongoing.

The work of the Research Center is comparable to that of an industrial design studio, with the difference that some of the Domus Academy projects may have a long and important research and brainstorming process before the initiation of the actual design of models, samples and prototypes. This makes these experiences particularly significant in regard to the conceptual creative phase.

In what follows, I make reference mainly to one of the projects recently undertaken at the Domus Academy Research Center. This project has been studied in depth by a team of the Cooperation Technology Laboratory of the University of Milan, in collaboration with some of the members of Domus Academy (namely, Marco

Susani, Director of the Research Center, and Claudio Moderini) within the Esprit Long Term Project Desarte (Covarrubias Gatica, De Michelis, and Leiva-Lobos, 1997). It was, moreover, discussed with the other Desarte partners (in particular Ina Wagner and Ruediger Lainer). Here I present and comment on some of the outcomes of that analysis and discussion.

The observed project is a research project for a company I call Fantasy, in order to maintain confidentiality between Domus Academy and its customers. Fantasy is a major Italian manufacturer of electrical switches for the home that is now considering entering the new market of *smart houses* through the production of electronic systems that control several different devices in the home. The project was commissioned by the marketing department of the company, but people from the R&D department were also involved. The company appointed one project leader on its side, plus another contact person who was mostly responsible for all communication with Domus Academy. The project had the aim of totally rethinking the idea of house switches, introducing the "interface design" concept, considering not only external shape but also access to the "software" functions. So, the Fantasy project needed innovative skills of conceptualization and rendering that required different innovative tools and methods.

Four members of Domus Academy played major roles in the Fantasy project:

- Marco (director of the Research Center) was appointed project leader, maintaining relations with the client.
- Mario (another design master at Domus Academy) was the other senior designer in the Fantasy project: he has almost the same level of skills and experiences as Marco and frequently collaborates with him in Domus Academy projects.
- Jozeph (a senior designer, at the Research Center for four years) was appointed project manager. He was responsible for coordinating the team and for respecting delivery deadlines.
- In Suk Il (a young designer temporarily working at Domus Academy) was the operative designer.

Other designers and graphic designers occasionally participated in some phases of the Fantasy projects, providing it with specialized skills (iconographic research, graphic rendering, model making, etc).

The Workplace and the Artifacts Populating It

DA operates on the top floor of a building outside Milan. The Research Center is located in a large (open space) laboratory where all the projects going on concurrently are hosted. The walls of the laboratory (as well as the doors of the cabinets) are fully decorated with photographs and drawings (figure 8.3). Each project occupies a portion of the laboratory constituting its work-space: the walls around the work-space of the Fantasy project are decorated with some pictures characterizing it (in particular, the different scenarios conceived by the project team at its beginning are represented through highly evocative images). The decoration of the Fantasy project work-space (as well as of any other project going on at the

Figure 8.3. Various Projects Are Ongoing at the Domus Academy Research Center

Research Center) captures the attention of visitors and of designers involved in the other projects and informs them of what is going on, acting as a trigger for crossfertilization and exchange of opinions. This cooperation style (peripheral participation; Lave, and Wenger, 1991) is stimulated by the master designers of Domus Academy.

The pictures decorating the work-space of the Fantasy project portray the smart house scenarios the designers have conceived. Jozeph's desk (with its work station) is near his assistant's (called the hot desk because that's where the work is really going on). In the background is Marco's office, whose door is almost always open. Near the desk Jozeph keeps some folders where he records and files the tracking of the project. Jozeph is responsible for maintaning the memory of the project, and in formal and informal meetings he updates the other designers about its evolution. Figure 8.4 shows the work-space.

The work-space of the Fantasy project is also populated by a large variety of artifacts: resources, tools, communication media. The latter (mainly telephone and e-mail) connect the physical work-space of the Fantasy project to the spaces where other actors are working (the clients, the master designers, etc.) and to various types of electronic archives (of Domus Academy as well as of other information sources), creating a virtual extension of it, where immaterial artifacts also become recognizable (plans, rules, etc.) The artifacts populating the virtually extended work-space of the Fantasy project define the potential for action of its designers. It should be emphasized that industrial designers do not substitute pencils, paper, and physical models with computer-based tools and electronic documents.

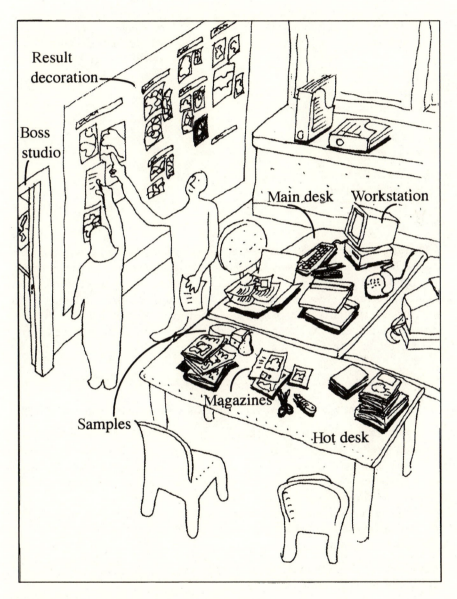

Figure 8.4. The Fantasy project work-space

The objects populating the Fantasy project work-space are:

Resources
  Magazines and Journals
  Draft design paper
  Various materials for physical modeling
  Different kinds of archives (also through Internet)

Tools
  Pencils and papers
  Cameras
  Work stations with a suite of productivity tools
  Tools for image processing
  A photocopy machine

Intermediate Outcomes
  Project folder (containing: letters, messages, notes, sketches, pictures, etc.)
  Archived material (activity reports, technical drawings, etc.)
  Samples

Immaterial Artifacts
  Project work-plan
  Domus Academy organizational rules
  Category matrices

Media
  Telephone, fax
  LAN (local area network) with Internet access

The *category matrix* is a peculiar immaterial artifact used in many steps along the process. It allows one to represent concepts and design problems in a structured way. In general, during a project several matrices are used, crossing different categories (for example, house types) and restrictions (for example, control requirements). In brief, a category matrix is a tool used to realize three important activities in a creative design process: developing ideas to their full potential, focusing the project, and suggesting further developments.

Observing the Evolution of the Fantasy Project

The Fantasy project was developed following a plan constituted by eight main phases.

- Preliminary contact with the client
- First meeting with the client
- Idea generation
- Researches
- Samples elaboration
- Strategy presentation and rendering
- Prepresentation
- Final presentation

Here I focus my description of the Fantasy project on the phases from idea generation to strategy presentation and rendering.

Other projects, continuing until product development, have two further phases that were not developed in the case of Fantasy:

- Engineering
- Final engineering

During the phases of the Fantasy project just mentioned, the Domus Academy team was involved in a diversified set of activities, among which the following can be considered the most characteristic.

First, almost every week the team has a session of joint collaboration, where Marco and/or Mario discuss with Joseph and In Suk Il the work the latter have previously done. During these meetings all the participants draw sketches of the new switches they are conceiving, evaluate the samples already prepared, and define the activities to be performed in the future. These activities are merged into a conversation where, on the one hand, the master designers continuously recall the clients' requests (frequently repeating their exact phrases) in order to avoid the design deviating with respect to their expectations; and on the other, they simulate the behavior of typical users of a smart house defined at the beginning of the project. At the end of these meetings each participant signs and collects his drafts in his folder, while Jozeph makes copies of those considered relevant for the project and puts them in the project folder. Even if the work style is highly collaborative, the project is managed in such a way that a fair recognition of individual contributions is granted.

Second, Jozeph and/or In Suk Il, while developing the drafts and creating samples, are frequently interrupted by other Domus Academy designers and occasional visitors. Their reaction to visits and interruptions is generally polite and patient; they explain what they are doing, making reference to the pictures on the walls, to the samples already created, and to some drafts they consider representative of their work, and they discuss the remarks, suggestions, and questions of the visitors, evaluating their impact on their design. Visits and interruptions are not considered lost time but rather are taken as occasions for learning, both through listening (they learn new ideas, new points of view, new options) and through speaking (they learn how to communicate their design effectively).

Third, the customers are not visiting the team while it is designing (the external visitors just mentioned are not involved in the project). This fact is not casual but is an organizational choice made by the Domus Academy Research Center, aiming to separate the designers, while they are creating, from the customers. The objective is to grant the team maximal freedom in their creative design, preventing customers from possibly conditioning choices. The separation has some drawbacks, because communication with the customers may diminish to such an extent that the latter lose awareness of what is going on and of what is expected. During the project the master designers—Marco and Mario—keep contact with the people from the Fantasy company alive in order to avoid a crisis situation.

Fourth, when deadlines are imminent the designers switch from an open-minded, creative collaboration to a more focused activity, devoted to the preparation of the deliverables. During these short periods (one to two weeks) the team expands to include graphic designers, who collaborate in the preparation of documents and multimedia presentation, and eventually experts in physical modeling, who prepare the samples to be exhibited at the meeting with the customers. During this phase the attention of the team, in particular of its most expert members, Marco and Mario, is focused on making the design comprehensible to the customers. In some sense, deliverable preparation plays a stabilization role in the design process (Cusumano and Selby, 1997). Again, in this period the conversations going on within the team simulate customers' reactions to the deliverables in order to improve communication with them. During this phase, even if Marco leaves Milan for other commitments, the team tries to remain in touch with him in order to have his advice about any relevant decision to be taken: the lack of adequate communication media sometimes causes dramatic breakdowns, and relevant improvements of the communication infrastructure of Domus Academy are considered necessary by the members of the Research Center.

Fifth, a peculiar feature of the Domus Academy design style (and of the Italian industrial design school) is the fact that the designers do not limit themselves to designing some product prototypes but create a new concept for the products to be designed. The presentation of the project outcomes is not only a presentation of some prototypes but also a visualization of the new concept, to which they make reference. Presentation is therefore highly evocative and expressive, avoiding the (hyper)realism allowed by rendering systems. As mentioned, this broad project scope was clearly stated in the Fantasy case. Frequently, however, customers (in particular, non-Italian customers) do not understand it. The separation just described between the designers and the customers can, obviously, be considered a major factor in the problems arising with customers.

Sixth, a final comment on computer usage by the Fantasy team. They frequently collaborate in a way free of computers. While creating, the designers work with pencils, paper, walls, materials, and so on. The computer role is limited to peripheral activities. In fact, computers are used as information retrieval tools in Web sites, for internal e-mail communication when direct communication is impossible, and for rendering design ideas to clients. Finally, they are used as word processor for internal and client documents.

I will now discuss the preceding observations from the viewpoint of knowledge creation.

A first point to be taken into account is the double role of the master designers in Fantasy. They are both clients and performers in the design process. In other words, when interacting with the other designers of the team they are both socializing (when they participate in the design itself) and externalizing (when they discuss and evaluate the design choices from the viewpoint of customer requests and of the smart house scenarios defined at the beginning of Fantasy).

A second point is that the occasional visitors and the other Domus Academy designers are acting as coperformers within Fantasy, since they have a peripheral participation (Lave, Wenger, 1991) in it. In this case the situation is that the Fantasy team socializes with them, but socialization is obtained through a rich externalization/internalization process. In particular, socialization with the other Domus Academy designers gives rise to a knowledge-sharing process that gives homogeneity to the design performances of Domus Academy (see the earlier discussion of organizational knowledge sharing).

A third point is that the preparation of the deliverables, as well as their presentation to the customers, is an externalization process, where the outcomes of the design are made comprehensible to the latter. Its criticality is due to the policy of keeping customers away from the creative design phase. It is as if there were two work-spaces in a design process: the creative work-space, populated only by the designers (but by all the Domus Academy designers), and the customer-performer work-space, where the designers of the Fantasy team interact with their clients. The problems that arise from the separation of the two work-spaces highlight the need for an effective permeability between the two spaces, so that the respective knowledge creation processes do not diverge. Figure 8.5 shows what is needed in terms of crossing the boundaries between the two spaces.

Computer-Based Systems for Supporting Knowledge Creation

From the preceding analysis, it is possible to derive some lessons with respect to the development of computer supports for cooperative work or, in other terms, groupware systems (Ellis, Gibbs, and Rein, 1991). This new family of applications is rapidly growing, both in terms of the products offered on the market and in terms of the research prototypes under development in laboratories devoted to computer-supported cooperative work (CSCW). Members of this family can be considered (the list is not exhaustive): synchronous and asynchronous multimedia communication systems, from active mail systems to video teleconferencing systems; coordination systems, from (multimedia) conversation handlers to workflow management systems; systems for knowledge sharing from organizational memories and/or repositories to collaborative hypermedia systems; and collaborative editors and group decision support systems.

Even if all these systems can be useful in some occasions—since they allow us to overcome the obstacles that spatial and temporal distance creates to effective cooperation—they are only components of a support system for cooperative processes, unable in isolation to make the difference with respect to traditional communication and information-processing tools or individual productivity packages.

A support system should be able to support its users in participating effectively in the cooperative process where they are engaged. In other words, its aim is not to embody and/or reflect their organization but to improve their effectiveness while

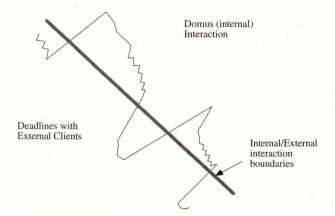

Figure 8.5. Crossing of boundaries

participating in the process. This requires that the system supports their awareness of the context where they are situated and provides them with any tool and/or resource they may need when and where they need it. Moreover, the context where they are situated is both spatial and temporal: on the one hand, it is constituted by all the artifacts populating the (virtual) space they occupy; on the other, it is constituted by the history of the cooperative process they are performing and of its expected future, that is, by of the already performed actions and conversations and of the ongoing conversations and actions.

Awareness (Agostini et al., 1996) of the context where she is situated is obtained by an actor sometimes through its visibility (i.e., through the explicit knowledge about it she shares with the persons with whom she is cooperating) and at other times through its transparency (i.e., through the tacit knowledge about it she shares with the persons with whom she is cooperating). A system supporting cooperative processes should therefore provide its users with the following services, independently of their mutual spatial and/or temporal distance (the list is not exhaustive; see also (Agostini, De Michelis, and Grasso, 1997):

- recording all the events characterizing a cooperative process together with the documents generated and exchanged in it, linking them in such a way as to reflect the history of which they are a part;
- recording the knowledge created by learning from past experiences, helping users to design and change the plans they can use to perform their activities and to enact them when needed;
- situating, in any moment, users in the appropriate context, making them accessible to knowledge about the cooperative process where they are performing.

In order to support awareness, in terms of both visibility (explicit knowledge) and transparency (tacit knowledge), the system should be able, on the one hand, to let its users access its knowledge base easily, providing them with the explicit knowledge they need in order to perform (e.g., providing a user with a document created by another actor some time before), and on the other hand, to let them use its knowledge base so as to make transparent to them the tacit knowledge they need to perform (e.g., connecting a user with the person she is looking for without asking for her current address). The effectiveness with which the system supports awareness depends on the virtual extension it provides to the work-space of its users, creating a virtual vicinity when they need transparency and linking separated work-spaces to a common knowledge base when they need visibility.

Taking into consideration these services from the knowledge-creation point of view (see the previous sections), we can see that they should be provided together with specific supports for the various types of social interaction or, in other terms, for the various types of positional relations through which knowledge is transformed.

To maintain the discussion at a rather general level, the following considerations offer some hints on the requirements that support systems for cooperative processes should satisfy in order to support knowledge creation within them effectively.

- *Socialization* among performers requires the creation of a common virtual space for the performers of a cooperative process, where they can continuously see each other in a natural and spontaneous way, so that at any moment they are updated on what is happening, of what the other actors are doing, and/or of the changes they are making to their common work plan. Tele-working and tele-cooperation projects that do not take this requirement into account are significantly exposed to serious problems, if not failures.
- *Combination* among customers requires a joint editing system, since combination of explicit knowledge can be considered the creation of a joint document, with all the problems deriving from the management of conflicting update requests by different customers, from the maintenance of the consistency among the different parts of the document and so on. Joint editing a document is not univocally associated with combination among customers (sometimes a document is the outcome of the cooperative process itself), but the latter can be considered the most demanding situation for joint editors, since in general one cannot assume any level of socialization among customers.
- *Externalization* and *internalization* between customers and performers require the creation of a communication space lying between the full asynchrony of the joint editor system and the full synchrony of the common virtual space. Neither full asynchrony nor full synchrony are useful for the relations between customers and performers, since they end up with a modification of the mutual positions of their participants. But internalization emphasizes the need for strict, direct communication between its participants, while externalization separates the moment in which the knowledge is made explicit by performers from that in which it is acquired by the customers.

These requirements for computer support systems for cooperative processes outline them as platforms integrating several different communication media and knowledge bases, together with the "intelligent" agents needed for maintaining the consistency of their information and for delivering the services needed by their users. But some of the characteristics of cooperative processes and of knowledge creation within them call for some more demanding requirements that deserve particular attention.

In the previous sections I have observed that:

1. the participants in a cooperative process change over time;
2. each participant continuously switches between acting and communicating;
3. each participant, at any moment, is engaged in different cooperation types, depending on her position in the process and on the positions of the other participants with whom she is cooperating;
4. the actors switch continuously between different cooperation forms, as well as between different knowledge transformation types;
5. collaboration, as well as internalization and externalization occurring within it, shifts between synchronous and asynchronous communication.

Moreover, we can also observe that the participants in a cooperative process do not share a unique image of its spatial and temporal context as well as of the knowledge created within it, due to the fact that none of them participates directly in all its actions and interactions.

All these observations are relevant with respect to support systems for cooperative processes, because they underline the fact that during the evolution of a cooperative process each of their components continuously moves from center to periphery and in the reverse direction (Brown and Duguid, 1994). Following Brown and Duguid, we can say that these movements are not sustainable by the users if the components of the support system are not enriched by effective *border* resources, helping the users switch among them without losing awareness of the context where they are cooperating.

Moreover, Brown and Duguid claim (1994) that borders develop into resources when the artifacts have "continuity" and when the users constitute a "community." Without elaborating further on the ways in which the participants in a cooperative process can be considered a community, we refine continuity in the framework of the support systems just described in terms of three qualities of the virtually expanded work-space they create: openness, multiplicity, and continuity (De Michelis, 1998).

Openness requires that the system supports the participants in a cooperative process, despite the fact that they are changing dynamically over time, helping to maintain in the process the knowledge of those who are leaving it and helping the newcomers to fully participate in it. Openness requires, on the one hand, that the system is as standard, portable, and interoperable as possible, and on the other hand, that it offers differentiated services to central and peripheral participants.

Multiplicity requires that the system, for example, supports not only the knowledge created within a cooperative process but also the personal image each one has of it. More generally, it requires that the system maintains multiple images of the knowledge created within it and situates any action or conversation in its right context.

Continuity requires that the system does not create any obstacle to the movements of its users with respect to the position they occupy in a cooperative process, their acting and/or interacting, and, finally, their roles in the knowledge-creation process. Continuity requires smooth transitions between synchronous and asynchronous communication; between communication and action; between peripheral and central participation. The above requirements outline some features characterizing a new generation of computer-based systems. Designing them uses experience, creative design, and technological innovation, all of which cooperate with and influence each other. In this sense design itself becomes a knowledge creation process.

References

Agostini, A., G. De Michelis, and M. A. Grasso. 1997. "Rethinking CSCW Systems: The Architecture of Milano." In *Proceedings of the Fifth European Conference on Computer Supported Cooperative Work*, edited by J. A. Hughes, W. Prinz, T. Rodden and K. Schmidt. Dordrecht, The Netherlands: Kluwer. Pp. 33–48.

Agostini, A., G. De Michelis, M. A. Grasso, W. Prinz, and A. Syri. 1996. "Contexts, Work Processes and Workspaces." *Computer Supported Cooperative Work: The Journal of Collaborative Computing* 5(2–3): 223–50.

Argyris, Chris, and Donald A. Schön. 1978. *Organizational Learning.* Reading, Mass.: Addison-Wesley.

———. 1996. *Organizational Learning II.* Reading, Mass.: Addison-Wesley.

Ashby, William Ross. 1956. *An Introduction to Cybernetics.* London: Chapman and Hall.

Brown, John Seely, and Paul Duguid. 1991. "Organizational Learning and Communities of Practice: A Unified View of Working, Learning and Innovation." *Organization Science* 2(1): 40–56.

———. 1994. "Borderline Issues: Social and Material Aspects of Design." *Human-Computer Interaction* 9(1): 3–36.

Covarrubias Gatica, E., G. De Michelis, and E. Leiva-Lobos. 1997. "Augmenting and Multiplying spaces for Creative Design." In *Proceedings of Group '97*, edited by S. C. Hayne and W. Prinz. New York: ACM Press. Pp. 177–86.

Cusumano, Michael A., and Richard W. Selby. 1997. "How Microsoft Builds Software." *Communications of the ACM* 40(6): 53–61.

Davenport, Thomas H. 1993. *Process Innovation: Reengineering Work Through Information Technology.* Boston: Harvard Business School Press.

Davenport, Thomas H., S. L. Jarvenpaa, and M. C. Beers. 1996. "Improving Knowledge Work Processes." *Sloan Management Review* 37(4): 53–65.

De Michelis, G. 1995a. *A che gioco giochiamo—Linguaggio, organizzazione, informatica.* Milan: Guerini.

———. 1995b. "Computer Support for Cooperative Work: Computers between Users and Social Complexity." In *Organizational Learning and Technological Change*, edited by C. Zucchermaglio, S. Bagnara, and S. Stucky. Berlin: Springer. Pp. 307–30.

———. 1996. "Co-decision within Cooperative Processes: Analysis, Design and Implementation Issues. In *Implementing Systems for Supporting Managerial Decisions: Concepts, Methods and Experiences*, edited by P. Humphrey, L. Bannon, A. McCosh, P. Migliarese, and J-C. Pomerol. London: Chapman and Hall. Pp. 124–38.

———. 1997. "Work Processes, Organizational Structures and Cooperation Supports: Managing Complexity." *Annual Reviews in Control* 21. New York: Pergamon Elsevier International. Pp. 149–57.

———. 1998. *Aperto, molteplice, continuo.* Milan: Dunod.

De Michelis, G., and Mario A. Grasso. 1994. "Situating Conversations within the Language/action Perspective: The Milan Conversation Model." In *Proceedings of the Fifth Computer-Supported Cooperative Work Conference.* New York: ACM Press. Pp. 89–100.

Ellis, C. E., S. J. Gibbs, and G. L. Rein. 1991. "Groupware: Some Issues and Experiences." *Communications of the ACM* 34(1): 39–58.

Hammer, Michael. 1990. "Reengineering Work: Don't Automate, Obliterate." *Harvard Business Review* 68(4): 104–12.

———. 1996. *Beyond Reengineering.* New York: HarperBusiness.

Hammer, Michael, and James Champy. 1993. *Reengineering the Corporation,* New York: HarperBusiness.

Keen, Peter G. W. 1991. *Shaping the Future: Business Design through Information Technology.* Boston: Harvard Business School Press.

Lave, Jean, and Etienne Wenger. 1991. *Situated Learning: Legitimate Peripheral Participation.* Cambridge, England: Cambridge University Press.

Medina-Mora, R., Terry Winograd, Fernando Flores, and R. Flores. 1992. "The Action

Workflow Approach to Workflow Management Technology." In *Proceedings of the 4th Computer Supported Cooperative Work Conference*. New York: ACM Press. Pp. 281–8.

Nelson, Richard R., and Sidney G. Winter. 1982. *An Evolutionary Theory of Economic Change*. Cambridge: Harvard University Press.

Nohria, Nitin, and R. Gulati. 1994. "Firms and Their Environments." In *The Handbook of Economic Sociology*, edited by N. J. Shelser and R. Swedberg. Princeton: Princeton University Press. Pp. 529–55.

Nonaka, Ikujiro, and Hirotaka Takeuchi. 1995. *The Knowledge-Creating Company*. New York: Oxford University Press.

Senge, Peter M. 1991. *The Fifth Discipline: The Art and Practice of the Learning Organization*. New York: Doubleday Currency.

Walsh, J., and Gerardo R. Ungson. 1991. "Organizational Memory." *Academy of Management Review* 16(1): 57–91.

Winograd, Terry, and Fernando Flores. 1986. "*Understanding Computers and Cognition*." Norwood, NJ: Ablex.

PART III
TRANSNATIONAL KNOWLEDGE CREATION

9

Multinational Enterprises and Cross-Border Knowledge Creation

D. ELEANOR WESTNEY

Over the last two decades, the model of the multinational enterprise (MNE) has changed dramatically, especially in terms of the nature and role of knowledge creation. From the 1960s into the early 1980s, the dominant perspective in international business viewed the MNE as developing a knowledge-based advantage in its home country and then exploiting it by extending its production system into geographically dispersed markets (see, for example, Vernon, 1966; Buckley and Casson, 1976; Dunning, 1981; Rugman, 1981). From the mid-1980s on, however, studies of the MNE have increasingly shifted their focus from the questions of why, how, and where a firm ventures beyond its home country borders to the emergent advantages of an established international network of subsidiaries (Bartlett and Ghoshal, 1986; Kogut, 1983; Kogut, 1985; Nohria and Ghoshal, 1997; Solvell and Zander, 1995). Chief among these advantages is a greater capacity for generating innovations. In other words, the focus of the study of the MNE has shifted from viewing geographic dispersion as a result of knowledge creation to seeing it as a source of knowledge creation.[1]

The shift in focus has reflected both the growing attention to innovation and knowledge creation in theories of strategy and organization in general (Nelson and Winter, 1982, and Nelson's 1995 review article) and changes in MNEs themselves—that is, it reflects both theoretical and empirical developments. One of the key features of the evolution of the MNE in the last decade has been the growing internationalization of R&D. As a result of the evolving technological capabilities of long-established subsidiaries and, perhaps even more strikingly, of the large-scale cross-border mergers and acquisitions of the 1980s, many MNEs increasingly found themselves with sizeable R&D centers outside their home country (Hakanson, 1990). A growing body of research on the internationalization of R&D has blossomed under the dual stimuli of managerial concerns with effective management of dispersed technology development units and scholarly interest in the internationalization processes of R&D, the last major function of the MNE to go abroad.[2] As international strategy in the 1980s came to focus heavily on the Triad of the highly industrialized economies, and as MNEs developed an established network of increasingly capable subsidiaries there, one of the key organizational questions became how MNEs could leverage their existing network for competitive advantage, rather than where and how they expanded their presence.

The advantages of the MNE in knowledge creation rest on one or more of the following characteristics:

1. *Variety in environmental stimuli:* because MNEs are by definition active in more than one national environment, they are exposed to a wider variety of customer, competitor, and technology stimuli to innovation than are domestic firms (see, for example, Ghoshal, 1987:431). The MNE here functions as a *global scanner*, in Ray Vernon's terms (Vernon, 1979:261), sensing and responding to a diverse array of environmental signals.
2. *Dispersed innovation centers*: the established MNE contains centers that generate innovations for local use in a variety of locations. The MNC can identify and select those that have potentially wider applicability and ensure their adoption in other locations. The MNC here is seen as a *selection regime*, in the terminology of population ecology, selecting for and proliferating certain innovations.
3. *Joint knowledge creation*: the dispersed innovation centers can combine their resources and capabilities to create knowledge jointly, in a variety of ways.[3] In this context, the MNC functions as a *knowledge-creating network*.

The fact that the MNE contains knowledge widely dispersed across its various local subsidiaries does not necessarily mean that it has developed this third capability. The geographic dispersion of R&D provides only the *potential* for joint knowledge creation; not all MNEs with international R&D centers have developed the organizational capability for realizing that potential. Nonaka has identified this cross-border synergistic process as "global knowledge creation" and sees it as the key process of globalization (Nonaka, 1990:82).

This essay explores the patterns and nature of cross-border knowledge creation in the R&D function. We should note that this is a deliberately narrow focus on one aspect of the more general topic of multinational knowledge creation processes. Of the four types of multinational innovation processes identified by Bartlett and Ghoshal (1986; 1989) and elaborated in Nohria and Ghoshal (1997), only one involves "joint cross-border knowledge creation" processes in the R&D function: their "globally-linked" pattern, or what Nohria and Ghoshal call global-for-global. The other three types—local-for-local, central-for-local, and locally leveraged (or local-for-global)—center on single-location knowledge creation rather than cross-border interactive knowledge creation, at least as far as the R&D function is concerned, although they may involve *crossfunctional* joint knowledge creation. This essay focuses on the questions of how widespread cross-border knowledge creation is within the R&D function, first within firms with internationally dispersed R&D units and then between firms and external foreign sources of technology, and what organizational and managerial systems support cross-border knowledge creation within companies that have a geographically dispersed R&D function. Finally, I suggest some concepts for analyzing cross-border knowledge-creation processes.

Cross-Border Knowledge Creation in Firms with International R&D Units

During the 1980s and 1990s, studies of the internationalization of R&D—that is, the establishment or acquisition of R&D centers outside a company's home base—

suggested that cross-border interaction in knowledge creation is increasingly important in MNEs. But in fact, most studies map the geographic dispersion of R&D rather than the level of cooperation in technology development across the dispersed units, whether the analyses are based on patenting (e.g., Cantwell, 1989) or on surveys of companies (e.g., Casson, 1991). An R&D center outside a company's home base may indeed be engaged in joint knowledge creation with the parent R&D organization or even with other dispersed R&D centers in the company. Alternatively, it may be engaged in quite autonomous knowledge creation, either as the sole "center of excellence" for a product or technology within the company or as what Ronstadt (1977) called the indigenous technology unit (ITU), whose mandate is primarily developing products for the local market. There are also a handful of studies of global new product development projects that involve cross-border knowledge creation (e.g., Bartlett and Ghoshal, 1990; Nonaka and Takeuchi, 1995:chap. 7; Hedlund and Ridderstrale, 1995), but such projects are clearly not typical of their companies' knowledge-creation activities, however strategically important they may be. In other words, although there is a widespread belief that cross-border knowledge creation is important, we have little data to tell us how extensive it is.

A recent research project at MIT provided an opportunity to explore this issue and a number of related topics. In 1994–96, together with Tony Frost (then also of MIT, now at the University of Western Ontario), I conducted a survey of the global management of R&D under the auspices of the Industrial Research Institute (IRI) based in Washington, D.C., whose member companies account for roughly 80 percent of the industrial R&D spending in the United States. One-third of the association's member companies agreed to participate: seventy U.S. firms and twelve foreign-owned firms with R&D centers in the United States (ten European companies and two Asian). Of the seventy U.S. firms, forty-three had R&D centers outside the United States. (We called this kind of company FIRDUs—that is, *firms with international R&D units*—not out of a perverse desire to add yet another acronym to the MNE literature but to reduce writer and reader fatigue over the constant reiteration of "firms with international R&D units.") The other twenty-seven U.S. firms did not have R&D centers outside the United States, although most were "multinational enterprises" in the classic definition of the term, with sales and production outside their home country; we called this type of firm the HRDU—firms with *home-based R&D units* only.

The unit of analysis in this study was not the company but the technology development unit—that is, one level below the company/function level that has been the usual focus of organizational studies of the internationalization of R&D, and a level above the individual project level that has been the focus of studies of knowledge creation. Obviously, the project level is best suited to the analysis of knowledge-creation processes, but the organizational capabilities that sustain the capacity for knowledge creation are best studied at the organizational level. However, in multibusiness, multinational companies, the R&D function has increasingly been segmented into distinct organizational units linked to a specific business area or (in the case of corporate R&D) technology area. Given the resulting intracompany variation, a company-level analysis is too coarse-grained to capture much of the information necessary to understand better the development of the organizational systems that sustain cross-border knowledge creation. Therefore, despite the many problems involved, we elected to direct our study to the R&D unit or, rather, the technology development unit.

Our pilot study revealed that our initial label "R&D unit" met some resistance from some of the participating companies, who eschewed the connotation of "blue-sky academic research" that they associated with the use of "research" (as in "R&D unit") and preferred the more neutral term "technology development unit." We defined this as a "technical unit engaged in any stage of the technology development process, from fundamental research to design, development, engineering or modification of products, processes, or technologies," specifically omitting technical units engaged primarily in technical service and support. In other words, we focused on units engaged in technical knowledge creation, both radical and incremental, and in this essay I use the terms "R&D unit" and "technology development unit" interchangeably in describing them. The IRI representative from each of the eighty-two participating companies identified a set of unit heads within the company as appropriate targets for the study, and questionnaires were mailed from MIT to these individuals. A total of 318 responded, giving a response rate of 77.4 percent. The questionnaire was followed by a set of over forty face-to-face interviews in units in the United States, Europe, and Japan.

Although we found that in many companies technology development units were quite specialized in terms of product or technology, most, even those that were relatively small, covered more than one stage of the R&D value chain (which we operationalized by a question asking about the importance of various types of technology development in the unit's current mandate). Table 9.1 shows the distribution of units in terms of the four core activities: developing basic or fundamental technology; developing breakthrough new products; developing new generations of current products; and process innovations.[4]

Only thirty of the units (fewer than 10 percent) had a single mandate (one additional unit identified a fifth activity, "modifying products developed by other units," as its only important mandate in the value chain). Somewhat surprisingly, there was no significant relationship between the size of the unit in terms of the number of technical personnel and the number of mandates it covered. In our interviews and our presentations of the data for the IRI members, it became obvious that this finding reflected the fact that many companies have cut their R&D organization into smaller units that are directly linked with individual businesses and cover the entire R&D value chain for a single business or product family, in order to increase their responsiveness to market pressures.

The 318 responding units were distributed across five categories, depending on ownership, dispersion of R&D, and location, as follows. We had three categories of United States–owned units: those in firms without international R&D units (HRDUs); the home country (i.e., United States–located) units in firms that did have international R&D units (FIRDUs); and units in the U.S. FIRDUs that were located abroad (primarily but not exclusively in Europe). We also had thirty-three units that were located in the United States but belonged to non-U.S.-owned FIRDUs, and twelve of their home country units.The map of responding units was as shown in figure 9.1.

Table 9.1. Vertical Technology Scope

Basic research	**Breakthrough products**	**Next generation products**	**Process innovations**	103	33.8%
Basic research	**Breakthrough products**	**Next generation products**	Process innovations	26	8.6%
Basic research	**Breakthrough products**	**Next generation products**	**Process innovations**	44	14.5%
Basic research	**Breakthrough products**	Next generation products	**Process innovations**	16	5.3%
Basic research	Breakthrough products	**Next generation products**	**Process innovations**	12	3.9%
Basic research	**Breakthrough products**	Next generation products	Process innovations	9	3.0%
Basic research	**Breakthrough products**	**Next generation products**	Process innovations	18	5.9%
Basic research	Breakthrough products	**Next generation products**	**Process innovations**	32	10.5%
Basic research	Breakthrough products	**Next generation products**	Process innovations	8	2.6%
Basic research	Breakthrough products	Next generation products	**Process innovations**	5	1.6%
Basic research	**Breakthrough products**	Next generation products	**Process innovations**	1	0.3%
Basic research	Breakthrough products	Next generation products	Process innovations	3	1.0%
Basic research	**Breakthrough products**	Next generation products	Process innovations	4	1.3%
Basic research	Breakthrough products	**Next generation products**	Process innovations	8	2.6%
Basic research	Breakthrough products	Next generation products	**Process innovations**	15	4.9%
Total				304	99.8%

This table presents the ways in which mandates are clustered—the entries in boldface are the mandates undertaken by units in that category.

Table 9.2 provides further information on each of these five categories of units. The companies covered a range of industries and reflected, to some extent, IRI participation: supplier industries were strongly represented, especially the chemical industry. Over one-third of the units (37 percent) were from the chemical industry; and 23 percent were from engineering and machinery. Of the remainder, 14 percent were in drugs and medical equipment, 9 percent in materials, and 9 percent in consumer products. Only 2 percent were in electronics, and 6 percent were classified as "other." This means that the industries that have been best represented in published case studies of cross-border new product development processes (consumer products and electronics) were much less well represented in our study, in favor of more "mature" industries where one might expect the pressures for cross-border interactions in technology development to be less strong.

Nevertheless, we found cross-border knowledge creation to be extensive. The most direct question could be asked in the FIRDUs. In the version of our questionnaire

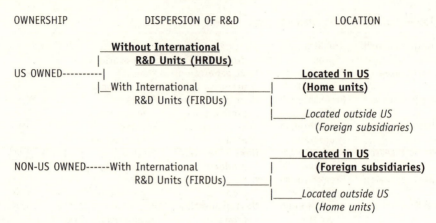

Figure 9.1. Map of responding units

tailored to such firms, we asked: "What percentage of the products and technologies your unit works on involve some form of collaboration with the company's technical units outside the country in which you are located?" Table 9.3 shows the distribution of the responses. These data support the belief that there is widespread cross-border interaction in knowledge creation in firms that have internationally dispersed R&D organizations. As one would expect, in the United States–owned companies, foreign units report a higher level of cross-border interaction in technology development than do the home country units. Over 40 percent of the home

Table 9.2. Categories of Responding Units: HRDUs and FIRDUs

Type of Unit	Number of Responding Units		Average Size (No. of Technical Employees)	Average Age (Years Since Est.)
U.S. firms—home-based technology development units only (HRDUs)	53	16.7%	106.3	27.6
U.S. firms with international technology development units (FIRDUs)—home units	149	46.8%	213.4	31.3
U.S. firms with international technology development units (FIRDUs)—foreign units	71	22.3%	52.1	16.4
Non-U.S. firms with international technology development units (FIRDUs)—U.S.-based units	33	10.4%	125.0	13.8
Non-U.S. firms with international technology development units (FIRDUs)—home units	12	3.8%	121.2	11.1
Total	318	100.0%	146.5	24.8

Table 9.3. Level of Cross-Border Knowledge Creation in FIRDUs, by Category*

Percent of Products/ Technologies Involving Cross-border Cooperation	U.S. FIRDUs— Home Units (n = 146)	U.S. FIRDUs— Foreign Units (n = 68)	Non-U.S. FIRDUs— U.S. Units (n = 33)	Non-U.S. FIRDUs— Home Units (n = 12)
None	3.4%	0	0	0
Less than 25%	43.8%	13.2%	33.5%	25.0%
25–50%	26.0%	22.1%	27.3%	33.3%
50–75%	26.7%	64.7%	39.4%	41.7%
Total	99.9%	100.0%	100.2%	100.0%

*Question (only on questionnaires for firms with international technology development units): Approximately what percentage of the products and technologies your unit works on involve some form of collaboration with the company's technical units outside the country in which you are located?

units report cooperating with foreign R&D units on less than 25 percent of their products or technologies. Nearly two-thirds of the foreign units, on the other hand, interact with R&D units outside their country of location for more than half of their product/technology portfolio. Given that the overwhelming majority of these foreign units are in Europe and that many have interactions with other European units in their company, this is perhaps not surprising. The foreign-owned R&D centers in the United States fall between the home country and the foreign units of the U. S. companies: one-third are relatively autonomous (this reflects a broader pattern in the data—units in this category are very United States–focused and less integrated with the rest of their company on a number of dimensions, a pattern that is perhaps not surprising, given the size and scope of the U.S. market). We cannot view the very small number of home units of non-U.S. firms as a group that is comparable to the U.S. firms' home units: the number is too small, and the very fact of their participation in a United States–based study indicates their very strong international orientation. Of course, we cannot claim that the U.S. home units are "typical," since they were selected by their company representatives as units that might have an interest in participating in a study of global technology management. But the fact that more than half of these units are involved in cross-border interactions with foreign units in the company for over one-quarter of the products or technologies on which they are working indicates extensive cross-border knowledge creation.

This study provided evidence that cross-border knowledge creation is extensive, both across units within MNEs and between those units and external partners in other regions. But the survey instrument was not well suited to probing the nature—as opposed to the extent—of cross-border knowledge-creation processes. For that kind of information, we relied on the interviews, in which we asked for examples of recent cross-border technology development. These examples were not detailed case studies but very brief descriptions of recent cross-border cooperation, ranging from (for example) a major four-year new product development project involving technology units in the United States, Europe, and Japan to an interaction of a few weeks' duration in which a local subsidiary in Europe worked with the business unit headquarters' R&D organization in the United States to modify a product and get it appropriately field-tested. In the course of the interviews, it became increasingly clear that while the cross-unit product development project was the dominant form of international knowledge creation, it was by no means the only one. Knowledge creation was occurring outside specifically cross-unit projects—as, for example, when someone from one unit flew to another unit to help solve a particular problem or to learn more about a particular set of customer needs.

This was reflected in the responses to a set of questions in the survey about the reasons for sending people abroad to other units in the company. These data are presented in table 9.4, which divides the responding units into three categories: low cross-border interaction (those with 25 percent or less of their products and technologies involving cooperation with other company units outside the country in which they are located); medium cross-border interaction units (25–50 percent) and high interaction units (more than 50 percent). While project-related travel

Table 9.4. Reasons for International Travel of Technical Personnel in FIRDUs, by Level of Cross-border Interaction*

	High Cross-Border Interaction Units (n = 101)	Medium Cross-Border Interaction Units (n = 66)	Low Cross-Border Interaction Units (n = 92)
Work on a joint project with another unit	90.1%	74.2%	64.4%
Follow a project from R&D to manufacturing	86.1%	81.8%	63.0%
Transfer technology (including "knowhow") *from* your unit *to* another unit	80.2%	72.2%	55.4%
Transfer technology *to* your unit *from* another unit	64.4%	56.1%	41.3%
Learn about another unit's products or technologies	65.3%	74.2%	55.4%
Learn about customer or market requirements	60.4%	65.3%	54.3%
Use specialized or expensive equipment	31.7%	39.4%	18.5%
Coordinate plans about future products/technologies	93.1%	72.7%	53.3%
Review goals, budgets, or recent performance	50.5%	50.0%	22.8%
Evaluate the progress of a project	64.4%	62.1%	41.3%
Fill a position that could not be filled locally	27.7%	25.8%	10.9%
Technical training or career development	60.4%	66.7%	32.6%
Management training or career development	43.6%	48.5%	22.8%

*Question: For your technical unit, how important are each of the following reasons for *sending* personnel *outside the country in which you are located*? Responses on 1–5 scale where 5 = very important. The table presents the percentage of each type of unit rating the reason 4 or 5.

clearly predominates, especially in the high interaction units, more general learning—about technology and markets, and technology transfer—is also important, and is almost as important in the medium and low interaction units as in the high. And of course, administrative coordination of various kinds is also a major reason for travel—again particularly in the high interaction units. But the key point to draw from these data is the range and variety of cross-border knowledge creation activities in MNEs.

The IRI sponsors and participating companies, however, were of course less interested in the extent of cross-border knowledge creation than in how to manage the process more effectively. We used both the questionnaire and the interviews to explore the question of how companies strengthen their cross-border knowledge-creation capabilities.

In the 1990s, the concept of organizational capabilities has been increasingly used in the analysis of strategy (see, for example, Aaker, 1989; Prahalad and Hamel, 1990; and Stalk, Evans, and Shulman, 1992) and of technology management (e.g., Leonard-Barton, 1992). Several terms were used as this perspective evolved—resources, invisible assets, strategic assets, capabilities, core competences. Gradually, however, the field has converged on the term "capabilities" and on several defining features: capabilities develop over time, involve complex interactions among resources (Amit and Schoemaker, 1993) and across levels (Leonard-Barton, 1992), and are a source of competitive advantage in large part because they are hard to imitate. And one of the reasons they are hard to imitate is that they involve dynamic interactions across levels within the organization: the level of individual skills and capabilities, the routines of the work process, and two organization-level variables: organizational systems (for R&D, human resource management systems, project management systems, and resource allocation systems are particularly crucial) and organizational culture.[5] While a study such as the MIT-IRI study, which focuses on organizational units rather than projects, is not able to illuminate significantly the first two levels of analysis (the individual and the work process routines), it is useful for analyzing the organizational systems level. The following section examines the extent of internal cross-border knowledge-creation patterns in the U.S. FIRDUs and the organizational systems that support them.

Cross-Border Knowledge-Creation Capabilities in Firms with International R&D Units

The organizational systems used to link units in a geographically dispersed R&D system are key elements of cross-border knowledge-creation capabilities. As one of the leading European scholars who has studied the internationalization of R&D, Arnoud de Meyer of INSEAD, has put it, "Learning about different markets, different problem-solving methods, different sources of technological progress, different culture, different competitors, and the rapid diffusion of that learning through the organization is definitely enhanced by creating an international network of R&D laboratories" (De Meyer, 1992:169). Drawing on work by De Meyer (especially De Meyer, 1991) and on input from the sponsoring committee of the IRI, we developed a list of ten mechanisms used to link technology development centers located in different countries into such a network, and asked the survey respondents in the FIRDUs to tell us whether they had used them and how they rated the effectiveness of those they did use (obviously this question was omitted from the version sent to the HRDUs).

Not surprisingly, virtually everyone uses the standard communications links of frequent long-distance interpersonal communication through phone, fax, and e-mail, and short international visits. But for other mechanisms, such as personnel transfers and some of the resource allocation systems, the percentage of units where they are not used is relatively high—almost half, in the case of short-term transfers of personnel. Therefore, we calculated an "effectiveness ratio," which is the percentage of those units using the particular mechanism that rated it as effective (either 4 or 5 on a 5-point scale). Table 9.5 presents the percentage of FIRDU units rating the mechanism as "effective," the percentage not employing each particular mechanism, and the effectiveness ratio for those that did.

Not surprisingly, the standard long-distance communications links (phone, fax, and e-mail) were virtually universally employed and received a high effectiveness

Table 9.5. Mechanisms in FIRDUs for Linking Technology Development Units in Different Countries

Linking Mechanism	Percentage rating "Effective"	Percentage "Not Tried"	Effectiveness Ratio*
Information Technology			
Frequent communication by phone, fax, e-mail	73.1%	1.5%	74.2%
Video conference	76.9%	15.9%	91.4%
Human Resource Management Systems: Travel			
Short visits (< 3 weeks) by technical personnel	80.2%	2.7%	82.4%
Short-term transfers (1–6 months) of technical personnel	38.6%	44.4%	69.4%
Long-term transfers (> 6 months) of technical personnel	48.1%	37.7%	77.2%
Resource Allocation and Decision-making			
System for allocating costs and benefits of joint activities	13.6%	38.1%	22.0%
Frequent meetings of top-ranking managers	46.7%	7.7%	50.6%
Different but complementary areas of expertise	40.2%	11.6%	45.4%
Some overlap of areas of technical expertise	41.4%	5.0%	43.5%
Designating a single unit as worldwide leader within a business or technology	48.1%	23.1%	62.5%

*"Effectiveness ratio" calculated by taking the percentage of those who used the mechanism who rated it as effective.

rating. The major exception in terms of effective ratios was among the foreign sub-sidiaries in the United States (a breakdown not shown in table 9.5), who gave the "frequent communication by phone, fax, and e-mail" a startlingly low effectiveness ratio of 51.5 percent, a low rate that holds for this group regardless of the amount of cross-border interaction on technology development (it is only 54 percent even for the units for whom more than half of their products and technologies involve cooperation with R&D units outside the United States). While one might first be tempted to look to a cultural explanation (for instance, that the home country busi-ness cultures of these units may be less comfortable with such arm's length com-munications mechanisms than the U.S. firms), in fact it seems to be related to a pattern revealed in other indicators in the survey and in the interviews: a very strong orientation among these units to the local U.S. market and a high proclivity for autonomy from parental control (which presumably also includes resistance to parental efforts at regular communication). These units were also less enthusiastic about the other virtually ubiquitous linkage mechanism, short visits; the effective-ness ratio among the foreign-owned units in the United States was 10 percent lower than the units in the U.S. FIRDUs, either at home or abroad.

The highest effectiveness ratio went to video conferencing. Our interviews re-vealed that R&D managers viewed this as a very useful way to reduce travel for meetings, although not to eliminate it. Moving people is still, however, the key mechanism for linking R&D units, and in this function short visits are key to the communications networks, receiving the second highest effectiveness ratio and being used by virtually all the units. The data from another of the survey questions reveals this even more strongly. We asked unit heads to tell us approximately what percentage of their technical personnel had traveled in the past year to technical units in the company outside the country in which they were located. These data are presented in table 9.6. For roughly 80 percent of all the FIRDU units in all cat-egories, 10 percent or more of their technical staff had traveled internationally within the R&D network at least once in the past year; more startlingly, in the U.S. FIRDUs 40 percent of the home units and 60 percent of the foreign units reported that a quarter or more of their technical personnel had done so. Not surprisingly, there was a relationship between this travel ratio and the size of the unit, but pri-marily for the units with very high travel ratios (50 percent or more): 31 percent of the units with under fifteen technical employees had a travel ratio of over 50 per-cent, compared to 20 percent of the units with sixty or more.

Most of this travel is of course in the form of short visits. But in addition, compa-nies transfer technical people on longer assignments. We distinguished two types of people movement that involve formal transfers of technical personnel: transfers of under six months (called short-term transfers) and those of more than six months (long-term transfers). Based on preliminary discussions, we learned that six months is usually the cutoff point in terms of whether the transfer is viewed as "temporary" and therefore not needing the re-establishment of the person's household in the new location. Long-term transfers had a higher effectiveness ratio but also a high pro-portion of units who didn't use them. Short-term transfers were even less common, and more of the units were ambivalent about their effectiveness. Neither type of transfer received as high an effectiveness rating as short visits.

Table 9.6. Proportion of Technical People Traveling across Borders, by Category*

Percent of Technical Personnel Traveling Internationally	U.S. FIRDUs— Home Units (n = 143)	U.S. FIRDUs— Foreign Units (n = 64)	Non-U.S. FIRDUs— U.S. Units (n = 33)	Non-U.S. FIRDUs— Home Units (n = 12)
None	3.5%	12.5%	3.0%	0
5%	18.9%	15.6%	15.2%	18.2%
10%	37.1%	10.9%	30.3%	9.1%
25%	26.6%	21.9%	30.3%	45.5%
50% or more	14.0%	39.1%	21.2%	27.3%
Total	100.1%	100%	100%	100.1%

*Question: During the past year, approximately what percentage of your unit's personnel took at least one trip: (a) (for FIRDUs) to another technical unit in the company outside the country in which you are located? (b) (for HRDUs) outside the country in which you are located?
0%   5%   10%   25%   50%   75%   100%
Chi-square: differences significant at p = .000 level.

The interviews clarified the different roles of these three types of cross-border people movement. Short visits, obviously, had a clearly targeted mission and were best used to solve problems (either technical or managerial coordination problems) or to maintain relationships that were supplemented between visits by other forms of communication, such as video conferencing. Short-term transfers were tied to specific projects and, like short visits, had a clear target. They were seen as effective for transferring technology, either into or out of the unit. Long-term transfers, on the other hand, are most effective in building individual cross-border capabilities, in terms of a deep understanding of a different business and technical environment and the development of lasting personal networks across units. However, they were seen to have high costs, both literally (in terms of the costs of re-establishing a household in a new country), and in terms of the problems they create for managers. Long-term postings are not usually tied to a specific project, and therefore the "host" unit has to find a role for the incoming person; the "sending" unit usually has to replace the person and then find a role for him or her upon return. Moreover, the growing number of dual career households in the United States was frequently cited in interviews as a factor making technical personnel less flexible in taking long-term transfers abroad.

Short-term transfers do not have these disadvantages, but several managers pointed out in the interviews that people were less likely to return from them with a broad understanding of the local business and technical environment and that they developed less dense and sustained personal ties (since they viewed themselves and were viewed by others as "transients" rather than members, however temporary, of the unit). As several managers pointed out, if a company were systematic about using a mix of short-term transfers and visits, repeated postings and visits to the same international site might well serve as a functional equivalent of long-term transfers in terms of their effect on individual border-crossing capabilities, but few

U.S. companies have the human resource management systems in place in their R&D organizations to make such long-term planning possible.

In fact, most companies do not use short- and long-term transfers as functional equivalents: nearly half the units (46.1 percent) use both, and over a quarter (28.7 percent) use neither; 15.9 percent use short-term but not long-term transfers, and only 9.3 percent use long-term transfers and not short-term. Of the companies that use both, over half see them as equally effective (57.1 percent—but as effective for different purposes, as the preceding discussion indicates); 17.6 percent see long-term transfers as effective, but not short-term, and 9.2 percent see only the short-term transfers as effective. The remaining unit heads—a surprising 11.8 percent of those using both types—did not view either as particularly effective.

The balance among the different modes of moving people across borders in R&D is especially noteworthy, given the fixation of studies of human resource management in the MNE on the expatriate manager (that is, on long-term transfers). In the R&D function, the cross-border movement of technical people is much more extensive for short visits and for transfers (those dubbed long-term here, as well as the short-term transfers) that are much shorter than the three to five years normal for expatriate managers. For the most part, this cross-border movement of R&D personnel has none of the infrastructure of cross-cultural training and mentoring provided in many companies for "expats." For the knowledge-creating company, improving the effectiveness of the much more numerous short-term transferees and the engineers sent into new cultural and technical environments for short visits— and often on short notice—is much more important than further improving the infrastructure for the much less numerous (and in many companies shrinking) number of longer term expatriates. In our interviews, managers provided some suggestions of how to do this, such as providing designated "local mentors" who have the formal responsibility of helping the visiting engineer or scientist to understand the local environment and improve his or her interactions in it. This is an arena that would benefit from much more extensive and systemic research.

For the resource allocation and decision-making systems, the lowest effectiveness ratio, to our surprise, went to "systems for allocating the costs and benefits of joint activities." In work with several companies prior to this study, we had found that the absence of such a system was often cited as a serious source of problems, and yet, although such systems are in place for 60 percent of the units in this study, they don't seem to work very well. One inference is that these data confirm the view that the geographic dimension of decision-making is a fundamental problem in product-based business-unit structures; another is that companies might be advised not to invest heavily in trying to construct systems for allocating costs and benefits among geographically dispersed units, but to rely instead on strengthening other means of cross-unit coordination.

The low effectiveness ratio given to "frequent meetings of top-ranking managers" was less surprising, given how widely managers in MNEs today complain about the level of travel required for meetings. Although these are widely used, they were not highly valued for effectiveness by half the units. We used two additional resource allocation systems variables that we thought would be closely and inversely related:

"different but complementary areas of expertise" and "some overlap of areas of technical expertise." We hoped by this question to discover whether units were using a strategy of differentiation of technical expertise or of redundancy. In fact most units reported using both: only twenty-one units (8.1 percent) reported having overlapping areas of expertise but not different but complementary areas, and only five (2.0 percent) reported the reverse. Either we didn't ask the question clearly enough, or the overlap reported confirms the need for some redundancy even with a differentiation strategy, in order to assure absorptive capacity in technology interactions (Cohen and Levinthal, 1990).

Designating a single unit as the worldwide leader for technology development within a business unit or technical area was used by more than three-quarters of the units' companies, but only two-thirds of them found it effective. There were, as one might expect, significant variations by category: units in the home country found the idea more attractive than the foreign subsidiaries, probably because they were more likely to be designated as the leader. The effectiveness ratio among U.S. FIRDUs' home country units was 68.9 percent, whereas it was 57.1 percent among the United States–owned subsidiaries abroad. It fell to 36.7 percent among the United States–located subsidiaries of non-U. S. MNEs, but their parent company units gave it a 100 percent effectiveness rating!

It may seem somewhat redundant, but it is also useful to look at these ratings by the units' level of cross-border interaction in technology development. Like table 9.4 above, table 9.7 divides the responding units into the three groups of low, medium, and high interaction. For all ten mechanisms, the percentage of units without experience of the mechanism falls as the cross-border interaction level rises. This is especially noticeable for video conferencing, which is used in virtually all the high interaction units. For several variables, the effectiveness ratio also rises with the level of cross-border interaction, as we would expect (especially for frequent meetings of top managers). However, there are some interesting departures from this expected pattern. The effectiveness ratio for long-term transfers is very high in the high interaction units and significantly higher than for medium interaction units; however, for short-term transfers the ratio is lower and is virtually equivalent to the ratio given by the medium interaction units, suggesting that the linkages and individual capabilities created by long-term transfers of people are most valuable when interaction levels across units are high. More surprising is the curvilinear relationship for two mechanisms: a system for allocating the costs and benefits of joint activities, which is most valued by the medium interaction units and least by the low and the high, and designating a single unit as worldwide leader, which exhibits the same pattern. Both suggest that formal allocation systems may be most useful when interactions across borders rise above a certain level, but that as interaction rises to higher levels, they have more difficulty satisfactorily dealing with the complexities.[6] This is a point made by both Gunnar Hedlund and by Bartlett and Ghoshal in their discussions of the "heterarchical," less formalized management systems appropriate for companies with very dense levels of cross-border interdependencies.

An additional organizational system variable about which we enquired in the questionnaire proved to have an interesting, though not unexpected, relationship

Table 9.7. Usage and Evaluation of Cross-border Mechanisms Linking Dispersed Units in FIRDUs, by Level of Cross-border Interaction*

Type of Cross-Border Linking Mechanism	Low Cross-Border Interaction Units (< 25%) (n = 92)		Medium Cross-Border Interaction Units (25-50%) (n = 66)		High Cross-Border Interaction Units (> 50%) (n = 101)	
	"Not Tried"	Effectiveness Ratio	"Not Tried"	Effectiveness Ratio	"Not Tried"	Effectiveness Ratio
Frequent communication by phone, fax, e-mail	4.4%	60.9%	0	75.7%	0	85.15%
Video conference	29.7	84.4	12.1	93.1	5.9	95.8
Short visits	6.6	72.9	0	84.6	1.0	90.0
Short-term transfers (1–6 months)	57.8	57.9	43.9	73.0	34.0	71.9
Long-term transfers (> 6 months)	50.0	73.3	34.8	67.4	29.6	84.1
Frequent meetings of top managers	17.8	37.8	3.1	46.0	2.0	63.3
System for allocating costs and benefits of joint activities	44.3	14.3	49.2	37.5	26.0	21.6
Different but complementary areas of expertise	16.9	18.9	7.7	56.7	10.1	58.4
Some overlap of areas of technical expertise	4.4	60.9	0	75.7	0	85.1
Designating a single unit as worldwide leader within a business or technology	42.2	53.8	12.1	72.4	14.3	58.3

*Question: Consider your unit's interactions with the company's technical units *outside [the country of location]*. In the last two years, how effective was each of the following factors in contributing to a good working relationship with them? Response categories: 0 = "Have not tried"; then a five-point scale where 1 = "not at all effective" and 5 = "very effective."

with cross-border knowledge creation. We asked the respondents to evaluate the importance of a set of factors in how they personally were evaluated and rewarded as R&D unit managers. The responses varied considerably both by the level of cross-border interaction in technology development and by the category of unit (United States–owned FIRDUs, home country and foreign, and non-U. S. FIRDU units in the United States). The data for the three factors that exhibited significant differences by interaction levels are presented in table 9.8.

In the U. S. FIRDUs, both home country and foreign units, the unit heads in high interaction units (those in which over 50 percent of their products or technologies involved cooperation with other company units outside their country of location) were much more likely to assert that cross-unit cooperation was an important factor in how they were rewarded than were low and medium cross-border interaction units. The foreign unit heads were somewhat more likely to believe that cooperation played a role in their evaluation, perhaps because the units with whom they were most likely to be cooperating were the home country units closest to headquarters and therefore likely to have influence in the evaluation process. On the other hand, the non–United States–owned unit heads were much less likely to believe that international cooperation was significant in their evaluation and reward, regardless of level of cross-border interaction. These data are from a single point in time, and it is notoriously dangerous to try to infer causality from correlation. But these data do provide some support for the view that behavior that is rewarded is more likely to be observed than behavior that is not. The fact that a number of the other survey indicators show that the non–United States–owned units resisted cross-border integration efforts and were strongly locally oriented is unlikely to be independent of their view of how their heads are evaluated.

In summary, then, the MIT-IRI survey revealed that cross-border knowledge creation was extensive and that the movement of people played a key role, in terms of short visits and short-term transfers, as well as longer term expatriate assignments of the conventional type. The different modes of moving people have different effects on the development of organizational capabilities and impose different costs on sending and receiving units, and this aspect of cross-border knowledge creation cries out for more detailed research and analysis in the future. The development of management systems to support cross-border knowledge creation seems to be more difficult when interaction levels—hence presumably the complexity of interactions—are high.

Cross-border knowledge creation is not, of course restricted to the dispersed internal network of the MNE. Let us turn now to the exploration of external cross-border knowledge-creation links.

Cross-Border Knowledge-Creating Links with External Organizations

Since the mid-1980s, technology development links with organizations outside the company, both at home and abroad, have become an increasingly important aspect of knowledge creation for many companies. International external tech-

Table 9.8. Basis for Evaluating and Assessing the Performance of Unit Managers*

Level of Cross-Border Interaction	U.S. FIRDUs—Home Country Units (n = 145)			U.S. FIRDUs—Foreign Units (n = 67)			Non-U.S.-FIRDUs—Units in United States (n = 33)		
	Low	Medium	High	Low	Medium	High	Low	Medium	High
Units' degree of cooperation with other units in the company	27.5%	23.7%	52.6%	22.2%	20.0%	62.8%	9.1%	22.2%	23.1%
Business unit/division performance in the market in which the unit is located	75.4	63.2	46.2	66.7	40.0	32.6	54.4	62.5	69.2
Business unit/division performance world-wide	50.7	65.8	71.8	41.4	33.3	53.5	18.2	44.4	46.2

*Question: Please indicate how important each of the following factors is in determining how you personally are rewarded (i.e., compensated, promoted, or otherwise recognized). Responses on a 1–5 scale where 1 = "not at all important" and 5 = "very important."

nology linkages are an especially important tool for internationalizing the knowledge-creation processes of firms that do not themselves have international R&D units.

In the questionnaire, we asked respondents if their units had engaged in joint technology development projects in the past two years with six types of organizations in each of the three major regions: North America, Europe, and Asia. The organizations were: a general category of "alliances, joint ventures, and consortia"; "competitors" (both these two categories we considered to be "horizontal alliances" involving similar firms); customers and suppliers (these two constituted "vertical" linkages); universities and public research institutes; and technical consultants (these last two being different kinds of "expert organizations"). The data we collected on external alliances are less informative than the information we gathered on internal cross-border knowledge creation, since we asked only about whether the unit has engaged in technology development projects with external organizations in other regions, not about the importance or the effectiveness of these activities.

Even so, the results are striking. If we focus particularly on the international links of the two categories of United States–owned units located in the United States, the HRDUs and the home units of the U.S. FIRDUs, we find an impressive international reach for both, with surprisingly little overall difference between them. A very high proportion of both had some kind of knowledge-creating linkage with organizations in Europe (75 percent of the HRDUs and 79 percent of the FIRDUs), and about half had at least one link with an external organization in Asia (47 percent and 57 percent, respectively). But as these figures indicate, the linkages of both types of units are much denser in Europe than in Asia, and there are some interesting differences between the two types of units, as one can see from that data presented in table 9.9. One observation from these data may be worth noting. In the 1980s, critics of U.S. antitrust policies asserted that it was easier for U.S. companies to engage in technology development alliances with foreign companies than with other U. S. firms, much to the detriment of U.S. national competitiveness. This was clearly not true by the mid-1990s: both the HRDUs and the FIRDU units were more extensively involved in such linkages at home than abroad, for all six types of cooperative links, including those with competitors.

The comparison of the patterns of external technology cooperation in Asia with that in Europe provides some food for thought. The HRDUs are less active in Asia than in Europe on all six linkages. The FIRDUs are as active in horizontal links in Asia as they are in Europe, but they are less likely to maintain vertical links (with customers and suppliers) in Asia. And both are much less likely to maintain "expert linkages"—that is, with universities and government labs or with technical consultants—in Asia than in Europe.

This last pattern suggests one explanation for the lower level of cooperative links in Asia: continuing scepticism about the degree to which technology development in Asia is original, valuable, and distinctive. One interviewee, when asked about his unit's lack of technology links in Asia, replied that all the Asians' technology came from the United States in the first place, that he felt that his unit was more likely to lose technology than gain it by such technical links in Asia, and that there really wasn't as much of interest there as he found in Europe. Other interviews sug-

Table 9.9. Cross-border Technical Cooperation with Outside Organizations in Europe and Asia by Home Country Units in U.S. Firms—HRDUs and FIRDUs*

Type of Cross-Border Joint Technology Development Partner	United States HRDU	United States FIRDU	Europe HRDU	Europe FIRDU	Asia HRDU	Asia FIRDU
Horizontal Cooperative Links						
Alliance, JV, or consortium	60.4%	57.4%	49.1%	39.9%	26.4%	39.9%
Competitor	35.8%	25.7%	22.6%	12.8%	9.4%	13.5%
Vertical Cooperative Links						
Customer	77.4%	78.4%	39.6%	52.7%	22.6%	33.8%
Supplier (not owned by company)	64.2%	75.0%	22.6%	45.9%	15.1%	18.2%
Cooperative Links with "Expert Organizations"						
University or public research institute	86.8%	73.0%	28.3%	41.2%	7.5%	8.1%
Technical consultant or contractor	83.0%	81.1%	35.8%	35.8%	7.5%	14.2%

*Question: During the past *two* years, has your unit participated in product, process, or technology development activities with any of the following organizations?

gested other explanations. One is that a regional approach whereby a center or an alliance in one country in the region provides wider geographic access—a strategy increasingly common in Europe—is less viable in Asia, where the national technology systems are less interactive than in Europe. Moreover, Asia is less well-established operating terrain for U.S. firms than Europe, and many units have not had the time to develop the knowledge of potential partners and the cross-border capabilities in Asia to engage as effectively in extended alliances there. And for U.S. firms, Japan, which is the undisputed technology leader in Asia, poses more formidable problems of language and access to centers of expertise than do most European countries.

The salience of the familiarity and access factors may be gauged by looking at the difference in the Asian linkages of home country units in U.S. FIRDUs whose companies have technology development units in Asia and those whose companies do not (table 9.10). The cooperative linkages of the firms with technology development units in the region are comparable to those in Europe (virtually all the companies in the U.S. FIRDU group do have technology development centers in Europe, and so a similar comparison in that region is not possible)—with the exception of the expert organization linkages, which remain significantly lower in Asia. But these data suggest that having a unit in the region can provide a "bridge," in terms of both information and support for developing a cooperative relationship, which is lacking for the HRDUs and the units in firms without such a center.

We can also compare the local cooperative knowledge-creation links of FIRDU subsidiaries in order to assess how "embedded" they are in local technology systems. These links are not, of course, themselves cross-border links, but they extend the technology reach of the local technology development subsidiaries of the MNE and thereby provide extended resources for intracompany knowledge-creation pro-

Table 9.10. Relationship between Joint Technology Development Networks in Asia and R&D Centre in the Region

Type of Partner	With Center (n = 123)	Without Center (n = 26)
Alliance, JV, or consortium*	44.7%	15.4%
Competitor**	16.3%	0
Customer*	39.0%	7.7%
Supplier (not owned by company)**	21.1%	3.8%
University or public research institute	8.9%	3.8%
Technical consultant or contractor	16.3%	3.8%

*Chi-square test significance level < .01.
**Chi-square test significance level < .05.

cesses. They also, as table 9.10 suggested, can provide a cross-national "bridge" for their parent organizations into the local technology system. As table 9.11 shows, these units are deeply embedded in their local technology systems, and in very similar fashion. Even the Asian units (although their number is very small and we cannot make statistical significance tests with so small a sample) have developed local external knowledge-creation partnerships to an extent virtually indistinguishable from their counterparts in Europe and comparable foreign-owned units in the United States. Although we have no control group for the U.S. FIRDU subsidiaries, we can compare the non-U.S. FIRDU subsidiaries located in the United States with the HRDUs and the U.S. FIRDU home units. When we do, we find there is no statistically significant difference in terms of technology development linkages with local organizations, at least on this admittedly coarse-grained measure.

One further issue that these data allow us to explore is whether the kind of external knowledge-creation links that companies create abroad is similar to the kind they develop at home. We must remind ourselves that we are working with a very coarse-grained measure here—simply having or not having a technology develop-

Table 9.11. Local External Technology Development Linkages, FIRDU Subsidiaries

Type of External Partner	Non-U.S.-Owned FIRDUs—R&D Units in U.S.— U.S. Links (n = 33)	U.S. FIRDU Units in Europe— with European Links (n = 55)	U.S. FIRDU Units in Asia— with Asian Links (n = 8)
Alliance, JV, or consortium	48.5%	43.3%	75.0%
Competitor	27.3%	28.3%	62.5%
Customer	87.9%	56.7%	75.0%
Supplier (not owned by company)	72.7%	61.7%	62.5%
University or public research institute	81.8%	65.0%	62.5%
Technical consultant or contractor	63.3%	58.3%	62.5%

ment cooperative link with a certain category of external organization. But the data are suggestive (table 9.12). Table 9.12 divides the United States–owned, United States–located units—the HRDUs and the U.S. FIRDU home country units—into eight categories for the three most common external partnerships, the "alliances, JVs, and consortia"; customers; and universities. The eight categories are: those that have no links, domestic or international, with that type of external organization; those that have only domestic (i.e., U.S.) partners; three categories of those that have U.S. and international partners (U.S. and European; "Triad"—that is, U.S., European, and Asian; and U.S. and Asian); and three categories in which the unit has international but not domestic partners (European partners only, Asian only, and European and Asian). The most immediately obvious observation is how few units have links with international but not domestic partners. The number is largest for the "alliances" type of partner: eight HRDU units and twenty-two FIRDUs (15 percent of the total in both cases). For customers and universities, none of the HRDUs and only a very small fraction of the FIRDUs have international but not domestic partners (5 percent and 3 percent, respectively). The figures are very similar for the other three types of partners, which are not presented here only for reasons of space. Moreover, it is striking how few of the units, in either HRDU or FIRDUs, have links at home and in Asia but not in Europe. The pattern seems to one of incremental internationalization in external technology cooperation, comparable to the incremental pattern found in the process of expanding operations internationally in production (see, for example, the classic Johanson and Vahlne, 1977). In external networking across borders, R&D units, like the companies in developing their international capabilities in general, build their border-crossing capabilities over time.

The issue of border-crossing capabilities raises a final issue about external knowledge-creation linkages: do R&D units use them as a substitute for internal international knowledge-creation links? Clearly for HRDUs, they can serve as a func-

Table 9.12. Alliances at Home and Abroad: HRDUs and U.S. FIRDU Home Units

Location of Joint Knowledge-Creation Links with External Organizations	Alliances, JVs, Consortia		Customers		Universities	
	HRDUs (n = 53)	FIRDUs (n = 149)	HRDUs (n = 53)	FIRDUs (n = 149)	HRDUs (n = 53)	FIRDUs (n = 149)
No external JKC links	24.5%	26.8%	22.6%	16.7%	13.2%	23.5%
U.S. links only	22.6	17.4	37.7	28.2	54.7	33.6
United States plus Europe	18.9	12.1	17.0	18.1	24.5	31.5
United States plus Europe plus Asia (Triad)	18.9	22.1	22.6	30.2	3.8	6.7
United States plus Asia	0	6.0	0	2.0	3.8	1.3
Europe only	7.5	4.0	0	3.4	0	3.4
Asia only	3.8	9.4	0	0	0	0
Europe plus Asia, no United States	3.8	2.0	0	1.3	0	0
	100%	99.8%	99.9%	99.9%	100%	100%

tional equivalent to or substitute for their own R&D units abroad. But in FIRDUs, are the units that are less engaged in international joint knowledge creation internally more likely to engage in external linkages as a substitute? The data in fact indicate the opposite: that the units with low levels of intracompany joint knowledge creation are also less active in external linkages. For the 149 United States–owned FIRDU home units, the correlation between the five-category raw data for cross-border internal technology cooperation and the twelve-category variable for the total number of types of external technology partnerships outside the United States (six each in Europe and Asia) is .379 (significant at a level of $p < .001$). Table 9.13 provides the same data in a reduced and more visually interpretable format. This strongly suggests that a common core of border-crossing capabilities, particularly in terms of moving people and knowledge across borders, undergirds both internal and external international knowledge-creating networks, and that units develop and use that core in both contexts.

Cross-Border Knowledge-Creation Processes in R&D

We now move beyond the data gathered from the MIT-IRI study to look somewhat more conceptually at the processes of joint cross-border knowledge creation in the R&D function in MNEs.

In one of the few explicit discussions of the basic principles of cross-border knowledge creation to be found in the literature on MNEs, Ikujiro Nonaka has defined *global knowledge creation* as "global synergy of the local tacit knowledge and the global articulate knowledge" (1990:86). Clearly a core element of global knowledge creation is, as Nonaka makes clear, bringing together knowledge that is geographically dispersed. But as he also indicates, "local" and "global" can have two very distinct dimensions. One is the *location* of the knowledge (where it is); the other concerns its *nature* (the kind of knowledge it is). In terms of location, "local" usually means situated in a single subsidiary outside the central R&D organization, whereas "global" means that it is located centrally (by "central" one usually means in the home country, where most firms still have most of their innovative activity

Table 9.13. Relationship between External and Internal Interaction in Knowledge Creation, Home Country Units of U.S. FIRDUs

External Technology Partnerships Outside the United States— Number of Types	Low Internal Cross-Border Interaction (25% or Less of Technology) (n = 69)	Medium Internal Cross-Border Interaction (25% or Less of Technology) (n = 38)	High Internal Cross-Border Interaction (25% or Less of Technology) (n = 39)
0-1	46.4%	23.7%	12.8%
2-5	40.6	52.6	41.0
6 or more	13.0	23.7	46.2
	100%	100%	100%

concentrated, particularly R&D, but in the transnational or "network" model of the MNE it can mean widely shared in the network). The *location* of knowledge can be most usefully be described in geographically specific terms.

The *nature* of "local" and "global" knowledge is a more complex issue. Nonaka sees local knowledge as tacit and global knowledge as explicit. While we found that this was often the case in the various examples of international knowledge creation we collected, it was not always so. Sometimes locally situated knowledge was highly explicit: for example, knowledge of the projected future needs of local customers, or local national standards. And much of the centrally located knowledge is tacit. A more consistent distinction in terms of the *nature* of knowledge seemed to be between knowledge that was *location-specific* (that is, applicable to and in a specific, circumscribed local context) and knowledge that was, for want of a better term, *generic* (that is, applicable in and to all similar contexts). Location-specific knowledge can indeed be tacit, but it can also be explicit: for example, national regulations governing electrical transmission standards, the kind of building materials that function best in the British housing industry, or the preferences of French manufacturers in terms of the functionality of production equipment. Generic knowledge can vary by context, but only when the contexts themselves can be described in general rather than idiosyncratic terms: for example, the boiling point of water varies by altitude, but "altitude" is itself a generic descriptor of context ("x feet above sea-level," as opposed to "at the top of Mount Rainier"). In technology terms, generic knowledge that varies by context can include such examples as the technologies needed for motors operating in extremely polluted or humid environments, the kind of operating system needed to support complete nonalphabetical scripts in software programming, or the miniaturization technologies needed for products in markets that prefer small-scale, space-saving attributes. There is a dynamic interaction between generic and location-specific knowledge akin to that between tacit and explicit knowledge: often generic knowledge is expanded by the need to incorporate or explain location-specific knowledge (for example, the development of technologies needed for motors operating in extremely polluted environments can be derived by examining carefully the motors that work best in Mexican factories). And location-specific knowledge is expanded by applying generic knowledge to particular contexts.

Nonaka's definition does, however, alert us to a very important point: like tacit knowledge, location-specific knowledge is difficult to move across borders and to share across locations, largely because an understanding of the local context is often necessary to give it validity. This difficulty is compounded by the fact that in most contexts generic knowledge is seen as being "higher order" knowledge than location-specific knowledge. This can be a source of some tension in cross-border, as in crossfunctional, interactions. And although ideally the distinction between location-specific and generic is objective, in practice it is not uncommon for location-specific knowledge to be seen as generic by its holders, especially in the MNE's home country. In particular, engineers and scientists in R&D units often see technology-related knowledge—especially their own knowledge—as generic and market-related knowledge as location-specific. This causes problems when the technical knowledge is in fact location-specific (i.e., it applies in the product or process context in which the engineers are located but not another location, where surrounding conditions may vary considerably)—a fact that most technical people are very reluctant to recognize.

One example concerns a product that is usually seen as among the most internationally standardized in the world: the color television set. When Japanese companies first began trying to sell their sets to Western distributors, they were astonished to hear complaints about the quality of the color, which they regarded as superior to that of many Western manufacturers. Considerable investigation showed that whereas most Japanese viewers watched television under overhead fluorescent lighting, most Americans watched it in rooms lit by standard bulbs, and most Europeans watched television in dark rooms. Color quality varied considerably depending on the lighting conditions under which the set was watched. The "generic" knowledge about color quality held by the Japanese R&D organizations turned out to have a larger element of location-specific knowledge than they had realized. Note that this was a technical problem—the maintenance of colour quality under a wide variety of lighting conditions. Considerable further technology development on generic technologies for improving and increasing the range of color quality was necessary to develop a product whose color could be adjusted to fit the requirements of various markets.[7]

This example exemplifies the classic mode of joint cross-border knowledge-creation in R&D, indicated by Nonaka's definition of global knowledge creation as the synergy between local tacit and global explicit knowledge: *combining generic knowledge located in the central R&D organization with location-specific knowledge in various subsidiaries to produce locally tailored products.* In this mode, the key role of the local R&D unit in a dispersed network is to be the repository of location-specific knowledge, in explicit rather than tacit form as much as possible, to facilitate the combining process, which can take place primarily at the center, in the local subsidiaries, or, increasingly, in a "virtual co-location" setting (where there are dense communications links across two or more locations), with varying degrees of central and local participation. As the example of the color television set indicated, often the location-specific knowledge demands further development of generic knowledge to produce appropriate products or processes. In HRDUs, combining dispersed location-specific and central generic knowledge is not, as a rule, cross-border knowledge creation within the R&D function, since the location-specific knowledge is usually supplied by local marketing people (especially those in technical sales and support) or local manufacturing personnel; the cross-border aspects of the knowledge-creation process are therefore crossfunctional. There are cases, however, where R&D personnel are dispatched to other locations to absorb location-specific knowledge and bring it back to the center for the knowledge-combining process. A well-documented example is provided by the development of the Nissan Primera described in Nonaka and Takeuchi (1995).

A second pattern of joint cross-border knowledge creation is that of *combining generic knowledge from several locations.* Two of the reasons given for the increased internationalization of R&D over the last decade assume that the target of geographic expansion is generic technical knowledge, rather than local adaptation capabilities: the increased dispersion of centers of scientific excellence around the world, and the shortage of scientists and engineers in the home country, which can be addressed by hiring technical personnel in other countries (Westney, 1991;

Granstrand, Hakanson, and Sjolander, 1992; Howells, 1995). Where the dispersed generic knowledge is complementary, joint knowledge creation has potentially high payoffs. A well-documented case of this is the development of liquid detergent in Proctor and Gamble, where technical centers in Europe, North America, and Japan contributed the complementary generic knowledge that they had developed in order to respond to the particular needs of their local markets (Bartlett and Ghoshal, 1990). Granstrand, Hakanson, and Sjolander pointed out that "[c]reating and maintaining technological competitive advantage increasingly require access to a wider range of scientific and technological skills and knowledge than is available in the home market" and that consequently we increasingly see foreign R&D units that are "charged with the creation and renewal of core technological capabilities" (1992:9). This involves not only combining dispersed generic knowledge in the context of specific projects to develop new products or product platforms but also another mode of combining geographically dispersed generic knowledge: the creation of ongoing "competence communities" to link geographically dispersed specialists of various types in an ongoing learning community to sustain and develop generic knowledge in key technologies.

Yet another—and much less studied—mode of joint cross-border knowledge creation involves sharing location-specific knowledge. One of the oft-cited advantages of the MNE is its internal variety—to review the earlier quotation from Arnoud de Meyer, "learning about different markets, different problem-solving methods, different sources of technological progress, different culture, different competitors" (De Meyer, 1992:169). Much of this knowledge is location-specific, but this does not mean it is not relevant for other locations. There are two kinds of joint knowledge creation based on dispersed location-specific knowledge. One is *using location-specific knowledge as a base for developing generic knowledge*, through abstraction and hypothesis formation and testing. (For example, why does a certain material work better in the high-humidity, high-pollution environment of a certain tropical metropolitan market?) A second mode is *moving directly from location-specific knowledge to location-specific knowledge through analogy*. (Certain kinds of customers prefer X features in the product in France—what kinds of customers in the United States might be like them? This kind of motor works best in Mexico City—what environments in the United States are like Mexico City?)

In summary, then, we can identify at least four distinct cross-border knowledge-creation processes:

1. Combining centrally located generic knowledge with locally dispersed location-specific knowledge to add value to products and improve processes (the "classic" mode);
2. Combining generic knowledge from two or more locations (the "transnational" mode);
3. Joint cross-border interactions using location-specific knowledge as a base for generating generic knowledge for transfer to other locations;
4. Using analogy to apply location-specific knowledge from one location to another.

The first process can occur in a number of venues, from the major cross-border project to relatively short "technology transfer" interactions. The second usually revolves around large-scale cross-border joint projects. We know much less about the third and fourth modes, because they have been less studied, but our interview-based examples suggest that they are more likely to occur as a by-product of the interaction of people across borders in various ways, rather than in specific projects.

Although adding yet another category to the typology of knowledge may seem to be unnecessary elaboration, the distinction between generic and location-specific knowledge can help to address some key issues in international knowledge creation. For example, we saw earlier that different kinds of travel seem to be effective in different contexts. Given the assumption that location-specific knowledge is more difficult to share across borders than generic knowledge, and that tacit location-specific knowledge is the most difficult to share, then we can suggest that fitting travel patterns to the kind of knowledge sharing is one way to make better use of cross-border travel of technical personnel (see table 9.14). Information technology links and short visits may well be adequate for sharing explicit generic knowledge across borders, whereas sharing tacit generic knowledge might benefit from short-term transfers. Sharing explicit location-specific knowledge may be accomplished through a combination of visits and short-term transfers, whereas sharing tacit location-specific knowledge may be the venue where long-term transfers are most effective. It should be possible to test these relationships empirically.

Finally, one of the most difficult questions facing MNEs today is how geographically dispersed their R&D ought to be. No company can afford to match the dispersal of R&D to the dispersion of markets or even of production; most companies have, and will continue to have, a smaller proportion of R&D abroad than of either production or sales. One answer has been the extent to which the technology-related knowledge needed to compete effectively is geographically dispersed and locally embedded. Indeed, it is now a commonplace to say that much useful knowledge is locally embedded, with the implication that one must have a physical presence there (usually in the form of an R&D unit) to gain access to that information. But "locally embedded" can have several meanings:

Table 9.14. The Nature of Knowledge and the Type of Cross-border Interaction for Effective Joint Knowledge Creation

	Explicit Knowledge	Tacit Knowledge
Generic knowledge	*Information technology Links* *Short visits*	*Short-term transfers*
Location-specific knowledge	*Short visits* *Short-term transfers*	*Long-term transfers*

1. a high proportion of tacit knowledge;
2. a high proportion of location-specific knowledge;
3. knowledge dispersed among several local organizations;
4. any combination of the preceding.

How one goes about gaining access to such knowledge will be greatly affected by which of these aspects is applicable.

The key factor is indeed the level of dispersion of relevant technological knowledge. But given the relative ease with which explicit generic knowledge can be transferred across borders, it is useful to make some finer distinctions. The geographic dispersion of tacit generic knowledge is a more important motivator for the internationalization of R&D than that of explicit generic knowledge. An even more important criterion is the level of value added by location-specific knowledge to the products and processes of the business. The higher that level is, and the greater the proportion of tacit location-specific knowledge within that level, the greater the potential advantages of the geographic dispersion of knowledge-creation capabilities.

To summarize the main argument: cross-border knowledge creation is extensive in MNEs, and in all likelihood will increase in importance over the coming years. Studying new product development projects probably remains the most promising locus for research aimed at understanding the processes of international knowledge creation. But this should not be the only level of analysis. Research on the development of cross-border capabilities at both the organizational systems level and at the level of the border-crossing individuals—moving across borders on short visits and short-term transfers, as well as long-term expatriate assignments—is an essential complement to project-level research and has relevance for cross-border learning well beyond the R&D function.

Notes

1. Defining "innovation" and "knowledge creation" is a notoriously difficult task. In this essay I use the term "knowledge creation" instead of "innovation," although the meaning of the two is very close (knowledge creation referring more to the process and "innovation" either to the process or the outcome). Knowledge creation or innovation is here considered in the context of the particular firm in which the specific knowledge—usually a product or a process (material or organizational)—is developed, regardless of whether that knowledge is "created" in the sense of never having existed anywhere before.

2. The lead on this kind of research was taken by European scholars, and much of the European research on the topic is represented in Granstrand et al. (1992).

3. Andreas Gast and Don Lessard in a recent working paper (1996) have pointed out that capabilities in dispersed locations can be complementary or similar; joint knowledge creation in the first case enhances the scope of the MNE, and in the second enhances scale.

4. There are obviously great differences across industries and companies in how these different categories of technology development are defined; in this study, given the range of industries and companies covered, we left it up to the responding individuals to decide on their unit's portfolio of activities, without providing more detailed definitions.

5. This three-level (individual, work process, organization) typology builds on and modifies somewhat Dorothy Leonard-Barton's very useful (1992) model.

6. It is worth noting that this pattern holds across the categories for the "worldwide leader" mechanism: for the U. S. FIRDU home units, the effectiveness ratios across the levels of interaction from low to high are 51.4 percent, 81.8 percent, and 71.9 percent.

7. I am indebted for this illustration to Takeyoshi Ohgai, formerly an executive of Matsushita and now enrolled in the doctoral program at Kobe University's Institute of Management Research.

References

Aaker, David A. 1989. "Managing Assets and Skills: The Key to a Sustainable Competitive Advantage." *California Management Review* 31(2): 91–106.

Amit, Raphael, and Paul J. H. Schoemaker. 1993. "Strategic Assets and Organizational Rent." *Strategic Management Journal* 14(1): 33–46.

Bartlett, Christopher A. 1986. "Building and Managing the Transnational: The New Organizational Challenge." In *Competition in Global Industries*, edited by Michael E. Porter. Boston: Harvard Business School Press. Pp. 367–404.

Bartlett, Christopher A., and Sumantra Ghoshal. 1986. "Tap Your Subsidiaries for Global Reach." *Harvard Business Review* 64(4): 87–94.

———. 1989. *Managing across Borders: The Transnational Solution*. Boston: Harvard Business School Press.

———. 1990. "Managing Innovation in the Transnational Corporation." In *Managing the Global Firm*, edited by Christopher A. Bartlett, Yves Doz, and Gunnar Hedlund. London: Routledge. Pp. 215–55.

Buckley, Peter J., and Mark C. Casson, 1976. *The Future of the Multinational Enterprise*. London: Macmillan.

Cantwell, John A. 1989. *Technological Innovation and Multinational Corporations*. Oxford: Blackwell.

Casson, Mark C. ed. 1991. *Global Research Strategy and International Competitiveness*. Oxford: Blackwell.

Cohen, Wesley, and Daniel Levinthal. 1990. "Absorptive Capacity: A New Perspective on Learning and Innovation." *Administrative Science Quarterly* 35(1), 128–52.

De Meyer, Arnoud. 1991. "Tech Talk: How Managers Are Stimulating Global R&D Communication." *Sloan Management Review* 32(3): 49–58.

———. 1992. "The Management of International R&D Operations." In *Technology Management and International Business: The Internationalization of R&D*, edited by Ove Granstrand, Lars Hakanson, and Soren Sjolander. Chichester, England: Wiley. Pp. 163–79.

Dunning, John. 1981. *International Production and the Multinational Enterprise*. London: Allen and Unwin.

Gast, Andreas, and Donald Lessard. 1996. *Managing Multi-point Learning in the Multinational Firm*. Working paper, Sloan School of Management, Massachusetts Institute of Technology.

Ghoshal, Sumantra. 1987. "Global Strategy: An Organizing Framework." *Strategic Management Journal* 8(5): 425–40.

Granstrand, Ove, Lars Hakanson, and Soren Sjolander. 1992. *Technology Management and International Business*. Chichester, England: Wiley.

Hakanson, Lars. 1990. "International Decentralization of R&D: The Organizational

Challenges." In *Managing the Global Firm*, edited by Christopher A. Bartlett, Yves Doz, and Gunnar Hedlund. London: Routledge. Pp. 256–78.

Hedlund, Gunnar. 1986. "The Hypermodern MNE: A Heterarchy?" *Human Resource Management* 25: 9–35.

Hedlund, Gunnar, and Jonas Ridderstrahle. 1995. "International Development Projects: Key to Competitiveness, Impossible, or Mismanaged?" *International Studies of Management and Organisation* 25(1/2): 158–84.

Howells, Jeremy R. 1995. "Going Global: The Use of IT Networks in Research and Development." *Research Policy* 24(2): 169–84.

Johanson, Jan, and Jan-Erik Vahlne. 1977. "The Internationalization Process of the Firm—A Model of Knowledge Development and Increasing Foreign Market Commitments." *Journal of International Business Studies* 8(1): 23–32.

Kogut, Bruce. 1983. "Foreign Direct Investment as a Sequential Process." In *The Multinational Corporation in the 1980s*, edited by Charles P. Kindleberger and Daniel B. Audretsch. Cambridge, Mass.: MIT Press. Pp. 38–56.

———. 1985. "Designing Global Strategies: Comparative and Competitive Value Added Chains." *Sloan Management Review* (26)4: 15–28.

Leonard-Barton, Dorothy. 1992. "Core Capabilities and Core Rigidites: A Paradox in Managing New Product Development." *Strategic Management Journal* 13 Special Issue (Summer): 111–25.

Nelson, Richard. 1995. "Evolutionary Theorizing about Economic Change." In *The Handbook of Economic Sociology*, edited by Neil J. Smelser and Richard Swedborg. Princeton: Princeton University Press. Pp. 108–36.

Nelson, Richard, and Sidney Winter. 1982. *An Evolutionary Theory of Economic Change*. Cambridge, Mass.: Harvard University Press.

Nohria, Nitin, and Sumantra Ghoshal. 1997. *The Differentiated Network: Organizing Multinational Corporations for Value Creation*. San Francisco: Jossey-Bass Inc.

Nonaka, Ikujiro. 1990. "Managing Globalization as a Self-renewing Process: Experiences of Japanese MNEs." In *Managing the Global Firm*, edited by Christopher A. Bartlett, Yves Doz, and Gunnar Hedlund. London: Routledge. Pp. 69–94.

Nonaka, Ikujiro, and Hirotaka Takeuchi. 1995. *The Knowledge-Creating Company: How Japanese Companies Create the Dynamics of Innovation*. New York: Oxford University Press.

Prahalad, C. K., and Gary Hamel. 1990. "The Core Competence of the Corporation." *Harvard Business Review* 68(3): 79–91.

Ronstadt, Robert. 1977. *Research and Development Abroad by U. S. Multinationals*. New York: Praeger.

Rugman, Alan M. 1981. *Inside the Multinationals: The Economics of Internal Markets*. London: Croom Helm.

Solvell, Orjan, and Ivo Zander. 1995. Preface to "The Dynamic Multinational Firm." *International Studies of Management and Organization* 25(1/2): 3–16.

Stalk, George, Philip Evans, and Lawrence E. Shulman. 1992. "Competing on Capabilities: The New Rules of Competition." *Harvard Business Review* 70(2): 57–69.

Vernon, Raymond. 1966. "International Investment and International Trade in the Product Cycle." *Quarterly Journal of Economics* 80(2): 190–207.

———. 1979. "The Product Cycle Hypothesis in a New International Environment." *Oxford Bulletin of Economics and Statistics* 41: 255–67.

Westney, D. Eleanor. 1991. "Organizational Change and the Internationalization of R&D." In *Transforming Organizations*, edited by Thomas Kochan and Michael Useem. New York: Oxford University Press. Pp. 245–60.

10

Knowledge Creation and the Internationalization of Japanese Companies

Front-Line Management Across Borders

KENICHI YASUMURO
D. ELEANOR WESTNEY

The distinctive patterns of knowledge creation in Japanese firms and their enormous contribution to the competitiveness of Japan's leading companies has been one of the central themes of Ikujiro Nonaka's work for over a decade (Nonaka, 1985). To oversimplify his argument considerably, he sees Japanese companies as both excelling in and heavily dependent on creating and enhancing tacit knowledge, in contrast to Western companies' reliance on explicit knowledge. There is a growing body of work illuminating Japanese knowledge-creation processes, including many of the essays in this book. However, relatively little of the work on Japanese knowledge creation explicitly addresses the implications for the internationalization processes of Japanese firms. What happens when firms whose patterns of knowledge creation have been generated in the tacit-knowledge-valuing Japanese context set up subsidiaries in an explicit-knowledge-valuing society like the United States?

Exploring this question requires the addition of at least one further dimension to the study of knowledge creation: Who creates knowledge, and where in the organization is it created? Most of Nonaka's empirical work has focused on knowledge creation in new product development projects. But Japanese firms have built much of their competitive advantage through knowledge creation in production (using the term in the broadest sense) and in customer service. This essay argues that many of Japan's leading companies have developed distinctive patterns not only of *how* knowledge is created but also of *where* knowledge is created in the organization. These distinctive patterns of the locus of knowledge creation are identified here as "front-line management," and we suggest that internationalization processes are affected in significant ways by the extent to which a company has developed the management and knowledge-creation patterns of front-line management.

This essay first analyzes the issue of who creates knowledge in companies and where knowledge creation is located, and then presents a model of "front-line management." We then explore the relationships between front-line management and patterns of internationalization, and we use a data-set of 147 Japanese manufacturing multinational enterprises to explore these relationships. Finally, we discuss the implications for further research.

National Variations in the Morphology of Knowledge Creation

One of the key features of the multinational enterprise (MNE) is that it operates in a number of diverse environments (Ghoshal and Westney, 1993). Analysts of the MNE have proposed various ways of characterizing this diversity. Strategic variables are perhaps the most widely used in the international management literature: the well-known Integration-Responsiveness framework, for example, in which the key variable for analyzing the differences across national contexts is the pressure for local responsiveness (Prahalad and Doz, 1987), or Bartlett and Ghoshal's use of the concept of the "strategic importance" of the local environment (Bartlett and Ghoshal, 1989). Cultural variables have also been employed, especially Gert Hofstede's four-variable typology of country environments (Hofstede, 1980).

But another set of variables that differentiates environments concerns knowledge creation. Nonaka has consistently contrasted Japan with Western societies in terms of the value Japanese place on tacit knowledge, compared to the Western, "Cartesian" preference for explicit knowledge (Nonaka, 1990; Hedlund, 1993). But there are also distinctions across Western societies. Lessem and Neubauer, for example, categorized the Anglo-Saxon orientation to knowledge creation as pragmatic, the French-Nordic as rational, the German as holistic (a characterization they also apply to Japan), and the Latin-Italian as humanistic (Lessem and Neubauer, 1994).

Knowledge orientation constitutes only one aspect of broad societal effects on organizational knowledge creation processes. It is also important to recognize how consistently class distinctions in a society and the related status and power differences in organizations are associated with patterns of knowledge exploitation and creation. In modern industrial societies, class structure is linked to and legitimated by differences in the kind of knowledge embodied in different occupational classes and broad class categories such as managers and workers, blue-collar and white-collar, salaried and hourly employees, or exempt and nonexempt personnel. And as even the names of these categories indicate, class position is closely associated with organizational position, particularly position in the large formal organizations that dominate the economy and provide most of society's most highly rewarded and highly regarded jobs. These broad class categories are linked to different modes of knowledge mastery and knowledge creation. Formal educational qualifications and a mastery of codified—that is, explicit—knowledge (planning, budgeting, technology, financial engineering, etc.) characterize those occupying the upper level of organizations; tacit knowledge such as manual skills in manufacturing and "salesmanship" for service people tends to characterize those at lower organizational levels.

Societies vary enormously in how they evaluate and reward different kinds of work. Many analysts have observed, for example, that in the United States, despite strongly democratic and meritocratic ideologies, the distinctions between managers and workers are pronounced. The difference between workers and managers in U.S. industry, for example, is embodied in different kinds of evaluation and reward systems and symbolized in the currently fashionable terms the *nonexempt* and the *exempt* workforce. The nonexempt workers prefer a standardized wage system and equal treatment, with a strong emphasis on seniority; the exempt employees favor differentiated reward systems that reflect one's knowledge base and ability. The nonexempt employees usually prefer employment at one site throughout their work lives; the nonexempt employees usually expect to be transferred across sites (if not to move across companies) in the pursuit of their careers. And as researchers like William Lazonick and Ronald Dore have pointed out, managers have long been considered an integral part of the core resources of the company in the Anglo-Saxon economies, while workers traditionally have not (Dore, 1973; Lazonick, 1990).

These differences in rewards and in work experience are closely related to the different knowledge-creation modes that characterize the two groups. In the classic U. S. organizational hierarchy, workers are viewed as developing varying levels of skill and tacit knowledge; managers are educated in explicit analytical knowledge management. While individual workers can and do develop high levels of tacit knowledge-creation capability, the translation of this knowledge into explicit knowledge is the prerogative of the managers, the expert staff, or the professional consultants. In Taylorist approaches to production, for example, the engineer or efficiency expert analyzes "best practice" at the work site and translates this tacit knowledge into an explicit model that can then be disseminated to other workers—a translation that the workers themselves are assumed to be incapable of making.

In any company, critically important knowledge resides in the workplace—on the factory floor, within sales and service organizations that deal directly with customers, at the "bench" in the R&D lab. But companies—and, more important for our current discussion, countries—differ systematically not only in how this knowledge is used to generate new knowledge but also in the extent to which valued new knowledge is created in these "front lines" of the company. We believe that one of the most important features of the most admired Japanese companies is "front-line management," in which the workplace is recognized and valued as the center of knowledge creation and in which knowledge-creation resources (both explicit resources such as analytical methodologies and tacit knowledge) and processes (the processes described in detail in Nonaka [1990] and Nonaka and Takeuchi [1995]) are concentrated at the front line of the company. The "front line" is the factory floor, the "bench" of the engineers of the R&D lab, and key points of direct interaction with important aspects of the environment, particularly in sales and marketing organizations that interact with customers in the broadest sense (including retailers and wholesalers as well as end users).

Front-line management involves the following features:

- A high value assigned to knowledge generated on the front line, in terms of management attention, and the concentration of knowledge-creation resources, both tacit and explicit, at the front line
- The assignment of significant levels of discretion and response capability to front-line units and individuals (e.g., the capacity of individual salespeople to commit the company to nonstandard customer services in order to make a sale, or the capacity of individual engineers to go out and fix a customer problem at the customer site, without consultation and specific authorization from management)
- Diffuse responsibility for problem identification and solution generation

- An egalitarian work culture, which minimizes differences across statuses and ranks in the company

These general features can be seen in a number of specific indicators, including: ease and frequency of communication across formal ranks and statuses (e.g., manager and worker, blue- and white-collar); extensive and detailed information flows across departments and functions; low levels of formalization of procedures and decision-making rules; the frequent movement of people across units, on temporary as well as permanent rotations and on short visits.

There is a striking contrast between this model and the Weberian ideal type of bureaucracy, with its clearly-defined rights and responsibilities for each individual position, its vertical information flows, the concentration of organizational knowledge in written files and formalized procedures, and the strong emphasis on control and routinization. There is also a contrast with the actual operation of traditional U. S. industrial organization, which exemplified the Weberian model in many respects and which located knowledge creation in specialized staff units (such as market research, process engineering, quality control and inspection, purchasing, and strategic planning) and in management positions (Chandler, 1977). The contrast between the locus of knowledge creation in Japanese and traditional U.S. industrial management became obvious in the 1980s with the efforts by U.S. firms to emulate Japanese methods of quality control: a far greater role was played in the United States by private consultants, specialized quality control units, and (eventually, and as a key element in many companies) by top management (Cole, 1989; Kearns and Nadler, 1992).

The concentration of knowledge creation in the front line of organizations has become one of the distinguishing features of the best Japanese companies, but it is not synonymous with "Japanese-style management," although it shares several of its features (Okubayashi et al., 1994, for example, provides a recent discussion in Japanese of the differences between the management paradigm emerging in Japanese companies in the last few years and the older paradigm of Japanese-style management). Many of the traditional features of Japanese-style management—the *ringisei* decision-making process, the enterprise union, and the seniority-based reward system in particular—are not integral elements of front-line management. Others, such as the system of so-called permanent employment, symbolize a commitment to employees and a high valuation on their accumulated knowledge and knowledge-creation capabilities, blue-collar as well as managerial employees, that is central to front-line management. And still other features are practically as well as symbolically integral to front-line management. As several analysts have pointed out, Japanese organizations have extended to blue-collar workers many features that are confined in most Western organizations to managerial reward systems (security of employment, participation through bonuses in the economic performance of the company, salaried rather than hourly reward packages, and a sense of membership in the company). They have also incorporated into managerial reward systems some of the features traditionally associated with blue-collar organization, especially the emphasis on seniority in promotion and reward systems that is rooted in the recognition of the importance of length of experience in developing an individual's tacit knowledge base.

This egalitarianism (for want of a better term) and the elimination of many aspects of class segmentation in traditional Japanese management have been important factors in the development of front-line management.

Japanese Multinational Corporations and Front-Line Management

The international reach of Japanese companies has obviously changed considerably since the first systematic studies of Japanese multinational companies (MNCs) were conducted in the 1970s by Yoshino (1976), Tsurumi (1976), and Yoshihara (1979). However, two questions have continued to dominate the study of the internationalization of Japanese firms ever since. One is the extent to which Japanese MNCs differ significantly from Western MNCs—U.S. and European alike—in terms of the prevailing variables used in the analysis of multinational corporations. The other is the extent to which Japanese companies going abroad introduce into their foreign operations the patterns of organization that have been dubbed Japanese-style management. The two questions are of course closely linked: to the extent that Japanese MNCs do differ from their Western counterparts, one possible explanation is the effect of distinctive organizational patterns developed at home. But over time, both the focal variables in the analysis of MNCs and the definitions of the essential features of Japanese organizational patterns have changed considerably.

In terms of the first question—the distinctive features of Japanese MNCs—early studies tended to build on the key variables of the highly influential Harvard Multinational Enterprise Project of the late 1960s: the destination of foreign direct investment, control systems (including the use of expatriate managers and headquarters-subsidiary relationships), organizational structure, and ownership patterns (for a more detailed review of this literature, see Westney, 1999). Some of the features identified as distinctively Japanese in the analyses of the 1970s (such as the channeling of investment to developing countries rather than the highly industrialized markets and the preference for joint ventures over wholly owned operations) proved to be characteristic of the early stages of the multinationalization process (that is, life-cycle effects) rather than persisting features of the Japanese MNCs. Since the mid-1980s, the central focus of concern in the analysis of the MNC has shifted from the ownership and control patterns so emphasized in the 1970s and early 1980s to a concern with strategies for cross-border integration, local responsiveness, and—most relevant to knowledge creation—learning and innovation (Bartlett and Ghoshal, 1986; Hedlund, 1986; Ghoshal, 1987). But continuously, from the mid-1970s to the mid-1990s, analysts identified a set of distinctive features that apparently persisted over time and across the life cycle of Japan's MNCs (at least to date). The most frequently observed (and criticized) is the relatively high proportion of Japanese expatriates in top management positions in the foreign subsidiaries. In addition, the following characteristics have been observed in a number of studies over time:

- A much higher proportion of expatriates in functional as well as top management roles than is found or expected in Western MNCs (Tsurumi, 1976; Yoshihara, 1979; Okumura, 1989)

- Dense communications flows between local operations and the Japanese parent organization (Tsurumi, 1976:250; Kujawa, 1986)
- An organizational structure that differs significantly from the "country subsidiary" characteristic of traditional Western MNCs: manufacturing and marketing subsidiaries are incorporated separately within each country, and often different local companies are set up for different businesses that are housed in Japan within the single parent company structure (Yoshihara, 1979; Kagono and Campbell, 1994).

These three features are not only highly interrelated; they are also knowledge linked, as several researchers have noted. More than two decades ago, Michael Yoshino, for example, attributed the fact that in the Japanese manufacturing subsidiaries he studied in Thailand, Malaysia, and Taiwan Japanese managers tended to occupy almost all key positions to a combination of the need for Japanese language mastery (in order to communicate effectively with the home base), the Japanese manager's need to have key subordinates "who share the same work style," and the high level of tacit knowhow involved in operations (Yoshino, 1976:167–8). In a study of the international manufacturing operations of Japanese electronics firms conducted at virtually the same time, Yoshi Tsurumi found an average of one expatriate plant manager and six to eight Japanese engineers and managers per plant, and he attributed this extremely high expatriate ratio to three factors: a technology transfer process that emphasized "face-to-face communication and learning by doing"; the fact that each expatriate had dense personal knowledge of only one aspect of the production process, requiring what he called a task force approach to technology transfer; and the prevalence of what he called multilateral base-touching across individuals, functions, and units in Japan and abroad (Tsurumi 1976:190–97).

The third feature noted—the distinctive organizational structure of Japanese MNCs—has been much less studied than the first two, perhaps because the persistence of this structure became apparent at virtually the same time that the focus of attention in the study of MNCs shifted away from the analysis of formal structure toward a process-oriented model of cross-border integration. One obvious outcome of the establishment of multiple subsidiaries, differentiated by function and by product sector, is that it simplifies and clarifies cross-border functional lines of communication, facilitating the dense communications characteristic of Japanese MNCs. In one of the few explicit discussions of this issue, Kagono and Campbell link it to the attributes of what we are calling front-line management: they argue that the smaller and more focused units encourage managerial innovation and entrepreneurship (1994:120). But not all Japanese companies actually realize these advantages of innovation and entrepreneurship from the differentiated structure; several analysts in the late 1980s and early 1990s in fact argued that the lack of such locally based innovation was a key weakness of Japanese MNCs to date (Bartlett and Yoshihara, 1988; Okumura, 1989; DeNero, 1990). One reason for this disagreement is that although virtually all Japanese companies rely heavily on expatriate managers and dense parent-subsidiary communications, not all have built the capabilities associated with front-line management.

The variations across companies in the adoption of front-line management also explain the fact that although the findings on the "distinctively Japanese" MNC patterns listed here have been consistent across time and across industries, the findings on the second major research question—the implementation of "Japanese-style," home country–based management patterns—have been mixed and inconsistent. One reason for the variety of findings is of course the great variety of definitions of what constitutes the core of "Japanese-style management" within Japan itself. From the earliest studies, it was clear that the patterns initially defined as the distinctive features of Japanese-style management—enterprise unions, seniority-based rewards and promotions, and permanent employment (Abegglen, 1958)—were not being transferred abroad. But it was equally clear that many other features were being adopted and adapted into local subsidiaries: Tsurumi, for example, found what he called "the creation of Little Japans" in factories, in terms of production procedures (1976:194). However, during the first decade of research on Japanese MNCs, there were only a handful of studies focused on work organization (e.g., Johnson and Ouchi, 1974). Most analysts, in keeping with the established focus of International Business research, focused on managerial decision-making and control systems rather than the factory floor. It was when Japanese companies began investing heavily in North America in the mid-1980s that scholarly attention was systematically drawn to the international transfer and adaptation of patterns of work organization in Japanese MNCs. From then on, the stream of research on work organization in Japanese-owned factories in the United States and Europe has grown and has focused increasingly on specific work practices (for example, Kujawa, 1986; Abo, 1994; Campbell and Burton, 1994; Kenney and Florida, 1993; Kim, 1995; Beechler and Bird, 1999). These studies have found considerable variation across industries and across companies. The only consistent finding has been that blue-collar workers seem to have adapted to the work organization of Japanese overseas plants more easily and with higher satisfaction levels than local managers.

Despite the lack of consistent findings across the various empirical studies, those who study Japanese MNCs (and those employed in them) recognize that the organizational patterns in local subsidiaries are strongly affected by the patterns that the company has developed at home: that is, there is a strong "home country effect" on Japanese MNC organization. Some of these home country effects are quite consistent across time and across industries and companies; others show considerable variation across companies. But it is important to note that this variation is not random. We would argue that many, if not most, of the consistent home country effects are related to the widespread reliance in Japanese organizations on tacit knowledge and its associated organizational patterns. We suggest that much of the systematic variation across companies in home country effects is explainable in terms of the level to which the parent company has developed front-line management patterns in its home country organization. We argue that those companies characterized by front-line management at home will adopt similar patterns in their subsidiaries abroad, both because managers see these patterns as crucial to the company's competitiveness, particularly to the continuous innovation processes on which such companies rely so heavily, and because of what Richard Scott has called cognitive institutionalization: as Michael Yoshino pointed out as early as 1976, managers in these companies take front-line management patterns for granted as the way to manage and cannot easily conceive of managing in any other way.

The following section presents the results of an exploratory study of Japanese MNCs conducted by the first author of this paper and examines the differences in organizational patterns adopted abroad between companies that score high on front-line management practices at home and those that do not.

Empirical Analysis of Subsidiary Organizational Patterns in Japanese MNCs

In 1994, the Kansai Productivity Center (*Kansai Seisansei Honbu*) sponsored a questionnaire study of Japanese MNCs that covered management practices and organizational patterns that they employed at home and in their subsidiaries abroad. The target group of companies was selected by examining of published data on Japanese firms and identifying those companies that fell into any one of the following three groups:

1. Companies listed on the Tokyo Stock Exchange that had manufacturing subsidiaries (with ownership ratios of 25 percent or higher) in more than three countries
2. Unlisted companies with five or more manufacturing subsidiaries (with ownership ratios of 25 percent or higher)
3. Service companies with wholly owned foreign branches or sales subsidiaries in more than three countries (liaison offices were not counted)

This process identified a set of 640 companies, to whom questionnaires were mailed in September 1994; 199 companies returned completed questionnaires, for a total response ratio of 31.09 percent. The analysis in this essay uses only the data from the 147 manufacturing companies in this sample. Of these 147 firms, 39 had fewer than one thousand employees in Japan, 58 had one thousand to five thousand, 24 had five thousand to ten thousand, and 26 had more than ten thousand. Two-thirds of the firms belonged to one of three major industry categories: 37 (25 percent) to electrical machinery (including precision manufacturing), 31 (21 percent) to general machinery (including transportation equipment), and 28 (19 percent) to light industry (including food and textiles).

The questionnaires asked one respondent from each company to assess, on a scale of 1 to 5, the importance of twenty-five specific organizational patterns and practices associated with front-line management in its operations in Japan. The scores on these twenty-five items were totalled to provide a Front-line Management (FLM) Score for each company, with a possible maximum score of 125. This score provided the basis for assigning each company either to the High FLM group (made up of companies with a total score of 85 points or more) or to the Low FLM group (companies with scores of less than 85). This yielded a group of sixty-nine High FLM and a group of seventy-eight Low FLM companies. The questionnaire also used the five-point rating scale to assess the importance of a number of organizational patterns and practices in the company's foreign subsidiaries. The average scores on these questions were then compared for the High and Low groups, to test for statistically significant differences between them.

Key descriptive statistics on the number of foreign subsidiaries and the number of local rather than expatriate presidents of those subsidiaries for the two groups are provided in table 10.1. The High FLM group had a larger number of foreign subsidiaries (a difference that was significant at the .10 level), a finding that was not surprising, given that we would expect a front-line management company to value a direct organizational presence in its markets to provide a direct "front line" through which to learn in that environment. Moreover, because this analysis used the existence of foreign manufacturing subsidiaries abroad as a criterion for inclusion in the study, it left out the kind of firm included in Yoshihara's pioneering 1979 study: the export-oriented firm that keeps manufacturing at home. We would expect that this group of firms would score even lower on the Front-line Management measure than the Low FLM group included in the study.

However, there was no statistically significant difference between the two groups in their reliance on expatriate managers. Both groups were more likely to have a local president in a sales subsidiary than in a manufacturing subsidiary, but even in sales, the most "local" function of the multinational corporation, the ratio of local presidents was not high. Overall, in the Low FLM group, 25 percent of the foreign subsidiaries on average had local presidents; the High FLM group had a somewhat higher average at 31 percent, but the difference was not significant.

These findings are consistent both with those of the very early studies of Japanese MNCs and with more recent studies: Japanese MNCs continue to have a high proportion of expatriates in key management positions in their foreign subsidiaries, regardless of their commitment to front-line management. The persistence of this pattern, despite vociferous local criticism, exhortation to change from management scholars (e.g., Bartlett and Yoshihara, 1988), and repeated declarations by top managers in Japanese companies of their commitment to *genchika* (localization), indicates that this pattern has deep roots in Japanese organizational systems. We believe that it is linked to the key roles of managers in the information and knowledge-creation systems of the Japanese firm (Nonaka, 1990). In a multinational system involving close integration between the activities of home and local operations and across various local subsidiaries, shared values at the top manage-

Table 10.1. Internationalization of the Firm and the Localization of Top Executive Position

	Average Scores	
	Low Group (n = 78)	High Group (n = 69)
Average number of foreign subsidiaries*	9.10	16.28
Average number of local national presidents (production subs)	0.91	1.64
Average number of local national presidents (sales subs)	1.33	3.39

*Indicates t-test for difference of means significant at p < .10.

ment levels are critically important in providing the base for communication and integration, as scholars of the MNC have been arguing for the last decade (Hedlund, 1986; Prahalad and Doz, 1987; Bartlett and Ghoshal, 1989). As Nonaka has argued, tacit knowledge management and decision-making on the basis of dense information-sharing and shared experience are characteristic of firms in the Japanese context. And several studies have shown how uncomfortable professionally trained, explicit knowledge–oriented Western managers are with this mode of management (Kano, 1980a; Yoshihara, 1989; Nonaka and Takeuchi, 1995).

Although this reliance on tacit knowledge is shared across Japanese companies and is reflected in the absence of significant difference in the localization of top management in the High and Low FLM groups in this study, it is likely that the role of the expatriate manager, and therefore the reasons for maintaining a high proportion of expats, differs between the two groups. In the Low FLM group, the key factors probably lie in the need for managers to participate in the home country–centered communications and decision-making systems, as Bartlett and Yoshihara (1988) suggested. But in the High FLM group, a more significant factor might well be the role required of top managers in a front-line management system. They need to be actively involved in encouraging knowledge creation at the front line of the organization, and in minimizing the status distinctions between categories of workers and types of knowledge, distinctions that are often embedded in local culture and shared at the deepest level by local managers. There is in fact some indication of a difference in top management roles in subsidiaries in the High and Low FLM groups in some of the data from this study.

The questionnaire also inquired about two other features of international structure that we would expect to differ significantly between the two groups: the mother-daughter factory system and direct horizontal communications between foreign subsidiaries (table 10.2).

The mother-daughter factory system in Japanese firms, especially in the auto industry, has received considerable coverage in the popular North American press. The "mother" factory in Japan provides the physical and organizational templates for the "daughter" factory in a foreign country and trains not only its technicians but often key members of its blue-collar labor force. The relationship often evolves over time. In the first stage, the mother factory, the largest in size and equipped with the latest technology, transfers its technologies to the daughter factory and provides on-the-job training for its employees. In the second stage, the daughter factory often

Table 10.2. The Mother-Daughter Factory System and Direct Cross-subsidiary Information Sharing

	Low Group (n = 78)	High Group (n = 69)
Percentage reporting application of mother-daughter factory system	15.4%	20.3%
Percentage reporting direct information exchange across foreign subsidiaries	62.8%	71.0%

develops the capabilities to support newer factories in the same country or region. And in the third stage, the mother and daughter factories form a mutual learning network on a global basis. This kind of "global factory network" provides an arena for rapid joint knowledge creation and the transfer of both tacit and explicit knowledge through the sharing of "front-line" experience. This relationship is often more informal than formal. We would expect the pattern to be more widely used in the High FLM group than the Low.

As table 10.2 shows, however, the proportion of companies in the sample reporting the use of the mother-daughter factory system is surprisingly low for both groups: 15 percent in the Low group and 20 percent in the High group, a difference that is not statistically significant. It may well be that this system is, like the use of expatriates, more closely linked to tacit knowledge factors than to front-line management and therefore differs little across the two groups. The low level of adoption suggests that it is most suited to extremely complex production processes (like automobile assembly) involving high levels of tacit knowledge. Again, further investigation could explore these patterns more deeply.

In the "new" models of the MNC developed since the mid-1980s (the heterarchy of Gunnar Hedlund, the multifocal MNC of Prahalad and Doz, the transnational model of Bartlett and Ghoshal), the expansion of direct horizontal communications across subsidiaries is a key change from older models, which were characterized either by low levels of cross-border communications from largely autonomous, locally oriented subsidiaries or by vertical communication between parent and subsidiaries. The new pattern of cross-unit horizontal communications would seem to be especially compatible with front-line management, which features dense horizontal communications within each unit. We found no significant difference between the Low and High groups in the study in the existence of patterns of horizontal cross-unit communications: a high proportion of companies in both groups report such communication patterns (although the number in the High group is slightly greater). However, the questionnaire asked only about the presence or absence of such patterns; future studies more narrowly targeted on communication would be necessary to uncover differences in the volume and kind of cross-unit interactions between the two groups.

Vertical communications between parent company and foreign subsidiaries were also a target of inquiry in the questionnaire, which asked respondents to rate seventeen mechanisms of communication on a five-point scale (where 1 = unimportant, 2 = less important, 3 = neutral, 4 = important, and 5 = very important). The results are presented in table 10.3, which orders the mechanisms in terms of their rank order for the High FLM group. The High group's average importance score was significantly higher than that of the Low group for twelve of the seventeen mechanisms, suggesting that the volume and range of means of cross-border communications in the High group is indeed (as we expected) greater than in the Low group. But although the importance ratings were different, the rank order was quite similar for the two groups. Fax communications were the most important, followed by phone communications. Interestingly enough, the newer communications of video conferencing and computer networks were much less important, nether having an average rating above 3 (neutral); indeed, the computer networks were ranked next

Table 10.3. Method of Information Exchange between Parent and Foreign Subsidiaries

	Average Scores	
Means and Methods	Low Group (n = 70)	High Group (n = 68)
1. Information exchange by fax**	4.53	4.75
2. Information exchange by telephone***	4.36	4.72
3. Business trips to foreign subs.**	4.17	4.44
4. Business trips from foreign subs.**	3.60	3.94
5. Manuals for new product and production knowhow (reverse scoring)***	2.93	3.49
6. Information exchange by audio-visual devices (e.g., video conferencing)	2.62	2.91
7. Personnel interchange with subsidiaries***	2.26	2.85
8. Inquiry into foreign subsidiary by parent	2.70	2.85
9. Organization of international project teams**	2.36	2.81
10. Company-wide campaign for new product and latest technology*	2.36	2.77
11. Employee training in the human resources center**	2.23	2.68
12. Social meetings of worldwide executives	2.33	2.65
13. Publish a company journal in English	2.52	2.63
14. Interchange of public relations and advertising personnel**	2.23	2.62
15. Interchange of merchandisers**	2.22	2.62
16. Information exchange by computer networks**	2.13	2.57
17. Worldwide quality control circle meetings	2.20	2.31

Average scores are on a five-point scale of evaluation, where 1 = "unimportant," 2 = "less important," 3 is neutral, 4 = "important," and 5 = "very important." The number of respondents in the "low" group changes across these tables because not all respondents provided all the information necessary to compile the data.
***Indicates t-test for difference of means significant at $p < .01$; ** at $p < .05$; * $p < .10$.

to last for the High group. Face-to-face communications through business trips to and from the subsidiary was much more important, being ranked third and fourth respectively for both groups.

The division into the High and Low FLM groups was based on their implementation of front-line management in their operations in Japan, and the issue of whether they actually introduced front-line management patterns into their foreign operations was a key concern of the questionnaire study. The questionnaire asked respondents to rate the importance in their foreign subsidiaries of ten policies associated with front-line management (table 10.4). As we would expect, the companies whose scores on front-line management at home put them into the High FLM group had significantly higher scores than companies in the Low FLM group on all ten measures used to assess front-line management in the subsidiaries. In the High FLM group, the average score for eight of the ten items was over 4; none of the items averaged over 4 in the Low FLM group. Indicators of dense information flows and front-line knowledge-creation activities such as *kaizen* (continuous improvement) movements, quality control circles, and suggestion systems were all significantly

Table 10.4. Implementation of Front-line Management in Foreign Subsidiaries

	Average Scores	
Key Features of Front-line Management	Low Group (n = 72)	High Group (n = 68)
1. Management through open access and information (e.g., product volume, defect rates, productivity)***	3.76	4.41
2. Management by walking around***	3.72	4.25
3. Manuals and job descriptions in local language***	3.76	4.24
4. Recreation and parties planned by each workplace***	3.69	4.24
5. "Kaizen" (continuous improvement) movement***	3.67	4.15
6. "Keep workpace clean" movement***	3.58	4.12
7. Quality control circle activities***	3.61	4.10
8. Suggestion system***	3.56	4.02
9. Use of project teams**	3.29	3.67
10. Use of first names rather than titles**	2.99	3.32

Average scores are on a five-point scale of evaluation, where 1 = "unimportant," 2 = "less important,"
3 is neutral, 4 = "important," and 5 = "very important."
***Indicates t-test for difference of means significant at $p < .01$; **at $p < .05$.

more important in the subsidiaries of the High group. Managers were also much more likely to manage "by walking around" and establishing a visible presence at the front line in subsidiaries of the High FLM group, an indicator of the difference between the two groups in subsidiary manager roles (HRM) that we discussed earlier.

Human resource management (HRM) policies in the broadest sense are critically important for front-line management, and the survey found significant differences between the two groups on six of nine indicators used to assess HRM policies for foreign subsidiaries (table 10.5). The High FLM group ranked five of these policies at an

Table 10.5. Human Resource Policies for Foreign Subsidiaries

	Average Scores	
Human Resources Management Policies	Low Group (n = 71)	High Group (n = 68)
1. Equal treatment of employees (single status)	4.17	4.28
2. Management by objectives (MBO)**	3.89	4.14
3. Management-labor union cooperation**	3.73	4.04
4. System of in-house awards**	3.68	4.02
5. Promotion from within	3.85	4.00
6. Regular employment of college graduates	2.59	3.84
7. Bonus system	3.56	3.84
8. Permanent employment arrangement (as in Japan)**	2.61	2.94

Average scores are on a five-point scale of evaluation, where 1 = "unimportant," 2 = "less important,"
3 is neutral, 4 = "important," and 5 = "very important."
**Indicates t-test for difference of means significant at $p < .05$.

average of 4 or higher, the Low group only one. There was no significant difference between the two groups on the most highly rated indicator, equal treatment of employees (symbolized by the use of a single category of employee) or on one of the other top five items, promotion from within. But the companies in the High group were significantly more likely to emphasize management by objectives, management–labor union cooperation, and internal reward systems. Perhaps even more worthy of note is the fact that none of the HRM practices traditionally identified as "Japanese-style management"—permanent employment, seniority system, or bonus system—were among the items rated highly by either group.

A central element of HRM is the education and training provided for employees. The questionnaire asked the respondents to assess the importance of seven mechanisms for training employees in the subsidiaries on a five-point scale. The results are presented in table 10.6. For all but the least important of the training mechanisms, the average importance was significantly higher for the High group of companies than for the low. On-the-job training was most important for both groups of companies, but it ranked as much more important for the High group. On-the-job training is important for virtually all Japanese companies but it is a central feature of front-line management. Although explicit knowledge can be acquired through formal classroom education, either prior to recruitment into a company or at training and educational facilities within and outside the company after recruitment (off-the-job training), tacit knowledge is best acquired on the job. The High FLM companies ranked multijob training on the job through the elimination of detailed job classifications second, but the Low group ranked it considerably below off-the-job training in the local training center. Training outside the company was the least important for both groups of companies.

The questionnaire also asked the respondents, as executives of the parent company, to give their own evaluation of the effectiveness of the education and train-

Table 10.6. Education and Training for Local Employees

Training Policies	Average Scores	
	Low Group (n = 72)	High Group (n = 67)
1. On-the-job (OJT) training in the workplace***	4.17	4.54
2. Elimination of detailed job classification in favor of small number of classifications and multijob training***	3.06	3.67
3. Off-the-job training in the company training center**	3.36	3.66
4. OJT in the parent organization*	2.94	3.25
5. Off-the-job training in the parent organization*	2.60	2.93
6. Sending employees to outside training centers and postgraduate courses**	2.09	2.49
7. Dispatching employees to outside tasks such as community service, etc.	2.43	2.40

Average scores are on a five-point scale of evaluation, where 1 = "unimportant," 2 = "less important," 3 is neutral, 4 = "important," and 5 = "very important."
***Indicates t-test for difference of means significant at $p < .01$; **at $p < .05$; *$p < .10$.

ing programs of subsidiaries on nine different dimensions on a five-point scale. These data are presented in table 10.7. On all but one of the nine variables, the executives in the High FLM group rated the subsidiary programs as significantly more effective than did their counterparts in the Low group. They gave average ratings of over 4 to three of the nine items, whereas none of the items received a rating of 4 or higher from the Low FLM group. The highest rated item for the High group was a central element of front-line management: instilling a culture of continuous effort for quality improvement. The most highly rated item for the Low group was a much more task-focused factor: workplace safety. Clearly, at least in the view of the parent company executives, the education and training programs in subsidiaries in the High FLM companies were more effective than those in the Low and seemed to be more oriented to instilling the knowhow and culture of front-line management.

The survey provides evidence that Japanese companies differ in the extent to which they have adopted the patterns of front-line management and that those differences have a significant and far-reaching effect on their internationalization patterns. As anticipated, some of the distinctive features of Japanese MNCs, particularly the use of expatriate managers, seem to be common across Japanese MNCs, regardless of their level of adoption of front-line management. But the introduction of Japanese-based home-country patterns into local subsidiaries, particularly in terms of work organization, human resource management, and workforce train-

Table 10.7. Evaluation by Parent Company Executives of the Results of Education and Training Programs in Overseas Subsidiaries

| | Average Scores | |
| | Low Group | High Group |
Objectives	(n = 57)	(n = 62)
1. Continuous effort for the improvement of quality***	3.39	4.33
2. Risk management in the workplace to eliminate hazardous work**	3.93	4.21
3. Thorough comprehension acceptance of factory culture and order***	3.65	4.02
4. Management knowhow in promoting group activities (e.g., quality control circles)**	3.65	3.98
5. Means of building team spirit and team activities**	3.68	3.94
6. Partnership between engineers and workers on the shop floor**	3.60	3.92
7. Rigorous procurement management for materials and parts**	3.35	3.87
8. Thorough comprehension and acceptance of corporate philosophy**	3.51	3.82
9. Environmental management for pollution prevention	3.60	3.79

Average scores are on a five-point scale of evaluation, where 1 = "almost no result," 2 = "relatively poor result," 3 is neutral, 4 = "relatively good result," and 5 = "very good result." The number of respondents in the "low" group completing this part of the questionnaire is particularly low, and suggests that the gap between the low and high group may be even greater than the data suggest, since those executives most critical of their companies would be reluctant to respond (more reluctant than executives who felt less critical). ***Indicates t-test for difference of means significant at $p < .01$; **at $p < .05$.

ing, seems to vary considerably across companies, depending on their adoption of front-line management systems at home. Companies with strong front-line management systems at home placed a stronger emphasis on information sharing between parent and foreign subsidiaries, on the introduction of front-line management systems into their foreign operations, on an egalitarian approach to local employees, on education and training for locals, and on the dissemination of front-line management philosophy and culture to their subsidiaries.

Directions for Future Research

Over the last two decades, Western managers and management scholars alike have come to recognize and admire the capabilities exhibited by Japan's leading companies in continuously improving quality, productivity, and products; rapidly responding to customers; and coping with volatile exchange rates and changes in the business environment. These capabilities are rooted in a management system that emphasizes knowledge creation at the front line of the organization, where knowledge creation resources are concentrated and where tacit and explicit knowledge is shared and combined regardless of the formal organizational position or status of those involved.

This front-line management system is not equally characteristic of all Japanese companies, as this essay has demonstrated. Some companies have gone much further than others in developing and applying its principles and organizational patterns. Those companies that have been most active in developing front-line management at home have made great efforts to introduce it into their subsidiariues abroad, efforts that in the view of their Japanese executives have been quite effective. But we need further research into the processes by which front-line management is introduced into a number of different social contexts, with widely differing class structures and knowledge-creation systems. The challenges to the system would probably be very different in, for example, Indonesia and France. The issue of the relationships among knowledge-creation processes, the loci of knowledge creation in organizations and in society, and their associated status systems within the firm and within the larger society (in the form of class systems) is one that has been surprisingly neglected by research on both comparative business systems and on international business.

Front-line management, in terms of its general principles, is far from being uniquely Japanese. Recent changes in U.S. management—signaled by such terms as *re-engineering, empowerment, the high commitment organization*—can be seen as moves toward a form of front-line management, but one that combines its general principles with deeply embedded aspects of the U.S. business system, including a strong emphasis on explicit knowledge, professionalized "expert" managers, and low job security. The different form taken by front-line management in different societies, and the effects of these different forms on multinationals from various countries, are topics on which further research will contributed to our understanding of the development of multinational corporations, the evolution of business systems, and the evolution of systems and processes of knowledge creation.

References

Abegglen, James C. 1958. *The Japanese Factory*. Glencoe, Ill.: Free Press.

Abo, Tetsuo, ed. 1994. *Hybrid Factory: The Japanese Production System in the United States*. New York: Oxford University Press.

Bartlett, Christopher A., and Sumantra Ghoshal. 1986. "Tap Your Subsidiaries for Global Reach." *Harvard Business Review* 64(4): 87–94.

———. 1989. *Managing across Borders: The Transnational Solution*. Boston: Harvard Business School Press.

Bartlett, Christopher A., and Hideki Yoshihara. 1988. "New Challenges for Japanese Multinationals: Is Organization Adaptation their Achilles Heel?" *Human Resource Management* 27(1): 19–43.

Beechler, Schon L., and Allan Bird. 1999. *Japanese Multinationals Abroad*. New York: Oxford University Press.

Campbell, Nigel, and Fred Burton, eds. 1994. *Japanese Multinationals: Strategies and Management in the Global Kaisha*. London: Routledge.

Chandler, Alfred D. 1977. *The Visible Hand: The Managerial Revolution in American Business*. Cambridge: Harvard University Press.

Cole, Robert E. 1989. *Strategies for Learning: Small-group Activities in American, Japanese, and Swedish Industry*. Berkeley: University of California Press.

DeNero, Henry. 1990. "Creating the 'Hyphenated' Corporation." *McKinsey Quarterly* (4): 153–73.

Dore, Ronald P. (1973). *British Factory, Japanese Factory: The Origin of National Diversity in Industrial Relations*. Berkeley: University of California Press.

Ghoshal, Sumantra. 1987. "Global Strategy: An Organizing Framework." *Strategic Management Journal* 8(5): 425–40.

Ghoshal, Sumantra, and D. Eleanor Westney. 1993. Introduction to *Organization Theory and the Multinational Corporation*, edited by Sumantra Ghoshal and D. Eleanor Westney. London: Macmillan. Pp. 1–23.

Hedlund, Gunnar. 1986. "The Hypermodern MNC: A Heterarchy?" *Human Resource Management* 25: 9–35.

———. 1993. "Assumptions of Hierarchy and Heterarchy, with Application to the Management of the Multinational Corporation." In *Organization Theory and the Multinational Corporation*, edited by Sumantra Ghoshal and D. Eleanor Westney. London: Macmillan. Pp. 211–36.

Hofstede, Gert. 1980. *Culture's Consequences: International Differences in Work-related Values*. Beverly Hills, Calif.: Sage.

Johnson, Richard T., and William G. Ouchi. 1974. "Made in America (Under Japanese Management)." *Harvard Business Review* 52(5): 61–69.

Kagono, Tadao, and Nigel Campbell. 1994. "Organizational Perestroika: Intra-company Markets in Japanese Multinational Corporations." In *Japanese Multinationals: Strategies and Management in the Global Kaisha*, edited by Nigel Campbell and Fred Burton. London: Routledge. Pp. 113–22.

Kano, Akihiro. 1980a. "Akio Morita and his Sony Corporation." *President* 9 (September).

———. 1980b. "Sony America." *President* 10 (October).

Kearns, David, and David Nadler. 1992. *Prophets in the Dark*. New York: Harper.

Kenney, Martin, and Richard Florida. 1993. *Beyond Mass Production: The Japanese System and its Transfer to the United States*. New York: Oxford University Press.

Kim, Choong-Soon. 1995. *Japanese Industry in the American South*. London: Routledge.

Kujawa, Duane. 1986. *Japanese Multinationals in the United States: Case Studies*. New York: Praeger.

Lazonick, William. 1990. "Organizational Capabilities in American Industry: The Rise and Decline of Managerial Capitalism." *Business and Economic History* (2nd series, 19): 35–54.

Lessem, Ronnie, and Franz-Friedrich Neubauer. 1994. *European Management Systems: Toward Unity out of Cultural Diversity*. London: McGraw-Hill Books.

Nonaka, Ikujiro. 1985. *Kigyo Shinka-ron* (Corporate evolution: Managing organizational information creation). Tokyo: Nihon Keizai Shimbunsha.

———. 1990. *Chishiki-sozo no Keiei* (A Theory of Organizational Knowledge Creation). Tokyo: Nihon Keizai Shimbunsha.

Nonaka, Ikujiro, and Hirotaka Takeuchi. 1995. *The Knowledge-Creating Company: How Japanese Companies Create the Dynamics of Innovation*. New York: Oxford University Press.

Okubayashi, K., N. Shoumura, A. Takebayashi, M. Morita, and N. Uebayashi. 1994. *Jukozo Soshiki Paradaimu Josetsu—Shinsedai no Nihonteki Keiei* (Introduction to the paradigm of flexible organization structure: A new generation of Japanese-style management). Tokyo: Bunshindo.

Okumura, Akihiro. 1989. "Guro-barize-shon to Nihonteki Keiei no Shinka." In *Guro-baru Kiko to Kaigai Shinshutsu Butai: Takokuseki Kigyo to Kokusai Soshiki*, edited by Akihiro Okumura and Mikio Kato. Tokyo: Tokyo Daiichi Hoki Shuppan KK. 15: 318–31.

Prahalad, C. K., and Yves Doz. 1987. *The Multinational Mission: Balancing Local Demands and Global Vision*. New York: Free Press.

Tsurumi, Yoshi. 1976. *The Japanese Are Coming: A Multinational Interaction of Firms and Politics*. Cambridge, Mass: Ballinger.

Westney, D. Eleanor. 1999. "Changing Perspectives on the Organization of Japanese Multinational Companies." In *Japanese Multinationals Abroad: Individual and Organizational Learning*, edited by Schon L. Beechler and Allan Bird. New York: Oxford University Press. Pp. 11–29.

Yasumuro, Kenichi. 1994. *Takokuseki Kigyo Bunka*. Tokyo: Bunshindo.

Yoshihara, Hideki. 1979. *Takokuseki Kigyo Ron*. Tokyo: Hakuto Shobo.

———. 1989. "The Bright and the Dark Sides of Japanese Management Overseas." In *Japanese and European Management: Their International Adaptability*, edited by Kazuo Shibagaki, Malcolm Trevor, and Tetsuo Abo. Tokyo: University of Tokyo Press. Pp. 18–30.

Yoshino, Michael Y. 1976. *Japan's Multinational Enterprises*. Cambridge: Harvard University Press.

PART IV
INTERFIRM RELATIONS

11

Coevolution of Interorganizational Relations

TOSHIHIRO NISHIGUCHI

The purpose of this essay is to discuss and develop a new coevolutionary model of organizational relations. In this model, well-formed interorganizational relations are best thought of as poised on the edge between exploitation and symbiosis. Thus they are constantly fluctuating between competition and cooperation, forever being redefined. New value and knowledge will emerge from the destabilizing interaction of the two systems that coevolve in a spiral manner over time. This twister may be a direct product not of dialectics (thesis-antithesis-synthesis) but rather of an interplay between structures within a structure, in which the interaction of parts constitutes the whole.

Traditionally, exploitation and symbiosis systems have been perceived as dichotomous and thus at best accommodated in a bipolar manner. In contrast, in the new interpretation that follows, a dynamically unstable order subsuming the two systems is seen as archetypical for coevolutionary creation. This essay emphasizes the self-referential aspect of coevolutionary mechanisms that enable effective interorganizational relations.

The first section discusses epistemological premises, traditional systems theory, complex dynamical systems, and some key concepts, including field, organizational reflection, strategic process, result information and process information, functional skills, and contextual skills. The second section discusses exploitation and symbiosis systems, as well as mechanisms of interorganizational coevolution, followed by implications and conclusions in the final section.

Epistemological Premises

Self-Referential Relationships

Not remote from Maturana and Varela's (1980, 1998) idea of autopoiesis (self-production), Haken's synergetics (1981, 1996) and Prigogine's dissipative structures (1980) is the theory of the physical ground of self-organization. Drawing on

The author wishes to thank Yaichi Aoshima, Dirk Baecker, Alexandre Beaudet, Jonathan Brookfield, Michael A. Cusumano, Takahiro Fujimoto, Martin Kenney, Ken Kusunoki, Jens Laage-Hellman, Ikujiro Nonaka, Stefan Thomke, D. Eleanor Westney, and Georg Fredrik von Krogh for their valuable comments.

experiments with lasers, thermodynamic behavior, and chemical reactions, this theory has inspired socioeconomic and organizational applications, including those performed by Luhmann (1984) and von Krogh and Roos (1995). Although propo- nents of self-referential epistemology in social sciences may differ in their tones and stances, the idea essentially comes down to this: the governing mechanism of socio- economic relationships among individuals and groups ultimately resides within the constituents' mutual relationships. Haken (1981) further suggests that there is dis- tinctive regularity in the emergence of an order. Emerged order is maintained by the invisible hand of its constituents, whose interaction collectively constitutes the con- trolling hand. The whole system is, as it were, a self-worked marionette, a self-designed watch, or a legendary giant who lifts himself up by pulling on his bootstraps (Dawkins, 1986; Gell-Mann, 1994). The controller or the ultimate regulator of socioeconomic phenomena is thus the self-referential relationships that arise from complex interac- tions among individuals, groups, and organizations in society.

The interconnecting relationships among social components are a driving force that creates order, coordinates changes in the relationships themselves, and main- tains the system once emerged. These relationships are revisited when the system is in a transitional state and a new order is generated by altering connections of the existing relationships. In this reordering process, numerous new combinations of local linkages emerge, promoting new forms of exploitation and symbiosis among constituents that in turn shape the global configuration of a new system.

Evidently, we are going through increasing uncertainty in the current business environment concomitant with increasing technological complexity and intensi- fying global competition. In many industries, as a result of the downfall of tradi- tional markets and radical restructuring, past common sense is rapidly turning into today's nonsense. Instead of familiar business organizations separated by owner- ship and functional attributes, moreover, a range of new flexible interfirm institu- tions, such as crossfunctional task forces and risk-sharing partnerships irrespective of equity holding, have been assuming greater prominence. These new institutions are establishing and demonstrating a novel way of combining hitherto remote or unrelated resources in the direction of a deeper sharing of benefits and losses across traditional boundaries. Under these premises, this essay explores traditional systems theory as compared with a new approach to complexity and argues that conditions for new interorganizational institutions are on the rise, entailing coevolutionary systems of exploitation and symbiosis.

Traditional Systems Theory and a New Approach to Complexity

According to Parson's classical systems theory (1951), a society is a self-regulat- ing system that adapts to change by reordering its institutions in order to maintain a balance among them and keep the system working effectively. This mechanism can best be understood by analogy to the physiology of the body. When the body is in good order, it is able to respond effectively to environmental changes. In response to rising or falling external temperature, for example, the body mobilizes certain physiological mechanisms (e.g., the sweat glands) to keep its own temperature stable. This is called homeostasis (self-stabilization). As the well-functioning body mobilizes certain mechanisms to stabilize its internal state in response to external change, so does the social system reorder its institutions to adapt to external shocks. The system may become dysfunctional, however, when environmental change is too drastic to cope with. For instance, if outside temperature surpasses a physiological limit, the bodily mechanism will be thrown into disequilibrium (Giddens, 1993). Johnson (1964, 1966) claims that the disequilibrium in societies is a necessary condition for the rise of revolution.

Increasingly, the traditional homeostatic view of systems has been questioned as a result of new evidence and interpretations proposed by researchers of chaos theory and complexity. Chaos theory deals with unpredictable and seemingly random behavior occurring in systems expected to be governed by deterministic laws. In such systems, the equations that describe the way the system changes with time are nonlinear and involve several variables. Complexity is concerned with the levels of spontaneous self-organization of a system. Complex systems are those in which collections of agents seeking mutual accommodation and self-consistency somehow manage to transcend themselves, acquiring collective properties such as life, thought, and purpose that they might never have possessed individually (Waldrop, 1992). In complex dynamical systems with very high but finite degrees of freedom (e.g., the brain, human body, and ecological systems), it is possible for each interacting mode to make the system unable to converge toward one invariant set and to force it to jump among stable modes (Tsuda, 1991). In a symbiotic network consisting of genes with respective mutation rates, the states with high mutation rates can emerge as structurally stable yet dynamically chaotic, whereas a state with zero mutation rate is stable only in an isolated gene. Ikegami and Kaneko (1992) have proven that in such symbiotic networks weak chaos appears, whereby dynamic stability is realized. Such a dynamically stable state in complex systems with high degrees of freedom and weak chaos is called homeochaos (Kaneko, 1995, 1996; Kaneko and Tsuda, 1996). Homeochaos induces an elastic balancing of entrainment (synchronization) and desynchronization among constituents of a complex system, whose process is not invariant but plastic. Importantly, this process would be history dependent. Thus, according to Tsuda (1991), a context-dependent processing of information may be represented as a path- or orbit-dependent emergence of collective modes, where chaotically itinerant motion among quasi-attractors would take place. This universality is called chaotic itinerancy and may be thought of as a history-dependent, itinerant motion of elements within the complex system.[1]

Going beyond a rather static, mechanistic stylization of homeostasis, homeochaos is considered to be important for complex systems ranging from biological organisms (e.g., the brain) to socioeconomic and ecological systems attempting to achieve structural stability while maintaining variety. Just as Gleick (1987) calls chaotic stability a moving equilibrium, the concept of homeochaos emphasizes dynamical stability, the balance point of order and chaos (the edge of chaos). Although some of its assumptions and applications are still debated (Kauffman, 1993, 1995), this approach to complexity appears to be opening up a new horizon for various disciplines to explore the working of complex systems.

Applied engineers have been actively incorporating new knowledge on complex nonlinear systems into the designing of engineering systems. For example, intelligent multiagent systems in which multiple robots self-regulate mutual relationships (Miyake, 1996), and net-based cooperative controls for autonomous distributed systems (Nagao et al., 1996) are similar, in that mutual entrainment between a system of engineering and its immediate environment results in producing ba (a field), which consists of, and at the same time subsumes, both entities in an insepa-rable manner in action.[2] Furthermore, these new systems of engineering are based on a new design philosophy that assumes that response to unpredictable change in the environment can be better managed by the real-time, self-organizing adjust-ments of constituents among themselves than by central control and planning.

This new approach starts with the following premises and questions. Given un-familiar circumstances, a living creature can still find situational meaning in them and take appropriate action. This is strange because the surrounding environment clearly has a larger degree of freedom than the living creature and therefore repre-sents an essentially unpredictable entity from the creature's standpoint. If so, what strategy does the creature follow so as to cope with this kind of uncertainty?

The new approach answers the foregoing as follows. A living organism has an inseparable relationship with its environment through its own physical commit-ment expressed by action, and it constructs a meaning for certain objects in the outer world that provide "affordance" to those who perceive them (Neisser, 1976; Gibson, 1979). The organism thus is constantly working toward a new equilibrium or co-herence on the border between itself and the environment. In other words, rather than designing its own system functions by predetermining a range of expected phenomena and preparing corresponding algorithms, the living system generates information in real time and constructs an adaptive design of its own in response to the changing situation.

This new engineering philosophy represents an antithesis to the traditional ap-proach in the designing of artificial intelligence systems where a designer would play a Godlike role by arbitrarily separating a system from its environment, defining algorithms and measurements of the collection of phenomena to be treated, and determining a class of system functions to be engineered.

Users of traditional artificial intelligence systems were getting increasingly frus-trated because of the systems' limited capacity to successfully adapt to unprogram-mable change in the environment and inability to reorder system functions in the face of exponentially complex external disturbances. Newell and Simon's informa-tion-processing approach (1972) was no exception to this conventionalism because it was preoccupied with defining a "problem space," in which operational and problem-solving techniques and initial and critical conditions were predeter-mined, whereas unidentified elements were ignored as noise. To the confusion of many users of artificial intelligence systems, however, problems of significance were usually not preordained but discovered ex post, and these accidental problems could not be determined ex ante as a problem space (Saeki, 1988).

In contrast to the traditional approach, a new intelligent multiagent model, as mentioned earlier, has been proposed, in which a self-generated field conditions, and is at the same time conditioned by, the functional distribution of individual units (e.g., a collection of group-forming, walking robots that autonomously adjust relative po-sitioning in real time through entrainment) (Miyake, 1996). This type of design by self-referential emergence is considered to be particularly effective in highly unpredictable environments and opens up a new dimension for self-creating the critical conditions not from the standpoint of the designer but of the system itself.[3]

Organizational Field

Let me briefly discuss the concept of the organizational field as it relates to the emergence of organizational reflection and interorganizational coevolution. In general, a field refers to a region or space in which a given effect (e.g., magnetism) exists. As a harbinger of applying the concept of the field to social psychology, Lewin (1946) defined a field as the coexisting whole of collective facts that are deemed interdependent and claimed that a living space representing a person and her realities must be regarded as a field in psychology. An editor of Lewin's collected papers, Cartwright (1951) pointed out that Lewin's concept of the field has *scaling*, for example, in personal psychology an individual's living space is the field, and in group or social psychology a group's (or a societal) space consisting of a group (or a society) and its perceived environment constitutes the field.

Translating the concept of the field (or ba) into organizational study, Itami (1991, 1992a, 1992b) defined it as a situational framework for the creation of order in macroscopic information in which participants in the exchange share among themselves at least a part of the following three elements in frequent and dense information interaction: agenda (information concerning what?); interpretation code (how should one interpret information?); and information carrier (what media carry the information?); As a critical system, the field can be delineated by membership, physical space, or common themes, thus liberating the definition in part from sheer physical constraints.

Using an Itamian framework of ba (the field), Nishizono conducted fieldwork on the renowned small-firm network in Ohta Ward of Tokyo and remarked: "there are no definitive planners [within the small-firm network of Ohta Ward], and yet an order emerges from the active interaction of people there" (1996:122). This is a precise description of what Haken (1981) calls cooperative phenomena, in which individual elements autonomously move around under no unified controls and yet a certain order emerges out of the whole system (Matsuda, 1995:143).

An organizational field may be thought of as a conceptual space in which continual entrainment and/or covibration among constituent elements promotes the emergence, registration, and storage of process information. In contrast to result information, the generated process information there could be extremely dense, like a neutron star. The field is a critical determinant of organizational reflection (Lewin, 1951).

From a strategic viewpoint,[4] proportional to the degree of external turbulence and uncertainty, the synapses of an organizational reflective strategy will explore by necessity interactions of a requisite variety with external organizations in different culture media. This is because it would be reasonable to assume that increasing external uncertainty can break the critical limits of the self-sustaining mechanisms of an organization, which should be compensated for by alliances with other organizations in different fields.

What is prescribed here is a shift from homeostasis as a passive, adjustive mechanism to homeochaos as an emergent, creative mechanism. In this context, a clustered control model of outsourcing (Nishiguchi, 1994) may be perceived as a system to make possible cocreation between organizations, allowing for differentiated sharing of the collaborative outcomes that accrue. In this system the possibility of an internecine struggle for resources is constrained by the phasic differentiation of interacting organizations. The field that differentiates exerts critical influence on interorganizational relations.

Coevolution of Interorganizational Relations

Exploitation and Symbiosis Systems

Based on their contribution to proliferation rates (i.e., to what extent the existence of a certain species affects the rise and fall of another species' offspring, and vice versa), ecological relationships among species can be divided into three: exploitation, competition, and symbiosis. *Exploitation* refers to a relationship in which one species gains whereas the other suffers. *Competition* refers to one in which two coexistent species hamper each other's proliferation, whereas *symbiosis* helps it. Biological relationships are logically exhausted by these three. These relationships are a product of natural selection, resulting from what Maynard-Smith calls an evolutionary stable strategy (ESS) adopted by the "selfish gene" aiming at producing as many self-copies as possible (Dawkins, 1989; Matsuda, 1995).

Needless to say, one needs to be cautious about unconditionally importing ideas of biological theory to social sciences. Uncritical recourse to analogies must be avoided. As Parsons (1964, 1966) points out, however, it would not be entirely unreasonable to try to interpret social evolution as an extension of ecological evolution despite substantive differences in the mechanisms of development. For both types of evolution can be understood in terms of what he calls evolutionary universals, which refer to any types of development that possess great survival value and are sufficiently important to further evolution, arising on more than one occasion in different conditions. In the organic world, vision is a good example of an evolutionary universal. In human society, language is the most significant evolutionary universal followed by other important universals such as religion, kinship, and technology. These universals leverage social evolution and differentiate selection. According to Parsons, social evolution can be interpreted as a process of progressive differentiation of social institutions. According to Haken's synergetics (1981, 1996) and Luhmann (1984), moreover, because human society is composed not of tangible matters but rather of relationships among individuals, groups, and organizations, it is possible further to reinterpret social evolution as a process of progressive change of those relationships.

Another critical concept that can be adopted from ecology is *coevolution*, signifying a process of parallel and relational evolution between ecologically complementary or interdependent species such as insect-pollinated plants and pollinating insects. Coevolution is caused by the selection pressures that each exerts on the other.

The concept of coevolution offers useful analytical leverage for examining interorganizational and outsourcing relations in particular. The prime contractor and the subcontractor need not be regarded as head-to-head competitors. By definition, the subcontractor's task is a partial contribution to the prime contractor's major contract. Insofar as the outsourcing relationship is concerned, the two do not compete for exactly the same market with the same product or service. Moreover, insofar as there is scope for repeated (as opposed to one-shot) games it is very unlikely that there will be an exploitative relationship reaching an extreme stage in which the prime contractor (the predator) kills off the subcontractor (the prey). This is because the former's survival depends on the latter's survival, and therefore a policy of neither sparing nor devouring prey is an evolutionary stable strategy.

Under these premises, interorganizational relations, with special focus on outsourcing, can be examined, using ideal typical models of exploitation and symbiosis. The procedure of analysis is as follows. First, the two systems will be put side by side and compared item by item. Next, a new vision will be presented in which these two systems are perceived not as completely separated and independent entities but as constituting a coevolutionary part of a nested structure in which the two systems are dynamically intertwined through entrainment, generating new life on the edge of a twisting whole-surface interaction.

On the basis of existing studies and discussion in this chapter, table 11.1 summarizes the characteristics of the exploitation and symbiosis systems. Needless to say, ideal typical (as opposed to real) attributes in a Weberian sense are shown here, and they are not intended to be the descriptions of reality as it is. They are better to be understood to form a useful conceptual tool to analyze the observations of complex phenomena.

Decision-making in the exploitation system is largely a top-down, unilateral process under central control of the prime contractor that is primarily concerned with deployment of *functional skills* and collapsed *result information*. By contrast, decision-making in the symbiosis system draws heavily on real-time, interactive processes among constituents of both the prime contractor and the subcontractor on the basis of their *relational skills* and the accumulated *process information*.[5] Real-time, interactive activity is considered to be an essential part of meaningful strategy emergence in a symbiotic system.

In the exploitative mode of relationships there are clearly discernible boundaries between organizations, and information processing is done sequentially, whereas in the symbiotic counterpart, organizational delineations are essentially boundaryless (as exemplified by interfirm crossfunctional teams), and information is processed in parallel and concurrently. The latter characteristic finds its analogue in the parallel distributed processing of recent computers, as opposed to early computers' "von Neumann bottleneck," a phenomenon in which only one instruction at a time could be executed and only one result at a time could appear in the accumulator (Dennett, 1990). The recent trend from delineative, sequential processing to crossfunctional, concurrent engineering, especially in the area of product development, can better be understood in terms of reordering of elements and evolution of relationships (Nishiguchi, 1987; Clark and Fujimoto, 1991).

Table 11.1. The Two Systems of Interorganizational Relations

	Exploitation System	Symbiosis System
Decision-making	Central	Constituent
	Unilateral	Synergetic
		Self-reflective, retrospective
Skills	Functional	Relational
Information	Result	Process
Information processing	Serial	Parallel
	Sequential	Concurrent
Organization	Delineative	Boundaryless
		Crossfunctional
Control structure	Arm's length	Clustered
Safeguard	Bidding	Single or parallel sourcing
	Multiple sourcing	Risk sharing
	Short-term contracts	Profit sharing
Requirements	Bargaining	Commitment
Objectives	Distribution	Cocreation
	Survival	Coadvancement
Attributes	Dichotomous	Permeable
	Antagonistic	Absorptive
	Win-lose	Win-win
	Mechanistic	Organic
	Dead end, cul-de-sac	Open-end
	Homeostasis	Homeochaos

Outsourcing mechanisms of the exploitative mode are characterized by an arm's-length control structure based on the principle of "hire many and control them by division." By contrast, symbiotic outsourcing adopts a clustered control structure according to the principle of requisite variety. (For more discussion on this, with evidence, see Nishiguchi, 1987, 1994). In the latter the prime contractor and its selected suppliers of excellence form a first-level cluster, where the dynamism of the field activates real-time interaction among the constituents, so as to hammer out an exemplar of best practice. The mother gene, as it were, is generated in the prime cluster and then passed onto subordinate clusters. What is important in this transfer process is that the principal cluster neither orders nor instructs the details of the design prevailing through the whole clustering system. Rather, as Madelbrot's fractal His-Purkinje network, a labyrinth of branching pathways organized to be self-similar on smaller and smaller scales, can be explained with transparent simplicity by a few bits of information, or as DNA (deoxyribonucleic acid) achieves its goal by the coded instructions of an organism's genes that can govern and specify a repeating process of bifurcation and development without specifying the vast number of bronchi, bronchioles, and alveoli or the particular spatial structure of the resulting tree (Gleick, 1987),[6] the archetypical instructions within the clustering mechanisms are issued, so to speak, as a recipe with a reasonable degree of freedom.

What is important is that such instructions are given as a mere recipe with a degree of freedom and its implementation is delegated to respective constituents of the clusters. Therefore, variations and mutations will emerge out of the same recipe. Analogously, such a multilayered clustering system allows for the emergence of agile dynamics, as when a conductor's *einsatz* triggers the full orchestra's tutti or the slight move of a fish instantly redirects a whole school of fish.

In the exploitation system, safeguards against organizational dysfunctions and paralysis in outsourcing are bidding, multiple sourcing, and short-term contracts, whereby an order of the same specifications may be sourced to several bidders, subject to market forces. The prime contractor's bargaining power can be maximized by rotating short-term contracts, whereby bidders and contract winners may be frequently changed based on the result information, for example, the price. In contrast, in the symbiotic system a small number of select suppliers meeting the requirements of requisite variety are employed, usually under single or parallel sourcing arrangements built on long-term contracts (Richardson, 1993). The relations are based on the process information accumulated thorough deeper commitments such as design-in (early supplier involvement in design). The reason for parallel sourcing of certain categories of products and/or services (but usually with different specifications) is to proactively safeguard against potential moral hazards of a monopolistic single sourcing situation and to keep a level of requisite variety.

Furthermore, risk sharing in the form of suppliers' initial asset-specific investment of a nonrecurring kind or profit sharing between the customer and the supplier, for example, are safeguards of another kind against opportunistic behavior in the symbiosis system.

One critical requirement of the exploitation mode of outsourcing is bargaining, whereas that of the symbiotic mode is mutual commitment.

The ultimate objective of the exploitation system is a kind of zero-sum distribution where one party tries to secure as large a proportion of the share as possible at the cost of the other. By definition, the system is divisive, and its orientation dichotomous. A party tries to add a little more of its own share to the disadvantage of the other, and vice versa. By contrast, parties in the symbiosis system are inclined to cooperate to enlarge the pie itself in the spirit of cocreation and coadvancement. The system encourages them to be permeable, absorptive, and win-win oriented (Nishiguchi and Anderson, 1995).

The exploitation model makes the parties concerned antagonistic and win-lose oriented, the end result of its mechanistic logic bringing them to a cul-de-sac (dead end). Conversely, the symbiosis model is more organic, and its final destination is open-ended. Mechanisms of resource allocation in the exploitation model are based on homeostatis, while the symbiosis model relies on homeochaos to allocate resources. The former is adjustive, the latter emergent.

Mechanisms of Interorganizational Coevolution

Today, increasing outsourcing and its qualitative change, ranging from contract labor to contract design, engineering, and assembly, are widespread throughout the world. Along with these developments, the concern of management studies has been progressing from traditional corporate governance and intraorganizational learning to intercorporate governance and interorganizational learning (Dyer, 1996; Nishiguchi, 1996).

Customarily, it has been argued that one major reason for the marked interest in outsourcing in advanced economies is securing flexibility and stability in the face of increasing environmental uncertainty and the high cost of product development and manufacturing. Firms are highly aware of the need to externalize problems arising from market sources (e.g., the volatility and fragmentation of the markets) and technological sources (e.g., hypercomplexity of new technologies) so as to enhance resilience to fluctuations and upgrade their own capacity as survival machines (Berger and Piore, 1980; Piore and Sabel, 1984). A critical point missing in the traditional arguments, however, is that evolution of interorganizational relations cannot be accounted for merely in terms of an adaptive model responding to environmental changes. An organization learns and unlearns, processes and creates information. When organizations interact, there should surely emerge something more than just simple adaptation, something beyond simplistic competition and coordination. Interorganizational relations coevolve. This is the basic standpoint of this essay.

How do relations between organizations coevolve? What mechanisms are there to make it happen? On the basis of the foregoing discussion, a vision that I propose is condensed hypothetically into a twister model of interorganizational relations (see figure 11.1). In this relational structure, (1) a spiral structured exploitation system and (2) a spiral structured symbiosis system are intertwined, influencing each other at the edge of a whole-surface interaction. Each strand constitutes, as it were, a "stream within streams," a "structure within structures." These two strings come closer and drift apart, flow past each other and sometimes mutually entrain, forming a unit-like whole-surface stream, a big twisted river, a large structure, which can be called (3) a metamodel. The generative element of this metamodel is a dynamic "form" emerged from the entrainment of the two coils "nested" within the twister structure. On the critical edge of the two strings emerges new vibrancy. It is the inequality of the dynamically unstable mechanisms that drives coevolution. The double-helix structure seen here may resemble the archetype of life and emergence: DNA. But the analogy is limited to that of shape. This is because it is not reproduction but dynamism itself that the coevolutionary twister represents.

Metaphorically, within each stream of the double helix there are competing waves, and rhythms competing in waves. There are eddies, vortices, vortex trains, and turbulences seen as the "rolling" of one surface about another. Vortices signify instability, and instability means that a flow is fighting an imbalance within itself, and the inequality is an "archetype" of coevolution (Schwenk, 1976). The inequalities could be fast and slow, hot and cold, dense and tenuous, salty and fresh, hard and soft, viscous and fluid, acid and alkaline, male and female. At the boundary, life blossoms (Gleick, 1987). It is even possible to claim that the twister model may represent the self-recursive "will" of life that attempts to reveal the "self." In this sense, Schopenhauer's famous proposition, and the title of his masterpiece, "The World as Will and Representation" (1818), may indeed have found support here.

It would be erroneous to assume that this twister is a product of dialectics (thesis-antithesis-synthesis) because it consists of the effects of interaction among small

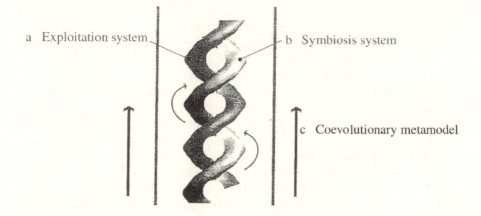

a Exploitation system

b Symbiosis system

c Coevolutionary metamodel

Figure 11.1. A Twister Model of Interorganizational Relations

streams within streams, small structures within structures, whereby phasic communications of the parts in themselves alone constitute the whole. Hypothetically, it could be said that within the exploitation stream and the symbiosis stream there are, respectively, self-recursive "nested" structures on a smaller scale, each beating different rhythms and recording its own small history. In this sense, this dual spiral model is essentially fractal. This twister evolves through chaotic itinerancy. It is the perpetual movement of the double strands that is the fundamental driving force of homeodynamic coevolution.[7]

Implications and Conclusion

Research Implications

The foregoing analysis provides important implications for future research on interorganizational relations. For one thing, traditional control mechanisms for interorganizational relations based on dichotomous determinants (e.g., make or buy, exploitation or symbiosis) may not be as useful as is customarily claimed because increasingly complex environments may readily challenge the validity of reductionist models. Restricting our view to outsourcing relations and in particular those in the automobile industry, it would be impossible to obtain a single-strand equilibrium among the various relationships as seen in table 11.1 because of the enormous complexity of the object and its components. For example, a typical automobile consists of approximately thirty thousand individual parts of radically divergent configurations, functions, prices, and materials. Furthermore, organizational responses to this complexity are broad. In 1986, for example, General Motors' North

American business alone operated five divisions (from Chevrolet to Cadillac), producing in total six million vehicles, of which there were thousands of variations derived from fifty "car series" (e.g., the Oldsmobile Cutlass, the Cadillac Eldorado) made up of nineteen "body families" (from the A type to the Y type) (*Automotive News*, October 27, 1986). In outsourcing, GM North America had six thousand buyers, controlling and buying parts and services directly from 37,000 suppliers (Nishiguchi, 1987, 1988). It was customary, moreover, that the same parts of the same automobile (e.g., metal subassemblies of a suspension system) were outsourced to four–five suppliers who were readily dropped depending on the results of annual bidding based on price, volume, and other contractual performance. Furthermore, GM's supply base was rapidly expanding from North America to Asia and Latin America in search of lower prices. Compared with GM's classical vertical integration, Toyota's cluster control model of outsourcing may be easier to administer, but ultimately the tasks are similar, and so there are few practical differences in the complexity of the management task.

In the face of these infinitely intertwined factors, how useful would it be to rely on the traditional information-processing approach that simplifies phenomena according to its own preferred format, by defining a "problem space" in which operational and problem-solving techniques and initial and critical conditions are predetermined, whereas unidentified elements are assumed away as default or noise? In today's turbulent environment, where the couplings and meanings of various elements are swiftly changing, to what extent are the algorithms and evaluative standards of the traditional approach consistently functional? As Ghoshal and Moran (1996) and Hodgson (1997) question, is it meaningful for today's businesspeople to hear the institutional economic exhortation (e.g., Williamson, 1975, 1985, 1996) that price, asset specificity, and safeguards are simultaneously determined at the agreement of a contract with the subsequent business operations automatically taken care of? To such questioning, few existing theories provide meaningful answers. There must be a theoretical limit, moreover, to applying linear calculations and projections to complex dynamical phenomena, a product of nonlinear interactions. As the aforementioned twister model of interorganizational relations suggests, a coevolutionary approach to complex dynamical systems may well indicate a viable avenue for new theoretical explorations.

To reiterate the points already made, as a stabilizing mechanism under weak chaos with a large degree of freedom for a system comprising many elements, homeochaos is thought to be important for achieving dynamic stability while maintaining variety. Homeochaos enables a requisite balancing of entrainment and desynchronization of the elements of a complex system, thereby inducing chaotic itinerancy or a path-dependent emergence of collective motion of the elements, each neither completely covibrating nor utterly desynchronized with one another (Tsuda, 1991; Kaneko, 1995, 1996; Kaneko and Tsuda, 1996). Instead of an equilibrium or a static constancy, a dynamical stability—a moving equilibrium—operates there (Gleick, 1987; Koga et al., 1996). A new theory to come must contribute to uncovering and analyzing such a process from the very logic of the process itself.

Although its concepts and applications are still being improved (Kauffman, 1993, 1995), a new approach to complexity is expected to widen the horizon for many disciplines, including management studies, which may have been suffering from hardened arteries stuffed with traditional, well-thumbed concepts and methodologies. Moreover, as Nishiguchi (1994) and Nishiguchi and Brookfield (1997) have carefully demonstrated, it is crucial to "historicize" a research perspective by going beyond a microeconomic world based on the principle of simultaneous determinacy of economic equations. It is hoped that a new theory will emerge that contributes not only to bringing forth a new outlook on the world but also to developing new evaluative standards for complex dynamical systems and new conceptual tools for sophisticated empirical research. There is an immensely fertile soil for new research in this field. The coevolutionary model proposed in this essay is but a modest start.

Managerial Implications

The foregoing discussion provides implications that are as much epistemological as practical. As already mentioned, we are evidently going through an unprecedented technological era in which the exponential speed of technological change renders Vernon's classical product cycle theory (1966, 1971, 1974) obsolete. Recently we have been witnessing some intriguing cases such as that of Windows 95, Microsoft's computer operating system software, whose sales record peaked on the first day of its sale. Not more than decades ago, industry standards were set by Kodak for film and by IBM for computers. But today, it is very difficult for any one firm to control industry standards. A new film standard called the advanced photo system (APM) introduced in 1996 was the product of careful strategic alliances between Kodak, the proposer, and Japanese competitors, including Fuji, Canon, Minolta, and Nikon. Many other traditional frameworks are rapidly collapsing, to be replaced by new ones, as exemplified by the diffusion of digital technologies, including the Internet and satellite broadcasting, which are rendering national borders less important. The advent of de facto standards, determined not by third-party regulatory organizations but by market competition and/or strategic alliances, does nothing but further this observable trend.

Under the circumstances, competence in managing interfirm relations is becoming increasingly important, going far beyond the simple pursuit of flexibility or cost reduction. Whether or not to make interorganizational relations exploitative, symbiotic, or some mixture of the two is an important strategic choice. Once, Porter (1980) successfully exhorted his "competitive strategy." It provided corporate managers with an analytical tool kit to help position their firm relative to competition; it encouraged them to obtain a superior position to competitors' or retreat if it would be too costly to do so. Today, however, to what extent is this type of dichotomous approach helpful? Would it not be the case that the present times are urging us to make a fundamental shift from a repellent "competitive strategy" to a "coevolutionary strategy"?

As discussed, the traditional view was that an individual entity in an ecological system is in a state of homeostasis in which it adjusts its own physiological conditions to changes of external environments. The foregoing discussion has pointed out, however, that homeochaos, rather than purporting to achieve some state of equilibrium through passive adjustments, instead represents the dynamical disequilibrium of a complex system in which constituent relationships are constantly redefined on the edge of their coevolution. This disequilibrium is the very source of life and advancement. Systems lacking this quality of dynamism are more inclined to extinction than survival.

What the twister model suggests is the necessity to strategically allow for and select conditions for the emergence of new self-referential coevolution on the edge between exploitation and symbiosis without definitively slanting toward either. In today's global aircraft development, for example, risk-sharing partnerships (in which major suppliers are made entirely responsible for initial nonrecurring investment) are becoming the norm. Prima facie, this practice may appear to originate in the symbiosis system, and yet this practice cannot be adequately understood without seeing an entrainment effect from the exploitation system, in that considerable proportions of the final product's failure, if any, will be directly incurred to suppliers. It has been reported that at the edge of this critical point, risk-sharing participants are unusually stimulated to contribute to the emergence of novel knowledge, innovation, and technological advancement that could not even be perceived in the old subcontracting model (for more details, see Nishiguchi, 1996). One example of such emergence is the Boeing 777. This large, twin-engine commercial aircraft was heavily codeveloped with risk-sharing partners as well as key airline companies and was first delivered in 1995. The aircraft was not only an immediate commercial success but also enjoyed an unprecedentedly high dispatch reliability in its first year of commercial launching. In a similar vein, the Gulfstream V and the Bombardier Global Express, new high-end, long-range business jets developed through deep engineering collaboration with risk-sharing suppliers, have both been enjoying a marked success.

Although the abrupt resignation in the autumn of 1996 of Inaki Lopez, sourcing mastermind and a vice-president at Volkswagen, somewhat clouded VW's new Resende plant in Brazil just as it opened, the very concept of the auto assembly plant that Lopez had developed was radical. The automaker, Volkswagen, provided plant buildings and belt conveyors; a small number of systems suppliers, each responsible for designated systems components, were persuaded to provide their own machinery and workers on site to produce VW-badge trucks at their own risk and cost. Similar to the aforementioned risk-sharing partnership, this radical move is another attempt at stimulating interorganizational coevolution in such a way as was previously unthinkable (*Business Week*, 1996; *Nihon Keizai Shimbun*, 1996; *Asahi Shimbun*, November 30, 1996; *Nikkei Sangyo Shimbun*, 1996; *IW*, 1997; Collins, Bechler, and Pires, 1997).

Under the arrangement, no payment is made to any of these on-site suppliers unless the VW-badge trucks they assemble pass VW's final inspection. The suppliers, therefore, collaborate because the incentive system pushes them to do so. Is this exploitation or symbiosis? Perhaps both. All in all, these examples suggest that "coevolution" is the key to understanding advanced outsourcing management that allows new relationships to emerge with no dedicated slant toward either exploitation or symbiosis.

Human beings are self-referential entities able to be conscious of being conscious. Groups and organizations that they form and the relationships among them are also self-recursive. Within human beings, and within a variety of relationships that they form, reside inherent capabilities for spontaneous self-creation. There, infinitely self-recursive evolution recycles within itself with the support of the self's profound commitment (Nonaka, 1986). The twister model of coevolution as proposed provides an excellent qualitative hint for interorganizational relations to invariably reveal contradictions, push actors into instability, and restart new order on the edge of moving equilibrium. The double-helix model provides a powerful cognitive structure to understand and promote the coevolution of interorganizational relations through participants' self-innovation and self-transcendence.

Conclusion

This essay has explored mechanisms and conditions of interorganizational management by a strategy of coevolutionary creation. Based on the premise that the determinants of socioeconomic phenomena are the working of the relationships per se among individuals, groups, and organizations, mechanisms of new strategic process were examined. Spontaneous decision-making through constituents' real-time interaction, retrospective sense-making, and synergetic entrainment in the "field" was identified as an important determinant of this process. I discussed how within the "field," which cuts physically and conceptually across the traditional boundary of hierarchy and the market, a combination of relational skills and process information emerges and is accumulated. It was further argued that an evolutionary prime mover is in essence the changing relationship of various constituents that differentiates and reorders itself.

Taking into account the foregoing, a new metamodel of interorganizational relations with primary reference to outsourcing was proposed and discussed. In this model, two ideal typical systems (i.e., the exploitation system and the symbiosis system) entrain and flow past each other in a double helix, from the dynamic edge of which emerges new life, resulting in the self-referential coevolution of interorganizational relations. It was further suggested that under the current turbulence of market fluctuation and technological advancement, the idea that a single best model may apply to all facets of phenomena as a panacea may no longer be tenable. Rather, it is argued that the coevolutionary model that subsumes and builds on dynamical nested structures (comprising an exploitation system that tends to distribution by bargaining and a symbiosis system that tends to cocreation by mutualism, each representing a necessary part of a moving equilibrium) may well assume overall a superior descriptive value for advancement. Furthermore, it is also suggested that the current circumstances may indicate an inevitable shift from a competitive strategy to a coevolutionary strategy.

I conclude with Seneca's proposition of two thousand years ago, whose message will probably be as pertinent two thousand years hence: "Nature created us to be related to one another."

Notes

1. Moreover, this process is considered to be a prerequisite for a hermeneutic (interpretive) process, as demonstrated in Shannon's (1951) classic experiment of *Vorverständnis*, or precognition, in which a collection of elements create a virtual partial wholeness, which in turn determines further elements for the increasingly efficient

interpretation of words, sentences, and paragraphs. This puts into perspective Marr's (1982) pragmatic definition of interpretation as an action to compute things related to complete information, based on virtual complete information inferred from the incomplete information.

2. The concept of the field is well established in physics, much developed in biology, and increasingly important in engineering. For a fuller account of the evolution of the concept of the field and its implications for management and organization studies, see Nishiguchi (1997).

Applying the concept of the field in engineering, Miyake (1996) simulated the self-organization of intelligent multiagents. In this experiment, nine walking robots were divided into three groups of equal numbers. Three robots were then arbitrarily removed from various positions at various times, resulting in the re-emergence of the initial three-group dynamics with the remaining six robots, which re-formed into three groups, each with two robots. This means that while walking, each intelligent robot self-generated its own physical coherence that emerged in real time through entrained walking rhythms with the neighboring robots, reinterpreted a newly self-organized field in accordance with the changing systems size, and accordingly self-regulated its own walking pace and patterns. Moreover, compensation effects of the individual robot's disappearance were consistently observed, regardless of the number and location of robots that were removed.

3. Needless to say, a preponderance of work by the Santa Fe Institute leads this new trend. See, for example, Cowan, Pines, and Meltzer (1994).

4. Although a full discussion goes beyond the scope of this essay, it is worth commenting on strategic process from a new standpoint consistent with the argumentative lines herein. In traditional strategic management literature, *strategy* has customarily been defined as the determination of basic long-term goals and objectives of an enterprise, the adoption of courses of action, and the allocation of resources necessary for carrying out these goals (Chandler, 1962). In this traditional framework, strategic planning and process are under the direct control of top management, and their implementation is a top-down process by fiat. In a similar vein to Taylorism, separation of planning and execution is the prescribed name of the game. Decision-making process and information flow are typically unidirectional along formal hierarchical lines, leaving little leeway for rank-and-file input in strategic process. If the environment is relatively stable or developing with reasonable predictability, there may be less of a problem in traditional recourse to the Chandlerian strategic process. Evidently, however, recent multifaceted disturbances such as the quick advancement of innovation, tendencies toward equalization of industrial power and access to information (e.g., the Internet), a surge of new entrants to the markets, and the resultant intensification of global competition, are all in all perceived to be making traditional strategic process increasingly questionable.

In line with recent skepticism on the traditional approaches, exploratory hypotheses in search of new dimensions are emerging. For example, a reinterpretation of the organization as an information-creating (in contrast to information-processing) entity has been put forward (Nonaka, 1988a, 1988b, 1989, 1990, 1994; Nonaka and Takeuchi, 1995; Von Krogh, Nonaka, and Nishiguchi, 2000). Characteristic of the theoretical basis of this emerging viewpoint is an emphasis on historicizing (Weick, 1979) as opposed to ahistorical simultaneous equations (Williamson, 1996); semantic meaning (Nonaka, 1994; Nonaka and Takeuchi, 1995) in contrast to syntactic meaning (Shannon and Weaver, 1949; Shannon, 1951); and holism or an emphasis on interacting wholes (Koestler, 1967, 1971; Koestler and Smythies, 1969; Jantsch,

1980; Bohm, 1976; Bohm and Hiley, 1994) as opposed to reductionism. Taking issue with the orthodox neoclassical standpoint, moreover, Nelson and Winter (1982) propose an evolutionary theory of economic change that is consistent with the view that knowledge creation can be interpreted as an act of innovation (mutation) in contrast to routine work (genes). Mutation and innovation may be common in their destabilizing quality to affect an existing order. Mutation in the natural world, however, randomly occurs perhaps even less frequently than a cycle of the vicissitudes of civilization. Innovation in human organizations, on the other hand, is a product of conscious efforts and accidents that emerges with much higher frequency. This distinction is important.

The foregoing urges a reexamination of traditional organization and strategy theory. Neither the existing interpretation of strategy as central planning and hierarchical implementation nor the classical systems theory that points to systems' homeostatic capacity provides sufficient prescriptions for today's corporations in the face of volatile markets and hypercompetition. Under the circumstances, it should be meaningful to revisit strategic process in a new light. Is it always the task of top management to plan, strategize, and hierarchically download implementation of planning and strategies? Or should there be alternative ways to organize strategic process under new arrangements? Is it invariably the case that interorganizational relations are to be governed by the more powerful at the cost of the less powerful? Or are there other methods to extract the best of partners?

Drawing on Weick's argument (1979) on retrospective sense-making, it may be legitimate to assert that organizations today may need to emphasize more and benefit from reflective capabilities of their constituent members active in the field (ranging from rank-and-file employees to middle-to-upper management), contributing to the strategic process. Because of an increasingly uncertain future, Chandlerian strategy based on long-term planning and formal, hierarchical execution appears to be less valid than in the past. Instead, there needs to be a new strategy formation process more resilient to uncertainty and less concerned with a foolhardy attempt to achieve a long-term goal that may become irrelevant by the time it has been attained. Seen this way, long-term goals are less ends than means to achieve a process. A new strategy based on constituents' reflective capabilities may represent a perpetual process of organizational learning, innovation, and knowledge creation that emerges from a chain of constituents' real-time self-organizing activities such as identifying and resolving localized problems that arise on the way to a long-term goal, with the result that ultimately a strategic path can be identified in retrospect in much the same way that chaotic itinerancy emerges. There, tacit knowledge (Polanyi, 1966) can be phasically converted into a mode of collective thinking through entrainment (e.g., dialoguing, languaging), contributing to the construction of a global system out of local communication and thus recording a history of interactions. There emerges a microcosmic world remote from the one based on the principle of simultaneous determinacy of economic equations.

An important condition here is that because this type of real-time strategy resorts to self-referential discovery and knowledge creation by constituent members, it cannot be successfully carried out if the top-down decision-making process prohibitively interfers. The new strategy cannot be expected to succeed without the constituents' autonomous entrainment, entailing a cycle of face-to-face contacts, dialogues, presentations, meetings, evaluations, reviews, and reflections. In terms of Nonaka's knowledge-creation theory (1994; Nonaka and Takeuchi, 1995; Von Krogh, Nonaka, and Nishiguchi, 2000), this process can be designated as a four-modal conversion model of organizational knowledge, comprising a loop of socialization, externalization, combination, and internalization. The process-based reflective strategy is a product of organizational synergetics a la Haken. Genuine controls reside with constituents rather than the ultimate authoritative point in the hierarchy. As such, this process-based strategy can be interpreted as "democratic" because the general will of constituent members may in the short run make small, isolated mistakes but will not in the long run bring losses to the constituent members themselves (Tocqueville, 1969 [1835]).

Using another expression, this real-time reflective strategy can be interpreted as "policy programing" rather than traditional "programmed policy."

This contrast between the traditional strategy of focusing on results and the new reflective strategy process can be better understood by a metaphor of sports versus budo (martial arts). The ultimate objective in sports is to win. Enhanced health and mental exhilaration are mere by-products. Insofar as competitive sports (requiring one's taking part in a match) are concerned, nobody strives to lose. One is somebody if she wins and nobody if she loses. In sharp contrast, in martial arts, in its original form at least, a loser bows thanks to a winner. This is because the winner gives the loser a chance to reflect on her own weaknesses, which in turn drives her to train more, enhance techniques, and master the secrets of an art.

What is the ultimate climax of sports? It is to win a championship cup, and in the case of the Olympic Games, to win a gold medal, and furthermore, to make a mark in history by achieving a world record. For the sake of such a victory, in which the winner experiences a temporal sense of glory, achievement, and greatness people endure years of hard training at the sacrifice of leading a normal human life. And a chance, if any, rarely comes. (Incidentally, there was a Japanese newspaper article that argued that after decades of internationalization, judo can no longer be considered an authentic budo because it has become, and degenerated into, a normal sport, as reflected by the series of rule changes that judo has experienced [*Asahi Shimbun*, April 20, 1996].)

Moreover, no matter how strong a player may be, with no matter how many world records, losing a critical match once is enough to render her meaningless. Consequently, the attainment of a gold medal often results in retirement because supreme achievement deprives one of the incentive to train further. The re-proving of one's worth would require the repeated attainment of a gold medal in the next Olympic Games, which is, needless to say, indeed a difficult task. Thus many winners retire after such an achievement.

In sharp contrast, budo is a never-ending learning process that is marked by a highly stylized *dan* grading system. Under this system, the tenth dan, the ultimate stage, is rarely awarded and even then in most cases only posthumously. Matches and the dan system in martial arts are mere rituals, institutions, even pretexts to help achieve higher goals. The ultimate objective of budo is *shugyo*, that is, the training itself, which includes mental training. Budo knows no retirement. For example, an eighty-year-old holder of the ninth dan of kendo (Japanese fencing) (the number of whom can be counted on one hand) is not a retired coach but an eternal player in active service and an unfinished seeker after truth who is infinitely approaching the state of absolute achievement. Interestingly, moreover, such an old man frequently beats a twenty-year-old fencer. In theory, the latter could simply overwhelm the former through forceful wielding of the bamboo sword (*shinai*). A true budo player, however, would not do that, because nothing could be learned by doing so. The essence of budo is to fight in accordance with, and only in accordance with, the very best of the opponent, not that of self. It is here that the possibility of eternal learning arises, where mechanisms that make budo truly budo are perpetuated. Spengler's (1926 [1917]) differentiation between "become" in the perfect tense and "becoming" in the progressive form can be seen here. The essence of budo represents an epistemological stylization of what process-based reflective strategy strives for.

The metaphor of sports versus martial arts can also be applied to interorganizational relations. For example, the traditional practice in outsourcing in the U. S. automotive industry of annual bidding and beating down prices represents an act of conveniently purchasing the functional skills of suppliers. (For more detail, see note 5, where a distinction between functional skills and relational skills is discussed.) Only result information is provided here. (Result information refers to a converging point of process information, or a type of irreversible, collapsed information that may be useful but whose noncontextual attributes deny retrospective decoding, as exemplified by the "price" in the market.) Prime contractors make their decisions without sufficient process information regarding by what process a certain bid came to be offered, whether a supplier is equipped with sound technical support to ascertain the prescribed level of quality, or whether the bidder is trying to cheat after obtaining a contract. Suppliers also make their own decisions based on limited result information provided by the prime contractor, for example, specifications of certain parts and materials, contract volume, and an acceptable price range. Suppliers are neither required nor even expected to take into account various contextual factors, for example, how the supplied parts are used, whether there is any scope for improvement, or whether there are alternative designs for cost reduction. The ultimate goal of each party is, as it were, to beat the other party by maximizing one's own gains and minimizing the profits of the other. This makes the trading relationship essentially antagonistic and drives the traders to behave opportunistically toward the dead end of a win-lose game (Nishiguchi, 1988, 1994; Nishiguchi and Brookfield, 1997). In contrast, Japanese outsourcing has over time evolved into something quite different, which relies on mechanisms of mutual trust and reciprocal long-term commitment among a smaller number of traders. This new order helps to create a profusion of process information and a sharing of organizational knowledge, which allows the competitors to pursue endless kaizen (continuous improvement) by means of institutionalized monitoring (e.g., target costing, value analysis [VA], value engineering [VE], suppliers' associations [kyoryokukai], supplier evaluation, and small group activities). The relationship under this new system is based on the principle of complementarity, driving the traders to collaborate toward the benefits of a win-win game. Drawing on a historical study of Japanese industrial sourcing and crossnational, comparative research, Nishiguchi (1994) and Nishiguchi and Brookfield (1997) provide systematic evidence that this is indeed the case: the buyer and the seller can profitably coevolve.

Reflective sense-making strategy that emphasizes the creation, sharing, and accumulation of process knowledge can further be seen in government-industry relations, as in the case of collaborative industrial policy-making in Japan. A series of legislation such as Kikai Kogyo Shinko Rinji Sochiho (the Machinery Industry Promotion Special Measures Law) and Chusho Kigyo Kindaika Sokushinho (the Small and Medium Enterprise Modernization Promotion Law), which produced notable results from the 1950s to the 1970s, are typical of this process-based strategy. At the implementation stage of these laws, originally drafted by officials of the Ministry of International Trade and Industry (MITI), the Ministry simply provided general guidelines (a "field" for dialogues between the government and industry) and a framework of financial support. The remaining detailing and progression of the industrial policy was spontaneously taken care of by industry participants, who, by means of a consensus-based process, codetermined specific targets, methods of achieving the targets, and mechanisms of information exchange and distribution. Moreover, there emerged frequent "reflective adjustments" among these participants in response to changing environments and resources available, often producing unexpected results, stimulating further the courses of the industrial policy, and eventually enhancing Japanese manufacturing industry to an internationally competitive level. According to MITI officials' own retrospective evaluation, although in the implementation of the industrial policy various targets were codetermined and operationalized by dialogues among industry participants, achieving the targets per se turned out to be secondary. More important, an abundance of information exchange among those involved took place in the process of trying to achieve those targets, and an international, comparative perspective and a benchmarking methodology, both then critically lacking in Japan, emerged from the participants' frequent foreign visits. The resulting level of the process information accumulated in industry over time went far beyond the scope of MITI officials' modest initial estimates. (This paragraph is largely based on a series of presentations and discussions at MITI's Study Group of Small and Medium Enterprise Problems [1995–1997], of which I was a designated member, and is also based on Yonekura, 1993a, 1993b).

The foregoing discussion and case evidence are consistent with the claim that reflective process-based strategy helps to produce abundant process information and relational skills shared among constituent members in the process of its implementation, the accumulation of which contributes to cultivating long-term organizational memory and organizational knowledge. This new type of strategy would probably be applicable to a broad range of interorganizational relations, including not only subcontracting relations and interfirm strategic alliances, but also government-industry relations.

5. Although the concept of skills could be infinitely classified depending on use, domain, and objective, it can be divided into two types for the purposes of this essay: functional skills and relational skills. *Functional skills* refer to those required and therefore used to perform specific tasks and achieve specific goals, and they can exist with or without relation to other skills. *Relational skills* refer to capabilities of a requisite variety to connect and reorder one's own and others' functional skills as necessary in a relatively localized field or context of activities. More concretely, this means that a person with relational skills can make full use of a human network based on her ample knowledge of who knows what, who can and is willing to be helpful in what, and who may use new information best in and out of an organization. By definition, relational skills bear a societal connotation.

Empirical researchers of interfirm relations are often impressed with the finding that in the same industry (under similar circumstances) two industry groups with evidently similar resources and governance mechanisms, for example, an automaker A's supplier base as opposed to its competitor B's counterpart, exhibit marked differences in performance. Despite few differences in observable attributes, it can often be the case that the automaker A's group is superior on all fronts, for example, in terms of product development, quality, cost, and profitability. To reemphasize, it is not only the automaker itself that is superior but also its supplier group.

Further examination often reveals that a well-managed group is sustained by an impressive accumulation of relational skills among constituent group members, involving tight interpersonal contacts and multilateral commitments across organizations. In contrast, a low-performing group is often found to be maintained by a mechanistic array of functional skills, fewer personal contacts, and unilateral commitments from suppliers to the prime contractor as designated by the latter. Dyer (1996), for example, measured face-to-face communication person-days between five U. S. and Japanese automakers and their suppliers and found that Toyota had the highest communication person-days, followed by Nissan, and, with a substantial margin, Ford, Chrysler, and General Motors, in that order, thus revealing an important aspect of Japanese outsourcing that prioritizes relational skills. It is argued that face-to-face communication with sufficient deployment of five senses and immediate feedback enables information exchange to occur that is superior to what arises from communication of an indirect kind (Daft and Lengel, 1986).

Just as human brain learning can be reinforced by a continuous pulse from synapses formed by previously separated axons of neurons as a result of repeated information input, so may interorganizational learning be promoted by the cultivation of rich relational skills made possible by frequent direct communication. Just like the human brain, where memory is a product of a physical networking of nerve cells (Margulis, 1990), so organizational memory could be an outcome of the entangling of relational skills resulting from direct human communication. It would not be unreasonable to assume, furthermore, that just like short-term memory, which is a mere physiological function of neurons' temporal interaction, can turn into stable long-term memory as a result of protein synthesized from intensified neuronic activity, so could short-term organizational memory be converted into long-term organizational memory by means of "institutionalizing" relational skills that previously belonged to a single individual. Once this institutionalization assumes a life of its own, influence, if any, from different personal capabilities and idiosyncrasies becomes minimal. A generating mechanism emerges, promoting an institution to spin off another, which reorders to produce yet another, and so on. For further details on institutionalized organizational memory that evolves, see Fujimoto (1997) and Nishiguchi and Beaudet (1998, 2000).

6. In this connection, Gleick (1987:110) cites a striking example: it was only after realizing that the phenomenal air-trapping capability of the natural product came from the fractal nodes and fractal branching of down's key protein, keratin, could DuPont and the United States Army finally start to produce a synthetic match for goose down. As such, fractal "scaling" is common not only in the natural world but also thought to be universal in morphogenesis, suggesting important implications for strategy and organization studies. It is reasonable to assume that a key to unlock the dynamics of the clustered control model may also reside in such fractal scaling.

7. In this light, a new word may be coined to mean a kind of coevolution that is neither wholly dependent on exploitation nor on symbiosis: "coevoloitation." An alternative term, de-emphasizing the evolutionary dimension, could be "exploibiosis."

References

Asahi Shimbun. 1996. (April 20): 1.
Asahi Shimbun. 1996. (November 30): 9.
Automotive News. 1986. (October 27): 1.
———. 1994. (August 1): 36.
Berger, Suzanne D., and Michael J. Piore. 1980. *Dualism and Discontinuity in Industrial Societies.* Cambridge, England: Cambridge University Press.
Bohm, David. 1976. *Fragmentation and Wholeness.* Jerusalem: Van Leer Jerusalem Foundation.
Bohm, David, and B. Hiley. 1994. *The Undivided Universe.* London: Routledge.
Bowman, Edward, and Bruce Kogut, eds. 1995. *Redesigning the Firm.* New York: Oxford University Press.
Brockman, John, ed. 1990. *Speculations: The Reality Club 1.* Englewood Cliffs, N.J.: Prentice-Hall.

Business Week. 1996. (October 7): 26–27.

Carmichael, L., ed. 1946. *Manual of Child Psychology.* New York: Wiley.

Cartwright, Dorwin, ed. 1951. *Field Theory in Social Sciences: Selected Theoretical Papers.* New York: Harper.

Chandler, Alfred D. 1962. *Strategy and Structure.* Cambridge, Mass.: MIT Press.

Clark, Kim B., and Takahiro Fujimoto. 1991. *Product Development Performance.* Boston: Harvard Business School Press.

Collins, Robert, Kimberly Bechler, and Silvio Pires. 1997. "Outsourcing in the Automotive Industry: From JIT to Modular Consortia." *European Management Journal* 15(5): 498–508.

Cowan, George A., David Pines, and David Meltzer, eds. 1994. *Complexity: Metaphors, Models, and Reality.* Reading, Mass.: Addison-Wesley.

Daft, R., and R. Lengel. 1986. "Organizational Information Requirements, Media Richness and Structural Design." *Management Science* 32(5): 554–71.

Dawkins, Richard. 1986. *The Blind Watchmaker.* New York: Norton.

———. 1989. *The Selfish Gene.* Oxford: Oxford University Press.

Dennett, Daniel C. 1990. "The Evolution of Consciousness." In Brockman (1990). Pp. 85–108.

Dunning, John H., ed. 1974. *Economic Analysis and the Multinational Enterprise.* London: Allen and Unwin .

Dyer, Jeffrey H. 1996. "Specialized Supplier Networks as a Source of Competitive Advantage: Evidence from the Auto Industry." *Strategic Management Journal* 17: 271–91.

Fujimoto, Takahiro. 1997. *Seisan shisutemu no shinka ron* (On the evolution of production system). Tokyo: Yuhikaku.

Gell-Mann, Murray. 1994. *The Quark and the Jaguar: Adventures in the Simple and the Complex.* New York: Freeman.

Ghoshal, Sumantra, and Peter Moran. 1996. "Bad for Practice: A Critique of the Transaction Cost Theory." *Academy of Management Review* 21(1): 13–47.

Gibson, James J. 1979. *The Ecological Approach to Visual Perception.* Boston: Houghton Mifflin.

Giddens, Anthony. 1993. *Sociology.* 2nd ed. London: Polity Press.

Gleick, James. 1987. *Chaos: Making a New Science.* New York: Viking Penguin.

Haken, Hermann. 1981. *Erfolgsgeheimnisse der Natur: Synergetik, die Lehre vom Zusammenwirken.* 2nd ed. Stuttgart: Deutsche Verlage-Anstalt.

———. 1996. "Synergetics as a Bridge between the Natural and Social Sciences." In Khalil and Boulding (1996). Pp. 234–48.

Hodgson, Geoffrey M. 1997. "The Coasean Tangle: The Nature of the Firm and the Problem of Historical Specificity." In Medema (1997). Pp. 23–49.

Ijiri, Yuji, and Isao Nakano, eds. 1992. *Business Behavior and Information.* Pittsburgh: Carnegie-Mellon University Press.

Ikegami, Takashi, and Kunihiko Kaneko. 1992. "Evolution of Host-parasite Network through Homeochaotic Dynamics." *Chaos* 2: 397.

Itami, Hiroyuki. 1991. "Joho no ba to shite no kigyo (The firm as an informational field)," mimeo.

———. 1992a. "Firm as an Informational 'Ba' (Interactive Field)." In Ijiri, Yuji, and Nakano (1992). Pp. 76–107.

———. 1992b. "Ba no manejimento josetsu (Towards the theory of management of 'Ba')." *Soshiki kagaku* (Organizational science) 26(1): 78–88.

Itoh, Masao, and Yutaka Saeki, eds. 1988. *Ninshiki shi kodo suru noh—noh kagaku to ninchi kagaku* (The cognizant and behavioral brain: cerebral and cognitive sciences). Tokyo: Univeristy of Tokyo Press.

IW. 1997. (March 17): 62–7.

Jantsch, Erich. 1980. *The Self-organizing Universe: Scientific and Human Implications of the Emerging Paradigm of Evolution*. Oxford: Pergamon Press.

Johnson, Chalmers. 1964. *Revolution and the Social System*. Stanford, Calif.: Stanford University Press.

———. 1966. *Revolutionary Change*. Boston: Little Brown.

Kaneko, Kunihiko. 1995. "Sogo naibu dainamikkusukei to shite no seimeikan—aisorogasu tayoka riron" (A view on life as internal dynamical systems: A theory of isologous diversification). *Gendai shiso* (Contemporary thought) 23(13): 86–97.

———. 1996. "Tayosei no kigen, iji, shinka" (The origin, maintenance, and evolution of diversity). *Keisoku to seigyo* (Journal of the society of instrument and control engineers) 35(7): 496–501.

Kaneko, Kunihiko, and Ichiro Tsuda. 1996. *Fukuzatsukei no kaosu teki shinario* (The chaotic scenario of complexity). Tokyo: Asakura shoten.

Kauffman, Stuart A. 1993. *The Origins of Order: Self-organization and Selection in Evolution*. New York: Oxford University Press.

———. 1995. *At Home in the Universe: The Search for Laws of Self-organization and Complexity*. New York: Oxford University Press.

Khalil, Elias L., and Kenneth E. Boulding, eds. 1996. *Evolution, Order, and Complexity*. London: Routledge.

Koestler, Arthur. 1967. *The Ghost in the Machine*. London: Hutchinson.

———. 1971. *The Case of the Midwife Toad*. London: Hutchinson.

Koestler, Arthur, and J. R. Smythies, eds. 1969. *Beyond Reductionism: New Perspectives in the Life Sciences*. London: Hutchinson.

Koga, Masaru, Kotaro Hirasawa, Masanao Ohbayashi, and Jun-ichi Murata, 1996. "Ippanka gakushu nettowaku ni okeru kaosu seigyo hoshiki" (Chaos control on universal learning network). *Keisoku jido seigyo gakkai ronbunshu* (Transactions of the society of instrument and control engineers) 32(6): 844–53.

Lewin, Kurt. 1946. "Behavior and Development as a Function of the Total Situation." In Carmichael (1946). Pp. 791–844.

Lewin, Kurt. 1951. *Field Theory in Social Sciences: Selected Theoretical Papers*. Edited by Dorwin Cartwright. New York: Harper.

Luhmann, Niklas. 1984. *Soziale Systeme: Grundriss einer allgemeinen Theorie*. Frankfurt: Suhrkamp.

Margulis, Lynn. 1990. "Speculation on Speculation." In Brockman (1990). Pp. 157–67.

Marr, David. 1982. *Vision: A Computational Investigation into the Human Representation and Processing of Visual Information*. New York: Freeman.

Matsuda, Hiroyuki. 1995. *"Kyosei" towa nanika* (What is symbiosis)? Tokyo: Gendai shokan.

Maturana, Humberto R., and Francisco J. Varela. 1980. *Autopoiesis and Cognition: The Realization of the Living*. Boston: D. Reidel.

———. 1998. *The Tree of Knowledge: The Biological Roots of Human Understanding*. Rev. ed. Boston: Shambhala.

Medema, Stephen, ed. 1997. *Coasean Economics: Law and Economics and the New Institutional Economics*. Boston, Mass.: Kluwer Academic.

Miyake, Yoshihiro. 1996. "Chiteki maruchi e-jento no kino bunsan to jiko genkyu" (Self-reference and diversity in the multi-agent system). *Keisoku to seigyo* (Journal of the society of instrument and control engineers) 35(7): 540–44.

Nagao, Yoichi, Hideaki Ohta, Hironobu Urabe, Shin-ichi Nakano, and Sadatoshi Kumagai. 1996. "Jiko bunsan shisutemu no tame no netto besu kyocho seigyo" (Net-based cooperative control for the autonomous distributed system). *Keisoku jido seigyo gakkai ronbunshu* (Transactions of the society of instrument and control engineers) 32(6): 967–74.

Neisser, Ulric. 1976. *Cognition and Reality*. San Francisco: Freeman.

Nelson, Richard R., and Sidney G. Winter. 1982. *An Evolutionary Theory of Economic Change*. Cambridge: Harvard University Press.

Newell, Allen, and Herbert A. Simon. 1972. *Human Problem Solving*. Englewood Cliffs, N.J.: Prentice-Hall.

Nihon Keizai Shimbun (Japan economic journal). 1996. (November 22): 22–3.

Nikkei Sangyo Shimbun (Nikkei industrial journal). 1996. (December 12): 10.

Nishiguchi, Toshihiro. 1988. "Sangyo kokka Amerika no fukken o uranau—biggu 3 wa jidosha shijo o dakkan dekiruka" (Foretelling the recovery of industrial America: Will the big three retrieve the auto market)? *Ekonomikkusu tsudei* (Economics today) (spring): 110–19, Tokyo: Shogakukan.

———. 1987. "Competing Systems of Automotive Components Supply: An Examination of the Japanese 'Clustered Control' Model and the 'Alps' Structure." Policy forum paper, International Motor Vehicle Program, Massachusetts Institute of Technology, May.

———. 1994. *Strategic Industrial Sourcing: The Japanese Advantage*. New York: Oxford University Press.

———. 1996. "Kyosei shinka no manejimento" (Coevolutionary symbiotic management). In *Autososhingu no jissen to soshiki shinka* (The practice and organizational evolution of outsourcing), edited by Diamond Harvard Business. Tokyo: Daiyamon-dosha. Pp. 123–201.

———. 1997. "Ba e no gakusaiteki sekkin" (An interdisciplinary approach to the field). *Business Review* 45(2): 14–35.

Nishiguchi, Toshihiro, and Erin M. Anderson. 1995. "Supplier and Buyer Networks." In Bowman and Kogut (1995). Pp. 65–84.

Nishiguchi, Toshihiro, and Alexandre Beaudet. 1998. "The Toyota Group and the Aisin Fire." *Sloan Management Review* 40(1): 49–59.

———. 2000. "Fractal Design: Self-organizing Links in Supply Chain Management." In Von Krogh, Nonaka, and Nishiguchi (2000). Pp. 199–230.

Nishiguchi, Toshihiro, and Jonathan Brookfield. 1997. "The Evolution of Japanese Subcontracting." *Sloan Management Review* 39(1): 89–101."

Nishizono, Haruka. 1996. "Ohtagata gijutsu shisutemu" (The Ohta-style technology system). Master's thesis, Hitotsubashi University, Kunitachi, Japan.

Nonaka, Ikujiro. 1986. " Soshiki chitsujo no kaitai to sozo—jiko soshikika paradaimu no teigen" (Creating organizational order out of chaos: a self-organization paradigm). *Soshiki kagaku* (Organizational science) 20(1): 32–44.

———. 1988a. "Creating Organizational Order Out of Chaos: Self-Renewal of Japanese Firms." *California Management Review* 30(3): 57–73.

———. 1988b. "Toward Middle-Up-Down Management: Accelerating Information Creation." *Sloan Management Review* 29(3): 9–18.

———. 1989. "Organizing Innovation as a Knowledge-Creation Process: A Suggestive Paradigm for Self-renewing Organization." Working paper, Haas School of Business OBIR-41, University of California at Berkeley.

———. 1990. "Redundant, Overlapping Organizations: A Japanese Approach to Managing the Innovation Process." *California Management Review* 32(3): 27–38.

————. 1994. "A Dynamic Theory of Organizational Knowledge Creation." *Organization Science* 5(1): 14–37.

Nonaka, Ikujiro, and Hirotaka Takeuchi. 1995. *The Knowledge-Creating Company: How Japanese Companies Create the Dynamics of Innovation*. New York: Oxford University Press.

Okazaki, Tetsuji, and Masahiro Okuno, eds. 1993. *Gendai Nihon keizai shisutemu no genryu* (The origins of modern Japanese economic systems). Tokyo: Nihon keizai shimbunsha.

Parsons, Talcott. 1951. *The Social System*. New York: Free Press.

————. 1964. "Evolutionary Universals in Society." *American Sociological Review* 29: 339–57.

————. 1966. *Societies: Evolutionary and Comparative Perspectives*. Englewood Cliffs, N.J.: Prentice-Hall.

Piore, Michael J., and Charles F. Sabel. 1984. *The Second Industrial Divide: Possibilities for Prosperity*. New York: Basic Books.

Polanyi, Michael. 1966. *The Tacit Demension*. London: Routledge and Kegan Paul.

Porter, Michael E. 1980. *Competitive Strategy*. New York: Free Press.

Prigogine, Ilya. 1980. *From Being to Becoming: Time and Complexity in the Physical Sciences*. New York: Freeman.

Richardson, James. 1993. "Parallel Sourcing and Supplier Performance in the Japanese Automobile Industry." *Strategic Management Journal* 14: 339–50.

Saeki, Yutaka. 1988. "Ninchi kagaku kara no sekkin" (An approach from cognitive science). In Itoh, and Saeki (1988). Pp. 10–30.

Schopenhauer, Arthur. 1969 (1818). *The World as Will and Presentation*. New York: Dover.

Schwenk, Theodor. 1976. *Sensitive Chaos: The Creation of Flowing Forms in Water and Air*. New York: Schocken.

Shannon, Claude E. 1951. "Prediction and Entropy of Printed English." *Bell System Technical Journal* 30: 59–64.

Shannon, Claude E., and W. Weaver. 1949. *The Mathematical Theory of Communication*. Urbana: University of Illinois Press.

Spengler, Oswald. 1926 (1917). *The Decline of the West*. London: Allen and Unwin.

Tocqueville, Alexis de. 1969 (1835). *Democracy in America*. New York: Harper and Row.

Tsuda, Ichiro. 1991. "Chaotic Itinerancy as a Dynamical Basis of Hermeneutics in Brain and Mind." *World Futures* 32: 167–84.

Vernon, Raymond. 1966. "International Investment and International Trade in the Product Cycle." *Quarterly Journal of Economics* 80: 190–207.

————. 1971. *Sovereignty at Bay: The Multinational Spread of U.S. Enterprises*. London: Basic Books.

————. 1974. "The Location of Economic Activity." In Dunning (1974). Pp. 89–114.

Von Krogh, Georg Fredrik, and Johan Roos. 1995. *Organizational Epistemology*. London: Macmillan.

Von Krogh, Georg Fredrik, Ikujiro Nonaka, and Toshihiro Nishiguchi, eds. 2000. *Knowledge Creation*. London: Macmillan.

Waldrop, M. Mitchell. 1992. *Complexity: The Emerging Science at the Edge of Order and Chaos*. New York: Simon and Schuster.

Weick, Karl E. 1979. *The Social Psychology of Organizing*, 2nd ed. New York: McGraw-Hill.

Williamson, Oliver E. 1975. *Markets and Hierarchies: Analysis and Antitrust Implications*. New York: Free Press.

————. 1985. *The Economic Institutions of Capitalism*. New York: Free Press.

————. 1996. *The Mechanisms of Governance*. New York: Oxford University Press.

Yonekura, Seiichiro. 1993a. "Seifu to kigyo no dainamikkusu: Sangyo seisaku no sofuto na sokumen" (Government-industry dynamics: a soft side of industrial policy). *Hitotsubashi daigaku kenkyu nempo shogaku kenkyu* (Commercial study: Research annual of Hitotsubashi University) 33: 249–92.

————. 1993b. "Gyokai dantai no kino" (Functions of trade associations). In Okazaki and Okuno, (1993). Pp. 183–209.

12

"Co-opetition" in the Japanese Aircraft Industry

SIGRUN CASPARY
TOSHIHIRO NISHIGUCHI

Knowledge creation is the key to Japanese entrepreneurial innovation (Nonaka and Takeuchi, 1995:3). It takes place on various organizational levels: within one company, between companies of one industry, and between companies of various industries. In cases where the development of an industry is thought to require government support, there is additional knowledge creation through the exchange between government and private industry. Strategic industries are one example of industries with massive governmental intervention.

Since its inception, the aircraft industry[1] worldwide has been supported by national governments in various ways, for four major reasons. First, it is a question of national prestige. Second, the industry possesses strategic character as a high-tech industry with spillover effects to other industries. Third, it is indispensable for the defense industry. Last, it is an obvious means for passenger and cargo transportation. The industry's importance for trade, business, and leisure is unbroken, and it has high growth prospects far into the next century (Piller, 1995:26–27). Thus, national governments will continue to be additional players that, depending on the extent of their intervention, promote or hinder the development of the industry.

Another chracteristic of this industry is its global market and oligopolistic structure, especially for commercial aircraft,[2] that impedes the market entrance of new companies. Comprehensive knowledge of international markets and competitors is essential in view of the colossal development and production costs and comparably long product cycles, which, again, prompt the call for government subsidies.

Throughout history, individual nations have placed emphases varying in scope and intensity on their industrial policy measures. The European nations, for example, heavily subsidized the multinational consortium Airbus Industrie, whereas the U. S. government granted only minimal support to the commercial aircraft industry and instead promoted military aircraft development (the "military-industrial complex").

In Japan, too, the aircraft industry has been labeled a strategic industry. The Ministry of International Trade and Industries (MITI) was applauded as well as criticized for its industrial policy measures aimed at nurturing target industries. In the case of the aircraft industry in Japan, and in contrast to Western counterparts, a unique interaction between governmental institutions and private companies emerged.

In addition, since the end of World War II, the global aircraft industry has shown a continuous trend toward concentration and integration. This is a reflection of the skyrocketing risks and costs of the development of commercial aircraft and aircraft engines and unpredictable market conditions due to enormous fluctuations in demand.[3] After the end of the Cold War in 1989, shrinking defense budgets in various countries also intensified this trend for military aircraft, as exemplified by several mergers and acquisitions and takeovers.[4] Several joint ventures have been established in this industry in order to reduce the risks of high costs and unpredictable market movements. Again, Japan appears to be the only country unaffected by this trend toward concentration.

We will analyze the characteristics of the Japanese aircraft industry in the light of differing views among statists, technonationalists, and flexible specialists, focusing on the interorganizational cooperation that has emerged since World War II. Furthermore, we take a close look at the knowledge-creation process within and between companies and in cooperation with governmental institutions, which differs strikingly from approaches in Western countries. We present various participants in the aircraft industry and respective industrial policy establishment, and we illuminate the cooperation and competition among companies and government institutions. In conclusion, we analyze the history of the Japanese aircraft development programs, thereby revealing the inevitable necessity for international commitment. Finally, we highlight the Japanese entrepreneurial contribution to knowledge creation worldwide through participation in international cooperations in aircraft and engine development programs.

The Japanese Industrial Policy

Since the early 1970s, the success abroad of Japanese products such as cars, motorcycles, household electronic appliances, and computers has led to a global discussion on industrial policy. The Japanese method of nurturing (*ikusei*) strategic industries through administrative guidance (*gyosei shido*) by MITI is considered to be one important contributing factor for the economic success of Japanese companies in conquering foreign markets (Johnson, 1986).

In his developmental state approach, Johnson (1986:320) identifies as MITI's key characteristics its "small size (the smallest of any of the economic ministries), its indirect control of government funds (thereby freeing it of subservience to the Finance Ministry's Bureau of the Budget), its 'think tank' functions, its vertical bureaus for the implementation of industrial policy at the micro level, and its internal democracy." The Japanese elite bureaucracy as a whole he calls the most important source for all political innovations, as they make the most important political decisions, write practically all the laws, and control the national budget. Johnson (1986:311) lists the chief mechanisms of the bureaucracy-industry cooperation:

> Selective access to governmental or governmental-guaranteed financing, targeted tax breaks, government-supervised investment coordination in order to keep all participants profitable, the equitable coordination by the state of burdens during

times of adversity . . . [and] governmental assistance in the commercialization and sale of products."[5]

The cooperation of government and industry has been institutionalized in "deliberating councils" (*shingikais*), formal "discussion groups" composed of bureaucrats as well as representatives of private companies, the academia and the mass media, which agree on industrial policy measures and their implementation. Political measures coordinated with the large companies left management and ownership in private hands, therewith providing more competition than possible under total state control while enabling MITI officials to intervene in the private sector. With this form of "administrative guidance" (gyosei shido), "government officials and representatives of banking and industry can coordinate their activities unconstrained by law and lawyers" (Johnson, 1986:312).

Nevertheless, Johnson's identification of MITI "as an industrial policy maker par excellence" (Callon, 1995:6) requires relativization. First, MITI has never been able to make its policy decisions independently of other governmental institutions. As we will show hereafter, other ministries have also played an important role. Second, industrial policy measures were differentiated for every industry and hence influenced their development with differing intensity and results. Third, there is no policy-making institution that other countries do not have. The difference lies in the way in which cooperation is organized among these institutions in order to implement particular measures. The consultation process for reaching a consensus among all participants is of similar importance to the results finally agreed on.

Nevertheless, the impact of industrial policy on the growth success of a particular industry has not been analysed in depth. For example, in Japan the aircraft industry was labeled a strategic industry as it was in other industrialized countries (NKUKK, 1987a:12); MITI introduced several laws and measures for its promotion. But in past decades, Komiya (1988:7) notes, "of such [i.e., strategic] industries, about the only one to date that has not been firmly established in Japan is the aircraft industry." It seems to be a contradiction that the MITI, praised as well as criticized for its successful nurturing policy in other "strategic industries," has not been able to promote the aircraft industry to the extent and scale one might have expected. In 1992, the aircraft industry in Japan only contributed 0.18 percent to the GNP, compared to 1.23 percent in the United States (NKUKK 1994b:12–3). "At best, policies resulted from a compromise forced on the bureaucracy, or even that business constrained the state." Hence, the "importance of state policies themselves, and the implications of business-state-relations in general, cannot be evaluated without situating them in the larger political context that surrounds industrial activity" (Friedman, 1988:30, 209–10). On the part of private industry, entrepreneurship also played an important role in the successful economic development of Japan. Here, industrial policy mostly focused on the big companies supervised by the vertical bureaus of the MITI. Nevertheless, it was not only big business that led the Japanese economy to success. Friedman showed that, for example in the machinery industry, the "flexible production" with its division of labor between a few big companies and the large number of small and medium-sized firms enabled a flexible response to changes in domestic and later international market demand. Because the airline industry experiences large fluctuations in demand at low production numbers, flexibility is necessary in that industry as well.

Samuels (1994) identified "technonationalism," the strive for technology for national security, as the leading principle for catching up with the Western nations that led to the success of the Japanese economic development. He considers the slogan "rich nation—strong army" (fukoku kyohei) of the late-nineteenth-century Japanese government, which serves as his book title, to be one clear expression of this technonationalistic behavior (Samuels, 1994:3). Taking the aircraft industry as an example of a strategic industry, Samuels argued that after World War II Japan nurtured the military industry, permanently enlarging the domestic content (kokusanka) of license production. Japanese companies targeted those technologies to be imported from the United States as those they were not yet able to produce domestically. Later, those technologies were transferred to the commercial sector for use in international codevelopment programs. "Technology-driven defense depended on political collaboration between MITI and the defense industry, and it was attended by MOF [Ministry of Finance] funding and JDA [Japan Defense Agency] deployment" (Samuels, 1994:167). The way Japanese companies managed to embed the defense production within commercial activities, gaining benefits through spinoff effects from the imported and later domestically developed high technology, is called the default option by Samuels because it was the only choice they had to build up a rich nation and a strong army.

Although we agree that spinoff effects initiated developments on the commercial side, there is still the question of the extent of those effects. The small number and size of military development programs never reached a quality level for military technology comparable to the United States. It was not technology per se that drove economic growth. It was the organization of companies, their way of commercialization of products and cooperation to improve business and trade, that led Japanese companies to success. Here again we must focus on the structure of government and private industry cooperation that enabled this kind of knowledge to flourish.

Ministries Influencing the Aircraft Industry

In Japan, the activities of the following ministries influenced directly or indirectly the performance and thus the knowledge creating process of the aircraft industry.

1. MITI's Aircraft and Defense Products Division under the Machinery and Information Industries Bureau is the vertical bureau (genkyoku) responsible for the coordination and regulation of business activities related to the manufacture and repair of aircraft and aircraft machinery. This division's policy aims to promote healthy development as well as to improve the technological base of this industry (MITI-ICO, 1994:77). In order to reach this goal, the division drafted several laws tailored to its national projects (e.g., the Aircraft Industry Law of 1952, the Arms Manufacturing Law of 1953, and the Aircraft Industry Promotion Law of 1958, revised in 1986). The Aircraft Industry Council was established as a "deliberating council" (shingikai). In this council all participants, that is, representatives of MITI and other ministries, industry associations such as the Society of Japanese Aero-

space Companies (SJAC), leading companies, academia, and mass media, bring in their knowledge to discuss current problems and future trends and proposals on industrial policy. This indicates how eager MITI officials were to provide the best framework for nurturing the aircraft industry as they wanted it to develop while conforming with Johnson's developmental state approach.

2. Nevertheless, the MOF also plays a decisive role in the industrial policy formulation process because of its responsibility for budgetary and financial questions. MITI is required by law to gain MOF's agreement on any activity that calls for government funding or the selection of financial institutions for provision of preferential loans and their conditions to private companies (Aircraft Industry Promotion Law, section 5.27; see Tsusho Sangyosho, 1995:1315). This fact, not mentioned in any previous analyses of industrial policy, proves that MITI cannot act independently but instead is dependent on the willingness of MOF to promote the respective industry. In contrast to, for example, the space or rail industries, MOF had always been reluctant to provide funds for aircraft development projects. This is is one crucial reason for the relatively small size of this strategic industry. In the case of the aircraft industry, the dependence on MOF is doubly significant. First, MITI does not have its own special budget for, for example, the promotion of commercial industrial development or the procurement of aircraft for governmental use. In the case of the first and only Japanese commercial passenger transport, YS-11, there were annual altercations about subsidies with the MOF (e.g., Maema, 1994:70, Umezawa, 1964:44). Legal restrictions limited the money available for the development and production of this national project aircraft (NKUKK, 1987b:42–3). Second, MOF's "minimal necessary defense" policy holds under strict control the amount of money available in the defense budget for military programs. The impact on aircraft production is elucidated hereafter.

3. The JDA influenced the development of the aircraft industry in being the most important single customer. Military demand always accounted for 70–90 percent of total aircraft production output.[6] Nevertheless, the prohibition of weapons exports under the Law for the Control of Exports (1959) reduced to zero the opportunity for companies to enlarge their military production base through sales abroad. Limited budgets, constrained by MOF's "minimal necessary defense" policy, restricted aircraft selection for JDA procurement and R&D activities, thus limiting the amount and types of aircraft to be built by the Japanese industry.

Formally, the supervision over military aircraft manufacturing is vested in the Aircraft and Defense Products Division of MITI. All procurement plans must be sanctioned by the Security Council of Japan. This council of several ministers under the chairmanship of the prime minister has the "civilian control" over all defense-related decisions. Note that the MITI minister only holds a consultative position within this council. Until 1986, this minister was not a member at all in the Defense Council (the preceding organization).

The nonofficial selection of number and type of aircraft is done within the JDA. In permanent consultation with company representatives on various levels, the prime contractors are preselected. In most cases, the JDA gives advice to the prime contractor on the percentage of work share that should be sourced out to the largest subcontractors. MITI officials again play only an advisory role. Where not subject to "foreign pressure" (see hereafter), JDA's plans on aircraft procurement (foreign, license production, or indigenous development) have passed the Security Council and the Diet with only little modificatio.[7] Being the sole customer of military aircraft, that is, 70 percent of the industry's output today, the JDA hence limits the central position of MITI in developing the aircraft industry argued by the statists.

4. The Science and Technology Agency (STA) is responsible for the Japanese R&D policy with respect to aircraft. The total prohibition of aircraft development and production under the United States occupation in 1945–1952 widened the technology gap for Japan at a time when jet engine technology in Europe and North America made rapid progress. From that time forward, STA policy was determined by the decision that it was too late for Japan to catch up with the Western industrialized countries in aircraft technology. In contrast, the gap in space technology was not considered to be too great for Japan to fill, since the race between the United States and the then Soviet Union for aerospace supremacy had just started. STA heavily promoted space R&D, thus limiting the available financial and personnel resources for (commercial as well as military) aircraft technology. This is another reason for the small size of the Japanese aircraft industry.

5. The Ministry of Transport (MOT) influences the development of the aircraft indirectly through market demand. First of all, MOT is responsible for the provision of air transport infrastructure: the number of airports is very low compared with countries in Europe and North America. Runway length determines the size of aircraft, which in turn influences the type and number of aircraft that can be sold and thus produced by Japanese manufacturers. In addition, MOT's tight regulations of national and international air transport service restricted the domestic market's growth, and, again the possible sales of aircraft to national carriers (Sakamoto, 1990:32–5). With a small and restricted domestic market, Japanese aircraft manufacturers had to rely on exports in the heavily competitive international aircraft market if they wanted to broaden their production base.[8]

Finally, we must include an external factor in our analysis of the Japanese aircraft industry. The United States influenced the development of this strategic industry in both military and commercial terms. In military terms, the equipment of the Japanese Self Defense Forces depends on the United States security policy (e.g., request for interoperability). Since the early 1950s, this sole ally promoted the technology transfer of military aircraft license production with an increasing percentage of Japanese content (*kokusanka*). With the emergence of Japan as a leading nation in terms of economy and technology, however, the United States increasingly restricted the flow of aircraft-related high technology to Japan. Instead, since the early 1980s, they sought to replace the one-way export of technology to Japan with a bilateral cooperation in the future development of weapon systems. At the same time, the huge surplus export of U.S. aircraft and related parts to Japan became a crucial but hardly mentioned element in the bilateral discussions on trade conflicts.[9] The United States influenced the Japanese aircraft imports and production numbers on the commercial sector as well. The appearance of a foreign factor made the development of the Japanese aircraft industry less predictable for government officials and companies and thus weakened the effects of MITI's industrial policy.[10]

In summary, the industrial policy of the aircraft industry is influenced by various ministries on the government side. MITI plays an important role but still has to coordinate its activities with other ministries. Of greatest importance is its dependency on MOF's agreement on financial measures for promotion. This stands in total contrast to the independent position of MITI as argued by the statists. Another striking fact is the lack of a coordinating ministerial institution, for example, for R&D policy. Although labeled a strategic industry, STA policy for aircraft was always small-scale, as was the range of military R&D activities that JDA was able to implement, because of budget constraints and U.S. influence on procurement decisions. Given this scenario, the role of private companies must be analyzed in greater detail.

The Aircraft Manufacturers

At first glance, the Japanese aircraft industry shows a structure to similar that of Europe and North America. There are a handful of large oligopolistic companies that are responsible for a large part of the manufacturing, assembly, and system integration. Today, there are five leading companies in aircraft manufacturing: Mitsubishi Heavy Industries (MHI), Kawasaki Heavy Industries (KHI), Fuji Heavy Industries (FHI), ShinMaywa (SMIC), and Japan Aircraft (Nippi). In the engine sector, the "big three" are Ishikawajima-Harima Heavy Industries (IHI), MHI, and KHI.[11] All of them source out the major portion of their business to a large number of subcontractors.[12]

Different is the fact that the "aerospace sector" of large Japanese companies accounts for only 10–20 percent of their overall business,[13] and aircraft-related activities again are only one part of aerospace. Within the aircraft sector, there was further competition for resources between commercial and military programs. As in the case of the STA policy already mentioned, several people in important positions in private companies also assumed that closing the gap in aircraft technology would be difficult, and they strongly promoted aerospace activities instead. Cooperation of all companies was the only possible solution (called by Samuels the default option) to achieve a sufficiently large-scale production to carry through big national projects.

The big manufacturers cooperated in several commercial and military programs, alternately as leading or prime companies or as subcontractors able to achieve a kind of "flexible production." In the commercial transport segment, for example, MHI, KHI, and FHI divided the airframe structure works among themselves. At the same time, the companies maintained a certain amount of independence in product niches.[14] In the jet engine sector, IHI emerged as the specialist for large aero engines, whereas smaller engines are the province of KHI and MHI.[15] Although characterized by small-scale production, the aircraft business can hardly be implemented as a side job, because of high development costs and a low rate of capital flow back. However, this division of labor enabled all companies to stay in the business. Some of the small and medium-sized subcontracting firms rely on aerospace demand to a higher percentage than do their mother companies. On the other hand, quite a number of companies admit that enhancing their reputation with their engagement in manufacturing aerospace parts is of greater importance than the prospects of making money in this business. For some firms, reputation ranks even higher than the prospects of achieving spill-over effects from the high-technology aerospace area to other business areas.

In contrast to other nations, however, in Japan there has never been any attempt to merge the activities of the existing large airframe manufacturers, and this is hardly likely in the future. With only few intrafirm resources available for aircraft-related products, the cost explosion in product development and manufacturing had caused many firms to seek low-cost solutions. The Japanese companies chose another way of knowledge creation to be able to stay in business: they combined interfirm cooperation with the transfer of manufacturing practices from other areas of their corporate business, enabling economies of scale even with low production rates. Thus, the spin-on of manufacturing and management practices became more important to aircraft business than the spin-off from high-tech aerospace to other business areas.

With reference to Brandenburger and Nalebuff (1996:4–5), this phenomenon of cooperation and competition within and among Japanese industries and with government institutions led to the choice of "co-opetition" as the title for this essay. Furthermore, co-opetition embedded the aircraft sector in the overall industrial structure without developing all the structural phenomena that caused the recent concentration process in other countries. Instead, Japanese companies became attractive partners in international codevelopment projects because of their experience in low-cost and high-quality production, intercorporate cooperation, and program management. Cooperation with other companies was institutionalized in semigovernmental organizations; it is described in the next section.

Aircraft Development and Semigovernmental Organizations

In Japan, all big aircraft and engine manufacturers joined to establish semigovernmental organizations in order to carry out national projects. This kind of organization is not to be found in other nations, because the manufacturers in Europe and North America, which are specialists, have been large enough to execute programs of their own.[16] Japanese companies devoted only a small percentage of their overall business activities to aircraft or engine development. Under the "administrative guidance" of MITI, semigovernmental institutions were established out of the necessity to concentrate the manufacturers' activities.

Nihon Jet Engine Corporation

Nihon Jet Engine Corporation (NJE) was the first semigovernmental institution, established soon after the readmittance of aircraft activities in July 1953. Three companies, Omiya Fuji Works, Omiya Precision, and Ishikawajima independently had requested financial support from MITI for jet engine development.[17] They were brought together in order to avoid "excess" competition and investment and to utilize jointly the existing scarce resources and facilities.[18] Shin-Mitsubishi was brought in under the administrative guidance of MITI (Maema, 1989:255–6). Each of the four companies contributed identical amounts of capital (40 million yen each) and personnel (ten people each) for the setup of NJE. Kawasaki joined under the same conditions in 1956 (NJE, 1967:14, Maema, 1989:258–9). Basic research for the J-1 engine was carried out on the basis of the first developments of Omiya Fuji Works (the JO 1 engine), but even though they agreed to cooperate, the company prohibited its engineers from giving all crucial data to NJE. Nevertheless, cooperation and knowledge sharing went more smoothly than expected because the engineers were led by a common goal: to develop a purely Japanese jet engine. MITI had promised to contribute capital as well but ultimately granted only 4 million yen in subsidies because the MOF insisted on substantial financial responsibility by the private companies. Without enough funding, NJE engine J-1 ended up only a quarter of the size of JO 1 and smaller than Ne 20, the jet engine that had been brought to first flight in August 1945. Lacking an appropriate commercial aircraft development program in Japan to install the engine, JDA finally agreed on the utilization of a NJE-developed engine on its first national trainer, T-1, in 1955. The project was enlarged and renamed J-3.

With the acceptance of J-3 by JDA, the question arose of which company would carry out the serial production. At first all participating firms refused because they feared the high costs for new manufacturing facilities, which would not be subsidized by the Japanese government. In view of the technical problems that were revealed during the development phase, Mitsubishi was not interested in such high-risk serial production, although the company would have gained enough support from politicians and bureaucrats to be named prime contractor (Maema, 1989:288). Kawasaki at that time owned the largest facilities for engine repair and overhaul, but also refused large scale engine production participation (Maema, 1989:294). Omiya Fuji already seemed to have decided on its withdrawal from engine development. Finally, the then president of IHI, Toshio Doko, decided, against dissenters within the company, that IHI would buy the blue prints and test engine from NJE. After the transfer of all activities concerning serial production of the J-3 to IHI's Tanashi works in 1959, NJE was disbanded.[19] Without the decision of JDA to install the NJE engine on its trainer F-1, NJE would have been disbanded much earlier. Japanese jet engines would have entered the market only very belatedly, if at all.

Here we stress the importance of the JDA in the initial development of the industry, whereas the reluctance of MITI, MOF, and financial institutions to provide sufficient funding for the J-3 project is one major reason for the sluggish start and the small size of this "strategic" industry. Although MITI encouraged cooperation in the initial phase of the project it withdrew its support for the engine project, which, in addition to the reluctant mood in the industry concerning serial production, hardly supports a "technonationalistic" interpretation for aircraft related-industrial policy at those times. Instead, it was the enterpreneurial courage of IHI's president, Toshio Doko, that got the serial production of engines under way. After that, the responsibility for the industry's development was largely transferred to private industry.

The V 2500

In the following period, jet engine development activities for civil aircraft remained low key, and license production of military engines became the main focus, with IHI taking the lead. In 1971, MITI tried to recover part of its influence in high-technology development programs by supporting a project called Fan Jet Research (FJR) under its Agency of Industrial Science and Technology (AIST) scheme. This FJR 710–type engine program was carried out in cooperation with the National Aerospace Laboratory (NAL) under STA. IHI was responsible for 70 percent of the work share, and MHI and KHI participated with 15 percent, respectively, in the R&D activities.[20] However, when reaching the test flight phase, Japan had to request the execution of high-altitude flight tests in a British national research institute because of the lack of facilities of this type and scale in Japan.[21] The tests proved such high technical quality for the FJR 710 engine that British Rolls-Royce (RR) afterward offered the Japanese a participation in the development of a similar engine. State-owned RR expected a substantial financial contribution from Japan toward the development costs, whereas Japanese companies hoped to gain crucial knowledge and expertise in technology and marketing from their British counterpart, a firm steeped in the tradition of engine manufacturing. In 1980, the joint venture company Rolls-Royce and Japan Aero Engine Ltd. (RRJAEL) was established, and codevelopment activities began.

Only a short time later, several factors led to a change in global aircraft and aircraft engine demand. The increased competition among American airlines as a result of the deregulation of U. S. air transport services in the early 1980s also had a strong impact on European carriers, not to mention the effect of the second oil crisis. The demand for larger passenger aircraft increased and thus the size of the RRJAEL engine had to be doubled, which doubled the estimated development costs to 200 billion yen (Maema, 1989:406). In the face of tougher competition between engine manufacturers, RRJAEL was no longer able to finance the program on its own and was forced to seek additional partners. After negotiations with all manufacturers, MITI, and the SJAC in the Aircraft Industry Council, the Japanese decided to carry out codevelopment with RR and the American Pratt and Whitney (P&W), with the latter bringing in its two partners, German Motoren- und Triebwerke Union (MTU) and Italian Fiat Avio.

Without a common project, cooperation in commercial engine research in Japan had been at low levels for more than a decade. With the prospect of MITI support for a large-scale national project and of international codevelopment with some of the world's leading engine manufacturers, IHI, KHI, and MHI agreed to set up a new semigovernmental institution. The Japanese Aero Engines Corporation (JAEC) was established in October 1981 with the goal of supporting and promoting R&D activities, testing, production, sales, and product support related to civil aero engines. The three manufacturers shared the capital and personnel—60 percent (IHI), 25 percent (KHI), and 15 percent (MHI), respectively—of this representative organization that coordinated the work shares between the Japanese companies and between Japanese and foreign companies.

In December 1983, the five "Program Sharing Partners"[22] established the joint venture International Aero Engines (IAE) in Zurich, Switzerland, which would be responsible for sales, marketing, and product support (including spare parts). Development and production (including up-front costs) of the fan jet engine for a 150-seat commercial transporter named V 2500 were to be carried out (in part jointly) at the partners' facilities. Thus, the IAE organization resembled that of the JAEC or that of the European Airbus Industry in the aircraft manufacturing sector. The five partners worked out a special overall business plan, including parameters for expected market development, sales, and after-sales business, as well as for changes in currency values. The work share was divided up between the JAEC (23 percent), RR and P&W (30 percent each), MTU (11 percent), and Fiat (6 percent). The Japanese work share of 23 percent was divided among the three companies IHI (60 percent), KHI (25 percent), and MHI (15 percent) (JAEC material received during an interview with T. Inoue, general manager, Small Turbofan Engine Department of the Japanese Aero Engine Corporation, June 14, 1996; Maema, 1989:407).

During the development phase, various problems arose because this was the first time for all partners to implement an international joint program. The Japanese companies were able to contribute their vast experience of knowledge creation in longstanding domestic cooperation (mainly in military engine license production) and project management in current international coordination. After five years of development at IAE, the first flight of V 2500 engines was successfully made on an Airbus 320 model at the Farnborough Air Show in September 1988. In comparison with other 150-seater engines, the V 2500 realized a noise reduction of 10 percent, a fuel reduction of 20 percent, and an exhaust reduction (carbon monoxide, etc.) of 70 percent (Maema, 1989:423). The total development costs approached 200 billion yen, with the Japanese share estimated at 50 billion yen (around 20 percent). The internationalization of the V 2500 engine program (and of the YX aircraft program, as discussed hereafter) effected a change in MITI's industrial policy. In 1986, the Aircraft Manufacturing Law was changed to enable the support of international development projects under the large-scale national program scheme. Under this new law, the International Aircraft Development Fund (IADF) was set up to provide loans of up to 75 percent of the total R&D costs under this scheme. The Japan Development Bank (JDB) was also enabled to provide additional loans at a preferential 4.3 percent interest rate. MITI introduced all measures it could to support the aircraft industry development. Nevertheless, MOF still asked for a high responsibility for private companies. The Ministry insisted on the repayment of all subsidies (including the interest subsidies) to both financial institutions after achieving profits from the sale of the engine. In addition, Japanese companies received no subsidies for any activity related to serial production—and in this point the Japanese case heavily differs from the Airbus one (interview with T. Inoue, General Manager, Small Turbofan Engine Department of JAEC, June 14, 1996).

As a result of the cooperation with Rolls-Royce, in the IAE, and further with General Electric (on several military programs), the Japanese company IHI, for example, doubled its aircraft engine business from 50 billion yen in 1976 to 100 billion in 1984 (Maema, 1989:409–10). Today, with a 20 percent share in overall business, IHI's aero engine activities have become an essential part of the core business, although the MOF had been reluctant to grant financial assistance.[23] It was the entrepreneurship of the company managers and the domestic and international cooperation with other manufacturers (KHI, MHI-GE, RR, P&W), and the SJAC and—to a lesser extent—with MITI on several commercial and military programs that enabled IHI's engine business to become what it is today in technology, quality, and reputation.

The National Project YS-11

The first national program for a commercial transport aircraft was initiated by MITI in 1956 in order to nurture the industry and to reduce the total import dependency on civil transport aircraft. The Aircraft and Defense Products Division of MITI formulated a special law for the promotion of the aircraft industry. With the support of politicians, the law was enacted in 1958 as the Aircraft Manufacturing Law. This law made possible not only the foundation of the Society for Research of Transport Aircraft Design (SRTAD) but also the contribution of government capital to this institution. Five famous designers of the war-time period were selected to lead the basic design work at SRTAD.[24] Once the national project was established, all companies gathered their forces and knowledge to bring the development of the passenger aircraft, called YS-11, to successful realization. The completion of the mock-up in 1959 led to further political support for a serial production. Because the SRTAD had been responsible solely for basic design activities, a new semigovernmental organization for the execution of manufacturing work had to be established. For this task, the Nihon Aircraft Manufacturing Company (NAMC) was founded, after the Aircraft Manufacturing Law was changed, enabling the provision of government capital for this new company. The companies received government loans of up to 75 percent for the R&D work on the YS-11 and up to 50 percent for the serial work. All subsidies were to be repaid after the product sales achieved profits. MOF wanted private companies to retain a large responsibility for high-cost and high-risk business such as aircraft manufacturing, although its was labeled a strategic industry by MITI and other ministries and associations.

In retrospect, the division of development and production work between two organizations proved to be a handicap for the YS-11 program. The slight experience of the renowned designers in commercial transport and their neglect to consider customers', that is, airlines', opinions in the configuration phase led to the necessity for modifications, causing the belated market entrance of the YS-11. In the meantime, competitor models had come up abroad and because of their prior availability had reduced the number of possible sales for the Japanese aircraft at home and abroad. Over time, the reputation of this first Japanese transport aircraft increased and proved that Japanese technology had reached a high enough level to compete in the global market segment for regional aircraft. Nevertheless, this success only proved to be real for Japanese manufacturing quality. Import substitution and export promotion strategy, as promulgated by MITI, was not achieved in the case of the YS-11.[25] Aircraft technology knowhow was too inferior to enable reliance on domestically developed products in the international aircraft market. Thus, foreign content of the aircraft (such as engines, avionics, raw material) remained high. Economies of scale could not be achieved because of small production numbers (Yamamura, 1995:111). In addition, the lack of experience in pricing and marketing led to a deficit in NAMC's balance of payments that was worsened by the limited opportunity to raising capital as laid down in the Aircraft Manufacturing Law. The belated implementation of political countermeasures for a reduction of the NAMC's deficit demonstrates the lack of experience in the companies and MITI, as well as the unwillingness of MOF to promote a national project in this strategic industry. The importance of government support with enough capital to enable an entry into this oligopolistic global market as a newcomer had been underestimated. The understanding that aircraft differed from other manufactured products with regard to development costs, sales conditions, capital flow back, dependency on global market development, timing of market entrance, and so on was inadequate on both the bureaucratic and the industrial side. In the end, the deficit at NAMC rose to 380 billion yen. In the repayment discussion, the two sides clashed. The companies asked for a large government contribution because YS-11 had been a national project initiated by MITI. The MOF wanted private industry to carry a larger burden.[26] Facing the huge deficit at NAMC, the Aircraft Industry Council reached a decision to stop the production of the YS-11 in 1972 (after having manufactured 180 aircraft) and to dissolve NAMC.[27]

The Large-Scale National Project YX/767

In the meantime, several plans for models to follow the YS-11 had been discussed at NAMC. Although R&D activities went on, both manufacturers and MOF were reluctant to engage in manufacturing of a follow-up model in the face of the financial failure of the YS-11. This special domestic situation was worsened by the international economic turbulence after the oil crisis that slowed the air transport demand and thus reduced the expected amount of supply and production numbers for the manufacturers. Apart from a plan for a national development project (e.g., a stretched version of the YS-11), there had been offers from European and American aircraft manufacturers to participate primarily as parts suppliers in their projects (KUMCK, 1985:40,170–3). The Japanese companies and MITI finally agreed on participation in an international joint development (50:50) proposed by the market leader, Boeing, which was looking for a partner to share the financial burden of high development costs. In addition, Boeing's plans for a large aircraft were similar to those of the Japanese side. Besides this, the Boeing people had been impressed by the quality of the manufacturing work in the YS-11 (Maema, 1994:452, 454). On the other hand, Japanese companies were attracted by the opportunity to learn new basic technology and manufacturing methods, as well as sales and after-sales knowhow, from the market leader.

In view of the repayment of NAMC deficits, there again arose a discussion on the amount of government support for a new national project in Japan. When Boeing learned that MOF was reluctant to allow subsidies for a codevelopment program, the company threatened to withdraw its offer for cooperation, which in the end made the MOF agree on an augmentation of financial support for the program

(Yamamura, 1995:178). This episode demonstrates the differences in standpoints concerning the necessity of governmental support in aircraft development. It was just during this period that in Europe several manufacturers gathered to establish the Airbus Industrie. It was heavily subsidized in order to enable the newcomer to break the market monopoly of the American companies Boeing, Douglas, and Lockheed for large transport aircraft. Consultations in the Aircraft Industry Council reached consensus that participation in international codevelopment programs (*kokusai kyodo kaihatsu*) afforded the most promising way to nurture the Japanese aircraft industry. Thus, MITI modified the Law for the Promotion of Aircraft Industry (1986) that initiated the foundation of the International Aircraft Development Fund (IADF). As already described, this fund provided semigovernmental organizations with loans up to a certain amount of a project's R&D work and paved the way for companies to procure additional loans from the JDB at a special interest rate. This measure revised the inadequate framework that had led to the financial disaster of the YS-11. Nevertheless, its provision for repayment of subsidies granted for R&D still left the private companies with a large financial burden.

Already in March 1972, a new organization, the Commercial Transport Development Corporation (CTDC), had been founded with the aim of carrying out R&D activities for a national project named YX (which later became the YX/767 project). CTDC was responsible for the coordination of activities with MITI and within the member companies, and it represented the Japanese in the negotiations with U.S. Boeing. Later on it also was responsible for the coordination of the manufacturing activities among all Japanese parties. MHI, KHI, and FHI became the three prime contractors holding the final responsibility for activities in which other Japanese companies were involved as subcontractors (e.g., SMIC under MHI and Nippi under KHI). The decision on the work share distribution for the three main contractors MHI, KHI, and FHI was made after Boeing had conducted several capability studies at their factories. In the beginning, CTDC and Boeing wanted to share the development and manufacturing work equally. However, with time, the Japanese side had to admit that their manufacturing resources were inadequate for a 50 percent participation as originally planned. Boeing, the stronger partner, was able to dictate the conditions, for example, the participation of Italian Aeritalia as a third nation and the reduction of CTDC's work share to 15 percent. Japan was forced to agree on the work share Boeing had selected, with no bargaining power if it wanted to stay in the program.[28] The influence of MITI on decisions of the configuration of this national project decreased to the same extent that the influence of the foreign partner, Boeing, increased. Nevertheless, during its negotiations with the American company, CTDC managed to maintain enough autonomy in the development work share to retain government support for the YX program as a national project. During the development phase, the IADF granted loans to an amount of 70 percent of the total budget necessary for project YX/767 as well as subsidies for the 4.85 percent interest rate on JDB loans (*Nihon Koku Uchu Kogyokai-Kaiho*, February 1989:6). The Japanese work share was divided among MHI, KHI, and FHI in terms of capital contribution with a distribution of around 60 percent:40 percent:1 percent and, finally, in terms of a different calculation for the work share, as 5:4:1 (KUMCK, 1985:246–9, 254).

Following the success of the first flight in September 1981, additional parts production, overhaul, and sales activities for the Boeing 767 were transferred to another semigovernmental organization, Commercial Airplane Company (CAC), established specially for those tasks in August 1983. This company did not receive governmental support, which indicates that the main responsibility for the execution of manufacturing remained with industry.

The Large-Scale National Project YXX/777

After the completion of the YX/767 project, Boeing confirmed to the Japanese companies that they "have become qualified sources for the manufacture of commercial transport components, enlarging their competitive posture and opportunities throughout the world" (KUMCK, 1985:502). Furthermore, Boeing invited the Japanese to participate in a bilateral codevelopment of a new project, YXX/777.[29] As before, both the negotiations with Boeing on the program as well as the domestic coordination of work share were to be managed by a semigovernmental organization. In December 1982, the CTDC was renamed Japan Aircraft Development Corporation (JADC) in order to define the area of activities executed in the company's name. In the YXX/777 project, the Japanese side managed to gain a 21 percent share (up from 15 percent in the 767 project) and to secure responsibility for a larger share of basic design work and marketing (for the Asian region) as well. These R&D tasks made its possible for MITI to declare the YXX/777 a national project, ensuring IADF loans on preferred conditions (again repayable after gaining profits after sales of the product).

From the beginning, Boeing assumed the leading position in deciding the model's configuration; the Japanese contribution here was much smaller than in the YX/767 project. Nevertheless, two additional Japanese companies, Nippi and SMIC, were named as prime contractors, in addition to the big companies MHI, KHI, and FHI, which had been selected in the prior project. Of the overall Japanese share of 21 percent, MHI held 45 percent, KHI 28 percent, FHI 22 percent (including the SMIC share), and Nippi 5 percent. As with the YX/767, MHI received the work for the aft fuselage sections, KHI for the front and middle fuselage sections, FHI for the under-wing fairing, and Nippi for the main wing ribs. Additional sections were the center wing box at FHI (taken over from the U.S. company Grumman), the passenger entry doors at MHI, and the cargo doors and the dome in the tail cone at KHI. MITI had no direct influence on the decision governing the Japanese work share but served only in an advisory capacity.

Facing stronger international competition from Airbus, Boeing introduced a new management concept for the development of the 777. Partners, such as (eight) airlines as launch customers;[30] vendors for engines, avionics, landing gear, and so on; and subcontractors were called in at an earlier stage of the product development phase than was common in the industry. Under this concept, a "Japan Mission" was established to study Japanese management techniques (e.g., at Toyota, Sony, Matsushita, and Canon). "Total Quality Management" and "Continuous Quality Improvement" were introduced at Boeing. Japanese aircraft manufacturers as well were able to make important contributions regarding product management, production process, and cost reduction—the result of domestic cooperation in prior national projects as well as the transfer of technologies from other business areas. For example, KHI introduced a new production process with lean methods, similar to the Toyota production system, that it had introduced earlier for its motorbike business (interview with M. Tsukamoto, Senior Staff Officer of Aerospace Group, KHI, March 28, 1996). In addition, several processes, for example, chemical milling and jigless riveting, were automated. Similar production practices had been introduced in newly established plants at MHI as well (interview with M. Niwa, Assistant Director, Business Department, Nagoya Aerospace Systems, MHI, March 27, 1996). For the first time, a positive trend appeared for the Japanese companies who were active in aircraft production with only a small percentage of their overall business.

Under the large-scale national project scheme, IADF sponsored up to 50 percent of JADC's R&D activities (again, repayable after gaining profits from aircraft sales) with additional loans from JDB at a 6.5 percent interest rate (in contrast to the V 2500 program, interest payments had been subsidized 100 percent). The development costs on the Japanese side reached 100 billion yen.[31]

In December 1990, joint development work on the Boeing 777 began. Of the 440 Japanese engineers engaged in the design work, 250 were sent as resident engineers to Seattle (at peak times). The prototype succeeded in first flight in June 1994. Following the completion of design work, the number of engineers at JADC was reduced to about forty people. The remaining design work was related to modifications of the basic model in view of the family concept of the 777 (stretched, short-, and long-range version) and was forecast to last until 2006 (interviews with W. R. Stroy, Business &Planning Manager, Boeing, June 16, 1995; with M. Yadoya, Managing Director, JADC, June 13, 1996).

The Merits of Co-opetition in the Japanese Aircraft Industry

In both the engine and the aircraft businesses, Japanese companies have managed to consolidate their position in the global market through both domestic and international codevelopment programs.

The expertise Japanese manufacturers gained during participation in such prior projects as the the V 2500 engine led in early 1996 to the choice of JAEC as a program-sharing partner by the world's market leader, General Electric (GE), in the development of a new aero engine for a seventy-seater civil aircraft (CF-34 8C). On the Japanese side, IHI is expected to carry out 90 percent of the work share, with KHI responsible for the remaining 10 percent. So far, MHI is not participating in the program.[32] Again, the JAEC was the coordinating organization between domestic and international participants, and MITI agreed to promote the program as a national project with IADF funding of 3 billion yen. With their decision to participate in international development programs in the early 1980s, Japanese companies, represented by a semigovernmental organization (JAEC), were able to reach an upgrading of their knowledge in technology and marketing. They further reached scale economies in joint sales on the global market while stabilizing their global position.

In the aircraft sector as well, JADC was again offered cooperation in Boeing's new project for a modified 747 version. Depending on the results of the ongoing negotiations launched in spring 1996 between Boeing and JADC on the Japanese work share, it was to be decided if this project could be supported as a national project under the MITI-scheme.[33] However, Boeing has not yet decided to launch the project.

Japanese companies, in addition to increasing their participation as parts suppliers for several McDonnell Douglas and Airbus programs, gained recognition as interesting partners in international codevelopment programs for their contribution of experience in project and production management. For a long time, the fact that only a small amount of their overall activities was devoted to aero engines seemed to have been a disadvantage because it forced Japanese companies to share most of the project with their "complementors."[34] In aerospace, the large companies themselves were forced to choose a strategy similar to the "flexible specialists" strategy of their subcontractors in order to stay in business. Besides spinoff effects from military aero engine production (Samuels, 1994:26ff), the Japanese companies have enjoyed spin-on effects by the transfer of intrafirm knowledge in cost-saving management and production technologies from other commercial areas. Those spin-on effects have already been a crucial factor in the development of the high-technology aircraft sector. They will increase in importance in future programs of aero engine development involving high cost and risk. Their extent is difficult to assess. Evidence of their significance is explicitly demonstrated in the change in the SJAC publications. For a long time, the high-tech aerospace industry was pictured as a tree rooted in quality, the manufacturing process, aerodynamics, engine technology, electronics, and systems control. Its branches extended into industries such as material, construction, leisure, shipbuilding, automobile, multimedia, and machinery (NKUKK, 1994b:7). Recently, this picture has changed to one with an aircraft in the center surrounded by all those areas, emphasizing the spin-on effect. For the aerospace sector, a separate picture is drawn.[35]

Without the collaboration of other companies, an individual Japanese firm was too weak to carry out a large-scale development project in aircraft or engine production on its own. MITI encouraged this intense cooperation among Japanese companies as well as with international partners, trying to achieve strong Japanese influence on this strategic industry. As a result, over time, Japanese companies managed to increase their work share in international codevelopment programs. These capabilities have been reached through ongoing co-opetition in domestic and international (commercial as well as military) programs and through the transfer of manufacturing and management practices out of other business areas. In this sense, it proved to be an advantage for the Japanese that they had no specialized aircraft manufacturing setup. In addition, all manufacturers managed to enlarge their output in aircraft and engine productions by enlarging their piece of the total "pie" of international codevelopments.

Conclusion

We have analyzed the role of the Japanese government in developing the strategic aircraft industry by means of the establishment of semigovernmental institutions. As we have seen, Japanese manufacturers have become reliable and indispensable partners in the global aircraft and engine industry.

The Japanese manufacturers developed out of necessity a method of knowledge creation that contrasted distinctly with the practices of their Western counterparts, as the following points make clear. (1) Japanese manufacturers started as latecomers after seven years of total noncommitment, during which period jet engine technology had rapidly developed abroad.[36] (2) Their aircraft divisions were only small business areas competing with other areas for scarce intrafirm resources. (3) The government's perception of support left most of the responsibility with the manufacturers. (4) Because of the small domestic market, Japanese entrepreneurs were forced to enter a highly competitive global market for commercial aircraft without the benefit of comprehensive knowledge. Thus, the cooperation of all national levels was a sine qua non condition.

Several interconnected levels of knowledge creation exist in the Japanese aircraft industry. The first level is that of interfirm knowledge creation, which encompasses the transfer of aircraft and engine-related technology knowledge into other areas and the reciprocal transfer of knowhow in production and management practices. Although the modest scale of aircraft-related business was initially thought to be a disadvantage, it initiated fruitful knowledge creation with other business areas. It is apparent that companies must not only have the best technology available but also be able to produce it at affordable prices. Today, therefore, commercialization in a global concentration process is the key even in military aircraft and engine industries, as mentioned earlier.

The second level is that of intrafirm knowledge creation. The necessity for cooperation among Japanese companies is the result of the modest size of their aircraft divisions in the face of colossal development and manufacturing cost and risks. Coopetition stimulated communication and exchange among industries that had been institutionalized in semigovernmental organizations. Over the decades, technological changes in component products such as engines, avionics, electronics, or landing gear has prompted the need to cooperate with other industries—for example, materials, electronics, and so on—on a supraindustrial level. The crossfunctional approach to product development has proven to be advantageous and has been emulated through the industry as the optimal practice.

The third level of knowledge creation was established within semigovernmental organizations as NAMC, JADC, and JAEC, where, with government support, a cooperation among companies and associations was institutionalized to carry out large commercial projects. Such organizations were nonexistent in Western aircraft industries. Nevertheless, changes in global market demand have prompted the establishment of similar organizations among competitors worldwide in order to implement single projects. Regularly convening deliberating councils consisting of representatives from ministries, companies, associations, mass media, and academia remain a uniquely Japanese institution. Their purpose is a dialogue on far-reaching national and international development features and the continual improvement of timely industrial policy. On this third level, MITI assisted the aircraft industry with special laws and measures, although its initial activities were based on outdated, prewar knowledge in which military aircraft dominated. It took both government officials as well as companies' representatives several years of trial and error to understand that new knowledge can only could be attained with state-of-the-art technology, already developed by the market leaders abroad. Still, the continuous dialogue and consensus on policy changes was fruitful. It led to the important decision and realization that the only possible way to gain new knowledge on technology, marketing, and sales while domestic development foundered was through an international commitment. Nevertheless, the Japanese government played an ambivalent role in the development of the aircraft and engine industry, which ultimately changed over time. MOF was reluctant to support the industry with large-scale subsidies. It thus left the responsibility for its development to the participating Japanese companies, which led to unique method of knowledge creation on the intra- and inter-firm level. STA, too, played only a subordinate role, focusing on matters other than aircraft-related R&D. JDA contributed to the aircraft industry's development with its procurement plans but was hindered in its ambitions by its small budget and the necessity to conform with the ordnance policy of the United States, the sole military ally (Otsuki and Honda, 1995:63). The prohibition of weapons exports reduced the military production base to the JDA demand. Thus, the Japanese aircraft industry could not achieve the magnitude usually expected from a strategic industry. Nevertheless, Japanese entrepreneurial skills enabled aircraft and engine manufacturers to develop methods of knowledge creation that qualified them as international participants in the global aircraft and engine market.

Japanese companies established a fourth level of knowledge creation through collaboration in international development programs. By contributing their experience and knowledge in product and management practices, they have benefited their foreign counterparts as well.

Thus, the development of the Japanese aircraft industry has centered on a combination including multilevel intra- and interfirm co-opetition and knowledge creation and cooperation of government institutions with domestic and international private companies.

Notes

1. Aircraft development and manufacturing is only one part of the aerospace industry. In the following, we focus on the commercial aircraft sector (the military sector is referred to only where necessary, and helicopters are excluded). The expression *aerospace* will be used only when inclusion of the space activities cannot be avoided.

2. The United States in the 1950s was the only market of a sufficient size to reach economies of scale with the sale of one passenger aircraft model (Todd and Simpson, 1986:50).

3. For an overview on the mergers and acquisitions in this industry since World War II, see Tomiura, 1995:158–62.

4. For example, Lockheed and Martin, Northrop and Grumman (all United States), Aerospatiale and Dassault, (scheduled for 1997) or, for smaller, commercial aircraft, Fairchild (United States) and Dornier (Germany) as well as Bombardier's takeover of Canadair, DeHavilland (all three Canada), Shorts (Ireland), and Learjet (United States).

5. Shortly after World War II, Kosai (1984:27) identified a "strong government and weak companies" (*tsuyoi seifu to yowai kigyo*); Similarly, Johnson (1986:133) speaks of "strong bureaucracy and weak companies."

6. In the late 1950s, more than 90 percent of aircraft sales were military (Arizawa, 1990:272; NKUKK, 1994b:53). Today the figure is still 70 percent (Arai, 1996:198). In 1991, the figure for the United States was 51 percent, for Germany 57 percent, for France 48 percent, and for the United Kingdom 55 percent (1989); only Italy (71 percent in 1989) showed a high dependence similar to that of Japan (NKUKK, 1993b:10).

7. Interview with H. Yamada, Senior Vice President of the Society of Japanese Aerospace Companies (SJAC) on November 11, 1994, Y. Hironaka, Counselor of Fuji Electric on June 12, 1996, and N. Miyazaki, Principal Deputy Director, Coordination Division, Equipment Bureau of JDA on June 20, 1996. As a member of the National Security Council, the Ministry of Foreign Affairs (MOFA) often expresses concern about the possible reactions abroad to Japan's defense activities, especially in the neighboring Asian states. In some cases, the decision-making process for industrial policy in the aircraft sector was influenced indirectly by this kind of foreign opinion. Only in one case did MITI make the final decision, when JDA was indifferent on which company to choose as prime contractor.

8. Today there are ninety (including military) airports in Japan, compared to, for example, fifteen international, seventeen regional, and one hundred sixty-six local airports and over seven hundred facilities for gliders and helicopters in Germany (Reuss, 1995:217–27).

9. From 1952 to 1991, aircraft related imports to Japan amounted to 6.68 trillion yen, nine times the exports in this period, or 69 percent of the overall production volume in Japan (NKUKK, 1993b:54).

10. A similar statement is made by Callon (1995:5–7) in his analysis of MITI's activities in high-tech industrial policy since 1975. Although oven on the Japanese side "technonationalistic" tendencies are not denied, Otsuki and Honda (1991:53) convincingly argue in their analysis of the FSX case that "technonationalism" cannot be extracted as a nationwide strategy for the promulgation of a Japanese defense and aircraft industry as proposed by the "technonationalists."

11. The fact that MHI and KHI are involved in both airframe and engine production is unique in the global aircraft industry. Although there had been a tradition in many European and North American companies of engaging in both areas, partly in air transport service as well, after World War II those companies were split into firms specializing in narrower areas.

12. For example, twelve hundred firms participate in the production of a fighter aircraft (Arai, 1996:198).

13. At KHI, the aerospace sector reached a share of 24.7 percent in 1992 with 26.3 percent of the company's employees (NKUKK, 1993a:219). In the same year, MHI was involved in aerospace with 16 percent of its overall activities and 14.4 percent of its employees (NKUKK, 1993a:337). The figures for FHI are 6.8 percent and 23.6 percent (NKUKK, 1993b:317), for IHI 17 percent and 23 percent (NKUKK, 1993a:199), and for SMIC 14.1 percent and 21.8 percent, respectively (NKUKK, 1993a:242). The only special manufacturer is Nippi, with 95 percent of its total output in aerospace activities (NKUKK, 1994b:301).

14. For example, KHI specialized on small helicopters (joint development with European Eurocopter); MHI maintained the business jet area (first with its own development of the MU-2 and the MU-300, and today as a partner in the Global Express program of Canadian Bombardier). SMIC is one of the few airship manufacturers worldwide, and Nippi specializes in main wing ribs.

15. This division in activities was reached via administrative guidance of MITI in order to prevent IHI from becoming a monopolist in engine manufacturing; see Maema, 1989:354.

16. If there was a necessity to call in partners, contracts are made only for one special project, or joint ventures are set up. Organizations similar to Japanese semigovernmental institutions with one coordinating head office in the center and production ordered in the facilities of the affiliated companies are, for example, the European Airbus Industry and the French-Italian-British Aircraft Industry Regional (AIR), although the participants here come from different countries.

17. In 1960 Ishikawajima Heavy Industries merged with Harima HI to form Ishikawajima-Harima HI (IHI).

18. In Japanese understanding, "excess" means "more than appropriate," and not "cutthroat," competition, as in most Western interpretations (Komiya, 1988:10–11; Ito et al., 1984:223–5; Goto and Irie, 1990:29).

19. After solving several technical problems, T-1 F-1 succeeded in first flight in May 1960. Development costs amounted to 1.58 billion yen. Later the J-3 engine was installed in the P-2 J surveillance aircraft, and in total about 250 engines were built (NKUKK, 1994b:40; Maema, 1989:300–2).

20. Maema, 1989:373–4. In 1981 a modified version of the FJR 710 engine was installed in STA's only short takeoff and landing (STOL) research aircraft, *Asuka*, but in the end only six engines of that type were built (NKUKK, 1994b:40).

21. Although SJAC, the JDA, and several companies had repeatedly requested funds for such R&D facilities, MOF refused governmental financial assistance for the reason that Japanese companies' activities had been license production that did not afford test facilities. Another reason was that the scale and number of Japanese development programs until that time were not considered large enough to pay back the huge investment in R&D facilities.

22. Sharing the program means sharing risks and revenues. A program-sharing partner is responsible for its part of the design work and for the up-front costs during the development and production phase. A subcontractor, in contrast, only gets a fixed price for the parts it manufactures mostly without having any design responsibility.

23. For example, IHI is responsible for the production of all jet engine shafts in the programs in which it participates; interview with T. Inoue, General Manager, Small Turbofan Engine Department, JAEC, June 14, 1996.

24. Hidemasa Kimura, a professor at Nihon University, Minoru Ota of Fuji HI, Shizuo Kikuhara of SMIC, Jiro Horikoshi of Shin-Mitsubishi HI, and Takeo Doi of Kawasaki Aircraft. They ironically were nicknamed "the five samurai," in reference to the film by Akira Kurozawa that was popular at that time, "The Seven Samurai"—rescuers who had little prospect of success. This gives some indication of the mood in the industry and the public opinion toward commercial aircraft development (Yamamura, 1995:42; Maema, 1989:321).

25. Initially, it was intended that domestic production of the YS-11 would be increased to 60 percent in order to replace several of the more than three hundred items imported at the beginning of serial production (foreign engines, propellers, and landing gear alone made up 50 percent of the import value of YS-11). However, Japanese technological knowhow proved insufficient in, for example, avionics and materiel, so that the goal of import replacement in the aircraft industry could not be reached to the expected amount (Umezawa, 1964:133–4; Yamamura, 1995:109–10; Maema, 1994: 281, 286, 288–9, 296).

26. In 1983, the responsibility for all remaining work concerning the YS-11 in service, such as product support, spare part sales, and maintenance work was transferred to MHI, where the final assembly had been done; on the division of YS-11 work share, see NKUKK,1987b:150.

27. The shifts in the currency exchange rate between the Japanese yen and the U.S. dollar alone raised the deficit by 17 percent. In the end, the government paid 24.577 billion yen and the participating companies 3.623 billion yen in order to reduce the NAMC deficit to zero (Yamamura, 1995:171–2).

28. KUMCK, 1985:180–2; Boeing looked for a risk-sharing partner for a 200 billion yen development cost program, but Japanese aircraft industry had only an annual output of 300 billion yen, including all military and space activities (KUMCK, 1985:122).

29. On the Japanese side, the project was called YXX; at Boeing, 777.

30. Among the eight launch customers for the Boeing 777 were United Airlines, British Airways, Cathay Pacific, and three Japanese airlines, ANA, JAL, JAS. Up to that time there had been only one launch customer for a new model and later airline customers faced the costs for additional design changes. Where not ohterwise cited, the information hereafter on "Working Together" is based on two lectures by Koji Hashimoto of ANA and Masaomi Kadoya of JADC entitled "B-777 Development under the 'Working Together' concept" at the 153rd monthly lecture in the series "Aircraft and Space" of the Japan Aeronautic Association, October 18, 1995, Tokyo.

31. With the Japanese share at 21 percent, total costs on the Boeing side are estimated to have reached 500–600 billion yen.

32. Even though MHI does not participate in the engine program, the company announced its cooperation with Canadian Bombardier on the development of a seventy-seat regional aircraft; *Nihon Keizai Shimbun*, August 13, 1996, August 14, 1996.

33. Interview with T. Sakaki, Managing Director, JADC, June 13, 1996; *Nikkei Sangyo Shimbun*, June 9, 1996.

34. Brandenburger and Nalebuff (1995:3–5) use this expression for partners with complementing business areas. For example, aircraft manufacturers and airlines are "complementors" because they need each other in order to be able to do business. As the Japanese aircraft companies are engaged with only a small portion of their business in aerospace production, they were forced to cooperate in order to reach scale and resources large enough to carry through large-scale projects. Thus they can be called complementing in the sense of Brandenburger and Nalebuff even though they belong to the same industry.

35. For the aircraft-centered picture, see NKUKK material received during an interview with H. Yamada, Senior Vice President, SJAC, February 16, 1996. On the commercialization of aerospace, see Horres, 1994.

36. On the Japanese aircraft production technology during the Pacific War, see Yamamoto (1994); for the technology gap to Western nations Japanese engineers saw emerging during the occupation period 1945–1952, see Doi (1989:250–1) and Maema (1993:60).

References

Arai, Hisamitsu. 1996. "Boei sangyo wa ikinokoreru ka" (Can the defense industry survive)? *Voice* (July): 196–205.

Arizawa, Hiromi, ed. 1990. *Showa Keizai-Shi (chu)* (Economic history of the Showa Period). Vol. 2. Tokyo: Nihon Keizai Shimbunsha.

Brandenburger, Adam M., and Barry J. Nalebuff. 1996. *Co-opetition*. New York: Doubleday.

Callon, Scott. 1995. *Divided Sun: MITI and the Breakdown of Japanese High-Tech Industrial Policy 1975–1993*. Stanford, Calif.: Stanford University Press.

Doi, Takeo. 1989. *Hikoki Sekkei 50Nen no Kaiso* (Memories of fifty years of aircraft construction). Tokyo: Kodansha.

Friedman, David. 1988. *The Misunderstood Miracle: Industrial Development and Political Change in Japan*. Ithaca: Cornell University Press.

Goto, Fumihiro, and Kazutomo Irie. 1990. *Sangyo Seisaku no Rironteki Kiso: 1990 nendai no Arata na Tenkai ni Mukete* (The theoretical base of industrial policy: Toward a new development in the 1990s). Tokyo: Kenkyu Shirizu 5, Tsusho Sangyo Kenkyusho, Tsusho Sangyo Chosakai.

Horres, Robert. 1994. "Entwicklungstendenzen der japanischen Raumfahrt—Kommerzielle und technologische Strategien" (Development tendencies in japanese aerospace—commercial and technological strategies). In *Asiatische Studien XLVIII. 1. 1994: Zeitschrift der Schweizerischen Asiengesellschaft: Referate des 9. deutschsprachigen Japanologentages in Zürich*, edited by Eduard Klopfenstein. Bern: Verlag Peter Lang. Pp. 619–35.

Ito, Motoshige, et al. 1984. Shijo no Shippai to Hoseiteki Sangyo Seisaku (Market failure and protectionistic industrial policy). In *Nihon no Sangyo Seisaku* (Industrial policy of Japan), edited by Ryutaro Komiya et al. Pp. 207–29.

Johnson, Chalmers. 1986. *MITI and the Japanese Miracle. The Growth of Industrial Policy 1925–1975*. Tokyo: Tuttle Books. Originally published 1982.

KUMCK (Koku Uchu Mondai Chosakai). 1985. *YX/767 Kaihatsu no Ayumi* (History of YX/767 development). Tokyo: Matsushi Insatsu.

Komiya, Ryutaro. 1988. Introduction to *Industrial Policy of Japan*, edited by Ryutaro Komiya, Masahiro Okuno, and Kotaro Suzumura. Tokyo: Academic Press Japan. Pp. 1–22.

Kosai, Yutaka. 1984. "Fukkoki" (The high growth period). In *Nihon no sangyo seisaku* (Industrial policy of Japan), edited by Ryutaro Komiya, Masahiro Okuno, and Kotaro Suzumura. Tokyo: Tokyo Daigaku Shuppankai. Pp. 25–43.

Maema, Takanori. 1989. *Jetto Enjin ni Toritsukareta Otoko*. (Men obsessed with aircraft engines). Tokyo: Kodansha.

———. 1993. *Man Mashin no Showa Densetsu (Ge)* (Stories of men and machines in the Showa period). Vol. 2. Tokyo: Kodansha.

———. 1994. *YS-11: Kokusan ryokyakuki o tsukutta otokotachi* (YS-11: The men who built the Japanese passenger transport aircraft). Tokyo: Kodansha.

MITI-ICO (Ministry of International Trade and Industry, International Communications Office), ed. 1994. *MITI Handbook 1994*. Tokyo: Japan Trade and Industry Publicity.

NJE (Nihon Jetto Enjin Kabushiki Kaisha), ed. 1967. *Nihon Jetto Enjin Kabushiki Kaisha Shashi* (History of the Nihon Jet Engine Corporation). Tokyo: Nihon Jet Engine Corporation.

NKUKK (Nihon Koku Uchu Kogyokai), ed. 1987a. *Nihon no Koku Uchu Kogyo Sengoshi* (Postwar history of the Japanese aircraft industry). Tokyo: Nihon Koku Uchu Kogyokai.

———. 1987b. *YS-11 no Seika* (Results of YS-11). Tokyo: Nihon Koku Uchu Kogyokai. March.

———. 1993a. *Koku Uchu Kogyo Nenkan. Heisei 5 nendoban* (The aerospace industry yearbook). Tokyo: Koku Nyususha.

———. 1993b. *Nihon no Koku Uchu Kogyo. Heisei 5 nenban* (The Japanese aerospace industry). Tokyo: Nihon Koku Uchu Kogyokai. March.

———. 1994a. *Koku Uchu Kogyo no Hatten o Shinko Suru Nihon Koku Uchu Kogyokai: Soshiki to Katsudo* (Promotion of the development of the aerospace industry by the

Society of the Japanese Aerospace Industry: Organization and activities). Tokyo: Nihon Koku Uchu Kogyokai.

————. 1994b. *Nihon no Koku Uchu Kogyo. Heisei 6 Nenban* (The Japanese aerospace industry). Tokyo: Nihon Koku Uchu Kogyokai. March.

Nonaka, Ikujiro, and Hirotaka Takeuchi. 1995. *The Knowledge-Creating Company. How Japanese Companies Create the Dynamics of Innovation.* New York: Oxford University Press.

Otsuki, Shinji, and Masaru Honda. 1991. *Nichibei FSX senso—Nichibei domei o yurugasu gijutsu masatsu* (The Japanese-American FSX war: A technology conflict shakes the Japanese-American alliance), Tokyo: Ronsosha.

Piller, Wolfgang. 1995. "On the Situation of the Aerospace Industry." In *Jahrbuch der Luft- und Raumfahrt* (The aerospace industry yearbook of Germany), edited by Tilman T. Reuss. Mannheim: SVA Südwestdeutsche Verlagsanstalt GmbH. Pp. 23–7.

Reuss, Tilman T., ed. 1995. *Jahrbuch der Luft- und Raumfahrt* (The aerospace industry yearbook of Germany). Mannheim: SVA Südwestdeutsche Verlagsanstalt GmbH.

Sakamoto, Teruo. 1990. *Gendai Kokuron* (Theory of present aviation). Tokyo: Seisando Shoten.

Samuels, Richard J. 1994. *"Rich Nation, Strong Army." National Security and the Technological Transformation of Japan.* Ithaca: Cornell University Press.

Todd, Daniel, and Jamie Simpson. 1986. *The World Aircraft Industry.* Dover, Mass.: Auburn House.

Tomiura, Eiichi. 1995. *Senryakuteki Tsusho Seisaku no Keizaigaku* (The Economics of the strategic trade policy). Tokyo: Nihon Keizai Shimbunsha.

Tsusho, Sangyosho, ed. 1995. *Tsusan Roppo 1995* (The 1995 MITI Code of Law). Tokyo: Marui Kobunsha.

Umezawa, Kyoji. 1964. *Tsubasa wa Yomigetta YS-11. Kokusan Puroppu-Jetto Ryokakki Kansei no Kioku* (YS-11 got wings: Memories of the completion of the Japanese prop-jet-passenger transport aircraft). Tokyo: Nihon Koku Shimbunsha.

Yamamoto, Kiyoshi. 1994. *Nihon ni okeru Shokuba no Gijutsu-Rodoshi 1854–1990* (History of technical work at the work place in Japan, 1854–1990). Tokyo: Tokyo Daigaku Shuppankai. Pp. 223–73.

Yamamura, Takashi. 1995. *YS-11 no Higeki—Aru Tokushu Hojin no Hokai* (The YS-11 tragedy: Collapse of a corporation with special rights). Tokyo: Nihon Horonsha.

13

Shukko (Employee Transfers) and Tacit Knowledge Exchange in Japanese Supply Networks

The Electronics Industry Case

JAMES R. LINCOLN
CHRISTINA AHMADJIAN

How Japanese companies manage purchase-supply relations has drawn considerable attention from scholars and practitioners. Indeed, the Japanese approach to supply chain management is now worldwide "best practice" in the automobile industry and in other strategic industrial sectors (Mitchener and Steinmetz, 1998). Close and long-term relations; high trust and mutual disclosure of information; and cospecialized investment in knowledge and other assets together comprise a supply management regime that has been much admired and copied (Womack, Jones, and Roos, 1990). In its ideal form, the Japanese model averts the Scylla of low-trust contracting and the Charybdis of full vertical integration under a corporate chain of command. Outcomes include: more and earlier supplier participation in customer designs; higher quality components; higher reliability of deliveries; and so on.

Precisely because Japanese supply chain practice has acquired this standing, however, it tends to be viewed as all the same. How Japanese companies and industries vary in their supply relations is seriously understudied. Moreover, the full array of coordination and learning mechanisms between suppliers and assemblers in Japan is not well documented. This essay draws attention to the phenomenon of shukko: the transfer of employees between firms and the role it plays in pooling the tacit knowledge stocks of supplier and customer. We also discuss a particularly tacit form of knowledge, spread by shukko, that enables close cooperation and smooth operation in Japanese supply chains: corporate and *keiretsu* culture.

Treatments of the effectiveness of Japanese supply chain coordination can be criticized as either too concrete or too abstract. Highly concrete are explanations that stress the role of formal systems like Just-In-Time (see, e.g., Nishiguchi and Beaudet, 1998). JIT is occasionally portrayed as an algorithm that can be "slapped on" production and procurement processes to yield good results. This ignores its embeddedness in a set of institutional arrangements, some of which are quite peculiar to Japan. Shukko is one such institution.

Other arguments for the success of Japanese supply partnerships place heavy stress on the role of "trust" in smoothing and stabilizing transactions (Sako, 1992;

Sako and Helper, 1998; Sitkin et al., 1998; Smitka, 1991). Trust is a rich concept, however, given to diverse interpretations. Economists see it as a forward-looking willingness to bet that a partner will not behave opportunistically. Psychological and sociological perspectives on trust stress its normative and affective, versus purely cognitive, side (Uzzi, 1996; Von Krogh, 1998). In this vein, Japanese management writers note the spirituality, obligation, even sentimentality that may be part of the "tacit knowledge" that one company has of another (Nonaka and Takeuchi, 1995). However, without analysis of the concrete actions that build trust—such as people from a manufacturer working hand-in-hand on-site for a sustained period with their counterparts in a supplier—trust is a "black box" defying both measurement and management.

Whether the focus is hard and formulaic models such as JIT or the soft and fuzzy ones that feature trust, research must address the processes that enable suppliers and assemblers to work with and learn from one another. In Japan, shukko transfers are key to how one organization in a purchase-supply relation aligns its goals and operations with another and taps the other's tacit knowledge base. Shukko is an observable phenomenon, although it cannot be understood in isolation. Of the conditions supporting shukko, the most important is cross-shareholding. A minority equity stake provides the receiving firm with investment capital, gives the equity holder some governance rights, and affirms to the outside world that a (keiretsu) partnership exists.

Japanese keiretsu-style supply relations are less contractual, arm's-length, and limited (in time, scope, etc.) than those in the West. They involve larger cross-firm flows of tacit knowledge—the inchoate, uncodified, even emotive and charismatic routines that underpin core competences. As with strong culture in a single firm, this blending of skills, habits, and values raises the speed and quality of the exchange, as each partner attunes to the work rhythms and styles of the other. An analogy is the socialization process described in symbolic interactionist social psychology as "taking the role of the other": one organization ("ego") takes on the identity and posture of a second ("alter") through embedding its people in alter's routines (Lincoln, Gerlach, and Takahashi, 1992; Lincoln, Ahmadjian, and Mason, 1998; Mead, 1962).

The Japanese Electronics Case

We focus on the Japanese consumer electronics industry. Like automobiles, electronics has been a highly strategic sector in Japan's export-led postwar economic development. Japanese electronics firms built up a huge competitive advantage on the strength of the quality, cost, and development time of their products. However, electronics is an industry in which the contrasts with Western component production and supply are less sharp than in the auto case. Japanese auto producers—Toyota in particular—evolved a highly distinctive model of production organization and supply chain management (Fruin, 1992). Relatively compact firms with narrow product lines (e.g., passenger sedans) specialized in design and assembly, while relying on an array of partners both to supply them with components and to fill out product offerings on a consignment basis (Fruin, 1992; Nishiguchi, 1994; Shioji, 1995).

Japan's electronics corporations, on the other hand, have broad product lines and decentralized divisional structures (Beer and Spector, 1981), are vertically integrated into parts-making and subassemblies, and deal at relative arm's length with a larger base of suppliers who participate less in design and development.

Even in autos, Japanese supply relations have been weakened by globalization, heightened competition, technological change, and macroeconomic stagnation (Ahmadjian and Lincoln, 1998). As Japanese companies move operations abroad or even within Japan to such remote regions as Kyushu and Shikoku, they have the opportunity and often the obligation to develop new supplier networks and scale down dependence on old ones. Yet the pains Japanese manufacturers take to smooth this transition—by easing old partners out slowly or into tangential lines of business—testify that longstanding obligations still carry weight in Japanese economic exchange. Moreover, some electronics companies—notably Matsushita—are reversing the drift from stronger to weaker supply relations. Matsushita is managing its supply chain in more strategic fashion than in the past, building closer ties to a smaller base of elite suppliers (Lincoln, Ahmadjian, and Mason, 1998).

Although collaborative development between assemblers and suppliers by all accounts played a critical role in the rise of Japanese manufacturing (Nishiguchi, 1994; Odaka, Ono, and Adachi, 1988), the trend is to less sharing and cospecialization. With worldwide diffusion of Japanese manufacturing techniques, manufacturers take excellence among suppliers for granted much more than in the past. Countertrends exist as well: the shift in Japanese domestic sourcing to larger suppliers with R&D and engineering capability (due to rising parts standardization and economies of scale, as well as global sourcing of low-tech parts) has spawned a new breed of Japanese supplier able to contribute greater value to the manufacturing process.

Supplier Participation in Design and Development

An influential paper by Imai, Nonaka, and Takeuchi documents close cooperation and mutual learning between Fuji Xerox, a major electronics firm, and its suppliers in the early stages of product development. Their informants said:

> We ask our suppliers to come to our factory and start working together with us as early in the development process as possible. The suppliers also don't mind our visiting their plants. This kind of mutual exchange and opennness about information works to enhance flexibility. Early participation on the part of the supplier enables them to understand where they are positioned within the entire process. Furthermore, by working with us on a regular basis, they learn how to bring in precisely what we are looking for, even if we only show them a rough sketch. When we reach this point, our designers can simply concentrate on work requiring creative thinking. (1985:351)

Yet such early and deep involvement of suppliers in manufacturers' product and process development is not the norm in Japanese electronics. We illustrate with case materials obtained through our own and others' interviews in several prominent

Japanese firms. Several reasons exist. Manufacturers make most electronic components in-house and use suppliers chiefly for lower tech materials such as packaging, plating, boxing, and so on.[1] Our informants said that the very fast development times and short product life cycles in electronics made it difficult to develop close ties with external suppliers. Another factor is the modular and standardized nature of electronic components, compared to the case of autos, where parts designs are often specialized to particular vehicle assemblies. This allows parts and subassemblies to be bought "off-the-shelf" from an external vendor or wholly designed either by the manufacturer or the supplier without much input from the other.

Sanyo, NEC, Nintendo

Involvement by outside suppliers in Sanyo's product development is fairly minimal. The R&D division told us that their value-engineering process does pool inputs from diverse functions, but suppliers do not participate at this stage; indeed, no outsiders do. Even after the design phase, direct supplier involvement remains low. Sanyo said, however, that purchasing representatives, who know the suppliers and can represent their interests, attend the meetings.

Sanyo engineers stressed that they can and do choose outside vendors over in-house units in sourcing high-value materials. For example, the audiovisual (AV) division in the early development stages of a large-scale integrated (LSI) system chip initially approached the internal semiconductors division but was turned down, so it went outside. The outside suppliers were not made members of the Sanyo AV team. The AV division discussed specs with them and negotiated prices. Sanyo said that suppliers do have the opportunity to innovate a process or product on their own, but cooperation in the actual innovation process is rare.

Nor do suppliers cooperate among themselves as in the auto industry, although formal supplier associations (*kyoryoku-kai*) are common to both industries (Lincoln, Ahmadjian, and Mason, 1998; Sako, 1996). NEC informed us that little transfer of specialized technology occurred among its suppliers. At the kyoryoku-kai meetings, some suppliers might present their successful technologies and allow on-site visits, but most remained very secretive. Moreover, whatever knowledge sharing took place among suppliers occurred without NEC's participation or guidance.

Nintendo is another electronics firm with a reputation for arm's-length treatment of suppliers. Nintendo managers said they are careful to avoid sole-sourcing for fear of fostering supplier dependence. Nintendo's specialized electronic games business is more cyclical and uncertain than that of more diversified makers, and it cannot be obligated to carry suppliers in lean times.

Toshiba

In his study of Toshiba's Yanagicho Works, Fruin (1997) observes that supplier involvement in Toshiba's designs depends on the maturity and complexity of the product. In rapidly evolving high-tech products, where Toshiba is intent on mastering the process of development and is on a steep learning curve, suppliers simply provide low-cost production capacity. In more mature and lower value-added products where the process is well understood and does not demand Toshiba's full design and engineering capabilities, development responsibility falls mainly on suppliers. Real sharing with suppliers occurs only when a mature product requires frequent redesign and modification. The design and production of key parts and subassemblies are then shifted to suppliers, but their activities must be closely integrated with Toshiba's own (see also Lincoln, Ahmadjian, and Mason, 1998; Nishiguchi, 1994:14).

Matsushita

The case of Matsushita is an interesting one that we explore in detail elsewhere (Lincoln, Ahmadjian, and Mason, 1998). Even within the Japanese electronics industry, Matsushita has a reputation for arm's-length dealings with a large supplier base, most of whom produce low-value parts and services (packaging, molding, painting, plating). Like Sanyo, Matsushita generally develops new products and processes with little collaboration by suppliers. Matsushita retains the designs and has suppliers build to blueprints.

Matsushita products use technically sophisticated parts and subassemblies. The suppliers are small and cannot afford the plant, equipment, and skills necessary to produce high-tech components. However, Matsushita, like other Japanese manufacturers, has been shifting its low-value sourcing overseas and eliminating domestic suppliers with low technological capability. Matsushita is training and assisting an elite corps of suppliers (the *kyoei-kai*, or mutual prosperity association) for this purpose. Similarly, NEC instructs the larger companies in its kyoryoku-kai in new technology that they are unlikely to develop on their own. For example, when suppliers were forced to find alternatives to the use of freon gas, NEC's *gijutsu shido* (technology training) center showed them how.

Compared with its old method of having suppliers work from a set of specs, Matsushita is encouraging suppliers to shape product design decisions early on. The responsibility of each Matsushita product division, encouraged and assisted by corporate purchasing, is to make very clear and specific requests for input by suppliers. The air conditioner division, for example, will begin with a set of drawings or a paper or wood model and ask suppliers for suggestions as to product form and function. The kyoei-kai suppliers benefit (gain a competitive advantage) from the early information they receive on Matsushita's product development plans and procurement needs.

As Matsushita's efforts to assist and motivate suppliers in developing special competencies bear fruit, the company is absorbing new technology from the most advanced suppliers. One supplier was utilizing a very precise method of gold plating, which, we were told, would take Matsushita five years to develop. Another had developed an innovative technique of plastic injection molding. Still another supplier of plastic television set casing had devised the method of punching tiny sound holes directly into the plastic, thus eliminating the need for speaker holes and netting. These cases exemplify suppliers' growing ability to leverage special competencies as they participate in Matsushita's product design process.

Despite this new commitment to more and earlier knowledge sharing with suppliers, our Matsushita informants saw the fast pace of the electronics industry as an obstacle to the success of the kyoei program. Because of ever-rising competitive pressures to shorten development times, some Matsushita managers felt they could design and build products faster if the effort to develop the kyoei-kai were abandoned and Matsushita simply made the high-tech parts itself.

The Role of Shukko (Employee Transfers) in Learning

Notwithstanding Imai, Nonaka, and Takeuchi's portrait of Fuji Xerox and Matsushita's program of mutual learning with its kyoei suppliers, the picture these interviews paint is clear: direct participation by suppliers in manufacturers' product and process development is the exception rather than the rule in Japanese electronics. Knowledge sharing between assemblers and suppliers is less extensive and direct than in the auto industry (Asanuma, 1989). Given the greater vertical integration and product diversity of consumer electronics firms, the value added by outsourced parts is lower, as is the technological competence of suppliers.

Still, one may underestimate the level of cooperation and learning by focusing too narrowly on the direct participation of suppliers in assembler designs. The exchange of tacit knowledge through informal means probably contributes the lion's share of interorganizational learning in Japan. The means we focus on is shukko—employee transfers—between Japanese companies. Shukko is key to the process of coordination between Japanese firms' purchase-supply and other partnerships. It is the assignment of employees from one company to either permanent or temporary stints on the shop or office floor of another. With all the discussion of trust in Japanese supplier relations, it is odd that the shukko phenomenon has gotten so little direct attention. Our interest is in the forms and purposes of shukko; the conditions—such as equity relations—that support or motivate it; and the degree to which it enables culture flows between firms.

There are two principal functions of shukko. One is to reduce labor costs by offloading redundant people to affiliated companies. This is common but controversial practice, for it smacks of dual-economy (niju kozo) exploitation of smaller, lower status firms by dominant core firms. Perhaps not surprisingly, Japanese managers tend to downplay this function. Government agencies such as MITI or the Fair Trade Commission are on the lookout for such abuse, as is the Japanese media, which has been highly critical of the practice (Nikkei Weekly, 1993, 1995). At an interview with Sanyo, we inquired about the use of shukko as a downsizing strategy. Our informant said: "I won't say that this does not happen, but practically, it has problems. If the parent sends excess people to the supplier because of temporary economic problems, the supplier is likely to be facing the same types of problems and then cannot take on excess people. This is not good for long-term performance."

The second role of shukko is in interorganizational knowledge exchange. Engineers employed by an assembler will work on-site at a supplier in order to assist it in meeting the assembler's quality and cost requirements (Asanuma, 1992; Clark and Fujimoto, 1991). Conversely, a supplier will locate its people at the assembler to ensure that components are designed and produced to the latter's specifications. Shukko also operates at higher levels as a monitoring and governance device wielded by external stakeholders such as a main bank, principal trading company, or industrial partner (Lincoln, Gerlach, and Ahmadjian, 1996). A perusal of the directors of most significant Japanese corporations will reveal a number of people who have spent large portions of their careers elsewhere. Rather like the intermarriage of Europe's royal families, they were dispatched to the new site to oversee, learn from, and influence the operations of the target firm.

Another role for shukko in knowledge creation is diversification into new product lines (Fruin, 1992; Nishiguchi, 1994:118). Japanese companies will cultivate a new business around, for example, a product innovation, then spin it off as a partially owned keiretsu affiliate (Gerlach and Lincoln, 2000; Takahashi, 1995). The former employees of the core firm are in effect shukko'd to the spinoff. When the international information network business of Kigyo Denki (our pseudonym for a large, old-line electronics company with strong ties to one of Japan's "big-six" horizontal keiretsu groups) was recently shifted to MIND, a five-year-old affiliated company, a number of Kigyo Denki employees went along.

The *tatemae*, or official word, on shukko in most Japanese companies is that learning and training are the goals. In our interview at Hitachi's Omika plant, which makes computer systems for large customers such as Tokyo Power or Japan Rail, managers stated that shukko was done to instruct Hitachi-affiliated companies in the use of Hitachi technology. Any cost reduction was a welcome but unintended consequence. They did acknowledge after some prodding that this depended somewhat on the affiliated company and its tie to Hitachi. Shukko to firms that provided lower tech engineering services (machining, plating) and in which Hitachi had no equity stake was motivated by labor reduction, and the people so transferred were mostly excess blue-collar. Also, not surprisingly, the amount of downsizing shukko goes up in bad times (e.g., the 1990s).

From a labor cost standpoint, the benefit to the dispatching firm (e.g., Hitachi) is not always great. In the case of temporary (*zaiseki*) shukko, it typically pays the entire wage of the transferred employee. In permanent (*tenseki*) shukko, the dispatching firm is responsible for the difference between the wage it paid the employee and the wage paid by the supplier. A small Kansai printing firm whose president and other executives were shukko'd in from "Kansai Credit" (our pseudonym for the financial subsidiary of a large Kansai-based electronics firm) pays one-half the incoming managers' salaries, and Kansai Credit pays the other half. Hitachi pays 20 percent of the salary of the shukko'd employee, and the affiliate pays the remainder. The payment ratio was 30:70 at Kigyo Denki. Our Hitachi informant said, "If there is a lot of shukko, the company has to pay a lot of additional wages. So workers' salaries do not go down. The 20 percent is a nontrivial cost."

The Ministry of Labor does an annual survey of over fourteen thousand workplaces employing more than five people. It contains very detailed information on employee departures, including shukko. We present the data from the 1996 survey; 1996 is the one strong year in a period of stagnation and recession that began in 1992 after the collapse of the speculative "bubble" and is now at crisis levels.[2] (We have produced, but for reasons of space do not present, comparable survey data for 1991.)[3]

Table 13.1 presents 1996 shukko rates as percentages of total employment, total departures, and total mandated departures by the gender of the employee, in-

Table 13.1. Shukko Rates Estimated from a Survey of Approximately 14,000 Establishments in 1996

	Males						Females					
	Originating Shukko			Returning Shukko			Originating Shukko			Returning Shukko		
	As % of Employment[a]	As % of All Departures[b]	As % of Mandated Departures[c]	As % of Employment	As % of All Departures	As % of Mandated Departures	As % of Employment	As % of All Departures	As % of Mandated Departures	As % of Employment	As % of All Departures	As % of Mandated Departures
All industries	.335	2.9	32.6	.279	2.5	27.5	.103	.59	12.5	.06	.35	7.42
Estab. size 1000+	.677	9.0	73.6	.096	1.3	10.5	.281	1.44	29.3	.03	.17	3.42
300–999	.229	2.7	30.4	.295	3.4	39.2	.043	.25	10.3	.04	.22	8.97
100–299	.278	2.6	31.2	.320	3.0	36.0	.023	.12	4.2	.06	.32	11.02
30– 99	.206	1.5	15.8	.387	2.8	29.7	.057	.32	5.9	.11	.60	11.03
5– 29	.218	1.4	18.5	.346	2.2	29.4	.031	.19	3.1	.06	.36	5.63
All manufacturing	.386	4.1	37.7	.126	1.3	12.3	.077	.50	6.9	.02	.12	1.67
Electronics	.502	8.5	42.6	.234	3.9	19.9	.069	.45	3.4	.01	.09	.69
Automobiles	.389	4.5	59.3	.073	0.9	11.1	.058	.40	8.3	.00	.00	.00

[a]Shukko departures as a percentage of male (female) employment; [b]Shukko departures as a percentage of male (female) departures; [c]Shukko departures as a percentage of all departures made "at the convenience of upper management" (excludes contract expirations, mandatory retirement, and expulsion for cause).
Source: Ministry of Labor, *Survey of Employment Trends*, Tokyo 1996, table 30.

dustry sector, and firm size.[4] An important distinction in these data is that between "originating" and "returning" shukko. The first is employees of the surveyed firms who were transferred out by those firms during the year. The second is people who had been shukko'd into these firms but in 1996 returned to their original employers. Note that all "returning" shukko are by definition temporary (zaiseki) shukko, but there is no way of knowing whether the "originating" shukko are permanent (tenseki) or temporary.

Firms originating shukko are rather different from those taking them in, if we can infer the volume of "taking in" by the number of returning shukko.[5] Manufacturing establishments shukko male employees at a rate exceeding that of all industries, and (contrary to our presumption of greater keiretsuization with auto), electronics firms shukko more than manufacturing as a whole and the automotive industry in particular. The picture is different for women: manufacturing in general and autos and electronics in particular shukko them at lower rates than is the norm for all industries. On the other hand, the pattern of establishment size differentials in originating shukko is the same for both genders. The largest firms (and plants) dispatch people, and the small and medium-sized firms take them. Establishments with more than one hundred employees shukko male employees out at two to three times the rate of smaller organizations—for women, three to five times. These differentials show up whether shukko is calculated as a ratio to all employment, all departures, or all mandated departures. Nearly three-quarters of all mandated departures from the largest establishments are shukko transfers, compared to fewer than 20 percent of workplaces in the 5–99 employee size range and around 30 percent in the 100–999 range. The pattern of returning shukko is very different. The lowest rate by far is found in the one-thousand–plus employee size class. Large plants thus routinely dispatch their people to jobs in other organizations, but the reverse flow is much smaller.

Thus, for male employees, originating shukko rates are higher and returning shukko rates are lower in manufacturing than in nonmanufacturing, in autos and electronics than in other manufacturing, and in big establishments than in small ones. Among women, rates of shukko are lower overall (implying higher layoff rates) and lower in manufacturing than in nonmanufacturing, although the pattern of establishment size differences is similar to that of men.

Much of what these data show makes sense in terms of the operation of the permanent employment system in the Japanese dual economy. Males, employees of large firms, and employees in core manufacturing industries are less likely to be fired and more likely to be shukko'd to affiliated companies. Women, smaller firm employees, and nonmanufacturing employees are less likely to be shukko'd, thus are more likely to be laid off. But shukko does not simply get rid of surplus people in a fashion that keeps an elite subset of them employed. Although the composition of shukko as originating (out) or returning (in) shifts markedly across industry and firm size classes, the two types together account for 4–10 percent of all (male and female combined) employee departures. This high level of transfer activity across an array of firm types and sizes identifies shukko as a pervasive mechanism of interfirm coordination and knowledge sharing in Japan. Big companies in key industries can demand that smaller and dependent firms give jobs to their surplus workers. As our interviews testify, however, shukko'd people retain their loyalty to the dispatching firm and act as bridge between it and the receiving *ukezara* (receiving firm; literally, "saucer for catching the overflow"). The transferees from big firms in core industries more often play the role of *sensei*—teacher or leader—in a learning partnership, whereas those from small firms are the *deshi*, or "pupils." This accores with the asymmetry we observe in the originating and returning shukko flows.

A sign that shukko serves a learning rather than cost-reduction purpose is when its volume varies with the product. A Hitachi manager noted: "System control (software) is very customer oriented. It is common to send [shukko] employees to customers. In hardware, it is not so useful, so there is less shukko." In addition, the length of time people are transferred depends on the complexity of the technology and the amount of learning required. Speaking of shukko to customers, our Hitachi informants said:

> When the product is a large industrial system the employee may stay three to six months, as was the case with JR. Nuclear and electrical power systems may transfer them for as long as two years. When a Hitachi employee is shukko'd to another company, he has to understand the precise meanings of that field so small mistakes can be avoided.

Likewise, if shukko is reciprocated between customer and supplier, the case for a mutual learning rationale is easier to make. In our visit to Hitachi, we saw entire sections where workers wore different-colored hats from the Hitachi standard issue. These workers were on loan from affiliated firms.

Although permanent, or *tenseki*, shukko for labor reduction purposes carries some negative "dual economy" connotations in Japan, it is widely preferred to the main alternative: outright layoffs. Sanyo managers said they did not want to lay people off as Pioneer Electric attempted to do in 1993 (an act that elicited such strong reaction from unions, the Ministry of Labor, and the press that Pioneer backed down; Lincoln and Nakata, 1997). But it does shukko redundant employees to jobs in domestic subsidiaries and other Sanyo *kanren gaisha* (affiliated companies).

For similar reasons, Japanese unions rarely oppose cost-reduction shukko. At an interview with Denki Rengo (Japan Federation of Electrical Workers), we inquired about the union position on shukko. In economic downturns, such as the 1986 *endaka*, the 1974 oil shock, and the early 1990s recession, they said, tenseki (permanent shukko) and *tenkin* (internal transfer or rotation) were common. The unions did not oppose it; indeed, they counseled workers to accept the transfers without complaint (due to weakening employment guarantees, plus a rise in dual-career marriages, resistance to mandatory shukko has been increasing). The unions see their role as facilitating the redeployment of people into growing sectors and ensuring that the processes of transfer and rotation are done under reasonable rules. Union involvement is also necessitated because collective bargaining agreements with electronics manufacturers often extend to suppliers and affiliates as well.

Shukko and Knowledge Sharing in Teams

The relative ease with which Japanese companies transfer workers within companies or shukko them between companies contributes to intra- and interfirm knowledge diffusion. As Hitachi managers described it, a relatively long-term on-site experience with a customer or supplier socializes Hitachi people in the tacit ways of a partner. Through direct exposure to the work rhythms and social networks of another firm, Hitachi employees develop a feel for how the partner operates without having to put that knowledge into explicit form (e.g., as a set of specs or memos). Nonaka and Takeuchi (1995) give a nice example of precisely this process. Matsushita Electric was designing an electronic bread maker but could not build one that kneaded the dough properly. Matsushita shukko'd an engineer on the project to work with one of Japan's premier breadmakers. Through learning and practicing on-site under the tutelage of a master artisan, the engineer was able to design a machine that effectively mimicked the baker's craft.

A downside to the shukko system is the "man in the middle" status of the transferred employee. Precisely because shukko'd people straddle the boundary between sending and receiving firms, they have difficulty balancing their dual commitments. A shukko'd manager at a supplier of Kigyo Denki said that people who began their careers with the ukezara firm often feel resentment toward those who arrived through shukko. Moreover, he said, given the strong cultures of Japanese companies, it is easier to deal with people who have "grown up" in the same company, for they have developed common ways of thinking. This manager said that he still keeps in touch with Kigyo Denki, but since he was in the United States for a period, he no longer knows many people there. This manager always used "we" in referring to Kigyo Denki and was forthright in saying: "I'm still a Kigyo Denki employee." He was one of approximately one hundred people shukko'd in from the Kyoto Works of Kigyo Denki, which employed some twenty-five hundred people.

Although companies prefer to stress the positive features (technology transfer and learning) of shukko over the less attractive ones (off-loading surplus people), most shukko serves a dual purpose. Companies do achieve cost savings, even with temporary transfers. But at the same time they intend that people learn from the experience—even if only by gaining a broader and more flexible outlook. Indeed, an intriguing speculation is that the recent increase in shukko for labor cost reasons may be raising cross-firm flows of tacit knowledge as well. Toyota told us that its transfers of employees to Toyota dealerships was not merely a cost measure but was intended to give its workers expertise in the sales end of the business, making them more sensitive to customer needs when they returned. (Japanese observers familiar with the situation, however, say that the dealers were less than thrilled to get the Toyota people. Used to factory ways, they lacked the skills and demeanor of salespeople.)

Still, many ukezara firms receive shukko'd workers gladly. Being, for example, Hitachi people, they are high-quality employees, and, as noted, either Hitachi or the Ministry of Labor will make up the difference in their wages. Thus, both sides benefit. The dispatching firm sheds excess labor while installing trained people with a partner who will monitor and guide its operations. The receiving firm gets an infusion of better human capital than it could recruit on its own, along with skills and values acquired in a superior company and business partner. The shukko'd manager at the Kigyo Denki supplier is an example. He worked eight years in Kigyo Denki's U. S. factory, then transferred to Oki Electric, where he spent three years before moving to his present post. It is unlikely that the supplier could have recruited someone with his experience and connections. Of course, the supplier pays a price in autonomy, as the incoming shukkos take over management positions otherwise held by homegrown people.

The case of a Kyoto subcontractor (*shitauke*) of Kigyo Denki shows how the various shukko forms intertwine. The subcontractor had several employees who had been shukko'd from Kigyo Denki, the production manager included. During a factory tour, we observed a number of Kigyo Denki people. The younger ones were on temporary (zaiseki) shukko and would go back to Kigyo Denki after the standard two-year term at the supplier. People over fifty, whether white- or blue-collar, generally do not go back. There was some reciprocity, however, for the supplier also shukko'd people to Kigyo Denki (two were there at the time of our interview). These, of course, were never permanent placements but were there for engineering training, some for up to four or five years. We were told that when the supplier begins a new business or installs a new process, some employees would be sent to Kigyo Denki for training.

While the smaller supplier and other satellite firms are not as disadvantaged by the shukko system as the usual dual-economy models suggest, there is still some real asymmetry in the distribution of benefits. If the interest of the dispatching firm is chiefly in lowering labor costs, it has an incentive to select the transferees from the bottom of its talent pool, so the receiving firm may not get the most productive people. The Kansai printing firm whose owner had recently made the decision to "join" the Kansai Credit keiretsu illustrates. The owner's biggest worry was cash flow, a problem solved by joining the Kansai Credit keiretsu. Upon the sale of the printing firm's shares to Kansai Credit, the latter company sent in three people, one as president. All three were over fifty and (in the founder's view) were not particularly competent. Despite a prestigious education, the new president had no experience in the printing business and had been the least successful member of his entering cohort at Kansai Credit.[6] The founder had been pleading with Kansai Credit to send some energetic young people.

The shukko'd Kansai Credit employees will stay until official retirement age and be replaced by new shukko. The founder acknowledged that a principal reason Kansai Credit purchased his company was so it could act as "ukezara" for Kansai Credit shukko. Eventually, as his company grows, it will absorb fifteen or more Kansai Credit people. He said that shukko is often a rationale for the creation or expansion of keiretsu. A family member worked for a life insurance company that had actually traded purchase prices for shukko rights. The insurer had an implicit agreement with a supplier of heating oil to increase the price of oil supplied by a fixed amount for every shukko'd employee received.

Equity Ties as Supportive Infrastructure

As this example suggests, extensive shukko to a supplier or other affiliated firm rests on a stable set of keiretsu relationships. Particularly important is cross-shareholding; the shukko'ing firm is apt to have an equity stake in the ukezara (recipient). Such investments bestow rights to board representation, a particularly important form of shukko (director dispatch, or *yakuin haken*). The assembler or customer, being a larger and higher status firm, has a greater investment and more members on the board of the supplier than vice versa (Lincoln, Gerlach, and Takahashi, 1992).

Equity ties facilitate other forms of shukko as well. Hitachi told us that companies in its *shihon* (capital) keiretsu have the same union and pension system. This compatibility of personnel practices makes interorganizational transfers much easier. However, unlike the auto industry, where capital relationships (*shihon kankei*) between customers and suppliers are the rule, in electronics their prevalence is highly variable.

Tables 13.2 and 13.3 present the results of an exploratory statistical analysis showing how director dispatch depends on reciprocity, equity and commercial relations, and firm size in the Japanese electronics and auto industries. The data, which pertain to 1993, are imperfect for this purpose since they refer to twenty-one electronics firms and twenty motor vehicles firms that were among Japan's

Table 13.2. Definitions of Variables and Descriptive Statistics for Observations on Pairings of 21 Electronics Firms and 20 Motor Vehicles Firms with 259 Large Japanese Financial and Industrial Firms in 1993

Variable	Description	Electronics (n = 4913) Mean (SD)	Motor Vehicles (n = 4876) Mean (SD)
Director(I)	Director on J's board came from I (= 1; else 0)	.0043 (.0653)	.0045 (.0667)
Director(J)	Director on I's board came from J (= 1; else 0)	.0062 (.0787)	.0060 (.0774)
Equity(I)	Log percent equity in J held by I if I a top-ten shareholder (else 0)	.0008 (.0167)	.0008 (.0128)
Equity(J)	Log percent equity in J held by I if I a top-ten shareholder (else 0)	.0011 (.0115)	.0022 (.0163)
Trade(I)	I sells to J (= 1; else 0)	.0111 (.1047)	.0109 (.1038)
Trade(J)	J sells to I (= 1; else 0)	.0154 (.1230)	.0189 (.1361)
Size(I)	Log total assets of I	13.762 (1.014)	13.159 (1.025)
Size(J)	Log total assets of I	13.040 (.982)	13.043 (.984)

Table 13.3. Probit Regressions of Director Transfer (Director[I]) on Reciprocity (Director[J]), Equity Ties, Trade Ties and Firm Size for Observations on Pairings of 21 Electronics and 20 Motor Vehicles Firms with 259 Large Financial and Industrial Firms

Explanatory Variable	Electronics Industry n = 4913[†]	Motor Vehicles n = 4876[†]
Director(J)	.260	.081
	(.780)	(1.549)
Equity(I)	7.023**	44.388***
	(2.600)	(3.47)
Equity(I)	2.042	2.801
	(1.432)	(5.159)
Trade(I)	1.08*	1.642*
	(.532)	(.724)
Trade(J)	.555	−.503
	(.318)	(.272)
Size(I)	.116	.301
	(.109)	(.216)
Size(J)	−.075	−.159
	(.039)	(.098)
Autoregression	48.547	48.281
term	(27.500)	(34.214)
Constant	−3.838**	−5.992
	(1.386)	(3.888)
X^2 (8)	65.48***	13767.38***
Pseudo R^2	.439	.827

Table entries are probit regression coefficients with robust standard error estimates (adjusted for clustering by firm) in parentheses. The autoregression term additionally controls for same-firm effects over dyads (see Lincoln, Gerlach, and Takahashi, 1992).
*p < .05; **p < .01; ***p < .001.
[†]Reduced by missing data.

259 largest corporations (fifty financials, two-hundred industrials, and nine trading companies; see Lincoln, Gerlach, and Takahashi, 1992). The observations are dyads—pairings of each firm in the industry with every firm in the set of 259. This would yield 5,439 electronics-based dyads and 4,980 auto-based dyads, but the actual numbers of observations are reduced due to missing data.

The means on the director, equity, and trade ties *sent* by electronics and autos firms are essentially the same. The means on equity and trade ties received, however, are somewhat higher in the auto case. The regressions in table 13.2 reveal more contrast between the industries. As expected under the assumption of greater keiretsuization of the Japanese auto industry, the effect of firm I owning an equity stake in firm J on the probability of I sending a director to J, while positive and significant in both industries, is much stronger in autos. The effect of a selling relationship—trade (I)—is also greater in autos, although the difference is smaller. There is no evidence of reciprocity in director exchange—the director (J) effect—in either industry. Similarly, a buying relationship—trade (J)—does not condition director shukko in either industry.[7]

The taking of equity stakes in the Japanese electronics industry typically occurs at the time of contracting with new suppliers. Buying shares as a way of cementing an existing relationship is more typical of autos (Asanuma, 1989). For example, the television production operations of Tokyo Sanyo Denki moved to Gunma prefecture in 1959. At that time, Sanyo made investments in various local companies in order to develop them as suppliers. The technological level of this area was already high, as it had been an aviation and textile center. Sanyo provided equity to help local firms convert their plant, equipment, and people so that they could serve Sanyo's procurement needs. Sanyo subsequently increased its capital participation in several firms.

As Japanese companies move operations offshore, they face problems finding suitable suppliers and may use capital investments as a development tool. Equity ties with foreign suppliers and distributors also help to overcome legal barriers or to gain entry to established business networks; for example, to build links to Chinese merchants in southeast Asia.

As our data suggest, companies without equity stakes in suppliers do less shukko. Matsushita, as noted, deals with a large number of suppliers in fairly arm's-length fashion. Matsushita said that they do not send equity, loans, or managers to suppliers. "We have no keiretsu," our informants in Matsushita Corporate Purchasing (Shizai Center) asserted.

NEC managers also told us that they rarely take equity stakes in suppliers, for NEC, too, claims to have no keiretsu of the auto industry sort and adheres strictly to a multisourcing rule. Their few capital investments in suppliers were made long ago. One originated with a bailout; two others were NEC spinoffs; still others are subsidiaries in lines of business that NEC hoped to expand (e.g., Toyo Tsushin in telecommunications). NEC has very little equity invested in small assembly subcontractors. However, in recent years several such firms had reached sufficient scale to be listed on the stock exchange. These requested and received NEC equity investments. Consistent with its infrequent use of capital relations, NEC shukkos sparingly. NEC does send personnel into suppliers on special missions—to improve quality, for example—but managers said such cases were rare. NEC will, however, assist suppliers in various ways. It will lend them equipment and help with overseas purchasing of hard-to-procure items.

On the other hand, Kigyo Denki, which shukkos extensively, holds shares in nearly one-thousand companies. Kigyo Denki also serves as a bank for its supplier network. Its loans go chiefly to troubled affiliates, since strong ones can get good terms from banks. Our informants felt the loans were a good investment, despite the low interest. Banks, they said, lend at a higher interest rate but tolerate more risk. If Kigyo Denki lends to a supplier, however, there is no risk, since Kigyo Denki will provide the company with business and not allow it to go bankrupt.

Shukko and Knowledge Sharing

Shukko is an extension of the familiar Japanese practice of rotating people through jobs and functions over a long (under the permanent employment system) career with the firm (Brinton, 1991). As a mode of knowledge diffusion both within and between firms, it rests on some important facilitating conditions. One is acceptance of team effort and sharing. Teams are the building blocks of Japanese organizations, and most observers agree that such collaborative pooling of skills and effort has figured significantly in Japanese competitive success. Team process is fundamental to organizational learning, our informants said. Discoverers of new technology will spread it to others, thus growing the knowledge base of the company. A key channel whereby new knowledge flows into existing teams is through the addition of shukko'd people with experience in a partner firm.

Our informants said that they had little difficulty getting employees to share innovations or ideas with others. We asked Hitachi why an employee might not hoard or appropriate knowledge in hopes of leveraging it in an entrepreneurial startup, Silicon Valley style. "No," they said. "This doesn't happen in Japan. An employee cannot leave to start his own company. In Japan, he has to stay in a big company."

Outside Japan, however, the norms differ, and managers expressed concern that globalization—offshore operations and recruitment of local employees—was bringing more people into the company who thought only of themselves. One manager said that when Hitachi instructs Chinese partners in new technology, they expect the technology to spread within China, as it would within firms and up and down supply chains in Japan. But the Chinese just hold the technology and do not spread it. This, he said, was very frustrating to the Japanese.

Managers also acknowledged that the weak economy and the decline of employment security were taking their toll on the Japanese knowledge-sharing system. When *katatataki* (the tap-on-the-shoulder signal that an employee should "voluntarily" resign) is prevalent, the innovator is much more likely to try to make himself valuable by hoarding knowledge.

One factor in the prevalence of shukko in Japan is that the permanent employment system severely constricts the interfirm flows of people and skills that in California's Silicon Valley, say, are governed by the labor market processes of firing, quitting, and hiring. Midcareer recruitment of employees with experience and knowhow at other companies generally has been taboo in Japan, although corporations are stepping up such hiring, particularly in hard-to-fill specialist fields (Lincoln and Nakata, 1997).

The Japanese practices of shukko (transfer) and tenkin (rotation) arguably show how keiretsu governance combines the best of market and organization principles (Dyer, 1996; Williamson, 1985). In shukkoing people to another firm, a Japanese company gains access to the knowledge base of the transaction partner. Even when the shukko is permanent (tenseki), the relocated employee still identifies with the dispatching company and stays in regular contact with it. Since shukko is administratively managed in a way that labor markets are not, it is likely that organizations, not just individuals, capture a significant share of the transferred knowledge assets and the returns they produce.

By contrast, when a skilled person quits or otherwise vacates a U. S. job, her tie to that company is effectively severed, and her loyalties (such as they are) quickly shift to the new employer. Not only may she thus deliver proprietary knowledge to a competitor, but her departure deletes a critical node in the knowledge network. A Hitachi manager who had worked in the United States at General Electric noted this problem. GE employees, he said, individually "owned" technology. A key person left a project this manager was on, thereby destroying it. No one else had the same grasp of the project. The GE team approached the departed employee for assistance, but he had lost interest in helping GE.

Culture Diffusion as Tacit Knowledge Sharing

Shukko transfers tacit knowledge between firms through socialization: employees of one follow the routines, perform the tasks, and forge personal ties in the other. As noted, shukko assumes the Japanese training model: people acquire broad skills and norms through job rotation and on-the-job doing. Some of what is learned this way also could be acquired through explicit knowledge sharing (e.g., classroom training), particularly of the technical or cognitive routines of innovation or production. It is apt to be least true of the normative and affective elements of an organizational culture. The "empathy" that one Japanese organization exhibits toward another—devotion, obligation, and commitment—like all sentiments is highly tacit. It is also a powerful force aligning the transacting organizations' strategies and operations, as it promotes high sensitivity in each to the requirements and rhythms of the other. In this last section, we give examples from our interviews of such cross-firm cultural processes. Our hypothesis is that shukko facilitates such flows; that is, the more shukko, the greater cultural affinity.

Shared values and sentiments are strongly implied in the idea that "trust" is essential to Japanese purchase-supply relations. Such normative or affective facets of trust augment or substitute for the cognitive and rationalist facets stressed in economics thinking. If people of one organization identify with and feel obligation to a second, less experience- or reputation-testing is required in order to forego hard contractual safeguards.

At Kigyo Denki, the culture that supports supply relations is much less that of the individual corporation than that of the horizontal keiretsu group of which Kigyo Denki was a part (Gerlach, 1992). Our informant said that Kigyo Denki, like its business group as a whole, is very conservative. People are smart but do not know how to use their abilities, for example, to enter new industries. However, Kigyo Denki's culture is supportive of someone who has an idea and puts effort into developing it. Kigyo Denki's affiliated companies have more young people with entrepreneurial drive. There is thus a certain symbiosis between the cultures of Kigyo Denki and its affiliates.

Part of keiretsu culture is the fictive kinship ideal of a cohesive "family" of corporations. This strengthens the network and ensures smooth, reliable transactions among members. A Kigyo Denki executive commented that such family values promote preferential trading: people want to keep purchases in the "family" (of keiretsu or equity-linked companies).

An example of interorganizational empathy and reciprocity is a Kigyo Denki manager's description of his efforts, as a shukko'd employee, to make Nihon Shohin (a pseudonym) profitable, a company in which Kigyo Denki had a 20 percent investment. The manager was pouring time into this not merely because it was a good business venture, but because he felt a moral obligation to assist Shohin and its employees. Shohin had served Kigyo Denki well in the past, so Kigyo Denki was bound to reciprocate:

> Once Kigyo Denki makes an investment in a company, we have a very important social responsibility. Nihon Shohin has eight hundred people, and I see the faces of all of these people and their families. I will do everything I can to make Nihon Shohin an excellent company. The employees of this company made a very nice contribution during the bubble years, so we are not going to cut them loose during a downturn. The ultimate goal is to make Nihon Shohin employees happy.

Our Kigyo Denki informants said that when suppliers are 100 percent dependent, they feel a strong sense of obligation to them. An equity relationship further increases that obligation. This, they said, is the distinctive "wetness" in Japanese economic relations. It is hard for a Japanese company to tell a long-term supplier that it can offer it no more business. This *kimochi* (mood, sentiment) is based on personal relations of *giri* and *ninjo* (obligation and human feeling).

Hitachi, on the other hand, told us that their corporate culture, both of the parent firm and of the larger Hitachi "group" of companies, was rather weak, compared, say, to Kigyo Denki or Toshiba. The reason was Hitachi's decentralized, very *kojo* (factory)-oriented structure. Formally, Hitachi had a *jigyobu-seido* (divisionalized system). In the usual case, the factory is part of a division (jigyobu). But at Hitachi, the factories are autonomous, and the jigyobu are weak. When each factory charts its own course, corporate- or division-level product strategy is hard to formulate. Thus, Hitachi lacks the strong corporrate culture of a Kigyo Denki or Toshiba that it could leverage to control or coordinate suppliers. Moreover, being a prewar company, it cannot invoke the charismatic vision of a postwar founder such as Matsushita Konosuke. A Sanyo manager said that the memory of the partnerships that built the business fostered cultural cohesion among postwar companies such as Sanyo. As he put it, "we grew up with our suppliers after the war, and thus we want to help them. Our kimochi [feeling, sentiment] is to preserve friendly relations with our suppliers."

Indeed, our Hitachi informants suggested that a benefit to them of shukko to customers and suppliers was the reform of Hitachi's somewhat hidebound culture. In our interviews, they made repeated candid allusions to Hitachi's rigid organization. By exposing Hitachi young people to the ways of other companies, they hoped that the next generation of Hitachi managers might be more flexible and open-minded than the present one.

Since purchase-supply relations are hierarchical and asymmetric—the customer has more power to fix the terms of the transaction—the source of such encompassing beliefs is often the culture of the customer. Matsushita's corporate culture, for example, derives mainly from the vision and teachings of the company's founder and first president, Matsushita Konosuke. In our visit to one sole-source Matsushita supplier of metal plating, the owner and cofounder (an *obaasan*—grandma—type dressed in kimono) talked at length about the great "heart" of Matsushita Electric and how inspired she had been by the teachings of Matsushita Konosuke. These "spiritual" qualities, she said, were the reason she and her deceased husband had devoted their lives to becoming reliable members of the Matsushita supply network.

Given Matsushita's reputation for "dry," even *kibishii* (strict, harsh) supplier relations, her comments were particularly interesting. The Matsushita supply chain does not have an encompassing culture apart from that of Matsushita Electric itself. However, that corporate culture is sufficiently strong and charismatic that it functions as a source of power and discipline over individual suppliers.

Descriptions of a parent company's relations with suppliers and affiliates as warm and personal, "wet" with emotion (*uetto*) versus cold and "dry" (*dorai*) came up often in our interviews with Japanese suppliers and customers. Some of Matsushita's reputation for being "dorai," even "kibishii" (severe, strict) stems from the Japanese stereotype of Kansai (Osaka area) firms and business people as colder, more money-oriented, and more prone to business haggling than Kanto (Tokyo area) business. Sanyo, another Kansai firm, likewise was reputed to be dry and kibishii in its dealings with suppliers (Lincoln, Ahmadjian, and Mason, 1998; Roehl, 1989).

Although our NEC informant did not imply that its source was NEC's Sumitomo group attachment, he did say that NEC group suppliers and affiliates had a culture that was very strong. NEC firms strongly identify with NEC and see themselves in competition with, say, the Kigyo Denki Group. This common identity kept the group competitive: a supplier cannot assume that because it is an NEC affiliate it can slack off and and NEC will always buy from it.

The examples of Matsushita and NEC suggest that alternative modes of supply chain governance may be functional substitutes. These companies make little use of equity ties and shukko and tend to deal with suppliers at relative arm's-length. On the other hand, their strong corporate cultures serve to promote cohesion and coordination across their supplier networks.

Conclusions

The widespread use of shukko in Japan has some significant implications for patterns of interorganizational learning. Shukko moves people up and down supply chains and to other affiliated firms, such as spun-off product divisions in which the parent firm maintains an equity stake (Gerlach and Lincoln, 2000). For obvious reasons, shukko does not channel people and knowledge between competitors. Nor, given Japan's traditional permanent employment system, do external market processes move many experienced workers between competing employers. The stigma of disloyalty that the employee and his family must endure is a sizable deterrent, but a greater obstacle is the reluctance of companies to hire midcareer people and treat them as regular employees. In the United States and other economies with more open and "efficient" labor markets, such labor flows are the routine consequence of employees quitting or losing jobs with one company and taking up new ones with a competitor. Much of the vibrancy and dynamism of Silicon Valley, for example, is credited to the role of established corporations like Hewlett Packard or Intel in training and grooming people who at some point jump ship (or, less often, are pushed overboard) into the arms of a competitor eager for the knowhow and sometimes the proprietary knowledge of the former employer. Other such people might apply their skills and energies to the founding and nurturing of an entrepreneurial startup that may grow to pose a significant competitive challenge to the established company they left. Our informants at Hitachi felt that, for these among other reasons, American companies were better at learning from competitors; "Hitachi observes the new products that competitors produce but it is hard to get information on their technology. That's why we go to America. In the United States yesterday's competitor is today's ally. The United States is more business-oriented. It doesn't work that way in Japan."[8]

As a method of coordinating goals and operations and exchanging knowledge and skill between affiliated or transacting organizations, however, the shukko mechanism may be without peer. It plays a major (if generally overlooked) role in forging the strong partnerships among banks, customers, suppliers, distributors, and even government ministries that have been an earmark of the Japanese network economy (Gerlach and Lincoln, 1998).

Notes

1. One indicator of in-house parts supply capacity in the major electronics firms is apparent to visitors on plant tours. Most of the machines in the VTR factory we visited were Sanyo-made.

2. GDP growth in 1996 was 3.8 percent; unemployment was 3.3 percent.

3. The pattern of shukko by firm size and industry is very similar in the two years. They differ in that departures for personal reasons (*kojin teki na riyu*) declined for males from 8.6 percent of employment to 7.2 percent and for females from 17.2 percent to 13.7 percent. Upper-management mandated (*keiei jono tsugo*) departures, on the other hand, rose for males from 0.74 percent to 1 percent of employment and for females from 0.58 percent to 0.82 percent. The change was mostly due to increased shukko: shukko as a percentage of employment increased 27.8 percent for both genders. "Layoffs" (inferred as total mandated departures minus total shukko) rose 11.7 percent for males and 14 percent for females.

4. Other reasons for departing are, for males: contract expiration (11.8 percent), mandatory retirement (8.9 percent), for cause (*honnin no seme*; 5.6 percent), personal reasons (e.g., marriage, child care; 62.5 percent), illness or death (2.3 percent). The figures for females are: contract expiration (8.8 percent), mandatory retirement (2.7 percent), for cause (3.8 percent), personal reasons (78.4 percent), illness or death (1.6 percent).

5. Also possible is that people shukko'd to big plants are more likely to remain permanently, but this is less likely. Our data are consistent with the common knowledge that shukko transfers flow down a firm-size hierarchy.

6. The status of the managers seconded to a supplier or other affiliated firm varies with the size and importance of that firm. Sanyo told us that most of its affiliated companies (*kanren gaisha*) have directors sent by Sanyo. If a firm has sales of one billion yen or more, Sanyo will send a *torishimariyaku* (director) or *kansayaku* (inside auditor). Firms below this size receive a *jigyo bucho* (operating division head).

7. This is a surprising result, since we would expect customers to shukko top managers to suppliers rather than the reverse. Such a pattern of buyers controlling sellers, however, is quite strong in regressions (not shown) in which equity tie is the dependent variable.

8. Clearly our informant had in mind *Japanese* competitors. Japanese firms go to considerable lengths to contain knowledge and skills from spilling over to competitors. Labor market rigidities, keiretsu obligations, and nontransparent auditing and reporting practices facilitate such secrecy. Obviously, Japanese firms have long been adept at borrowing and learning from Western competitors.

References

Ahmadjian, Christina L., and James R. Lincoln. 1998. "Changing Firm Boundaries in Japanese Auto Parts Networks." In *Corporate Governance Today*, edited by Mark J. Roe. New York: Sloan Project on Corporate Governance at Columbia Law School. Pp. 179–200.

Asanuma, Banri. 1989. "Manufacturer-Supplier Relationships in Japan and the Concept of Relation-Specific Skill." *Journal of the Japanese and International Economies* 3(1): 1–30.

———. 1992. "Japanese Manufacturer-Supplier Relationships in International Perspective: The Automobile Case." In *International Adjustment and the Japanese Firm*, edited by Paul Sheard. New York: Allen and Unwin (in association with the Australia-Japan Center). Pp. 99–124.

Beer, Michael, and B. A. Spector. 1981. *Matsushita Electric*. Harvard Business School case no. 9-481-146. Based on *Matsushita Electric Industrial Co. Ltd.: Management Control Systems*, by H. Ishido and K. Takahashio, Keio University, Tokyo, Japan.

Brinton, Mary C. 1991. "Sex Differences in On-the-job Training and Job Rotation in Japanese Firms." In *Research in Social Stratification and Mobility*. Vol. 10, Greenwich, Conn.: JAI Press. Pp. 3–25.

Clark, Kim B., and Takahiro Fujimoto. 1991. *Product Development Performance*. Boston: Harvard Business School Press.

Dyer, Jeffrey H. 1996. "Specialized Supplier Networks as a Source of Competitive Advantage: Evidence from the Auto Industry." *Strategic Management Journal* 17 (April): 271–91.

Fruin, Mark. 1992. *The Japanese Enterprise System: Competitive Strategies and Cooperative Structures*. Oxford: Oxford University Press.

———. 1997. *Knowledge Works: Managing Intellectual Capital at Toshiba*. New York: Oxford University Press.

Gerlach, Michael L. 1992. *Alliance Capitalism: The Social Organization of Japanese Business*. Berkeley: University of California Press.

Gerlach, Michael L., and James R. Lincoln. 2000. "Economic Organization and Innovation in Japan: Networks, Spinoffs, and the Creation of Enterprise." In *Knowledge Management: Comparative Perspectives*, edited by Georg von Krogh. London: Macmillan.

———. 1998. "The Structural Analysis of Japanese Economic Organization: A Conceptual Framework." In *Networks and Markets: Pacific Rim Strategies*, edited by W. Mark Fruin. New York: Oxford University Press. Pp. 293–321.

Imai, Ken-ichi, Ikujiro Nonaka, and Hirotaka Takeuchi. 1985. "Managing the New Product Development Process: How Japanese Companies Learn and Unlearn." In *The Uneasy Alliance: Managing the Productivity-Technology Dilemma*, edited by Kim B. Clark, Robert H. Hayes, and Christopher Lorenz. Boston: Harvard Business School Press. Pp. 337–76.

Lincoln, James R., Christina L. Ahmadjian, and Eliot Mason. 1998. "Organizational Learning and Purchase-Supply Relations in Japan: Hitachi, Matsushita, and Toyota Compared." *California Management Review*, Special Issue on Knowledge and the Firm, edited by Robert E. Cole, 40 (spring): 241–64.

Lincoln, James R., Michael Gerlach, and Christina Ahmadjian. 1996. "*Keiretsu* Networks and Corporate Performance in Japan." *American Sociological Review* 61 (1): 67–88.

Lincoln, James R., Michael L. Gerlach, and Peggy Takahashi. 1992. "*Keiretsu* Networks in the Japanese Economy: A Dyad Analysis of Intercorporate Ties." *American Sociological Review* 57 (5): 561–85.

Lincoln, James R., and Yoshifumi Nakata. 1997. "The Transformation of the Japanese Employment System: Nature, Depth, and Origins." *Work and Occupations* 24 (February): 33–55.

Mead, George Herbert. 1962. *Mind, Self, and Society.* Edited with an introduction by Charles W. Morris. Chicago: University of Chicago Press.

Mitchener, Brandon, and Greg Steinmetz. 1998. "After a Prolonged Skid, Mercedes Is Regaining Much of Its Prestige." *Wall Street Journal* (July 6): A8.

Nikkei Weekly. 1993. "Businesses Should Seek Other Options before Resorting to Personnel Cuts." (November 8): 6.

———. 1995. "Blue-chip Firms Tighten Hiring, Shift Workers to Subsidiaries." (June 12): 8.

Nishiguchi, Toshihiro. 1994. *Strategic Industrial Sourcing: The Japanese Advantage.* New York: Oxford University Press.

———. 1996. *Managing Product Development.* New York: Oxford University Press.

Nishiguchi, Toshihiro, and Alexandre Beaudet. 1998. "Fractal Design: Self-organizing Links in Supply Chain Management." Paper presented at the Conference on Knowledge Creation and Transformation, University of St. Gallen, Switzerland, June 26.

Nonaka, Ikujiro, and Hirotaka Takeuchi. 1995. *The Knowledge-Creating Company: How Japanese Companies Create the Dynamics of Innovation.* New York: Oxford University Press.

Odaka, Konosuke, Keinosuke Ono, and Fumihiko Adachi. 1988. *The Automobile Industry in Japan: A Study of Ancillary Firm Development.* Tokyo: Kinokuniya.

Roehl, Thomas. 1989. "A Comparison of U. S.-Japanese Firms' Parts-Supply Systems: What Besides Nationality Matters?" In *The U. S. Japanese Economic Relationship: Can It Be Improved?*, edited by Kichiro Hayashi. New York: New York University Press. Pp. 127–54.

Sako, Mari. 1992. *Prices, Quality, and Trust: Inter-firm Relations in Britain and Japan.* New York: Cambridge University Press.

———. 1996. "Suppliers' Associations in the Japanese Automobile Industry: Collective Action for Technology Diffusion." *Cambridge Journal of Economics* 20 (6): 651–71.

Sako, Mari, and Susan Helper. 1998. "Determinants of Trust in Supplier Relations: Evidence from the Automotive Industry in Japan and the United States." *Journal of Economic Behavior and Organization* 34 (3): 387–417.

Isaka, Satoshi, 1995. "Automakers Consider Worker Swaps: Flexible Use of Labor Becomes Vital Issue in Effort to Maintain Employment Levels in Car Industry." *Nikkei Weekly* (October 16): 8.

Shioji, Hiromi. 1995. "'Itaku' Automotive Production: An Aspect of the Development of Full-line and Wide-Selection Production by Toyota in the 1960s." *Kyoto University Economic Review* 65: 19–42.

Sitkin, Sim B., Denise M. Rousseau, Ronald S. Burt, and Colin Camerer, eds. *Academy of Management Review.* Special topic forum on Trust in and between Organizations, 23 (3): 381–640.

Smitka, Michael J. 1991. *Competitive Ties: Subcontracting in the Japanese Automotive Industry.* New York : Columbia University Press.

Takahashi, Peggy K. 1995. *Strategic Spin-offs and Organizational Change in the Japanese Electric and Electronic Equipment Industry*. Ph.D. dissertation, University of California at Berkeley.

Uzzi, Brian. 1996. "The Sources and Consequences of Embeddedness for the Economic Performance of Organizations—the Network Effect." *American Sociological Review* 61 (4): 674–98.

Von Krogh, Georg. 1998. "Care in Knowledge Creation." *California Management Review*, Special Issue on Knowledge and the Firm, edited by Robert E. Cole, 40(spring): 133–53.

Williamson, Oliver E. 1985. *The Economic Institutions of Capitalism*. New York: Free Press.

Womack, James P., Daniel T. Jones, and Daniel Roos. 1990. *The Machine That Changed the World*. New York: Macmillan.

14

Absorptive Capacity, Co-opetition, and Knowledge Creation

Samsung's Leapfrogging in Semiconductors

LINSU KIM

Most, if not all, firms in developing countries are engrossed in activities to catch up with advanced countries. Even the majority of firms in advanced countries are engaged in catching up, as not all firms can be pioneers of novel breakthroughs even in these countries. Nonetheless, research on organizational knowledge creation and innovation is concentrated mainly in advanced countries and is focused mostly on the pioneering process (Dodgson, 1993; Nonaka and Takeuchi, 1995; Utterback, 1994; von Hippel, 1988). Research on those subjects in the catching-up process, particularly in developing countries, is, however, scanty (e.g., Fransman and King, 1984; Kim and Kim, 1985; Kim, 1997; and Kim, 1998). Models that capture organizational knowledge creation and innovation in the catching-up process are crucially important not only to develop new theories relevant to developing countries but also to extend existing theories in advanced countries. This essay attempts to develop a model of organizational knowledge creation in the catching-up process in a developing country by empirically analyzing the vibrant history of technological transformation at the Samsung Electronics Company (hereinafter Samsung) as a case in point (Samsung, 1987).

Despite the skepticism that it lacked the technological capability to enter and remain competitive in the semiconductor industry, Samsung has leapfrogged from a mere producer of discrete devices to the most vibrant producer of dynamic random access memory (DRAM) chips in only a decade. Samsung has emerged as the largest memory chip maker and the seventh largest semiconductor maker in the world. Samsung's production increased from $83 million in 1985 to $5.2 billion in 1994. In memory chips, already dominant in 4-megabyte and 16-megabyte DRAM semiconductors, Samsung is ahead of Japan in 64-megabyte and 256-megabyte generations, while also attempting to crack more profitable applications-specific integrated circuits (ASICs).

Samsung's rapid surge in a decade raises several research questions. (1) How has Samsung expedited knowledge creation so expeditiously? (2) How does knowledge creation in the catching-up process in a developing country differ from that of the pioneering process in advanced countries? (3) How does knowledge creation in catching up differ between semiconductor and other industries? (4) Can other catching-up firms emulate Samsung's knowledge creation model? This essay briefly reviews theories related to knowledge creation and innovation. It then analyzes Samsung as a case in point to illustrate how the Korean firm has expedited knowledge creation and to answer these questions.

Conceptual Background

Knowledge creation, whether for imitation or innovation, takes place at two levels: individual and organizational. The prime actors in the process of knowledge creation are individuals within the organization. Knowledge creation in organizations is not, however, the simple sum of knowledge creation by individuals (Hedberg, 1981). Rather, it is the process that creates knowledge, which is distributed across the organization, is communicated among its members, has consensual validity, and is integrated into the strategy and management of the organization (Duncan and Weiss, 1978). Individual knowledge creation is, therefore, an indispensable condition for knowledge creation in the organization but cannot be the sufficient one. Organizations create knowledge only when individual insights and skills become embodied in organizational routines, practices, and beliefs (Attewell, 1992). Only effective organizations can translate individual knowledge creation into organizational knowledge creation (Hedberg, 1981; Daniel Kim, 1993; Shrivastava, 1983).

Absorptive Capacity

Knowledge creation is a function of an organization's absorptive capacity. Absorptive capacity requires a learning capability and develops problem-solving skills. Learning capability involves the development of a capacity to assimilate existing knowledge (for imitation), while problem-solving skills represent a capacity to create new knowledge (for innovation).

Absorptive capacity has two important elements: prior knowledge base and intensity of effort (Cohen and Levinthal, 1990). First, the prior knowledge base refers to existing individual units of knowledge available within the organization. Accumulated prior knowledge increases the ability both to make sense of and to assimilate and use new knowledge. Relevant prior knowledge base includes basic skills and general knowledge in the case of developing countries, but it includes the most recent scientific and technological knowledge in the case of industrially advanced countries. Thus, prior knowledge base should be assessed in its relation to the task difficulty involved (Kim, 1995).

Second, the intensity of effort refers to the amount of energy expended by organizational members to solve problems. It is insufficient merely to expose firms to relevant external knowledge without exerting effort to internalize it. Learning how to solve problems is usually built up over many practice trials involving related problems (Harlow, 1959). Thus, it requires a considerable amount of time and effort directed toward solving problems early on before moving on to more complex problems. Such effort intensifies interaction among organizational members that facilitates knowledge conversion and creation at the organizational level.

Knowledge Conversion and Creation

It is widely accepted that knowledge has two dimensions: explicit and tacit (Polanyi, 1966; Nonaka and Takeuchi, 1995). Tacit knowledge forms the core of the prior knowledge base at a firm. A firm may have some proprietary explicit knowledge such as firm-specific blueprints and standard operating procedures. However, they are useful only when tacit knowledge enables its members to utilize them. Much of the knowledge that underlies the effective performance in the organization is tacit knowledge embodied in its members (Howells, 1996; Nelson and Winter, 1982).

Knowledge creation in organizations takes place primarily through the dynamic process of four different modes of conversion between the two dimensions of knowledge. Tacit to tacit conversion (socialization) takes place when tacit knowledge within one individual is shared by another through training, while explicit to explicit conversion (combination) takes place when an individual combines discrete pieces of explicit knowledge into a new whole. Tacit to explicit conversion (externalization) can be said to take place when an individual is able to articulate the foundations of his or her tacit knowledge. Explicit to tacit conversion (internalization) takes place when new explicit knowledge is shared throughout the firm and other members begin to use it to broaden, extend, and reframe their own tacit knowledge (Nonaka and Takeuchi, 1995).

Figure 14.1 depicts the dynamic process of knowledge creation in the catching-up process. It shows how knowledge creation takes place through knowledge conversion that starts at the individual level and moves up in an upward spiral process to the organizational level. Knowledge creation tends to become faster and larger in scale, as more actors in and around the firm convert knowledge within and between themselves.

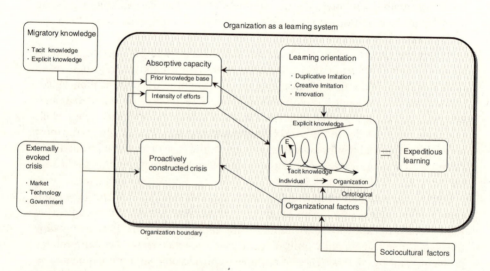

Figure 14.1. Dynamics of Organizational Learning in Catching Up
Source: Linsu Kim, "Crisis Construction and Organizational Learning: Capability Building in Catching-up at Hyundai Motor," *Organization Science* 9(4): 506–21.

Learning orientation also affects the process of knowledge conversion and creation. All organizations are learning systems. They learn as they develop, produce, and market products and services. All learning systems, however, have different patterns of learning orientations, which are the values and practices that reflect what is learned and where it occurs. Learning orientations determine the direction of the way organizations acquire, share, and utilize knowledge. In developing countries, learning orientation ranges from duplicative imitation to innovation (figure 14.1). This requires a different level of prior knowledge and a different degree of the intensity of effort. It also affects the spiral process of knowledge conversion.

Migratory Knowledge and Prior Knowledge Base

Figure 14.1 also shows that prior knowledge base affects the dynamics of the spiral process in knowledge conversion and that the organization can obtain knowledge from various external sources. In developing countries, foreign direct investment and foreign licensing transfer such explicit knowledge as technical specifications, designs, production manuals, and technologies as embodied in physical equipment. Training in both suppliers' and recipients' sites transfers tacit knowledge related to technologies transferred. Individual scientists and engineers migrating from one organization or country to another are also an important source of tacit knowledge; Badaracco (1991) calls it migratory knowledge. The acquisition of such migratory knowledge enables the organization to expand its prior knowledge base. Migratory knowledge alone is not, however, sufficient. It should also be matched with the high intensity of effort to enhance the organization's absorptive capacity.

Crises Construction and the Intensity of Effort

Cumulative or linear knowledge creation along the current trajectory can take place under normal circumstances. Discontinuous or nonlinear knowledge creation, however, takes place normally when a firm perceives a crisis and deploys a strategy to turn around the critical situation (Meyers, 1990). Organizations tend to engage in major changes mainly after they have been confronted with crises (Miller and Friesen, 1984; Tushman, Virany, and Romanelli, 1985). In such a case, the organization has to invest heavily in the acquisition of new migratory knowledge, as well as in knowledge-creation activities, to overcome the crisis in the shortest possible time. As the term "crisis" in Chinese (*wei ji*), which combines two characters, the first meaning "threat," the second "opportunity," some organizations manage to turn a crisis into an opportunity by expanding their absorptive capacity in a discontinuous manner and reap tremendous growth through their enhanced competitiveness. A crisis may be creative in this sense; otherwise, it is apt to become destructive.

Crises may stem from external sources, as shown in figure 14.1. Crises may be evoked naturally when a firm loses its competitive standing in the market and in technology. Literature abounds on market- and technology-evoked crises (e.g., Abernathy, 1978; Cooper and Schendel, 1976; De Greene, 1982; Meyers, 1990;

Miller and Friesen, 1984; Shrivastava, 1988; Tushman and Anderson, 1986; Utterback and Kim 1985). A crisis may also be generated deliberately by an external principal. In developing countries, particularly where the state plays an orchestral role in industrialization, the government could impose a crisis by setting challenging goals for firms in a strategically designated industry. Such an external change generates a crisis for top management but not necessarily for organizational members at the lower echelon.

Top management is also able to construct a crisis internally, either in response to or in the absence of an external crisis, as shown in figure 14.1. This type of crisis is called constructed crisis (Pitt, 1990). A crisis may be proactively constructed at the corporate or suborganization level. The former may be called a corporate crisis, while the latter may be called a team crisis. Crises constructed at Samsung are primarily team crises. Team crises may be more frequent and easier to manage than corporate crises. A team crisis may have more focused and clearer goals than a corporate crisis (Kim, 1998). The shared sense of the internally constructed crisis among organizational members enables the organization to draw on their energy, increasing the organization's total intensity of effort. This, together with high prior knowledge base, enables the organization to sustain its competitive position with high absorptive capacity. That is, the effective organization may frequently evoke proactively constructed crises and institutionalize the process and structure to make discontinuous knowledge creation possible and turn the crises into opportunities.

The intensity of effort focuses not only on learning by doing (Arrow, 1962) but also on learning by research (Kim, 1997). When technology involved is simple and mature, learning by doing may be sufficient. But when technology involved is near the frontier, as in semiconductors, learning by research plays a central role in sustaining competitiveness.

Internal Co-opetition and Absorptive Capacity

Internal co-opetition is another important dimension that facilitates knowledge creation within organizations. Co-opetition, a term coined by Brandenberger and Nalebuff (1996), is a hybrid of cooperation and competition. Interfirm competition and cooperation are essential to the innovation process (Teece, 1992). So is intrafirm cooperation and competition. The challenge to managers, therefore, is to find the right balance between the two. Figure 14.2 depicts how intrafirm cooperation and competition affect the dynamic process of knowledge conversion in two subunits in the catching-up process.

Intrafirm cooperation between subunits can give significant rise to the prior knowledge base of the firm, as shown in figure 14.2. The most meaningful cooperation may be information and personnel exchange. Information exchange disseminates explicit knowledge across the firm, while personnel exchange can elevate tacit knowledge base. In contrast, intrafirm competition between subunits to accomplish the same goal independently can induce the intensity of effort in R&D and information-searching activities. Unlike duplicative imitation of technologically simple products, such competition is productive in creatively imitating or generating technologically complex products.

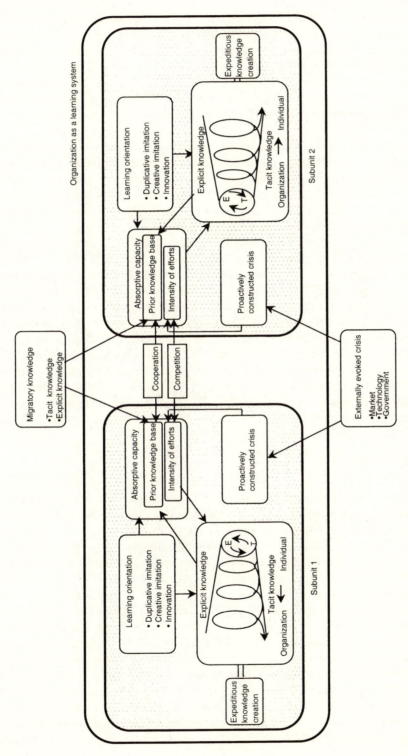

Figure 14.2. The Process of Knowledge Creation with Two Co-opetiting subunits

A case hereafter illustrates how the two elements (prior knowledge base and the intensity of effort) of absorptive capacity, migratory knowledge, externally evoked and internally constructed crises, and internal cooperation and competition affect knowledge creation at Samsung.

Samsung's Knowledge Creation in Catching Up

Korea's semiconductor industry traces its beginnings to the mid-1960s, when several multinational semiconductor firms—Signetics, Fairchild, Motorola, Control Data, AMI, and Toshiba—began assembling discrete devices in Korea in order to take advantage of the local cheap labor. The assembly operations required only about six months' training of unskilled workers, who transferred little design or engineering capability to Korea.

It was in 1974 when the first local semiconductor firm was established by a Korean-American scientist with a Ph.D. from Ohio State University and semiconductor design experience at Motorola. Samsung bought out the company during a financial crisis that occurred in the company's first year. With a large stake in consumer electronics, Samsung made the acquisition as a stepping stone to secure necessary prior knowledge related to semiconductors. The scientist-turned-entrepreneur provided Samsung with an even higher tacit knowledge base. His tacit knowledge was effectively transferred to Samsung engineers. This enabled the firm to progressively produce various transistors and integrated circuits on a small scale, largely for in-house consumer electronics. Samsung also established its Semiconductor R&D Laboratory in 1982, which focused mainly on reverse-engineering and assimilating technologies related to bipolar and metal oxide semiconductors (MOSs).

Foreign Licensing and Internal Cooperation for the 64K DRAM

Samsung then organized a task force in 1982 to formulate an entry strategy for very large–scale integrated circuits (VLSI). Its eight years of experience in transistor and integrated circuit production provided a platform for VLSI. However, it required a major technological leap to jump from the current form of operations: from 5 micron to 2.5 micron circuit width, from 3-inch wafer to 5-inch wafer, and from 1K/16K large scale integrated circuits (LSI) to 64K VLSIs.

The four-phase learning process—preparation, acquisition, assimilation, and improvement/application—identified by Kim (1998) in his study of knowledge creation in the Korea's automobile industry is also evident at Samsung. At the outset, Samsung took preparatory measures to acquire necessary migratory knowledge. The team spent six months collecting explicit knowledge related to 64K DRAM chips, analyzing the technology and market, and formulating plausible entry strategies. This significantly built up Samsung's prior knowledge on VLSIs. The team members then spent one month in the United States, meeting experts in the industry, particularly Korean-American scientists and engineers working in American semiconductor firms or teaching at American universities. They studied the market and industry structure and identified potential technology suppliers. Their prior knowledge enabled them to make sense out of discussions and observations during the trip.

The prior knowledge base developed during the preparation phase helped Samsung identify the sources of foreign technology and strengthen its bargaining power in negotiations with the foreign supplier. But Texas Instruments, Motorola, NEC, Toshiba, and Hitachi refused to transfer 64K DRAM technology to Samsung. The odds, however, seemed to be stacked in Samsung's favor: Samsung was able to find a number of distressed small semiconductor companies in the United States that were eager to sell what Samsung needed most—chip designs and processes—in attempts to obtain cash for survival. Samsung acquired 64K DRAM design from Micron Technology in Boise, Idaho, gaining both explicit and tacit knowledge related to VLSIs. Design for a high-speed MOS process was picked up for $2.1 million from Zytrex of California, which resulted in the transfer of explicit knowledge to Korea. These technologies from the small firms were, however, not production tested. This meant Samsung had to reinvent and translate them into production-viable ones. Samsung sent its engineers to these technology suppliers for training as a part of the technology transfer process, elevating Samsung's capability to assimilate the licensed technologies.

Samsung sequenced the assimilation of transfered technology from the easiest to the progressively more sophisticated: from assembly processes to process development, then to wafer fabrication and inspection. Samsung first imported three thousand 64K DRAM chips from Micron Technology to assemble in Korea. With eight years of experience in the assembly of LSI chips, Samsung assimilated VLSI assembly technology without many problems, but this experience enabled Samsung engineers to gain initial familiarity with the new product. Samsung's assembly operation easily reached the 92 percent yield ratio, on a par with Japan. Then Samsung went further, to assimilating design and process technologies.

Substantial technological capability and in-house research efforts were, however, required to translate tacit and explicit knowledge related to design and process technologies acquired from two American companies into a production operation with a high yield ratio. For this purpose, Samsung organized two R&D teams to work collaboratively in assimilating and commercializing the 64K DRAM.

Samsung set up an R&D outpost in Silicon Valley in 1983 and hired five Korean-Americans with doctorates in electronics engineering from Stanford, Michigan, Minnesota, and Notre Dame universities with semiconductor design experience at IBM, Honeywell, Zilog, Intel, and National Semiconductors. These scientists, plus about three hundred American engineers, including several designers who left Mostek, brought to Samsung the crucially important tacit knowledge to crack VLSI technology. Silicon Valley was a strategic location for the development of the 64K DRAM. A high density of scientists and engineers in the vicinity offered the rich source of critical information and expertise that Samsung needed. The outpost also provided opportunities for engineers in Korea to participate in training and research in the United States and enabled them to learn significantly about VLSI technology.

Samsung organized another R&D task force in Korea with Samsung engineers who were experienced in LSIs and trained on VLSIs at technology suppliers and two Korean-American scientists. The two scientists had 64K DRAM development experience at American companies and gave Samsung a significantly higher level of tacit knowledge. Active interaction between the outpost in Silicon Valley and the team in Korea, through training, joint research, and consulting, elevated significantly both the tacit and explicit knowledge within the Korean team in a very short period of time, resulting in the effective transfer of knowledge from Silicon Valley to Korea. This made Samsung engineers better equipped to assimilate VLSI technologies from Micron Technology and Zytrex. In short, Samsung had a deliberate strategy to upgrade its prior tacit and explicit knowledge, expanding its prior knowledge base.

As a means to intensify its effort, Samsung created a crisis by presenting the team with the very ambitious goal of developing a working production system for the 64K DRAM within six months. The team members lived together in a makeshift accommodation on the plant site and worked around the clock to assimilate imported technologies and develop processes. The team was so immersed in working on 64K DRAM that a Korean-American team leader confessed that he hardly slept any more than three or four hours a day for six months and stopped smoking and drinking (Samsung, 1987).

In such a crisis, the goal was clear to all team members. Personal dedication and long working hours expedited knowledge conversion at the individual level. The shared awareness of a crisis and determination to solve problems within the assigned time frame intensified close interaction among members. This, together with high prior knowledge, led to rapid knowledge conversion among the individual members and to a high rate of knowledge creation at the organizational level, enabling Samsung to have a high absorptive capacity. Samsung managed the crisis to become a creative, rather than, destructive process.

Beside the ad hoc meetings to solve spot problems, the task force team held regular daily meetings at 11 PM. This meeting, called eleven meeting, continued for several years. The "eleven meeting" later became the "nine meeting" and then the "seven meeting," as the sense of crisis dwindled. After individuals and smaller teams worked all day, they regularly met during the night to discuss and coordinate progress made, problems faced, and plans for the next day. These meetings facilitated the creation and diffusion of knowledge among members and across smaller teams (Choi, 1996).

Given previous experience in semiconductor production, Samsung engineers managed to assimilate and develop all but the eight core technologies needed for 309 processes in 64K DRAM production. After six months of hard work to make the crisis creative, the team in Korea assimilated the core technologies and succeeded in developing a working good die, which is a functionally operating wafer before packaging and reliability testing.

In constructing its mass production plant, Samsung set the ambitious goal of completing construction which normally required eighteen months in Japan, within six months. This created another major crisis for Samsung engineers. The construction team collected and studied technical information to raise its relevant prior knowledge. It then identified a Japanese firm that had previously built a Sharp semiconductor plant in Japan. This firm designed the plant for Samsung and supervised its construction. This provided Samsung with an opportunity to learn about the Japanese system. Samsung switched its in-house assimilation efforts from untested technology from Zytrex to Sharp's production-tested technology. Samsung emulated Sharp's system to expedite its process development. Engineers from Samsung's process development teams and from its construction subsidiary worked around the clock even on weekends and holidays. Despite the long series of trials and errors, the team successfully completed the construction of a working plant within six months. Whenever problems arose, inexperienced Samsung engineers, not knowing much about semiconductor mass production process, had to check from A to Z to identify the source of problems. Such repeated checks of the whole system also helped Samsung accelerate its technological learning (Choi, 1996).

Samsung hit the market with a 64K DRAM in early 1984, some forty months after the American pioneer and about eighteen months after the first Japanese version became commercially available. Korea became the third country in the world to introduce DRAM chips and significantly narrowed the technological gap with Japan and the United States.

Internal Competition for the 256K DRAM

Having met with success in mass production of 64K DRAMs in early 1984, Samsung again launched two task force teams—one in Korea and the other at its outpost in Silicon Valley—for 256K DRAM development, using internal competition between the two.

For the team in Korea, Samsung once again decided to license circuit design from Micron Technology to shorten the time gap in commercializing the 256K DRAM with Japan and the United States. This time it did not, however, have to license process technology. Experience in the developing process for 64K DRAMs provided an invaluable platform for developing the process for the 256K DRAM. Nevertheless, several challenging process technologies for 256K DRAMs—the development of process for 2 micron circuits, 200 angstrom thin oxide fabrication, 1.1 micro meter metal pitch and chemical etching, test program, and ceramic package assembly—imposed another crisis on Samsung. The team went through all of the available literature on the 256K DRAM process and underwent intensive training at its supplier's site, again significantly raising the team's tacit knowledge base. Then, as the team did for the 64K DRAM, its members entered the crisis management mode, working around the clock for eight months. The team succeeded in developing a working good die in October 1984, reducing Samsung's pursuit of the world's pioneer from four years for the 64K DRAM to two years for the 256K DRAM (see table 14.1). Mass production began in early 1986, about eighteen months after the first introduction by the advanced countries.

For the better prepared outpost team in Silicon Valley, Samsung, however, gave the same assignment without foreign licensing. The team had to compete with its counterpart in Korea in developing the whole range of the 256K DRAM, including circuit design as well as process design, independent of foreign design suppliers. This was also a major crisis in technological learning. The team spent seven months reverse engineering 256K DRAM chips developed by Japanese and American firms and studying literature on production processes. They completed the circuit design in April 1985 and a working good die in July 1985, about ten months after their counterpart in Korea. Silicon Valley and its surroundings, as mentioned earlier,

Table 14.1. Gap between Advanced Countries and Samsung in the Semiconductor Industry

	64K DRAM	256K DRAM	1M DRAM	4M DRAM	16M DRAM	64M DRAM	256M DRAM
Development Time							
Pioneer in U.S. and Japan	1979	1982	1985	late 1987	early 1990	late 1992	mid 1995
Pioneer in Korea	1983	1984	1986	early 1988	mid 1990	late 1992	early 1995
Gap	4 years	2 years	1 year	6 months	3 months	at par with Japan and U.S.	ahead of Japan and U.S.
Sample Shipment Time							
Pioneer in U.S. and Japan	1st half of 1980	2nd half of 1984	2nd half of 1986	2nd half of 1989	2nd half of 1991		
Pioneer in Korea	1st half of 1984	1st half of 1986	2nd half of 1987	2nd half of 1989	2nd half of 1991	2nd half of 1994	
Gap	3½ years	1½ years	1 year	at par with Japan and U.S.	at par with Japan and U.S.	First in the world	

Source: Compiled from data provided by Korea Ministry of Trade, Industry and Energy

provided an environment for team members to have effective interaction with the scientific and technical community.

The success of the Silicon Valley team had two important meanings. First, Samsung developed the technological capability to design a 256K DRAM circuit on its own, laying an invaluable platform for the subsequent development of the 1M DRAM. Through the relocation of personnel, design capability was effectively transferred to the Semiconductor R&D Center in Korea. Second, the quality of its working good die was better in terms of several important performance measures, such as soft error rate, electric static discharge, and information-processing speed, than the model acquired from Micron Technology, so Samsung adopted it as the 256K DRAM design for mass production in Korea.

Facing the entry of Samsung and other Korean *chaebols* into the 64K DRAM and 256K DRAM markets, Japanese semiconductor producers moved quickly to dump their 64K and 256K DRAMs at a fraction of the Korean producers' cost. This strategy worked early on, placing enormous financial strains on their American competitors. However, unlike the single-business semiconductor producers in the United States, cushions provided by cash-cow subsidiaries within the diversified Samsung kept its semiconductor subsidiary afloat during the financial crisis. Then Samsung and other *chaebols* received a stroke of luck. Japan acceded to export restraints on semiconductor trade with the United States. This and the subsequent move to the 1M DRAM by Japanese firms opened up new opportunities for Samsung and other Korean firms to penetrate the U. S. market, allowing them to emerge as dominant suppliers of the 64K DRAM and 256K DRAM. Increasing demand and short supply also pushed prices for the 256K DRAM from $2 in 1986 to $5 in 1988. The market remained firm for many more years, leading Korean semiconductor producers into the black and enabling them to establish themselves firmly in the semiconductor industry.

In short, by the time the 256K DRAM was completed, the technological capability of the Korean team had reached a par with that of its counterpart in the Silicon Valley. Both had enough capability to undertake R&D on their own without foreign assistance.

Internal Competition and Cooperation for the 1M DRAM

When development of the mass production system for the 256K DRAM was at its final stage, Samsung's R&D team shifted its research focus to the development of the 1M DRAM, in September 1985. Despite the fact that Samsung could purchase designs from an American firm, it decided to go on its own. Once again, the project was given to a team in Korea and a team at the Silicon Valley outpost. The project was in a sense competitive because they both were to work on the same project. It was in another sense cooperative because they were to exchange information, personnel, and research results.

Experience gained in the 256K DRAM development process provided a prior tacit knowledge base, but unlike the case of the 256K DRAM, Samsung had trouble securing explicit knowledge in the form of technical specifications, literature on production processes, and sample chips from pioneering firms in Japan and the United States. This preempted imitative reverse engineering.

Design and process development for the 1M DRAM required several significant technological changes from the 256K DRAM. They included, among other things, design shifting from N-MOS to energy-efficient C-MOS, resulting in notable complications, such as circuit width change from 2 microns to 1.2 microns, from double ploy process to triple ploy process, and accelerating the processing speed by up to 100–120 nanoseconds.

The task force team in Korea was headed by a Korean-American scientist and included five project teams: circuit design, unit process, devices, process structure, and test programs. Once again, research teams adopted the Korean style of crisis management, staying together in a makeshift housing arrangement and working around the clock. The team consulted extensively with scientists and engineers at universities and public research institutes in Korea and those abroad, including its counterparts in Silicon Valley. It was March 1986 when the team in Korea completed circuit design and July 1986 when it produced a working good die, narrowing the gap with the Japanese pioneer from two years for the 256K DRAM to one year for the 1M DRAM. The outpost team in Silicon Valley also successfully completed the 1M DRAM development about three months later, indicating that the locus of R&D capability had by then shifted from the outpost to the R&D center in Korea.

In an attempt to narrow the gap in marketing 1M DRAMs, Samsung took the risk of building a pilot mass production system in parallel with design R&D work. Although Samsung had gained substantial tacit and explicit knowledge in setting up mass production systems for the 64K DRAM and 256K DRAM, it was another crisis for its R&D and engineering teams. This time Samsung designed and constructed the production system, needing only some technical consultations from Japanese and American firms. Samsung began mass-producing the 1M DRAM in late 1987, a year after Japanese firms, but in time to catch the rapid rise in market demand.

But the road ahead was getting bumpier. In 1986, Texas Instruments filed a suit against Samsung and eight Japanese chipmakers charging infringement of patents for DRAM designs, while Intel filed a similar suit against Hyundai and its American design suppliers. Both Samsung and Hyundai ended up paying royalties on the past and future sales of their memory products. Work on the next generation of chips—the 4M DRAM—meant competition neck-and-neck with Japanese and U. S. companies in exploring the frontiers of semiconductor technology. As the stakes rose in the chip game, the field of players grew smaller worldwide, meaning that few, if any, of those left in the game could be counted on to sell state-of-the-art chip design technology to the Korean *chaebols*. So the Koreans had to tackle the design and process development of 4M DRAM and beyond on their own (Kim, 1997).

Summary and Discussion

This article presented the process of Samsung's leapfrogging from a mere assembler of discrete devices to the most vibrant and largest producer of memory chips in the world in a decade. Samsung first licensed both design and process technologies from financially troubled small American firms for the 64K DRAM but needed only design technology for the 256K DRAM. On the basis of these experiences, Samsung developed both design and process technologies for the 1M DRAM and subsequent chips on its own, rapidly displacing foreign assistance. Samsung made this possible by expediting knowledge conversion and creation through continuous enhancement of its absorptive capacity.

How does knowledge creation in the catching-up process differ from that of the pioneering process in advanced countries? First, catching-up firms, particularly those in developing countries, reverse the sequence of research (R), development (D) and engineering (E) of the advanced countries. Samsung first reverse-engineered (E) technologies related to 1K and 16K DRAM chips. It then undertook development (D) to assimilate 64K and 256K DRAM chips acquired through foreign license. When it had no place to turn to for licensing, Samsung undertook serious research (R) to develop 4M DRAM and beyond.

Second, catching-up firms can greatly benefit from relevant migratory knowledge available elsewhere in various forms. They can easily acquire prior explicit knowledge through literature review, observation touring, and foreign licensing. Explicit knowledge may easily be transferred through various means, but tacit knowledge to use it effectively cannot. One of the most effective ways of acquiring tacit knowledge is the hiring of experienced personnel from existing firms. Such experienced personnel make it possible for firms to assimilate imported technologies expeditiously.

Third, Samsung used proactively constructed crises as a major means of intensifying its effort. Goals may be more specific and clearer in catching up than in pioneering. The catching-up company can use crisis construction to reach goal consensus and identification and to generate enormous energy from organizational members in searching and converting knowledge at the individual and organizational levels. In contrast, the pioneering company has to work with a strategic ambiguity that provides only a broad direction (Nonaka, 1988) and has difficulty in identifying external sources of relevant knowledge. Consequently, learning in pioneering may be creative but not necessarily expeditious.

Expeditious knowledge creation is also evident in Hyundai's vibrant growth in the automobile industry (Kim, 1998). What are similarities and differences in knowledge creation in the catching-up process between Samsung in semiconductors and Hyundai in automobiles? There appear to be two similarities. First, the both firms expedited their knowledge creation by enhancing their absorptive capacity through the extensive use of migratory knowledge and crisis construction. Second, they advanced from one stage to the next through the four phases: preparation, acquisition, assimilation, and improvement of foreign technologies.

There appear to be four dissimilarities. First, there is a significant difference in the kind of migratory knowledge acquired. In automobiles, since the technologies involved in assembly operations and localization of parts and components were relatively simple, Hyundai acquired migratory knowledge mainly through literature, observation touring and the poaching of experienced technicians and low-class engineers. In contrast, Samsung had to hire high-caliber scientists and engineers in order to assimilate highly sophisticated design and process technologies. Second, the process of assimilation of imported technologies and generation of new technologies stemmed largely from learning by doing in the case of the automobile industry but from learning by research in the case of the semiconductor industry. Third, while the government was one of the major sources of externally evoked crises for the automobile industry in the early years, it was not in an appropriate position to impose a crisis on the semiconductor industry. Fourth, while Hyundai used a single task force team for each project, Samsung deliberately used two task force teams to work on the same project competitively and cooperatively. In short, all these dissimilarities appear to have stemmed from differences in the degree of technological sophistication between the two industries.

Can catching-up firms in other countries emulate Samsung's learning model? Yes and no. They can improve the effectiveness of knowledge creation by emulating the learning process illustrated in figure 14.2. But some of the implicit aspects of the Samsung case may be difficult to mimic, such as the availability of high-caliber scientists and engineers who can be recruited from abroad and their hard-working traits. The first is associated with prior knowledge base, the second with the intensity of effort.

First, firms in other countries cannot easily mimic the availability of high-caliber human resources. According to a United Nations report, Korea is one of only four developing countries that made a double jump from low-level to medium-level and from medium-level to high-level groups in terms of the human development index between 1960 and 1992. Korea also made the largest absolute increase and the highest score among the same four in 1992 (UNDP, 1994). The number of scientists and engineers per ten thousand people in Korea is the highest among the developing countries and closer to that of France and the United Kingdom, at least in quantity. Human resource development requires a long-term investment.

Second, firms in other countries cannot easily emulate the hard-working habit of Koreans and their long working hours. Such cultural traits stem from several factors. In terms of population density, Korea trails only Bangladesh and Taiwan. The cramped conditions and severely cold winters appear to have forced Koreans to work hard and long whenever possible in order to survive in an unfavorable environment. In addition, the older generation has been motivated by the memory of deprivation and hard times under Japanese occupation and the destructive Korean War. An obsession to "beat Japan" to settle old scores and national economic competition with North Korea are also major forces motivating Koreans. Such cultural and situational factors cannot be duplicated in other countries.

References

Abernathy, William J. 1978. *Productivity Dilemma*. Baltimore: Johns Hopkins University Press.

Arrow, Kenneth. 1962. "Economic Implications of Learning by Doing." *Review of Economic Studies* 29: 166–70.

Attewell, Paul. 1992. "Technology Diffusion and Organizational Learning: The Case of Business Computing." *Organization Science* 3(1): 1–19.

Badaracco, Joseph L., Jr. 1991. *The Knowledge Link: How Firms Compete Through Strategic Alliances*. Boston: Harvard Business School Press.

Brandenberger, Adam M., and Barry J. Nalebuff. 1996. *Co-opetition*. New York: Currency Doubleday.

Choi, Youngrak. 1996. *Dynamic Techno-Management Capability*. Aldershot, England: Avebury.

Cohen, Wesley M., and Daniel A. Levinthal. 1990. "Absorptive Capacity: A New Perspective on Learning and Innovation." *Administrative Science Quarterly* 35: 128–52.

Cooper, Arnold C., and Dan E. Schendel. 1976. "Strategic Responses to Technological Threats." *Business Horizons* 19: 61–9.

De Greene, Kenyon B. 1982. *The Adaptive Organization: Anticipation and Management of Crisis*. New York: Wiley.

Dodgson, Mark. 1993. "Organizational Learning: A Review of Some Literature." *Organization Studies* 14(3): 375–94.

Duncan, Robert B., and Andrew Weiss. 1978. "Organizational Learning: Implications for Organizational Design." *Research in Organizational Behavior*. 1: 75–123.

Fransman, Martin, and Kenneth King, eds. 1984. *Technological Capability in the Third World*. London: Macmillan.

Harlow, H. F. 1959. "Learning Set and Error Factor Theory." In *Psychology: A Study of Science*, edited by Sigmund Koch. New York: McGraw-Hill. Pp. 492–537.

Hedberg, Bo. 1981. "How Organizations Learn and Unlearn," In *Handbook of Organizational Design*. Vol. 1. *Adapting Organizations to Their Environments*, edited by Paul C. Nystrom and William H. Starbuck. New York: Oxford University Press. Pp. 3–26.

Howells, Jeremy. 1996. "Tacit Knowledge, Innovation and Technology Transfer." *Technology Analysis and Strategic Management* 8(2): 91–106.

Kim, Daniel H. 1993. "The Link between Individual and Organizational Learning." *Sloan Management Review* 35(1): 37–50.

Kim, Linsu. 1993. "National System of Industrial Innovation: Dynamics of Capability Building in Korea." In *National Innovation Systems: A Comparative Analysis*, edited by Richard R. Nelson. New York: Oxford University Press. Pp. 357–83.

———. 1995. "Absorptive Capacity and Industrial Growth: A Conceptual Framework and Korea's Experience." In *Social Capability and Long-Term Economic Growth*, edited by Bon-Ho Koo and Dwight Perkins. New York: St. Martins Press. Pp. 266–87.

———. 1997. *Imitation to Innovation: The Dynamics of Korea's Technological Learning*. Boston: Harvard Business School Press.

———. 1998. "Crisis Construction and Organizational Learning: Capability Building in Catching up at Hyundai Motor." *Organization Science* 9(4): 506–21.

Kim, Linsu, and Youngbae Kim. 1985. "Innovation in a Newly Industrializing Country: A Multiple Discriminant Analysis." *Management Science* 31(3): 12–22.

Meyers, Patricia W. 1990. "Non-linear Learning in Large Technological Firms: Period Four Implies Chaos." *Research Policy* 19: 97–115.

Miller, Danny, and Peter H. Friesen. 1984. *Organization: A Quantum View*. Englewood Cliffs, N.J.: Prentice-Hall.

Nelson, Richard R., and Sidney G. Winter. 1982. *An Evolutionary Theory of Economic Change*, Cambridge: Harvard University Press.

Nonaka, Ikujiro. 1988. "Creating Organizational Order out of Chaos: Self-renewal in Japanese Firms." *California Management Review* 30(3): 57–73.

———. 1994. "A Dynamic Theory of Organizational Knowledge Creation." *Organization Science* 5(1): 14–37.

Nonaka, Ikujiro, and Hirotaka Takeuchi. 1995. *The Knowledge-Creating Company*. New York: Oxford University Press.

Pitt, Martyn. 1990. "Crisis Modes of Strategic Transformation: A New Metaphor for Managing Technological Innovation." In *The Strategic Management of Technological Innovation*, edited by Ray Loveridge and Martyn Pitt. Chichester, England: Wiley. Pp. 253–72.

Polanyi, M. 1966. *The Tacit Dimension*. London: Routledge and Kegan Paul.

Samsung. 1987. *Samsung Bandoche 10 Nyun Sa* (Ten-year history of Samsung Semiconductor). Seoul: Samsung Electronics Company.

Shrivastava, Paul. 1983. "A Typology of Organizational Learning Systems." *Journal of Management Studies* 20: 1–28.

———. 1988. "Industrial Crisis Management: Learning from Organizational Failures." *Journal of Management Studies* 25(4): 283–4.

Teece, David J. 1992. "Competition, Cooperation, and Innovation: Organizational Arrangements for Regimes of Rapid Technological Progress." *Journal of Economic Behavior and Organization* 18: 1–25.

Tushman, Michael L., and Philip A. Anderson. 1986. "Technological Discontinuities and Organizational Environment." *Administrative Science Quarterly* 31: 439–56.

Tushman, M. L., B. Virany, and E. Romanelli. 1985. "Executive Succession, Strategic Reorientations and Organizational Evolution." *Technology in Society* 7: 297–314.

UNDP (United Nations Development Program). 1994. *Human Resource Development Report, 1994*. New York: Oxford University Press.

Utterback, James M. 1994. *Mastering the Dynamics of Innovation: How Companies Can Seize Opportunities in the Face of Technological Change*. Boston: Harvard Business School Press.

Utterback, James M., and Linsu Kim. 1985. "Invasion of Stable Business by Radical Innovation." In *Management of Productivity and Technology in Manufacturing*, edited by Paul R. Kleindorfer. New York: Plenum Press. Pp. 113–51.

von Hippel, Eric. 1988. *The Sources of Innovation*. New York: Oxford University Press.

15

Conclusion

Social, Technical, and Evolutionary
Dimensions of Knowledge Creation

IKUJIRO NONAKA
TOSHIHIRO NISHIGUCHI

How firms create, convert, transfer, and absorb knowledge to gain competitive advantage has been the focus of this book, with thirteen chapters each offering a part of the answer. Knowledge and knowledge creation are by nature complex and multifaceted phenomena, requiring a variety of concepts and approaches to explain and understand them. Nevertheless, we believe that the field of knowledge creation would benefit from increased unity of concepts and coordination of research efforts. In this concluding chapter we therefore briefly attempt to discern common threads uniting these chapters and research on knowledge creation in general. This will lead us to suggest a number of avenues that future research could take to advance this still emerging field.

The Embeddedness of Knowledge

A first area of unity is the view of knowledge as largely tacit and embedded in the social values and beliefs of individuals. This contrasts with the traditional view of knowledge as explicit information represented by scientific formulae or patents. Although the concept of tacit knowledge is not new, with Michael Polanyi (1966) among its early proponents, its refinement and application in business research is a relatively recent affair.

The knowledge-creation process is by extension a social process, embedded in a particular set of relationships among individuals, teams, and organizations. The end result of this process, represented by formulae, patents, and other forms of explicit knowledge, does not fully convey the intricacies of the highly interactive and delicate nature of knowledge creation. As a result, there is often a mismatch between the corporate strategies developed by top management and the actual knowledge-creation process carried out by the front-line actors in labs, factories, and distribution outlets. In the words of Brown and Duguid (1991), an often large gap separates canonical from noncanonical practice.

As many of the case studies included in this book demonstrate, many of the most innovating and successful companies leave considerable autonomy to front-line actors. Top management does not try to control or direct the knowledge-creation process itself; instead, it provides resources for individuals and/or teams to engage in experimentation and dialogue among each other and with external sources of knowledge such as customers, suppliers, and competitors.

Ba as a Platform for Knowledge Creation

This brings us to a second common ground of knowledge-creation research, particularly but not exclusively evident in the chapters on Japanese practice: the concept of ba. Although the concept is well introduced by Nonaka, Konno, and Toyama in chapter 2, it is worth emphasizing the difference between ba and ordinary social interaction. Everyone would agree that most if not all knowledge is created not by a single individual but through an iterative process of experimentation and dialogue involving several individuals. The concept of ba is useful to understand how the organic concentration of resources in a given space, which may be physical, virtual, and/or mental, *and* a specific time frame affects knowledge creation. Put differently, knowledge is created through real-time interaction in specific contexts, not just human interaction.

As demonstrated in the various chapters of this book, ba can be used to promote product innovation (e.g., at Maekawa Seisakusho and Microsoft), to absorb outside technology (e.g., at Samsung), or for joint, interorganizational projects (e.g., in the Japanese aircraft industry). Different strategies and priorities demand different ba, and even for a given strategy there is a variety of forms ba can take, but the underlying issue is the same: knowledge must be nurtured rather than managed. The top management of firms such as Maekawa, Microsoft, and Samsung and the MITI officials did not try to manage the knowledge-creation process directly, instead, they provided a platform where individuals could engage in meaningful dialogue and real-time interaction and thus share and create knowledge.

Technology and Communication

As emphasized in Part II, new information technologies (IT) have revolutionized the way products are designed, manufactured, and delivered. No serious firm can afford to ignore new communication technologies such as e-mail or design technologies such as CAD, which radically reduce the time needed to create and/or communicate knowledge. They open the way for the emergence of virtual or cyber ba discussed in the chapter 2. However, as recognized by all authors herein, face-to-face interaction remains crucial in most stages of the knowledge-creation or knowledge-transfer processes. A very telling example in this regard is the case of Boeing discussed in chapter 4, where state-of-the-art IT is used in conjunction with the colocation of engineers. In this sense, IT is one among several resources needed to support the knowledge-creation process. Technology must therefore be designed and implemented in accordance with these other resources, in particular human resources, and with the overall ba.

By the same token, the new ITs are important enough to warrant major transformations in the design of ba. As noted in chapter 4, this gives a chance for firms in the West and elsewhere to catch up with the ba-oriented Japanese firms, many of which are relatively behind in the use of IT. However, while the latter are learning to use these technologies more efficiently, the more technology-oriented Western firms must learn how to orchestrate meaningful social interaction among their employees and key suppliers. The lessons learned the hard way by General Motors, Volkswagen, and others, that is, that organization is often more important than technology, should be remembered in this regard (Shimokawa, Jürgens, and Fujimoto, 1997).

Coevolution of Organizations

While no one would deny the importance of *intra*organizational knowledge creation, there is now a wide consensus on the importance of interfirm, or *interorganizational*, cooperation in the emergence, refinement, transfer, and diffusion of new knowledge. As demonstrated in Parts III and IV, interorganizational projects may involve direct competitors, public institutions, suppliers, and/or customers. While previous research has tended to emphasize competition and/or exploitation among organizations, a theme of this book is that interorganizational cooperation is not only profitable but often necessary. It is increasingly rare for a single firm to possess either the financial resources or the technological capabilities to undertake alone the development of an entire product. From such cooperation emerge not only new products but also different (and often stronger) organizations. In other words, there is *coevolution* of the organizations involved, which learn together and from each other. As was also suggested, however, leading firms do not follow blindly either the competitive or partnership models, mixing cooperation and competition, trust and flexibility, exploitation and symbiosis. This apparently destabilizing interaction between contradictory approaches is in itself a major source of coevolution, as Nishiguchi suggested in chapter 11.

Avenues for Future Research

The emerging field of knowledge creation is clearly blossoming. This explains its richness and diversity but also its lack of cohesion. This book has attempted to identify common and unifying concepts that could benefit the evolution of the field, but there clearly remains much to be done. In particular, future efforts should be directed to further integrating key knowledge-creation concepts such as tacit knowledge, ba, care, coevolution, and so on. We need to know more about how these elements interact and how they could fit into a more unified theory of knowledge creation.

As suggested in chapter 14, our field would also benefit from increased attention to the many firms and regions not involved in state-of-the-art knowledge creation. In other words, we need to know more about how concepts such as ba and coevolution can help small and medium-sized firms and developing regions, where the accent is often on imitation, absorption, and incremental improvement rather than the development of radically new products or processes. This would also help us to differentiate knowledge creation and knowledge transfer, two key but often undistinguishable processes.

A final suggestion concerns the integration of technology and ba. As suggested by several authors, a promising avenue for practitioners is to combine face-to-face interaction with the new communication technologies. Researchers should further examine this trend, investigating where and how electronic networks are replacing human networks and what effects this is having on knowledge creation and transfer.

These are only a few possibilities; the field of knowledge creation can accommodate a very wide range of themes and approaches. We hope the reader will agree with us that it is also a fascinating subject, worthy of continued and persistent effort.

References

Brown, John, and Paul Duguid. 1991. "Organizational Learning and Communities-of-Practice: Toward a Unified View of Working, Learning, and Innovation." *Organization Science* 2(1): 40–57.

Polanyi, Michael. 1966. *The Tacit Dimension.* Gloucester, Mass.: Peter Smith. Reprinted 1983.

Shimokawa, Koichi, Ulrich Jürgens, and Takahiro Fujimoto, eds. 1997. *Transforming Automobile Assembly: Experience in Automation and Work Organization.* Berlin: Springer-Verlag.

Index